PENGUIN BOOKS

SAFARI

Bartle Bull was born in England and educated at Oxford. A student of Africa for over thirty years, he went on his first safari in Kenya in 1959 with the Polish hunter Stas Sapieha. At the time he was writing his Harvard College thesis on Rhodesia. A Fellow of the Royal Geographical Society and an active environmentalist, he has not hunted since 1967, preferring to scout the bush on horseback, like the nineteenth-century hunters, or to stalk on foot with no gun and no camera but with an armed companion. He has been on safari with Robin Hurt, the 'hunter's hunter', one of the finest professionals left in Africa.

Bartle Bull is a lawyer and lives with his son in New York, where he was formerly publisher of *The Village Voice*. He has recently published his first novel, *The White Rhino Hotel*, which is set in East Africa in the 1920s.

Safari has received great critical acclaim. The *Boston Globe* wrote: 'Bull brings a quality of scholarship to bear in an irresistibly beautiful book . . . Bull captures the feel and sight and smell and sound of the bush, animal spoor, brandy and tobacco and the smell of musky women, rotting meat and campfire smoke, wildflowers . . .'

SAFARI

A CHRONICLE OF ADVENTURE

BARTLE BULL

PENGUIN BOOKS

PENGUIN BOOKS

Published by the Penguin Group
Penguin Books Ltd, 27 Wrights Lane, London w8 5tz, England
Penguin Books USA Inc., 375 Hudson Street, New York, New York 10014, USA
Penguin Books Australia Ltd, Ringwood, Victoria, Australia
Penguin Books Canada Ltd, 10 Alcorn Avenue, Toronto, Ontario, Canada m4v 3b2
Penguin Books (NZ) Ltd, 182–190 Wairau Road, Auckland 10, New Zealand

Penguin Books Ltd, Registered Offices: Harmondsworth, Middlesex, England

First published by Viking 1988
Published in Penguin Books 1992
10 9 8 7 6 5 4

Copyright © Bartle Bull, 1988
All rights reserved

Printed in Singapore by Kyodo Printing Co. (S'pore) Pte Ltd

Title page: Head of Cape buffalo as preserved
by Captain Cornwallis Harris

CONTENTS

FOR
MY FATHER
BARTLE BRENNEN BULL
AND
ALL THE OLD AFRICAN HUNTERS
LONG HOME FROM THE HILL

EGYPTIAN MAIL

CAIRO

OCT. 17, 1940

Capt. Bartle B. Bull, M.P. for Enfield, leading his platoon somewhere in the western desert.

PREFACE

Even today, to visit Africa is a feast for the senses. The bush literally brings one's faculties to life, as you learn to see better, to smell for the first time, to be silent and to listen. Without sharing their diaries, it is difficult to imagine what it must have been like for the first Europeans on safari a century and a half ago. Despite generations of change, however, most of it imposed by a foreign world, the wildlife, the landscape and the people of Africa remain an exhilarating contrast to the world we still seek to escape.

Today, as before, the best safari is the one closest to nature. With a very few, very good friends. There is no substitute for walking until you have had enough, and then forgetting exhaustion as you spot the magnificent creatures that no imagination could have conceived. Elephant, rhinoceros, giraffe. Then stalking or crawling in close, until you smell the elephant or hear the rhino chew the acacia thorns. Finally, if you have learned to require neither a trophy nor a photograph, to respect the animal, to let it continue its life undisturbed, to leave it, quietly, as you found it.

The opportunity to write the first history of the African safari, to combine academic research with vital activity, to go from the lost folios in the basement of the old Cape Town library to buffalo stalks in the rich swamps of Tanzania, to share both the diaries of the lonely hunters of the 1880s and the camp fires of the last hunters of today, has been an adventure in itself. As with sailors or soldiers, the transport and the equipment have changed, but when the moment comes, things are still much the same.

I have been fortunate to have a family, and many friends, with a long interest in Africa. A Canadian grandfather, William Perkins Bull, who relished long, smoky evenings at the Garrick Club with Rider Haggard, hearing once again the tales of Haggard's early days on horseback in the Transvaal. An English father who spent the War in Ethiopia, Libya and Egypt, and brought me home from Addis Ababa a splendid knife, with an elephant carved on its still-sharp blade, which has passed forty years on my bedside table. An American son who taught English in a school in Botswana when he was sixteen, and has shared not only many a camp fire with me on five continents, but also canoes on the Zambesi, dugouts in the Okavango Swamp, horseback chases in Kenya's Northern Frontier District, and long stalks in Zimbabwe, scrambling up trees as the dust of a buffalo herd rose around us. He, too, loves Africa.

Itinerant authors need friends, and I have had them. In Cape Town the antiquarian bookdealer Irving Freeman shared his scholarship, and his wine. In

Johannesburg Clive Menell was generous, and Harry Oppenheimer's Brenthurst Library, a remarkable repository of Africana, opened its treasures. In Nairobi, and in London and New York, the resourceful Mouse McConnell pursued the trails of research.

In Kenya, the brotherhood of old hunters unfailingly extended themselves for me, particularly my friends Glen Cottar, Terry Mathews and Tony Seth-Smith. In London Michael and Marcia Blakenham provided me with patient hospitality, my spirited agent, Ed Victor, guarded the camp, and Timothy Best of Rowland Ward and Roger Mitchell of Holland & Holland opened their sanctums. Philip Cranworth, whose father and mine shared the desert and a flat in Cairo during the war, lent me his grandfather's scrapbooks. It was his grandfather, the redoubtable Lord Cranworth of this book, who first told me of Africa when he taught me croquet in Suffolk in the 1950s. In New York my patient law partners at Jones Hirsch Connors & Bull endured like elephants, always supportive, particularly my loyal friend Daniel Hirsch, and my most finely honed, all-seeing critic, Winfield P. Jones.

Others who earned thanks, each deserving more than mention, include that keen hunter Alex Brant; the gifted photographer George T. Butler, for his early encouragement; John Heminway for his experienced counsel; Wallace Dailey, the Curator of Harvard's Theodore Roosevelt Collection; F. William Free, for the gift of his taste; Eleo Gordon, for her superb professionalism in putting the book together; Susan Rose-Smith for graphic research; Frederick H. S. Allen, Alan Delynn, Iain and Oria Douglas-Hamilton, Michael Main, Nicholas Millhouse, Sarah Skinner, and the staff of the Royal Geographical Society for research assistance; Vincent Vallarino, for teaching me the art of organizing graphics; America's most distinguished firearms scholar, Larry Wilson, for his hospitality on safari; and James Kotsilibas-Davis, Dimitri Sevastopoulo and Sean Sculley for their thoughtful reading.

Of the many who helped generously, four made me envious, for each is the best at what he does. Robin Hurt, 'the hunter's hunter', Peter Mayer, my editor and publisher, Eugene Stavis, the scholar of film history, David Winks, the master gunsmith of Holland & Holland.

Most of all, I must thank my friends from the African camp fires, for they gave this book its heart: the friend of my youth, and spirited companion in all things, Michael Christian, now home from the hill; Stas and Didi Sapieha, who introduced me to the bush in 1959; Dominic Cadbury, Anthea Christian, Anthony Hardy, Charles McConnell, Barbara Peterson and James Wilkins; Alan Elliott, who recognized 'the dreary stare of a dog whose day is done'; Paul Connolly and John Stevens, who made a gift of the Zambesi; Robin Hurt; Ted Roosevelt, my fellow Yankee, who on safari was good at almost everything; and Bartle Breese Bull, my best and finest friend.

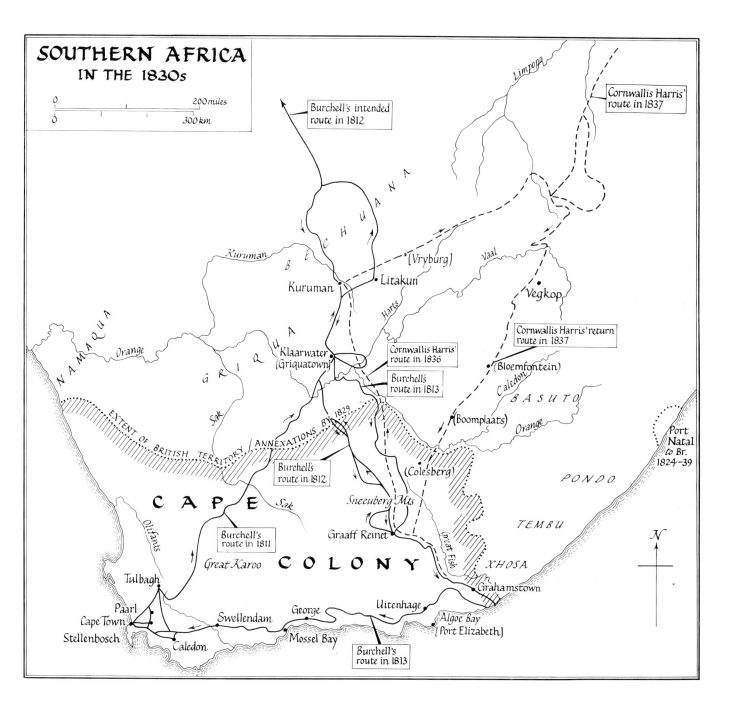

SOUTHERN AFRICA
IN THE 1830s

0   200 miles
0   300 km

Burchell's intended
route in 1812

Cornwallis Harris'
route in 1837

Limpopo

CHUANA

Kuruman

(Vryburg)

Vaal

Kuruman • • Litakun

Harts

• Vegkop

B E

Cornwallis Harris' return
route in 1837

NAMAQUA

Orange

G R I Q U A

Klaarwater
(Griquatown)

Cornwallis Harris'
route in 1836

Burchell's
route in 1813

(Bloemfontein)

Caledon

BASUTO

Sak

EXTENT OF BRITISH TERRITORY   ANNEXATIONS BY 1829

(Boomplaats)

Orange

Port
Natal
to Br.
1824-39

Burchell's
route in 1812

CAPE

Sak

(Colesberg)

PONDO

Burchell's
route in 1811

Great Karoo

COLONY

Sneeuberg Mts

TEMBU

Graaff Reinet

Olifants

Great Fish

XHOSA

Tulbagh

Grahamstown

Paarl

Uitenhage

Swellendam   George

Algoa Bay
[Port Elizabeth]

Cape Town

Stellenbosch   Caledon   Mossel Bay

Burchell's
route in 1813

N

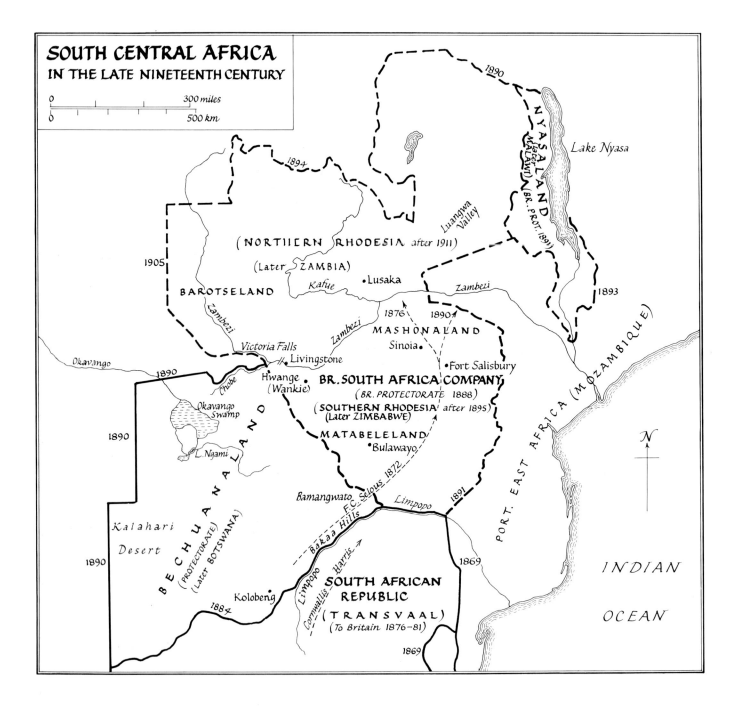

0   300 miles
0   500 km

1890

1894

NYASALAND
(MALAWI)
(BR. PROT. 1891)

Lake Nyasa

1905

(NORTHERN RHODESIA after 1911)

(Later ZAMBIA)

BAROTSELAND

Kafue

• Lusaka

Luangwa Valley

Zambezi

1893

1876   1890

MASHONALAND

Sinoia •

Zambezi

Zambezi

Okavango

Victoria Falls
Livingstone

• Fort Salisbury

1890

Chobe

Hwange
(Wankie) •

BR. SOUTH AFRICA COMPANY
(BR. PROTECTORATE 1888)
(SOUTHERN RHODESIA after 1895)
(Later ZIMBABWE)

Okavango
Swamp

MATABELELAND
• Bulawayo

1890

L. Ngami

F.C. Selous 1872

1891

B E C H U A N A L A N D

Bamangwato

Limpopo

PORT. EAST AFRICA (MOZAMBIQUE)

Kalahari

Desert

(PROTECTORATE)
(Later BOTSWANA)

Bakaa Hills

Limpopo

1869

Cornwallis Harris →

1890

Kolobeng

1884

Limpopo

SOUTH AFRICAN
REPUBLIC
(T R A N S V A A L)
(To Britain 1876-81)

1869

N

INDIAN

OCEAN

LADO ENCLAVE

ANGLO–EGYPTIAN SUDAN

Juba

Nimule

Rhino Camp

BELGIAN

CONGO
(Later ZAÏRE)

Lake Albert

Victoria Nile

1926
to KENYA

ABYSSINIA
(ETHIOPIA)

Lake Rudolf
(L. Turkana)

Marsabit
L. Paradise

NORTHERN   FRONTIER
DISTRICT

Matthews Range

UGANDA

KENYA
(Formerly BRITISH EAST AFRICA 1895–1920)

Eldoret

Baringo

Nanyuki

Mt Kenya

Lorian
Swamp

SOMALILAND
(later
SOMALIA)

Kampala
Entebbe

Nakuru

Gilgil

L. Naivasha

Nyeri

Tana

Lake Edward

Lake
Victoria

Mara
Bay

MASAI

Narok

Limuru

Aberdare Mts

Nairobi

Thika R.

Lake Kivu

MARA

Mt Suswa

L. Natron

Machakos

Ngong Hills

Yatta
Plateau

Lamu

Ngorongoro

Serengeti
Plain

RIFT VALLEY

Mt Meru

Mt Kilimanjaro

Voi

Malindi

Moyowosi
Swamp

Arusha

MASAI
RESERVE

Kilindini

Mombasa

TANGANYIKA
(Formerly GERMAN EAST AFRICA 1884–1919)
(Later TANZANIA)

(BR. MANDATE 1919–1961)

INDIAN

OCEAN

Tabora

Tanga

Ugalla

N

ZANZIBAR

Lake Tanganyika

EAST AFRICA
AFTER THE FIRST WORLD WAR

0   200 miles
0   300 km

Dar es Salaam

Ruvu

Selous Game
Reserve   • Beho Beho

WILD SPORTS

OF

Southern Africa.

W. C. Harris   Frank Howard

1. THE WITCHCRAFT OF THE DESERT

The First Safari, 1836

The descent of the African night is never forgotten. There is nothing more complete than to rest by a fire on a canvas seat, with tobacco and a drink, as the sky grows blue dark and the stars sharpen with the clarity peculiar to Africa, until the rim of the firelight seems surrounded by a second, outer world alive with the night sounds of contesting animals, and then to lie awake learning the language of the bush, the low, panting grunt of lion, the sudden rush of hooves as zebra or antelope flee, the menacing cough of a leopard defending its kill from hyena.

This fascination has held travellers since the first Europeans experienced the African bush before 1800. Today it is easier to visualize the surface of the moon than it was then to imagine the reality of Africa. The 'dark' of the African continent was the darkness of European ignorance. It took three months to sail from Southampton past the Madeira, Canary and Cape Verde Islands, crossing the Equator, passing east along the Ivory, Gold and Slave Coasts, and then south to the Cape of Good Hope. The River Nile, its origins a mystery, was a thousand miles longer than the distance between London and North America. With the exception of a few coastal enclaves, Africa was an immense unknown, a blank on the map three times the size of the United States, nine times the size of Western Europe. Thousands of Englishmen knew the hill resorts of the Himalayas long before even one of them had heard the thunder of Victoria Falls.

The game and the habitat waiting in Africa were the richest and most diverse in the world. Between Cape Town and Cairo was a landscape so vast and varied, so complex in its magnificence, that it made the moors of Scotland and the forests of Germany into tame and modest gardens. Even adventurers who had hunted in the Andes and the Himalayas, and had ridden the wide horizons of Australia, the American west and the Russian steppes, were dazzled when they found Africa, with elephants bigger than India's and a waterfall twice the size of

Title-page of *The Wild Sports of Southern Africa* by Cornwallis Harris

Early depiction of elephants in a swamp by George French Angas

Niagara. North from Cape Town, beasts unknown to Europe sheltered in the deserts of the Great Karoo and the Kalahari, the swamps of Bechuanaland, the tropical forests of the Congo, the mountains of Ethiopia and the dry bush of Somalia.

Outside Africa, the giant animals of prehistory had disappeared some four million years ago. But Africa one million years ago was still a land of giants. In east Africa alone, in the canyons of the Serengeti Plain, lie the fossils of over 150 vanished species, ox-like creatures at least twice as big as any buffalo, wild pigs the size of rhinoceros, five types of elephant, 30 ft crocodiles, immense tigers and giant sheep, and huge hippopotamus with pronounced eye sockets raised far above their faces. Then, as now, the diverse habitat of east Africa sustained the world's richest assortment of animal life. There, in steamy mangrove swamps and cool highland plateaus, in tropical forests and dry bush, in deserts and grasslands, these magnificent creatures evolved and perished, in what would one day become the heartland of the African safari.

When Europeans began to penetrate the interior of Africa in the early nineteenth century, animals were in such plenty that elephants foraged in herds of hundreds. At times antelope covered the savannah like a carpet. Lions were literally pests. One might see 150 rhinoceros in a day. Dedicating a lifetime to foxes and pheasants, or at best to stag and boar, European sportsmen saw in giraffe and elephant the animals of paradise. To the European hunter, Africa was Eden. Once there, many stayed until they died in the field. Others wrote and painted, seeking to capture the true value of the safari experience, the

Swamp scene with hippopotamus,
by G.F. Angas

exhilaration, the toughness, the freedom, the intimacy of hunter and animal, the direct connection between man and the detail of nature. Finally they went home, to speak and dream of Africa, creating the legend of the great safaris.

But it was a world that could not last. The great African safaris lasted for one century. From 1836 until 1939 unique conditions and eccentric individuals created a style of adventure that can never exist again. Abundant big game, ungoverned landscapes, suitable weapons, the lifelong habit of hunting, a zest for discovery and an appreciation of both hardship and luxury, all came together then in the vast bush of south-eastern Africa.

This is the story of that hundred years, and of the fifty that followed, a tale that began with the old hunters and adventurers who walked across Africa with their double rifles. Even today their ghosts linger outside the outer circles of the camp fires as stories are told in the African evening, and the greatest white hunter of them all, Frederick Selous, might still step into the firelight, leaning his ·450 Rigby against a tree, resting on his heels, describing the morning in 1878 when three great bull elephants chased him in the forests of Mashonaland.

Although English East India Company vessels anchored in Table Bay at the Cape of Good Hope as early as 1601, they established no base, and virtually no Europeans penetrated the interior of Africa until after 1800. Although the Cape was the fulcrum of the passage between Europe and Asia, England still failed to build a base after two of her sea captains claimed the Cape for James I in 1620. But in 1652 the Dutch East India Company founded the supply station that became Cape Town. At the time, lion, buffalo and elephant still inhabited the

very shores of Table Bay. For the next century and a half, Europeans were confined generally to Cape Colony itself, a territory ultimately the size of England and France, extending north from Cape Town. The Cape was the gateway to Africa, but it was tightly closed. Commercial and authoritarian, determined to manage its settlements under tight control, the early Dutch administration discouraged travel to the north. But the first *trekboers*, nomadic cattlemen of Dutch descent, drifted north between 1700 and 1720, beyond government control, often skirmishing with hunting communities of the tiny San, or Bushmen, who sometimes resisted their encroachment and raided their livestock.

Lions on the shore, Cape Province

Already a complaint was heard that was to become familiar during the next three hundred years: the game was being shot out and driven back. In the southern Cape peninsula itself the hippopotamus were destroyed by 1690, and Governor van der Stel complained to Holland that many colonists were preoccupied with hunting, instead of working to develop the economy. In the period 1700 to 1720, the first professional ivory hunters killed off the elephant in the south-western Cape, and turned their muzzle-loading muskets to the north-east.

Gradually, small numbers of defiant Dutch farmers, or Boers, described by Governor van Plettenberg in 1780 as 'rambling peasants', trekked north throughout the eighteenth century, often bringing slavery with them and shooting out the heavy game wherever they settled. Like their Virginian contemporaries, these early Afrikaaners forcefully asserted their own freedom while denying it to those around them. In 1795, one rebellious group, settling the remote village of Graaff-Reinet, prepared a declaration of their rights as free burghers, proclaiming 'That every Bushman or Hottentot shall for life be the lawful property of such burghers as may possess them, and serve in bondage from generation to generation.'

In 1806, Britain, at war with France and Holland, sent sixty-three warships and six thousand troops to terminate Dutch rule and occupy the Cape. The British administration that took charge continued the Dutch policy of discouraging both colonization and hunting to the north, requiring written authorization from the governor for any expedition beyond the Orange River, the principal border of the Colony. They hoped to retain a buffer territory of essentially unoccupied land north of the Orange River in order to prevent hostilities with the strong Bantu* tribes to the north-east and to limit British colonial responsibilities.

In the nineteenth century the British empire in Africa was often expanded despite the wishes of the London government, which knew that each colonial entanglement led to yet another imperial domino. The colonial engine was frequently driven either by ambitious individuals acting beyond their authority, like Cecil Rhodes or Chinese Gordon, by the dynamics of local events, by moralistic movements, whether evangelical or abolitionist, or by competitive European initiatives.

The first travellers to make their way into the interior were missionaries, explorers, traders, stockmen, prospectors, ivory hunters and empire builders. They did not come for the sport, for what came to be called a 'safari', a sustained sporting expedition in the African bush. Like many Swahili words widely used in east Africa, the term 'safari' has its origins in Arabic. There had been Arab traders and slavers along the coast since at least 1300. The root verb *safara* in classical Arabic means to unveil, hence to discover, or to enter upon a journey, and the noun *safariya* in Arabic refers to a voyage or expedition. The derivative word *safari*, used in Swahili to refer to any trip or journey, was not employed in

---

* Contrary to some contemporary usage, whether liberal or racist in implication, the terms 'black' and 'African' are not a substitute for 'Bantu'. Both Hottentots and Bushmen were black Africans, but they were not from the major Bantu peoples that dominated southern Africa. The term 'Bantu', correctly used, applies only to various African peoples who are thought to have originated in west Africa and to have intermingled with Hamitic and Nilotic peoples. Generally, the five major ethnolinguistic peoples of southern Africa, all Bantus, are classified as the Nguni (including Zulu, Swazi, Xhosa, and Ndebele or Matabele), Sotho (including Tswana and others), Venda, Tsonga and Lemba. For a thorough review of these ethnic and historical origins, interested readers are referred to the eight volumes of *The Cambridge History of Africa*, and to the works listed in the bibliography to Chapter 1 at the back of this book.

the sense of a sporting expedition until Europeans, in the late nineteenth century, began to hunt extensively near areas of east Africa that had been under Arab influence.

Finally, in 1807, a fickle English girl launched the sequence of events that began the great safaris. Lucia Green of Fulham agreed to sail to the island of St Helena to marry her fiancé William Burchell. In 1808 he eagerly awaited her, with the banns called and the ceremony arranged. On the way to St Helena, however, Lucia Green fell in love with her ship's captain. Burchell, his engagement cancelled, desolate, abandoned his post as botanist for the East India Company and, in 1810, inspired by meetings with travellers returning from Africa, sailed for Cape Town to start life again. Meanwhile, back in England, also in 1807, the man was born who would become the first of the great white hunters, William Cornwallis Harris.

Like so many travellers who stepped ashore on to the wooden jetty in Table Bay after a hard sea voyage, Burchell was seduced by the colonial charm of Cape Town and by the majestic amphitheatre of mountains in which the town reposes. He appreciated its orderly streets and Dutch houses, built of brick and faced with lime stucco, its horse races and elegant concerts. But he deplored the 'disgusting trade' that had imported the slaves he found around him. He noted that the proud Malay slaves despised the black slaves from Mozambique and Madagascar. Early settlers and merchants had imported slaves to the Colony because they found the Cape itself to be thinly populated, essentially only by aboriginal Bushmen and by diminutive Khoi or Hottentots, non-Bantu tribes of nomadic herdsmen, for the more warlike Bantu had not yet pushed down from the north in substantial numbers.

Hiking on the slopes of Table Mountain above Cape Town, gathering specimens with both hands, amazed that over two hundred species flourished in a single mile, Burchell found the country more rich in botany than he had ever imagined. A keen botanist since the age of thirteen, the son of a nurseryman and himself a former junior gardener at the Royal Botanic Gardens at Kew, Burchell now found himself at a botanical feast, surrounded by an opulent diversity unimaginable in England. This determined him to mount a sustained expedition inland to study the lavish flora and collect specimens. He intended to penetrate further north than any previous European. Although his motivation was science rather than sport, botany not hunting, this journey was to inspire the first true safari twenty-five years later, and in its elements it shared much with the great safaris that were to come.

Burchell occupied six months in planning his trip, securing permission, buying a sturdy Cape wagon and oxen, collecting supplies and hiring Hottentot assistants. His most difficult problem, before and during the expedition, was recruiting reliable Africans to accompany him. Too small a party would make him vulnerable to attack, and he decided to take no whites with him in order to avoid the discord that bedevilled many expeditions. The only alternatives were Hottentots, many of whom were already either employed or enslaved by the

W.J. Burchell in 1818, by J. Sell Cotman

A Boer trek-wagon crossing the mountains

25,000 Europeans in Cape Colony. Themselves fearful of the Bushmen and the warlike Bantu tribes to the north, however, and reluctant to undertake long and distant journeys, few Hottentots would join him.

For £88, about £1,400* today, Burchell commissioned the manufacture of a Cape wagon by one of the Colony's leading craftsmen. In 1663, when an official expedition first used a wagon to transport barter goods inland, the gruelling conditions broke it to pieces. The men, obliged to carry the goods themselves, revolted and walked back to Cape Town. From that date, during a century and a half of rough use, the Cape wagon was refined and strengthened. The resulting wagons, more durable and sophisticated vehicles than the prairie wagons that opened up the American west later in the nineteenth century, could be taken to pieces for transport across mountains and rivers. For generations, they were to be the backbone of every safari.

* At April 1988 conversion rates, £1 equals $1.75.

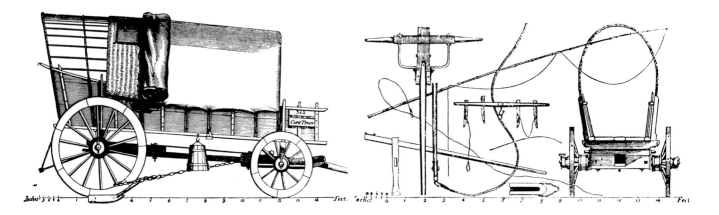

Fifteen feet long and 2 ft 9 in wide at its tapered bottom, with 5 ft rear wheels and 3½ ft front wheels, an upper shell of bamboo cane covered by a canvas sail, and the frame and moving parts made of iron and heavy planks and timbers, the Cape wagon was well suited to its work. Designed to endure vast stretches of the most brutal terrain, it employed an early version of independent suspension. Burchell noted that 'its principal advantage consists in its sides, bottom, and carriage not being joined together, admitting each part to play freely, to avoid the straining and cracking to which solid-built wagons are subjected'.

In addition to wagon stores, carpenters' tools, art supplies, four barrels of gunpowder, six muskets, a fowling-piece or shotgun, four pistols, a heavy rifle and a cutlass, Burchell loaded his wagon with sixteen categories of goods as presents to the chiefs and for bartering with the natives, including porcelain beads, blue check handkerchiefs, sheets of copper and, the greatest gift, tobacco. In all, the cost of outfitting the expedition, including the wagon, its contents and oxen, came to £800, roughly £20,000 in today's terms.

After a farewell dinner with the Earl of Caledon, the Cape governor, Burchell set out on 19 June 1811. He had never in his life spent one night out of doors. For the next four years he was to sleep on the ground or in his wagon. After spending the day forcing his wagons through difficult country, befriending Bushmen, treating wounds, hunting for food, moulding bullets, cutting specimens and painting portraits, he would play the flute and question his Hottentot companions in the frontier patois that was a rich stew of Dutch–Afrikaans, English and native languages. In this way, many Afrikaans words eventually passed into the English language, including boss, stoep, trek, swap and corral.

To remind himself of home and the rigour of the calendar, Burchell raised the British flag every Sunday, whether in the desolate karoo, as the Hottentots called a dry landscape, or in teeming Litakun, a village of Tswanas. The principal tribe of what became Bechuanaland, present-day Botswana, the Tswanas are a tribal group of the Sotho, one of the five major Bantu peoples of southern Africa, then all referred to, both pejoratively and not, as 'kaffirs', a term derived from the Arabic word *kafir*, or infidel.

As the first European to penetrate as far north as Lake Chue, near present-day Mafeking, close to the Botswana border, Burchell was determined to draw the finest existing map of southern Africa, eventually preparing a chart 7½ ft high by 8½ ft wide. To log each day's journey, he measured the exact length of ground

Depictions of a Cape wagon and its components by Burchell

20

the large wheels covered in a number of revolutions. Then he developed tables to indicate the rate of travelling per hour for each number of timed revolutions, which were marked by a leather thong tied around a spoke. At its best pace of eighteen revolutions of the wheel per minute, the wagon travelled 3 miles 390 yards an hour. Knowing the number of hours he travelled at a particular pace, he made remarkably accurate estimates of each day's progress, usually agreeing with his oxen that twenty miles was a full day's work.

They were not easy miles. Helping the oxen drag their loads through rough mountain passes, a jarring punishment often too severe for man or wagon, then forcing the sunken wheels through sand and mud, sharing his cattle's thirst through the heat of the Great Karoo, enduring driving rains, half-inch hailstones, cutting winds and sudden snowstorms, Burchell learned to persevere.

On quiet days, after repairing the wagon and recording specimens in his botanical ledger, often inventing Latin names for his discoveries, Burchell would write down Bushman or Tswana music, or work on his Tswana dictionary. As events required, he would pause to make ink from vegetables or rhinoceros blood, candles from the fat of sheep's tails, or blue paint from gum water and powdery iron ore. Exceeding his hopes, the yellow vegetable-dye ink retained its Sienese brightness for over ten years. The blue paint was perfect for his portraits, as it was made from the same mineral base as the *sibilo* dye the tribe used for adornment and insulation and so rendered exactly the Tswana skin colouring. Although Burchell made only a limited study of geology, he predicted that minerals would be the 'sleeping riches' of southern Africa. When his companions collapsed asleep, he would fix his course with his sextant, plot an eclipse, or study Jupiter's satellites through his pocket telescope in a night sky so much brighter than England's. Then he would retire to his wagon to write his journal, mixing the day's hunting tales with favoured lines from Horace and Virgil.

As the bush can, the journey changed him. At school in Surrey, Burchell had been considered puny and unathletic. His friends in Cape Town had warned him that, at 5 ft 4 in tall, his bodily strength was unequal to the task. But he felt stronger each day, hardened by constant exertion, impressing the Twsanas by his ability to lift 70 lb tusks easily in one hand. Reading the long volumes of his

diary, one senses him growing daily more resolute, more resourceful, wiser in his dealings with men and the bush. During his four-year expedition, he walked or rode 4,500 miles, collected 40,000 botanical specimens, made 500 drawings, 'discovered' at least four species of animals, and practised anthropology, medicine, taxidermy, music and navigation. Like generations of other Europeans, he considered that he had discovered something if he was the first white man to see it.

Burchell was not charmed by missionaries, commenting that perhaps the Africans should send missionaries to Europe. He observed that blacks educated by missionaries had the virtues of neither Africans nor Europeans. Some even proclaimed that since they were now Christians, other blacks should work for them. Burchell was prescient in understanding the mischief in depriving a people of their own communal beliefs without replacing them with something else by which they could live. Although he occasionally echoed the conventional European scorn for native 'superstitions', he was unusual in perceiving that 'the judgement of a European is often as much perverted by customs and prejudices as that of a Bushman'.

Living for years with ten Hottentots, he learned to appreciate or dislike them as individuals. Travelling among Bushmen, Hottentots and Tswanas, he developed an appreciation for each. He admired the meticulous circular reed dwellings and good nature of the Tswanas, although he resented their 'tobacco beggars' and insatiable importuning for presents. Tswana men made little

A south African mission of the period

distinction between a wife and a domestic slave. Generally they paid four oxen for a wife of their own tribe, but would pay ten for the more attractive Kora women, who kept their looks longer. He developed high regard for the skills, subtle culture and athletic grace of the Bushmen. These San hunters and gatherers, probably more intensely intimate with the finest details of nature than any other Africans, were feared by the Hottentots for their lethal poisoned arrows, were hunted like wild animals by the Boers to avenge cattle depredations, and were slaughtered by the Bantus, who invaded their hunting grounds. The artist in Burchell admired the Bushmen, the girls in ostrich-shell girdles, the boys, fishing with their spears, standing death-still in the water, motionless as herons.

Burchell was constantly impressed by the rich intricacy of nature in the bush, finding that 'nothing is wanting, nothing is superfluous, the smallest weed or insect is indispensably necessary to the general good. Nothing more bespeaks a littleness of mind, than to regard as useless all that does not visibly benefit man.' He was the first to observe that certain rare plants, like wild geraniums, develop noxious and even poisonous qualities to protect themselves from over-grazing. Like many great naturalists, he was himself a hunter, but lamented the excesses that by 1811 had already virtually eliminated elephant, hippopotamus, eland, rhinoceros and ostrich from most of Cape Colony.

Obliged to feed his men, with local tribes often hounding him for meat, tracking and hunting were everyday concerns. Without firearms, it was often difficult for the Africans to kill the heavier game, and the passing of a white man was an opportunity for feasting. Inevitably, Burchell was influenced by the tastes of his companions, agreeing that eland was the finest meat. He never acquired the Hottentot taste for zebra, however, which he ate only from necessity, always with the English prejudice against eating the flesh of horses or their cousins. Eating twenty-three species of antelope, several of which he 'discovered', including the sassaby and the brindled gnu or blue wildebeest, an ox-like antelope, Burchell averred that eland was even better than English beef.

Africa's largest delicacy, nearly six feet at the shoulder and weighing 1,500 lb, distinguished by a large dewlap and straight, spiral horns, eland suffered the misfortune of being favoured game for both Africans and Europeans. Faster than a horse when young, but easier to run down as they reached their imposing maturity, eland occasionally gored the horses that pursued them. Their great weight caused hunters to chase them towards camp before shooting them, an efficiency Burchell once regretted, when he sketched a wounded male with gentle black eyes just before his companions killed it.

In a dawn hunting accident, a musket exploded in the hands of Gert, a Hottentot, tearing away the palm and three fingers of his right hand. Bursting guns were a common hunting accident, especially in the heat of the chase. Normally loading free-hand, from powder horns and bullet pouches, instead of personally preparing a box of cartridges, eager hunters were likely to overload or even double-load. Burchell unsuccessfully urged his Hottentots to prepare their cartridges ahead of time, and he always maintained a supply in case of attack by a local tribe.

'Little, indeed, I knew of surgery', but faced with Gert's three fingers hanging by a strand of flesh, and dreading the job of later amputation, Burchell cut away the lost fingers and saved what he could. For weeks he treated the wound successively with Friar's Balsam, alum, vinegar, brandy and wild wormwood, making a healing plaster from candlewax and sheep fat. Eventually, his thumb and one finger serviceable, Gert was able to shoot again and to play the camp fiddle, an improvised violin made from a willow bowl, covered in sheepskin, mounted with a fingerboard and tail piece, strung with sheep's entrails and played with a horsetail bow. Near the end of the trip north, another Hottentot was run over by a wagon wheel and trampled by an ox, again developing Burchell's skills as a field surgeon.

Birds, from guinea fowl to the tasty kori bustard with a seven-foot wingspan and flesh superior to that of the wild turkey, provided a change in menu. Ostrich omelettes made a substantial treat, one egg equalling twenty-four hen's eggs. Once finding twenty-five eggs in a multiple nest scratched in the sand, with nine more eggs waiting in a surrounding trench as first food for the chicks, Burchell's companions prepared a feast. Often unfertilized, the outer eggs made better eating. One cock and up to five hens will share a nest, which can contain up to eighty eggs. Each Hottentot consumed an entire egg, expertly prepared to taste by piercing a hole at one end, inserting a forked stick with the ends pinched together as it entered the egg, and twirling the stick between the hands to scramble the egg as it cooked in its shell over the fire.

The finest bush orgy, however, was a hippopotamus feast, for a 3,500 lb hippo carries more fat than any other quadruped, and animal fat was the African's favourite food. The rich 'sea-cow pork' is so fatty over the hippo's ribs that, exposed to the sun, it melts like butter. Known as a 'river horse' by the ancients, and called a *zeekoe*, or sea cow, by the early Dutch settlers, a hippopotamus is more dense than water and can walk on the floor of a lake with its lungs full of air. The hippo generally lives in water by day, often with only its periscopic eyes probing above the surface, being able to stay down for five or six minutes, and regularly consumes over a hundred pounds of vegetation during its nocturnal excursions. Dangerous when surprised or cut off from their home waters, highly territorial, hippopotamus are difficult quarry for the lightly armed, and Bushmen hunted them by digging *kysi*-pits, animal traps, lengthwise along the hippo tracks that led to the water.

When it had been killed, its heavy skin was pulled back like planks from the sides of a ship and bushels of half-chewed grass were scraped from its stomach and intestines. The hippo then became a flesh market, as every man turned butcher. Strips of drying meat hung from bushes, and 'all around was carving, broiling, gnawing and chewing'. As the Hottentots devoured the animal, Burchell himself enjoyed a handsome hippo steak, while the friendly Bushmen drank bowls of melted fat, rejoicing over the offal, entrails and head. Nothing

A feast in the bush

was wasted. To extend the delight, a vat made of hippo hide was set in the wagon, with pieces of fat lying in salt. Cut into strips, the $1\frac{1}{2}$ inch thick hide was also preserved to make the thirty-foot ox whips whose crack could be heard for two miles, and for shorter whips, the brutally effective *jamboks*.

On more sedate occasions, Burchell relished the tongue of the black rhinoceros, or honey bartered from the Bushmen for tobacco, while his companions simmered a pot of blood over the fire, stirring it gently until it acquired 'nearly the consistence of liver'. His most sophisticated dish, a stew of eland, buffalo, hippo and camelopard, as giraffe were called, was served to him by the otherwise ungenerous missionaries of the Dissenting Missionary Society of London.

Burchell's diaries mention few encounters with dangerous game, possibly because the surviving pages cover less than half the time he was in the bush, but his observations on lion provide details of interest to later hunters. He was one of the first to document that lion are more dangerous during severe storms. Stimulated, their lethargy seems to leave them. Not intimidated by lightning and thunder, they prowl and hunt more aggressively, pursuing the distracted and unsettled animals around them.

One afternoon, carrying only his pistols, Burchell found himself confronting a large, black-maned lion, which the Hottentots said were more dangerous than the 'pale lion'. This prejudice, holding that the quality of a lion is determined by the darkness of its mane, rather than by its size, endures among hunters even today. Advancing to within a few yards of Burchell and appearing about to spring, the lion was surrounded by Burchell's dogs in a tight, yapping circle. Seeming to ignore them and looking only at Burchell, the lion suddenly flashed out a paw, killing two dogs with imperceptible exertion, and then made its escape after being lightly wounded.

Awakened a week later by the prodigious roaring of a lion, his oxen panicking and breaking loose from their ties, the deep, trembling noise resembling the sound of the earthquake he had survived in Cape Town, Burchell hurried to build up the fires. Later he ascertained that lions make this unforgettable din, different from their usual growling, by putting their heads low to the ground and sending the noise rolling along the earth.

Two 'discoveries' he did not enjoy eating were the quagga and the white rhinoceros, at four tons the second largest land animal, much heavier but far less dangerous than the black rhinoceros. Both types of rhino are in fact grey in colour, and often acquire the tones of the dust or mud in which they wallow. The square-muzzled white rhino, once known as 'Burchell's rhinoceros', is built for grazing and prefers the light scrub of the open savannah. One theory holds that this rhino is called 'white' because of the Afrikaans word *wid*, or wide, describing its broad mouth. The more aggressive black rhino favours thick thorn country, using its pointed, prehensile upper lip to seize the thorny branches and bark that form its prickly diet.

The quagga, sometimes known as 'Burchell's zebra', was a larger, heavier zebra, with smaller ears, and a fuller mane and tail. Even more equine than other zebra, with clear striping only on the head and neck, the quagga was to be an early victim of European extermination. Only seventy-two years after Burchell's initial recording of the *Equus quagga burchelli*, the last specimen died in captivity in Amsterdam in 1883.

In one thing Burchell failed, a failure that evidences the dark ignorance about Africa and her wildlife of nineteenth-century Europeans. Three weeks before setting out from the Cape, he wrote to his mother that he was certain to be paid at least £7,500 'should I be so fortunate as to discover the unicorn'. A giraffe skin recently had been sold in England for £1,500, over twice what it had cost to outfit Burchell's safari, and he calculated that a unicorn would fetch five times as much.

To Burchell, every spot on which his wagon stood was home. Evening camp became his greatest pleasure, his men mingling and laughing with the Bushmen around a camp fire, the exhausted oxen munching quietly, the sheep with their heads turned towards the firelight, baggage and guns hanging from trees, his horse tied to a branch, the dogs asleep in the shadows, including his favourite, Wantrouw, a keen expert in 'comparative anatomy' and the 'greatest canine traveller in memory'. As the fire died, the 'pale silvery light of the bright moon played upon the feathery foliage' and the star Sirius shone at its zenith as the 'romantic character of the scene kept me from sleep'.

Cape wagon as depicted by Burchell

Most of all, Burchell 'caught a spirit of enthusiasm which seemed like some fascinating power emanating from the strange objects which everywhere surrounded me'. Like the hunters who followed him, he relished 'the delightful sensation of unshackled existence that can never be recalled'. Back in Fulham, dedicating ten years to preparing his diaries and to classifying tens of thousands of specimens, Burchell was refreshed by his memories of trekking by moonlight in the cool brightness of the night, wrapped in his watch-coat. Later in life Burchell recognized that 'the perfection of Nature in the wilds of Africa was the irresistible motive which led me on'. Finally, although long celebrated as England's foremost exploring botanist, honoured by Oxford University, and with his work broadened by five years of research in the Amazon jungle, Burchell, ill and still alone, killed himself.

In 1813, while Burchell sat on the fore-chest of his wagon sketching flowers and animals north of the Orange River, the young Cornwallis Harris, who was to follow Burchell and found the tradition of the great African safaris, was learning to draw and stalking hare and deer in the Kent countryside. At the age of six, already fascinated by hunting, 'devoted to woodcraft from the cradle', he took Betsy, an old family blunderbuss, from the wall and shot sparrows over the neighbour's pigsty. Punished, he avenged himself at the age of seven by building a cross-bow and pricking the neighbour's geese with tiny, hand-carved arrows. Severely beaten, gun and bow confiscated, Cornwallis Harris determined to become the greatest hunter in the world.

At sixteen Harris sailed for Bombay as a second lieutenant in the military engineers of the East India Company. Army life in India made him hard and independent, able to ride all day and shoot from the saddle like an Afghan, training himself with a rifle to hit a soaring hawk at a hundred and fifty yards. Tough and artistic, he regretted that existing portraits of Indian wildlife lacked authenticity. Often his saddle carried more paints and brushes than food and water. Deep in the aromatic teak and sandalwood forests of the Abu Mountains, instead of shooting he would dismount to sketch the hill game of western India.

Like other nineteenth-century British adventurers, Harris became an eclectic combination of martial and creative talents. William Burchell's coloured engravings and diaries, published in London in 1822 and 1824 under the title *Travels in the Interior of Southern Africa*, finally made their way to India. This began the chain of inspiration that, for a century and a half, has drawn men to the safari life of the African bush, as the tales of each generation of hunter inspired the next.

From the moment Cornwallis Harris studied Burchell's accounts and luminous depictions of the landscape and animals of Africa, his life was changed. He would see in his 'dreams the slender and swanlike neck of the stately giraffe, bowing distantly to our better acquaintance'. Even when tiger hunting in Gujarat, mounted on Mowla-Bukhsh, 'whilst urging my elephant to his utmost speed in pursuit of a retreating tiger', his thoughts would turn to Africa. Just as

Major Sir William Cornwallis
Harris, by O. Oakley

Burchell was drawn by the botanical riches of Africa, so Harris was lured by the incredible wildlife that haunted his imagination.

Ordered to Cape Colony in 1836 to recover from an Indian fever, Cornwallis Harris determined to turn his two-year convalescence into a prolonged hunting expedition deep into the interior of uncolonized Africa. A generation or more before the legendary expeditions of David Livingstone, Richard Francis Burton, John Speke and Samuel Baker, Harris went for the sport of it. Instead of a rest cure, he planned the first African safari. Even before stepping ashore at Cape

Colony, after an eleven-week voyage on a large 'Indiaman', Harris had already recruited a fellow passenger and English sportsman, William Richardson of the Bombay Civil Service, to join him, 'heart, hand and purse'.

But South Africa was in turmoil. Both blacks and whites were on the move. To the north and east, the Zulus, a warlike tribe of the Nguni, the largest of the Bantu peoples of southern Africa, were exterminating their neighbours. In Cape Colony itself, 1836 was the first year of the Great Boer Trek. Under pressure from parliamentary abolitionists and public opinion in England, in 1828 the Cape authorities had decreed that all free natives had the same rights and protection as the settlers.

Then Britain's Slave Emancipation Act of 1833 ended slavery throughout the British empire, a quarter of the world, and required that the 36,000 slaves in Cape Colony should be set free by 1838. This Act launched the Great Trek. Believing they had toiled to build a civilized, truly Christian society in a barbarous wilderness, the Boers saw equality as a loss of their own rights, and emancipation as a theft of their property. They particularly resented the British missionaries, who, equally stubborn and moralistic, advocated the rights of the natives as 'fellow human beings'. The godfearing Boers, on the other hand, found in Genesis ix, 25, their justification for treating Africans as 'creatures', as the cursed 'sons of Ham'.

Three Boer scouting parties, secretly sent ahead in 1834, reported that the land north of the Orange River was fertile, rich with game and virtually unpopulated. This was probably a recent condition attributable to the internecine Bantu wars, both the Sotho massacres of the 1820s, known as the Mfecane, and the Zulu conflicts of the 1820s and 1830s. Finally, in 1836, two years after the Boer scouting parties, seven thousand hardy Afrikaaners, the Voortrekkers, determined to escape British colonial administration, struggled north in their wagons with their cattle and slaves, settling in what became the Orange Free State, Natal and the Transvaal.

While this resettlement was under way Harris and Richardson arrived in Cape Town, each attended by an Indian servant. Knowing the India of 1836 to be already a civilized centre of empire, rich in the luxuries of both East and West, and anticipating the savagery of Africa, Harris also brought his camping essentials, including his teapot, tent, drawing materials and a barrel of gunpowder.

The hunters planned to launch their safari from Graaff-Reinet, an immaculate Dutch village 370 miles north-east of Cape Town, but perhaps twice that by the route that circumvented the desert of the Great Karoo. Reaching Graaff-Reinet by coastal schooner, wagon and horseback, crossing two mountain ranges and the Fish River, the travellers were well broken in before the safari started, finding themselves received as 'Indian gentlemen' by the up-country Boers. Before they set out, Harris was robbed by a Boer farmer, lost an ox that strangled itself in the night, had a wagon overturn in the mountains, and was abandoned by his once faithful Muhammadan servant. The man 'preferred

The first safari sets out, by William Cornwallis Harris

returning to India to eat his curry with true believers'. Harris's plan was to penetrate rapidly as far as possible into the interior, and then find the best hunting ground, reaching at least as far north as the Tropic of Capricorn. In addition to general sport and adventure, Harris had two aspirations,

> Next to the slaughter of the proud giraffe, the desire nearest to my heart was to discover something new. Not a new lizard, nor a new rat, no, nor even – by which to immortalize myself as a naturalist – a new weasel; but an entirely new something or other, some stately quarry unknown to science and adorning no museum saving mine own.

Different hunters are drawn to different animals. To Cornwallis Harris, the giraffe represented the magic of African wildlife, the eccentric combination of qualities that caused it to be known in his day as the 'camelopard'. Harris was a student of wildlife mythology, and the giraffe was a chimera as fabled as the unicorn or sphinx. First displayed by Julius Caesar in Rome, the decorative giraffe featured in Roman circus games and triumphs. Later the giraffe became the ultimate gift, favoured tribute for the despot who had everything. In 1403 the Sultan of Babylon sent six ostriches and a giraffe to Tamerlane the Magnificent. In 1827, while Harris was in India, the Pasha of Egypt sent one each to the courts of France and England, the first giraffe seen in Europe since the one given to Lorenzo de Medici in the late fifteenth century.

With the Great Trek underway, wagons and horses were at a premium. Harris had great difficulty in accumulating two Cape wagons, forty-two draught oxen and a stud of twelve motley horses. Like most Indian veterans, he and his companion knew that an honest drink would be useful in the field. Compelled to dispense with the 'luxury of beer, so palatable to an Anglo-Indian', they packed in 'a few dozens of brandy, and a small barrel of inferior spirits for the use of the followers'.

Loading the baggage wagon with dried fish and cheese, axes and carpentry tools, spare metal parts for the wagons, 18,000 prepared bullets, pigs of lead and bullet moulds, and his own wagon with weapons, bales of coffee and chests of tea and barter goods, Harris compared them to ships proceeding to sea, with a long voyage ahead. Like the best English sailors of the period, the eight Hottentots engaged by the hunters, most of them former convicts, had to be pried from the gin shops before the safari could leave. After pawning the muskets with which Harris had equipped them, they collapsed into 'drunkenness and debauchery' and were 'loaded like pigs into the wagons they had been hired to drive'. One of the more sober Hottentots crashed one wagon into a house while driving out of Graaff-Reinet in the dark.

As Harris and his small safari travelled north, they first struggled through the high passes of the Snow Mountains, described by Burchell a quarter century before as 'the great portals by which the interior of Africa may be entered'. Making his way through falling snow and mountain streams crisp with morning ice, Harris was relieved to descend into the valleys, where he saw his first wildebeest, and, in an abandoned Boer farmyard, a wrinkled African smoking *dacca*, the narcotic wild hemp, through a bullock-horn water pipe.

Pausing at a prosperous farm, then and now the cornerstone of Afrikaaner life, Cornwallis Harris appreciated the legendary Boer hospitality, the sturdy *vruow* perpetually serving tea at an outdoor table, the patriarch surrounded by his bondsmen and the farms of his children, enjoying his own fruit brandy. The hearty dinner, swimming in sheep's-tail fat, was preceded by an extended grace, and the customary washing of the feet, as a slave carried the tub of water from one diner to the next. Noting that one tub served for all, and that the feet were then wiped on the tablecloth, the Englishmen, accustomed from boarding-school to bathing rarely, declined to participate. Deploring the 'primitive' Boer custom of eating at noon, observing a coffin hanging from the rafters among the dried meat and sausages, Harris remarked that 'to see one of these bleak abodes is to see all'.

The education available at Boer farms was generally restricted to one volume, the Old Testament. Occasional contributions were made by itinerant teachers, in this case a diminutive Frenchman, paid in food and cattle. With an Englishman's appreciation of French culture, Harris noted that the tutor, 'pedantic, disputatious and garrulous to the most wearisome extent . . . inherited all the grimaces and vivacity of his progenitors'. The Frenchman further annoyed Harris by flattering and courting the women of the household. When the tutor paused, the host would repeatedly denounce the British Parliament for reducing his farm to poverty by abolishing slavery.

On the seventh day of the safari, Harris came upon one of the miracles of the bush, a gathering of springbok, the only gazelle native to South Africa. Reddish, small-horned, two and a half feet at the shoulder, springbok are given to 'pronking', leaping over ten feet into the air, with back arched, legs extended and hooves bunched together. He paused to paint a portrait of nineteen springboks against the pink flowers and grey hills that spotted the plain, taken by the rich chestnut bands traversing their flanks, their elegant 'bird-like flight' and later, their succulent venison.

In his diaries, Harris recorded the 'myriads which covered the plains', confirming earlier reports of the poet Thomas Pringle that, driven by occasional droughts and famines in their heartland north of the Orange River, periodic migrations of springboks, known as *trekbokken*, swarmed south, literally covering the veld like locusts or American bison. Flocks of sheep in their path were swept away by the torrent, herdsmen were trampled to death, lions were seen stalking in their compressed phalanx. Farmers in the Snow Mountain region burned piles of manure along the margins of their fields to drive off the springboks at night, but dawn found the fields stripped bare. Later travellers were to affirm Harris's report, carefully estimating the trekbokken in the millions, occasionally documenting their desperate, thirsty marches into the ocean itself, where they perished of the salt water, and left the beaches red and tan, covered in bodies for stretches of thirty miles.

Plentiful as some animals still were in the Colony, Harris was mindful of the loss of free habitat and the overshooting of game already under way. He recorded that two antelopes, blesbok and hartebeest, were already reduced to a single herd each in the Colony, both under the protection of the British colonial government, as was the hippopotamus. The earliest efforts at game conservation in Africa had been enacted by the Dutch in 1657 and 1684, when each farmer was limited to one rhinoceros, hippo and eland per year.

Soon Harris was relishing the daily schedule that still characterizes safaris, rising at dawn with strong, dark tea, pushing hard all day, an evening feast, then drink and cigars by a fire as night settles in. Each day the practical demands of the safari required different talents, melting pigs of lead into bullet moulds, dragging an ox from quicksand, carving a new rifle stock after his horse fell and smashed it during a hard chase. Disappointed that his Hottentots were far inferior trackers to his hunting companions in India, Harris made a cast of the footprint of each African species and soon learned to distinguish them instantly. Each morning he lay awake listening, waiting for the rapid African sunrise, understanding now why Burchell wrote that 'nothing but breathing the air of Africa, and actually walking through it, can communicate the indescribable sensations which every traveller of feeling will experience'.

Leaving the borders of Cape Colony, the safari traversed over three hundred miles of mostly desolate plains, arid, free of vegetation, with only ostrich and occasional Bushmen relieving the stony landscape and baking saltpans, where the oxen died painfully from heat and hunger. These were not the Bushmen of Burchell's experience, threatened by Boer and Bantu, but still living by their own code in their own land. These seemed instead to be dispossessed, desperate survivors, driven where even they could not endure. Famished, they existed on roots, locusts and ant larvae, for safety living far from water, carrying a few drops in ostrich shells, sometimes resembling skeletons draped with wet cloth.

Gnu or wildebeest, by Cornwallis Harris

It seemed that the 'hand of these wandering outcasts is against every man, and every man's hand is against them'.

Refreshed by the startling contrast of the sparkling Orange River, three hundred yards wide, bordered in willows, Harris's small caravan struggled across, sheep and horses swimming, as double teams of oxen hauled the heavy wagons through the water, the baggage raised on elevated platforms. Moving north for the next month, the safari gradually entered richer country beyond the missionary station at Kuruman, where Harris met the Revd Robert Moffat, the future father-in-law of Dr David Livingstone.

Soon they were greeted by ocean-like expanses of waving grass, and clusters of flowering shrubs and mimosa trees. Near the lush banks of the Meritsane River, troops of Burchell's zebra mingled with herds of brindled wildebeests, mixed with sassabys and hartebeests, two large antelopes, as many as 15,000 in one scene, packed 'like a Manchester mob', until the landscape appeared a moving mass of game, the country 'actually chequered black and white with their congregated masses'. As Harris and Richardson galloped among the animals, excited as schoolboys, the sound of the rushing game resembled the din of a cavalry charge. Shooting as they rode, the horsemen were followed by four Tswana hunters who killed the wounded animals by pricking their spines with assegais, or spears, and then covered the bodies with thorn bushes to keep off the vultures. Destitute of cattle since their conquest by the Matabele, meat-hungry, the Tswanas were eager for the hunt. Matabele is a tribal name derived from the root '−tebele', meaning to 'drop from sight', as the Matabele in battle disappeared from sight behind their five-foot, oval ox-hide shields.

For Harris and Richardson, it was fine sport and good training, but it was not yet the land of the heavy, dangerous game that had drawn them to Africa. As they advanced into the territory of the earlier Bantu wars, they passed abandoned kraals, or village compounds, and broken huts, occasionally meeting the survivors of Sotho tribes, including the Tswanas that Burchell had known. Hardened in India by swarms of professional beggars, the hunters were not daunted by jostling groups of curious Tswanas, each demanding *muchuco*, tobacco. Since Burchell's day, tobacco, however, had lost value among the Tswanas due to its planting locally. Beads were now the favoured exchange for barter. Occasionally, pressed too hard by Tswanas who actually seized their property or intimidated their Hottentots, the hunters recovered by a show of force with their shotguns, sometimes falling back on that supreme confidence that is the silver lining of upper-class English arrogance, courageous in the belief that one educated Englishman can deal with the world.

Often Harris set off alone on foot or horseback to hunt or study game. Always he carried sketching materials in his cap. After shooting an animal he would repeatedly measure it with a tape and two-foot rule, checking its proportions, determined that his picture be true to nature. Generally he made careful drawings in the field or in his wagon, and painted in colour with a fine brush later. His tracking and stalking sharpened until he was far better in the bush than his Hottentot companions. Every day he adapted and improved a lifetime of hunting skills learned in England and India. Frequently he used the crotch of his staff as a gun rest, after tacking in obliquely as he approached his quarry while feigning another course. His determination to depict each animal's social behaviour in its true setting made him more alert and analytical both as artist and hunter. Each day he drew closer to Africa, completing the intimate connections between subject and artist, animal and hunter.

Obsessed with accuracy, deploring naturalist artists who worked from zoos or mounted trophies, Harris observed in the bush that the skin of certain antelopes, such as kudu, loses its lustre and hue almost immediately after death. To capture the true colour, with a wounded animal at bay, he would sometimes pause to paint his subject before he dispatched it. Stopping to do this with his first eland, struck by its beauty after a long chase on horseback, suddenly touched, as Burchell had been, by the appeal in its clear black eye, he was horrified when the Tswanas came running up and exulted in repeatedly stabbing the dying animal. Despite his regrets, he later agreed with them that 'the venison fairly melts in the mouth, the brisket is absolutely fit for a monarch'.

As Harris approached the Molopo River, desolate villages with broken stone walls, mounds of skeletons and the panic of his wagon driver announced the realm of the gifted tyrant, Mzilikazi, King of the Matabele. More important to Harris, the sport was improving. Lion were raiding the camp at night, killing sheep. Rhinoceros, hippopotamus and buffalo became plentiful. Bushy-tailed wild dogs hunted the hartebeest, successively sprinting after the antelope until the hungry pack finally ran it down. Large herds of game gathered to eat the new grass where the Matabele herdsmen had burned the withered grass to improve grazing.

Harris was particularly excited by his exhausting pursuit of three oryx, or gemsbok, agreeing with other observers that this antelope is the source of the unicorn legend, which he himself traced back to ancient Persia and Egypt,

Gemsbok, by Cornwallis Harris

through Plantagenet heraldry and the British royal arms. A powerful animal, with exceptional endurance and will to live, weighing 450 lb, 4 ft at the shoulder, with a tan body and black and white face, the oryx carries straight horns 3 ft long. Known to kill even lion when attacked, wounded oryx can be dangerous to approach. As Harris pointed out, seen in profile, or when one horn is lost, the oryx closely resembles the classic depictions of the unicorn fable.

The leader of a renegade Zulu clan, the Matabele or Abaka-Zulu, Mzilikazi was building the Matabele nation by the traditional methods. Killing every adult male in the tribes that resisted him, seizing their women and cattle, and absorbing their young men into his highly trained impis, or regiments, Mzilikazi had won the respect of both Africans and Europeans. Mzilikazi's impis were modelled on the disciplined impis created by Shaka, who had built the great Zulu kingdom twenty years before by organizing his followers and slaughtering his neighbours. Mzilikazi's Matabeles fought in tight ranks like a Roman legion, with a dense central mass and flanking units or 'horns' to surround the enemy. They used the short stabbing assegai that Shaka had invented for close fighting, on the same principle as the Roman short sword. Death was the penalty for losing an assegai in battle.

Like Shaka a highly intelligent and a careful planner, Mzilikazi was building a complex feudal system of military communities and vassal states, probably more efficiently organized than the white society of Cape Colony. On hostile terms with Dingane, Shaka's murderer, brother and even more bloodthirsty successor, and wishing to avoid the Europeans to the south, Mzilikazi had led his people on a seven-hundred-mile trek north-west from Zululand on the Indian Ocean to settle between the Vaal and Limpopo rivers, at the expense of the resident Tswanas. Behind him, his impis raiding voraciously as he advanced, Mzilikazi was proud to leave a two-hundred-mile trail through the eastern Transvaal empty of human life. Both Hottentots and missionaries warned Harris to avoid his kingdom, but Harris was determined to shoot in Mzilikazi's rich hunting grounds. He had come, after all, for the sport.

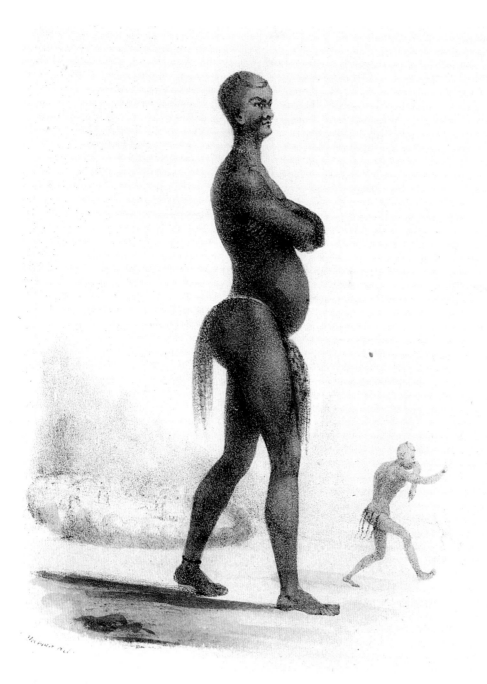

Mzilikazi, King of the Matabele, by
Cornwallis Harris

Between conquests Mzilikazi, the Black Bull Elephant, would emerge from
his seraglio of a hundred women in the royal enclosure, half a mile in
circumference, that his Sotho slaves had built of mimosa logs. His body
glistening with grease and hung with beads, he diverted himself by impaling his
victims on four-foot, inch-thick stakes and drinking heavy sorghum beer. The
Zulu and Matabele courts were celebrated for their royal herds and feasts of
beef, beans and pumpkins, pursuing the high standard set by a court glutton,
who earned his place by eating an entire goat at one sitting. Always wary,
seeking to extend his power, fearing enemies black and white, Mzilikazi did not
welcome visitors. Already he was skirmishing with the Boer settlers as they
encroached from the south.

Harris had prepared himself in Cape Town by packing into his wagon chests of beads, thin ropes of twisted tobacco, and a royal cloak, specially fashioned for Mzilikazi from rough cotton duffel, lavished with six fur capes hanging from the shoulders, lined in scarlet worsted and fastened by bone buttons and a crested brass clasp. The opportunity to present the gifts came one evening in October 1836.

The safari was making camp for the night five miles from the Matabele military town of Mosega, near a chain of swampy lakes where the rock-like heads of wallowing buffalo mingled with the tall tufted stems of the marsh grasses. Harris found that the dangerous Cape buffalo, $5\frac{1}{2}$ ft at the shoulder, weighing up to 1,800 lb, with poor eyesight and fair hearing but a keen sense of smell, gave good sport and decent meat. In a straight charge, because the hard base, or boss, of its thick horns spreads like a 'bulletproof casque' across its forehead, it was almost impossible to stop with the weapons of the day. Harris, not easily deterred, found parts of its tough hide 'impenetrable to a ball of unadulterated lead, more especially if propelled from a smooth bore'.

The Cape buffalo bears little resemblance to either its domesticated cousin, the water buffalo, or to the dwarf forest buffalo of west and central Africa. Once aroused, either by a rival in the season of love, or by a wound or disturbance, the Cape buffalo can be the hardest of all animals to put down. If adrenalin starts to flood the system, even cruel wounds will not deter the buffalo from a relentless and often crafty pursuit of its adversary, frequently circling and waiting in the tall grass to charge the enemy that follows its bloody trail.

Shortly after Harris returned to camp from pursuing a buffalo until his shoeless horse fell lame, four armed Matabele warriors strode into camp, bearing messages from Mzilikazi's deputy governor at Mosega. 'Tall, straight, well proportioned, of regular features, although of very dark complexion', the warriors impressed Harris as superior to any tribe he had yet seen. Their heads shaved and crowned with an *issigoko*, a circle of animal sinews blackened with grease, wearing leather girdles hung with leopard skins, they carried knobbed throwing sticks and short assegais.

Sharing the camp fire with his Matabele guests, Harris made friends over an immense beef dinner and presents of snuff. The men carried *qui*, or snuff, in a small gourd secured in a perforation cut in one ear lobe. An ivory sniffing spoon hung from the neck. Great draughts were taken in sharp breaths, until the tears flowed. Harris found that smoking was not a fashionable vice among the Matabele.

Advancing towards Mzilikazi's royal kraal, having sent a pound of beads ahead as a first offering, Harris learned that the king had ordered a five-thousand-man impi two hundred miles south across the Vaal River to destroy a party of invading Boer farmers at Vegkop. Undeterred, needing meat for a growing circle of Matabele guests, the Englishmen went after buffalo, pursuing the huge beasts on horseback into the swampy lakes, the water up to the horses' girths and the reeds reaching far above the riders' heads, unable to see the quarry, but following the noise as the buffalo rushed through the water. A general skirmish developed as the animals broke for the next lake. Turning, wounded and hard to stop, blood pumping from its nostrils, one buffalo charged Piet van Roy, a Hottentot hunter, smashing him down in the water and then dying under a karra tree as Harris galloped three miles round the lake to the rescue.

After the hunt, American missionaries based at Mosega reported that the king, encouraged by the beads, insisted that the hunters join him at once, declaring them to be 'his own white people'. The Americans, however, warned Harris of Mzilikazi's unspeakable atrocities and varied styles of execution, including decapitation, genital amputation, skewering and crocodiles. Annoyed that the king forbad his people to work for them, the Americans denounced the abject deference Mzilikazi required as 'little according with American notions of tolerance'. Aware that slavery still flourished in America even when it was dying in Africa, and himself an ardent abolitionist,* Harris was amused that, unlike other tribes, the haughty Matabele mocked the missionaries, ogling them as if they were 'wild beasts in a menagerie'.

On the way to the royal kraal, Harris got lost in a maze of Matabele hunting traps made of tall thorn branches set in the ground and broke the stock of his favourite double rifle when his horse fell violently in a hole, breaking its nose. Binding the stock with a strip of hide from the sassaby he had just killed, he was thrilled to come upon the spoor of camelopard, his first tracks of giraffe, shortly before killing a rhino that blocked the path.

Mzilikazi, 'the very beau ideal of an African chief', impressed the Englishmen when he visited their tent shortly after the safari made camp outside his gate. Naked except for a narrow leather girdle hung with leopard tails, he wore on his scalp three long turquoise tail feathers from a lilac-breasted roller, a bird also to be known as 'Mzilikazi's roller', as no man but he was allowed to wear its plumage. Tall, dignified, capable, cunning and greedy as a banker, Mzilikazi enthusiastically accepted the great cloak, a 2 ft mirror, coiled copper wire, 2 lb of Blackguard Irish snuff and 50 lb of his favourite red beads, known in the bead trade as *mangazi*, the Matabele word for blood. Accustomed to owning everything he saw, the sole possessor of all cattle, harvests, women and booty

* The British abolitionist movement is incorrectly remembered as a movement principally of preachers and moralists, of William Wilberforce, John Philip and David Livingstone. In fact, its broad support was probably more due to traditional British notions of individual rights than to Christianity, more to the Magna Carta than to the Bible. It was the officers of the Royal Navy who freed the slaves. They directly liberated at least 150,000 slaves, and fought the slave trade in the Indian Ocean and the south Atlantic from 1807 until the mid nineteenth century, even landing on the African coasts and destroying the slave barracoons. When the foreign ministers of Europe, carving up Napoleon's empire at the Congress of Vienna in 1814, asked the Duke of Wellington what England wanted, since Saxony and the Duchy of Warsaw were already spoken for, Wellington amazed them by requesting an end to the slave trade. Cornwallis Harris's generation of Indian Army officers were keen students of the Duke's military career in India thirty years before, and knew his reputation as a horseman, hunter and abolitionist. Wellington's leadership and attitudes influenced them far more than the clergy. Napoleon, on the other hand, in 1802 re-authorized slavery in the French colonies.

from the Molopo to the Limpopo rivers, the king was not satisfied. He wanted more, and Harris wanted to be the first white man to hunt freely throughout his realm, particularly after the great elephant herds of the Magaliesberg Mountains.

Well matched, for days Mzilikazi and Cornwallis Harris tantalized each other before the safari could proceed. The king personally snatched the red silk braces from the back of Richardson's Indian servant, Nesserwanjee Motabhoy. Still not satisfied, he took Harris's own shoes and the red tasselled cord off his pyjama trousers, rummaging on his knees through the wagons until the hunters closed a chest of beads upon the king's eager hands.

When Mzilikazi himself hunted animals, he did it in style. Deploying several thousand men in a vast circle enclosing many square miles, the king waited while they slowly converged, forcing together incredible numbers of excited game. As the men became a solid ring, the hunters fought to kill the desperate animals, displaying 'the most daring and dangerous sport that can be conceived'. Only the hyena were spared, as the Matabele acknowledged their supernatural powers.

Harris found that Mzilikazi's seraglio contained a captive concubine named Truey, daughter of Peter Davids, chief of the Griquas, the 'Bechuana Bastaards', a tribe of horsemen of mixed blood, part Hottentot and part white. Perhaps seventeen and wildly voluptuous, but oppressed by her role as Mzilikazi's favourite, Truey asked Harris to report to her father. Later the king gave Truey to her admirer, one-eyed Andries Africander, Harris's laziest and luckiest

Below left: Truey, the Griqua maid, by Cornwallis Harris

Below right: Andries Africander, by Cornwallis Harris

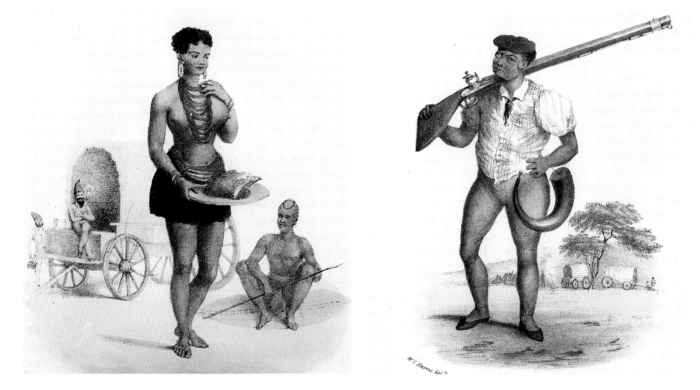

Hottentot. As further inducement for Andries to join his own retinue, the king gave Andries a hornless ox, also with a bad left eye to match his own.

Conversing through a chain of four interpreters, Mzilikazi proclaimed the English were his friends, and that William IV was the most powerful monarch after himself. He was evidently not aware of the severe limitations on the authority of the English king. At first Mzilikazi attempted to conceal news of the battle his impi had fought with the Boer trekkers at Vegkop only eight days before. Losing hundreds of Matabele warriors, but seizing 100 horses, 500 cattle and 50,000 sheep, Mzilikazi counted it a victory. The trekkers who survived considered it a Boer victory. Their fifty-eight wagons laagered in two concentric circles, the fifty outer ones chained wheel-to-wheel, with acacia thorns stuffed under the wagons, the men ceaselessly fired their muzzle-loaders at brave waves of Matabele. Shot and powder were loaded from open buckets by the women and children, including the young Paul Kruger, who later became president of the Boer Republic of the Transvaal. It was the laager technique that the Boers had first employed in the western Cape in 1685, and it was soon to be used in the American west.

Continuing to snoop and snatch in Harris's tent, Mzilikazi took the Indian's pocketknife, the chest of beads and Harris's heavy hunting boots. The loss of the boots later proved painful. Finally, Mzilikazi demanded the safari tent itself. Willing to part with anything save his sport, Harris promised the tent in exchange for licence to hunt and travel where he pleased. Sending his compliments to King William, giving Richardson a leopard-skin girdle and Harris his own greasy weasel-skin cloak in return for a Persian carpet, Mzilikazi cheerfully waved his guests on their way.

Pleased with Harris, Mzilikazi later welcomed the missionary David Livingstone, considering himself a friend of the British, and resisted the land-hungry Afrikaaners, who, after brutal battles, were soon to drive the Matabele north of the Limpopo River into what became Rhodesia.

Harris, however, was to miss his hunting boots. Later in the safari, riding with rough, untanned shoes made in camp, Harris caught a foot in his stirrup as he leapt down to shoot. His horse galloped off, dragging and kicking him, ripping the clothes from his back and the skin from his shoulders.

The day after leaving Mzilikazi, while hunting eland to feed a large party of Africans who were following the wagons, Harris, 'half-choked with excitement', spotted his first giraffe moving among the trees. Giving chase, his double-barrelled rifle in one hand, the giraffe 'gliding gallantly along like some tall ship upon the ocean's bosom, sailing before me with incredible velocity', Harris pursued the giraffe recklessly over broken, rocky ground, and twice dismounted to fire on the animal's hindquarters with no apparent effect. Finally the giraffe began to tire. As Harris came up to it, galloping hard, his horse fell into a pit, pitching Harris forward into an ostrich nest. The lashings of his rifle snapped with the fall, the stock hanging loosely from the trigger guard. Remounting his stunned horse, Harris tried to bind the rifle with his handkerchief so that he could shoot. Unable to get the hammer to come down on the brass nipple, he desperately sought a stone or knife to do the job, but he had lent his knife to a Hottentot to behead a hartebeest.

Frustrated, his dream of giraffe hunting eluding him, Harris instead collected twenty-three ostrich eggs, which the Hottentots carried by stripping off their trousers and tying up the bottoms to form sacks. Agreeing with Burchell that one ostrich equalled two dozen chicken eggs, he was amazed that some of his companions devoured two. After a hearty omelette, Harris built a blacksmith's forge and repaired the double rifle with the iron clamp of a storage box, binding it with the tightening green hide of an eland, aware that his life could be no more secure than his rifle.

While Harris was losing his first giraffe, Richardson narrowly escaped a wounded rhinoceros which was chasing his horse so closely that his second shot was fired with the end of the barrel actually in the rhino's mouth, so that the animal damaged the rifle as it fell. Continually pressed by the Africans for meat, early the next day Harris shot a large white rhino, which required six two-ounce bullets behind the shoulder before it collapsed. Retiring to the wagons for breakfast, he found a horde of visitors demanding snuff, particularly one old lady who inhaled from the back of her hand through a long wooden tube. Later, after crossing two deep rivers with steep banks, requiring the brake wheels to be locked as the wagons descended almost perpendicularly, the hunters met Mzilikazi's son Kulumane, an aristocratic lad, who immediately stole a clasp knife from one of the Hottentots.

Soon they crossed paths with Mzilikazi's impi returning from the battle at Vegkop. Driving the Boers' cattle before them, carrying wounded comrades on bullet-torn shields, the warriors passed by all day in groups of hundreds. In full battle regalia, in monkey-tail kilts, their joints hung with feathery ox tails, carrying the weapons of their dead as tribute to Mzilikazi, 'nothing could be more savage, wild and martial'. That evening the safari, travelling under the king's protection, shared camp fires with the exhilarated Matabele warriors, who feasted on beef, chanted the praises of Mzilikazi, and stamping, leaping and beating their sticks, danced to exhaustion.

As the safari moved southwards towards the Magaliesberg Mountains, hunting to feed his men, Harris became perhaps the first European to shoot a waterbuck, a 450 lb grey-brown antelope, 4 ft at the shoulder, with 3 ft curved horns and a distinctive white ring across its rump. Although it reminded him of India's stately sambur stag, Harris was disappointed by the poor quality and rank, carrion-like smell of the waterbuck's flesh. But he was thrilled to find, on the same day, the first traces of elephant: the giant spoor and mimosa trees torn up by the roots.

Moving on through the Magaliesberg Mountains, following the elephant trails, Harris was awed by the wild chasms, stupendous forests and lush beauty around him. Rhinoceros often obstructed the wagons and, in their flight,

charged without provocation, becoming so plentiful that three or four were killed in a day, even when efforts were made to avoid shooting. On one occasion twenty-two white rhinos were counted in a half mile.

On Guy Fawkes's Day, 5 November 1836, the camp made a huge bonfire and feasted on a fine buffalo that, wounded, twice charged Harris on three legs. With a four-foot spread of horns, the heavy animal made a handsome meal. The diners, 'gorged to the throat, and besmeared with blood, grease and filth from the entrails, sat nodding torpidly around the carcass, sucking marrow from the bones'.

Two days later, Harris, who had never seen an African elephant, found an immense footprint, six feet in circumference, indicating a bull elephant of about twelve feet at the shoulder, close to the maximum height, and probably weighing about six tons. Following the trail across the Sant River, eastwards along the Magaliesberg chain, and on for another eight miles, Harris finally gazed on a sight of 'intense, indescribable interest'. A rocky valley opened before him, a grand and magnificent panorama which beggars all description. The whole face of the landscape was actually covered with wild elephants. There could not have been fewer than three hundred within the scope of our vision. Every height and green knoll was dotted over with groups of them, whilst the bottom of the glen exhibited a dense and sable living mass . . . a picture soul-stirring and sublime.

Sending men ahead to drive the elephants up the valley towards them, Harris, Richardson and the Hottentots opened a running fire on the elephants that poured up the valley, killing and wounding many. With the weapons of the period it was only possible to stop heavy game with a single shot if the lead ball was hardened with tin or quicksilver, if the animal was hit at close range, perhaps fifty yards or less, and if it was struck in the brain. Even with modern rifles and cartridges, elephant and buffalo have been known to run hundreds of yards with a bullet in the heart. With the muskets of the Hottentots, it was still more dangerous. The Hottentots relied on numerous wounds, bloodletting and exhaustion. Harris records a rhinoceros that was hit twenty-seven times before it went down, and a bull elephant fifty times. One buffalo, a hind leg shot and dangling, lanced with assegais, shot eighteen times, charged violently until two final bullets brought it down. Often the hunting of heavy game had the character of a small battle, with many men shooting at many animals, instead of the clean kill approach of one-to-one hunting.

The day after this first elephant hunt, as he walked over the battlefield, contrite for the first time, recalling his favourite Indian hunting elephant, Mowla-Bukhsh, Harris felt remorse for the killing. A surviving calf, three and a half feet tall, hovered about its dead mother, making mournful piping notes and trying to raise her with its trunk. Finally it wrapped its trunk about Harris's leg and followed him to the wagons. Moved, Harris had it fed and cared for, but it soon died.

Traversing the Magaliesberg to the north, through rocky passes where only guy ropes stopped the wagons from crashing over precipices, and across swampy streams where the leather traces, already nibbled by crocodiles, twice snapped with the strain of the oxen, the safari moved along the west bank of the Limpopo, a hunter's paradise, searching for the elusive giraffe. On 19 November, mounted on Breslar, his best horse, Harris suddenly spotted thirty-two giraffe browsing in a wooded plain, 'sending the blood coursing through my veins like quicksilver'. Chasing them flat out for two miles, himself pursued by three rhino, struck by a projecting bough that tore his white Indian turban off his hunting cap, Harris finally drew alongside an eighteen-foot bull giraffe, its legs catching in the treacherous sands of a soft river bank. Reaching his rifle up with his right hand behind the animal's shoulder, he pulled both triggers. It was not enough. The giraffe, exhausted and bleeding, laboured on among the mimosa groves, Harris loading and firing from the saddle as Breslar, steaming, kept up. Pulling out in front, blocking the giraffe's path, Harris fired for the seventeenth time. The giraffe, 'tears trickling from his full brilliant eye', tottered to the dust.

Reverential, dazzled by the elegance and strength of the giraffe, Harris unsaddled Breslar and himself sank down. For two hours he admired the animal. Measuring it carefully, he took paper and pencils from his hunting cap and drew the splendid beast. Writing later, he recommended his method, 'boarding giraffe', to fellow hunters: due to the tough, $1\frac{1}{2}$ inch thick skin and the great speed of the big bulls, the only method was to get close, well-mounted, and then to gallop into the middle of the herd, select the largest and ride with it, firing until it fell.

By 1 December, after three months on safari, having crossed the Limpopo and advanced forty miles into what would one day be Rhodesia, the hunters reached the region of the Tropic of Capricorn. Harris's Matabele guides urged him to continue on for two moons to a great inland lake, evidently Lake Ngami, then thought to be one of the long-sought sources of the Nile. Tempted, but fearful that they could be delayed by the next rains and so exceed their military leave, Harris and Richardson checked their calculations, matching the daily log against their pocket sextant, which had been broken when a wagon overturned and now required a sheet of pasteboard as a false horizon. To follow their position on a map, Harris had explicitly copied the mileage method 'of the indefatigable Burchell'. As they turned south, he estimated that they were near the Tropic of Capricorn.

After passing clusters of famished Tswanas, their cattle long taken by Matabele conquerors, the safari spent the night in a Tswana kraal. Killing a rhino to feed his hosts, Harris watched the starving Tswana women divide the carcass, leaving nothing but a pool of blood. Several days later, the safari was interrupted by emissaries of Mzilikazi, demanding a percussion shotgun for the king. Promising to send the gun as he left the country, Harris instead addressed his compliments to the king, accompanied by brass wire, 144 regimental gilt buttons and a Toby jug, a pot to hold the royal beer, bearing five depictions of Toby Philpot, the proverbial drunken Englishman.

Having killed four hundred large animals, all over three feet at the shoulder, Harris and Richardson transported their specimens south, hunting as they went. Their Matabele guides and Hottentots were eager to return home, particularly the lovesick Andries Africander. Pursuing a wounded elephant one morning, carrying a heavy, primitive rifle with flint and steel, as his double rifle had been smashed again in another bad fall with his horse, Harris observed strange black antelopes in the distance. Checking with his pocket telescope, counting nine chestnut does and two coal black bucks, Harris realized at once that the antelopes were new to science. This was his second dream: the discovery of a new species. He raised the rifle, squeezed the trigger, and the heavy lock fell, but did not fire. Three times it failed, as the buck moved off. Dashing back to camp, Harris repaired his rifle and galloped back to take up the tracks. For three days, he followed the trail, finally shooting the larger male.

Cornwallis Harris's prize was the most beautiful of the world's antelopes, the sable, to be known for generations as the 'Harris buck'. Glossy black, with a snowy belly and white face with a black blaze, 500 lb, nearly $4\frac{1}{2}$ ft at the

Sable antelope, by Cornwallis
Harris

shoulder, the sable is distinguished by its distinctive colouring and immense
scimitar horns, which are often over 5 ft long, arching back over its shoulder.

Anxious to get this specimen properly preserved and back to England, his
oxen falling sick and his horses lean and weak, Harris announced that the safari
would now return to the colony by the unexplored route across the Vaal River.
The news was well received, particularly by Andries Africander and by
Nesserwanjee Motabhoy, who had endured not only Mzilikazi's thefts, but also
unscheduled fasting, as the Hindu had refrained from any meat that appeared at
all bovine, denying himself even the succulent eland. All hands celebrated the
news by the camp fire, with a wild-peppermint-tea party, accompanied by a
broken Hottentot violin.

At three in the morning on Christmas Day, 1836, after a brief rest in parched
country, the safari resumed its march, hoping to find water for the oxen before
the full heat of the day. Hunting ahead on Breslar, Harris became absorbed in
shooting in the midst of an enormous herd of stampeding antelope, before
stopping to skin his victims and sling the game over his saddle. By then he was
lost. The vast troops of animals had destroyed his tracks.

That night Harris spent huddled in the rain, after baking a guinea-hen in an
oven he had scooped deep in the ground to hide the flame from the Bushmen.
For two more days Harris searched for the wagons, surviving a fall into a six-
foot Bushman hunting pit, deep with mud that ensnared Breslar, before finally
finding the camp. As the safari approached Cape Colony, all thirty-eight of the
surviving oxen were stolen in the night by Bushmen, who validated the angry
tales of the Boers by vindictively leaving nineteen dead oxen, bloated almost to
bursting from poisoned wounds, and abandoning the other seventeen so
crippled as to be useless. Harris grieved particularly for his sturdy wheelers,
Holland and Oliphant, and his loyal leaders, Lanceman and England, lying in
their blood, who had hauled the safari through deserts, rivers and mountains.

Bartering tea and snuff, bullets and wheel grease with suspicious parties of
Afrikaaners, the safari secured enough oxen to drag the wagons back to Cape

Colony. Knowing that Dutch settlers had been attacked, the Boers resented the Englishmen's friendly relations with the Matabele, not appreciating that the king welcomed gifts, but not invaders. Returning further south, the safari came on a valley filled with the white canvas sails of Boer wagons, as the Afrikaaners gathered for the trek north, determined to take Mzilikazi's lands. Six days later the Boers defeated a Matabele impi at Mosega in the Transvaal.

Although reports of his death preceded him as far as Cape Town, Harris safely concluded his five-month safari in Graaff-Reinet on 24 January 1837, at a cost of seventy dead oxen and £800, now about £20,100. The safari had reached new territory. It passed near present-day Pretoria on the way home, and some believe that Harris and Richardson may have been the first white men to cross the Witwatersrand where Johannesburg now stands. Harris's collection, including two perfect heads of every game quadruped found in southern Africa, was a sensation in London. The handsome sable was first preserved in Cape Town by the French taxidermist, Monsieur Verreaux, and then proudly escorted to England by Captain Alexander of the 42nd Royal Highlanders.

The first man ever qualified to compare hunting in Africa and Asia, Cornwallis Harris noted that African rhinoceros were not covered in body plates, that female African elephants had tusks and that African lion had finer manes. But he wrote that African boar were inferior to their Indian cousins, which provided such fine pig-sticking, the cavalryman's sport of chasing boar on horseback with lances. Most interesting to big-game hunters, he compared the African lion to the Indian tiger as sporting animals. With similar skeletons, teeth and claws, both animals are surprisingly alike under the skin, the clearest distinction being that in a tiger's skull the nasal bones extend higher. The females of both species are most dangerous and fiercely protective when their cubs are still small, although both lions and tigers are known to eat their own young when famished. Harris judged that the African lion is better sport, although the Bengal tiger is even bigger and faster. Tigers are deflected by gunfire, even without being hit. Harris found that a charging lion, more confident, intrepid and determined, is diverted by nothing but death.

If only the African elephant could be trained as a hunting mount, Harris mused, Africa would provide ideal sport. He warned his fellow sportsmen that safari life in Africa was far harder and more dangerous, more wild and demanding, than the pampered life of the great Indian *shikars*, lavish hunting expeditions attended by large retinues, preceded by carpenters and specialized servants and housed in sumptuous oriental tents. Instead, hunters should welcome 'the toils, trials and troubles that beset the wanderer in the African desert'. In India, even the elephants were spoiled, groomed and well greased in their stalls. Were he to plan another safari, Harris wrote, he would bring horseshoes and a third wagon, to carry grain out and ivory back, as he had been obliged to abandon some of his tusks.

Concerned with the future of southern Africa, loving the land and the animals, fond of the Matabele if not the Bushmen, infected but not blinded by the Christian, European sense of superiority, Cornwallis Harris looked ahead. In 1838 he wrote that the migratory Boers,

> whilst they flourish, are the judges and avengers of their own cause. But their path is beset with perils. Thus far their course has been marked with blood, and with blood must it be traced to its termination, either in their own destruction, or in that of thousands of the native population of southern Africa.

By the time Harris sailed from Cape Town for Bombay in December 1837, eleven months after the end of the first safari, he had lived beyond his fantasy. His adventures and his art would dominate his life and create the standard for future safaris. For a century and a half, professional hunters would try, under easier circumstances, to cope with the problems he had mastered, seeking to find for themselves and their clients fragments of the safari world that Cornwallis Harris discovered. The elements of a safari would endure, but all would change.

Back in India, Harris found his brother officers, sportsmen and naturalists intrigued by his tales of Africa. Working from his diaries and drawings, he wrote the first book ever devoted exclusively to game hunting in Africa, *The Wild Sports of Southern Africa*, first published in Bombay in 1838 by the American Mission Press. This influential volume excited such interest in England and India that it went through five editions by 1852. Harris also published, in 1840, a folio of thirty-one coloured engravings, accompanied by descriptive texts and numerous line drawings, under the title *Portraits of the Game and Wild Animals of Southern Africa*.

The report of his safari established Harris's reputation, and in 1841 the British government asked him to lead a mission to Abyssinia to persuade the King of Shoa to enter commercial relations with England and end the slave trade. Now thirty-four, keen to return to the hunting grounds of Africa and eager to fight slavery, Harris walked four hundred miles from the Gulf of Aden through the wild Danakil Desert and across the mountains into the Abyssinian highlands to Ankober, the capital of the ancient Coptic Christian kingdom of Shoa. Well trained by Mzilikazi, Harris brought as tribute three hundred muskets and two cannon made in Calcutta, awkward but appealing presents.

Each year, the King of Shoa, Sahela Selassie, a fierce slaver and hunter, mounted an expedition against the Galla tribes, rather like an annual hunting trip, destroying their villages and enslaving the Galla women, particular favourites among the Arabs. The king was so impressed with Harris's hunting skill and bravery in the field that he befriended the Englishman. After a year and a half of fine hunting and intriguing, to the distress of his hated French rivals, Harris made some progress with his mission and in 1844 was knighted by Queen Victoria. The first of the great white hunters died an early death of the fever in India in 1848, but his art and words lived to inspire the next generation of adventurers.

> To wander through a fairyland of sport among a new and fabled creation amid scenes never before paced by civilized foot is so truly spirit-stirring and romantic, that in spite of hardships the witchcraft of the desert must prove irresistible.

2. THE OLD AFRICA HANDS

The Early White Hunters, 1840–60

Hunting the Cape buffalo, by Cornwallis Harris

By the mid-nineteenth century there was an explosion of interest in Africa. Most of the continent was not colonized by Europe until the last twenty years of the century, but individual curiosity and ambition preceded the rush for empire. Particularly in England, there was a fascination with exploration. With the Americas and India already spoken for, geographers and adventurers picked up the old challenge that lured Alexander the Great and Napoleon: finding the source of the Nile. Like discovering the New World or walking on the moon, this magical pursuit stimulated other efforts.

For some men the motivation was essentially imperial or commercial. For others, like Dr David Livingstone, it was a matter of Christian zeal. For Samuel Baker, Richard Francis Burton, James Grant and John Speke, the call was exploration and recognition. In every case, however, the efforts involved drew on the same skills and resources as those required for a sporting safari. Each of these men enriched the lore of African hunting and adventure, although their expeditions were not safaris in every sense. At the same time, less celebrated individuals, frequently inspired by Cornwallis Harris, were going for the true sport of it. With no cameras to record their safaris, many turned to sketching and diaries to document their days in Africa.

The great majority of early African hunters and adventurers were British, and though they tended to be eccentric and often lonely individuals, they had much in common. For many, the sporting, imperial and military ethics all flowed together in a boyish enthusiasm for outdoor adventure. For some, religious, scientific or artistic tastes added a dimension. They were men like Roualeyn Gordon Cumming, William Cotton Oswell and William Charles Baldwin, who thought nothing of taking a double-barrelled rifle and setting off

49

Hunting eland on horseback, by
Captain Henry Butler

alone on foot across Africa. Confined by Victorian conventions at home, they agreed with the Arabist and Nile explorer Richard Burton that 'the gladdest moment in human life is the departure upon a distant journey into unknown lands'.

Brought up in the hard-riding, sporting spirit of the British countryside, by the age of six they could clean a shotgun and load a musket. Collecting owls' eggs, breeding ferrets, snaring hares, a sharp-eyed fieldcraft was in their blood. As the fabled hunter Gordon Cumming explained in 1850, 'during these early wanderings by wood and stream, this strong love of sport and admiration of Nature in her wildest forms became an all-absorbing feeling'. As a young boy, his true delight, after fashioning a cap of tufted marsh rushes, was to pass summer nights alone in the Moray woods in the north of Scotland, studying the changing beauty of the forest at night, watching for the shadows of broad-antlered fallow deer, laying his head flat to the ground in order to see the darkened outlines better. It was a nocturnal taste he would pursue in Africa. Even before he went to Eton at eleven, Gordon Cumming took pride in the hunting trophies that crowded his room. Whatever else it did, early boarding-school made young men athletic and independent, and the outward-looking imperial ethic helped them to see Africa as a vast shooting estate.

Like Harris, Gordon Cumming was first drawn to India. At nineteen, with Eton behind him, he joined the Madras Light Cavalry, arriving in India in 1839 when Harris's first book was the talk of every officers' mess. But the Indian climate disagreed with him, and at twenty-three, having already hunted on four

'Dressed for Africa'. This outfit, designed by Samuel Baker and stitched by Florence Baker, was dyed with the juice of wild fruits

Below: A single barrel, four-bore, three-groove percussion rifle weighing 17 lb, made *c.* 1848 by Harris Holland (founder of the business) for Sir Samuel Baker, which he called his 'baby'. The rifle, trodden on by an elephant, was repaired with elephant skin around the hand and action

Extract from SIR SAMUEL BAKER'S "WILD BEASTS AND THEIR WAYS."

" My battery is one '577, one '400, and one 'Magnum Paradox,' No. 12. The 'Paradox' is a most useful weapon, as it combines a shot gun (shoots No. 6 shot with equal pattern to a best cylinder-bored gun) with a rifle that is wonderfully accurate within a range of 100 yards."

" No. I.—Struck a large Barra Singha deer upon the spine, and the bullet was found embedded in crushed bone "

" No. II.—Passed behind the shoulder of a full-grown bear, and struck the bone of another

bear below the shoulder joint, a few paces on the other side of the first wounded animal "

" No. III.—This went through a bear, and was found beneath the skin upon the opposite side."

Exact drawings from bullets forwarded by the late SIR SAMUEL BAKER, showing the power and penetration of the " Magnum Paradox " Gun built for him by us, and referred to by him in his letters to " The Field."

continents and looking for 'the life of the wild hunter – so far preferable to that of the mere sportsman', Cumming determined to hunt in Africa. In 1843 he transferred to Cape Colony with the Cape Mounted Rifles, another regiment whose young bloods were preoccupied with hunting and wild horsemanship. For Cumming, the pig-sticking and polo of Indian service were replaced by desperate gallops through herds of buffalo, and elephant hunting by moonlight.

Soon seduced by the bush, Gordon Cumming resigned his commission and began what may be the longest safari ever taken, five years, spending from 1844 to 1849 bush-bashing in what became northern Cape Province, the Orange Free State, the Transvaal and Bechuanaland. Already, times were changing. The hunters, the game, the natives, the transport, even the oxen were getting more sophisticated. As four-wheel-drive vehicles did a century later, the Cape wagons were getting larger and more elaborate, three feet longer than in Burchell's day. Side-pockets, rows of square canvas bags, hung along the sides, convenient for the day's necessaries. Pots and gridirons were lashed to a heavy wooden frame under the rear. The better wagons, like Gordon Cumming's at £60, boasted cap-tents, planed and riveted wooden arches to support the sail, but these were only too easily destroyed when a wagon overturned. The heavy game itself was in retreat, already virtually exterminated south of the Orange River or, like the elephant, forced to retire to the north. The lion historian Sir

Elephant hunting by moonlight, by Thomas Baines, 1862

Alfred Pease reports that the last lion shot south of the Orange River was killed in 1842.

Hunters and trekkers had now learned they were better off with tough little coastal oxen, zuur-veldt cattle, raised where the salt air kept the grass sour, instead of the heavier sweet-veldt oxen, bred on the lush grasses near the frontiers of Cape Colony. Survivors, the zuur-veldt oxen could feed where their spoiled cousins would soon perish.

Tobacco now served only for gestures, not for acquisitions, among the Tswanas and other Bantu tribes. Beads were still useful on safari. Manufactured at the glassworks in Venice, the beads were distributed by the London bead merchants Levin & Co., who specialized in this colonial necessity. Various colours and shapes were favoured by different tribes. But knives and hatchets, guns and ammunition, calves and she-goats, were the favoured currencies. European traders, who wandered among the Boer farms and the tribes of the frontier districts, had taught the Tswanas and others to bring in ivory, ostrich feathers and *karosses*, or leather cloaks. Although the price fell as the vogue faltered in Europe, ostrich feathers in 1845 fetched as much as £7 per pound, some seventy-five to ninety large feathers, nearly thirty times the cost of ivory by weight. (One pound of elephant ivory then sold for about five shillings.) Harder than elephant ivory, large hippo teeth, carved for dentistry and the finest inlaid furniture, were then selling at four times as much.

Mzilikazi, the ladies of Paris and the Bushmen were all decorated in the savage feathers of Africa, while the clubs of London rang to the sound of ivory

Ostrich on the veldt, by Henry Butler

dice and billiard balls, and to the chatter of false teeth which had once been the dentures of the hippopotamus of the Orange River. But dental fashions also changed. By 1892 Sir Samuel Baker advised that the respective prices of hippo and elephant ivory had nearly reversed, as fickle dentists forsook the sea cow.

An even more obsessive hunter than Cornwallis Harris, unsoftened by artistic interests, Gordon Cumming did not believe in going lightly armed. His armoury included his heavy boyhood rifle, a single-barrelled German carrying twelve shots to the pound (a twelve-bore), a Purdey double rifle that had served him well in the jungles of Hindustan, a light double rifle by William Moore, a two-grooved 'most perfect and useful' double by Dickson of Edinburgh, and three sturdy double-barrelled guns for rough work on horseback, when rapid loading and hard falls were part of the exercise. The guns themselves did not travel lightly, requiring ramrods, shooting belts, powder flasks, rifle holsters and the sound waterproof gun cases patented by Hugh Snowie in England. To keep them all firing, Cumming brought 400 lb gunpowder, 300 lb lead, bullet moulds, lead ladles, 50 lb pewter for hardening the balls for heavy game, 10,000 prepared bullets, 20,000 flints and 50,000 percussion caps.

Like Cornwallis Harris, Cumming was abandoned by his personal servant early in the safari. A cockney and former London cab driver with some experience of the interior, Long soon decided, correctly, that life with Cumming would be hard, being obliged to direct the Hottentots during the day and sleep on the ground in the bell tent at night. Infatuated with a dark-eyed laundress, Long deserted his master while they were still near the coast, 'inclined to worship at the shrine of Venus rather than that of Diana'. Cumming did not make the same mistake. Like other nineteenth-century English hunters, he was well trained at boarding-school to do without. Cumming's journal makes no reference to any involvement or concern with women or their absence. When Gordon Cumming twice writes of loneliness, it is because he lacks a companion with whom to exchange hunting tales. His only reference to native liaisons is to mention that when in 1848 the 91st Regiment moved from their camp at Colesberg, dark-eyed lovers wept hot tears as the men rode out to fight the Boers at Boomplaats across the Orange River. He had a careful eye, however, for the charms of the mixed-race Griqua girls. Once having smelled their rare perfume, extracted from roots found under bushes near the mouth of the Orange River, a man can never inhale it again without recalling 'the fine dark eyes and fair forms of these semi-civilized nymphs'.

Blessed with that savage core that the English suspect lurks deep in the hearts of their northern neighbours, Cumming in full cry hunted like a maddened Scot fighting to the death at the battle of Culloden. Reloading and firing from the saddle in his green and yellow Gordon kilt, bare arms and legs savaged by thorns and dark with blood, his vivid red beard falling over his shredded shirt and a hippo-hide whip swinging from his wrist, the dogs crashing through the forest as a wounded bull elephant raged after him, Gordon Cumming never had enough.

R. Gordon Cumming

Even the frontier Boers, a moderately unpolished lot themselves, were startled when this wild second son of a Scottish baronet rode up to their doors, drink in hand, looking 'like one escaped from Bedlam'. Isaac, a Hottentot hunting companion, who, with Cumming, survived an attack by two wounded buffalo, being barely saved when the dogs drew off the buffalo after his girth broke, told Cumming's men that the hunter's madness doomed all who followed him. Even today, when the old hunters of the Shikar Club gather to tell tales at dinner in London, they speak of Gordon Cumming. Did he in fact strangle animals with his bare hands when his rifle misfired, and, like a hyena, begin to eat them while they still lived?

After his first two years on safari, Cumming knew how to make himself tolerably comfortable in the field. When he left his safari camp, prepared to stay out until he got the elephant he wanted, he had one after-rider carrying a spare rifle and extra ammunition, and two men bearing water, a kettle, two American axes, sickles for grass cutting and leather sacks containing coffee, bread, sugar, salt and pepper, biltong, a wooden bowl, a spoon and his woollen nightcap. He found that small American axes were the best quality and the most suited to the tough but delicate task of chopping out tusks from the heads of hippopotamus and elephant. He wore a wide-brimmed hat secured by *riempies*, or leather straps, a coarse shirt, either a kilt or buckskin knee-breeches, and a pair of *veldschoens*, 'African brogues', made on safari. Not a man to welcome disagreement from his horse, he wore fierce 'persuaders' to spur his mount.

Dressed to kill, 6 ft 4 in tall, hard and powerful at 14 stone (196 lb), Cumming wore two heavy belts. From one dangled an eight-inch riempie, holding his loading rod, cut from a solid piece of rhinoceros horn. The larger girdle was a wide shooting belt, with four otter-skin pouches, possibly from his hunting days in Newfoundland, carrying percussion caps, a powder flask, balls and patches, two clasp knives, a compass, and flint and steel. Stuck into the hunting belt was his loading mallet, made of rhino horn. For elephant hunting, he usually carried his two-groove Dickson double rifle in his right hand.

Reading his five-hundred-page journal, it is easy to pity his prey when a vengeful Cumming sets off after the lion that ate Hendrick, his favourite Hottentot, leaving the man's leg behind on the trail, bitten off below the knee, with the shoe still on it. In perhaps no other hunting writer does one feel so strongly the mixture of love of the animal and love of the kill that is so confusing to non-hunters. After another lion hunt, deeply moved by the beauty and dignity of his quarry, he plucks a lock of the lion's rich black mane and places it carefully 'in my bosom'. Hunting the most handsome of all antelope, the Harris buck or sable, he writes, 'I was struck with admiration at the magnificence of the noble old black buck, and vowed in my heart to slay him, although I should follow him for a twelvemonth.'

In general, Gordon Cumming had more affection for the animals than for the Boers who occasionally crossed his trail. But he admired the durability and invariable hospitality of these early settlers. By the 1840s, the patterns of relationship between Bantu, Boer and British were permanently established. In 1843, as today, blacks voluntarily went south for long periods to work for the Boers, being paid in calves and she-goats. Travelling among the frontier Boers, Cumming won their acceptance with gin and kilts. Unfailingly, just as Harris made his way with beads and modern travellers do with tips, Cumming offered each Boer he met a brimming glass of gin at the moment of meeting, toasting his new friend and identifying himself as a 'mountain Scot'.

Appreciating the kilt and the generosity as conclusive signs that the traveller was not English, the Afrikaaners welcomed the implication that they shared oppression by a common enemy. The Boers tended, then as now, to regard the British as effete newcomers to their Africa. To them, lion were cattle-killing vermin, not vain trophies, but they were impressed by the ivory and splendid specimens that Cumming dragged about with him for years.

Anglo-Boer competition extended even to the spans, or teams of oxen. Cumming complained that the Boers wrongly assumed that their oxen were always superior to an Englishman's oxen. The Boers typically hunted with old single-barrelled *roers*, long, heavy muzzle-loaders, with which they were remarkably accurate. As British regiments in the 1840s moved into Natal to quell the Zulu in the Kaffir Wars, and to the Orange River to separate the Boers and the Bantu, the competition between Boer and British became more intense. Annoyed by the Boer assumption that the English were inferior shots, four of Cumming's friends in the 91st Regiment, all top shots, challenged any four Boers to a shooting competition, 'the Dutchmen getting, of course, jolly well licked'.

Afrikaaners indulged in little sporting sentiment about wildlife. Cumming particularly disliked their habit of continuing to riddle the lion after the cats were safely down, until the heads were 'shot all to pieces', when they had a Hottentot pull the tail to make certain the animal was dead. Cornwallis Harris, similarly, had complained that the Boers used to avenge themselves on the hyena that ate their sheep by trapping the hyena, then slitting one hind leg and hooking a heavy wagon chain to the sinew before releasing the animal. Its teeth broken by violent attacks on the chain, the hyena was baited with boar-hounds until it was killed. Even today, professional hunters in east and central Africa deplore the practices on some shooting safaris in South Africa. There, to ensure an easy bag, clients are frequently led up to known animals on private game farms. In the eastern Transvaal, farmers occasionally leave donkey carcasses near the edge of the Kruger National Park to lure lions over the fence. As one fourth-generation African, a professional hunter in Botswana, expressed it to me with the accurate and witty intolerance that often characterizes British colonial conversation, 'The Afrikaaner will shoot anything that walks, crawls, sweats, slithers or burrows.'

Cumming grew more at home with his Hottentots than with the Boers, daily risking his life with them on hunting trips, but generally disparaging the Hottentots as unreliable in the presence of alcohol or danger. Solid drinkers

Right: Hunting wildebeest and zebra, by Thomas Baines

Below: Crossing the river, by Thomas Baines

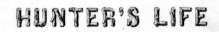

A

HUNTER'S LIFE

IN

SOUTH AFRICA.

BY R. GORDON CUMMING.

VOL. I.

The title-page of *A Hunter's Life in South Africa* by R. Gordon Cumming

themselves, most white colonists considered that alcoholism should be a European privilege. To Gordon Cumming, a lack of steadiness was the darkest sin. Angry that none of his armed Hottentots intervened while a leopard brutally mauled a friend, Cumming complained that one Hottentot had fired his musket into the air and jumped into the river, 'according to the established custom among colonial servants'. Under what he considered extreme provocation, such as when a wagon was needlessly overturned, a man smoked near the powder casks, or, worse, breakfast was not waiting after a dawn hunt, Cumming would revert to English schoolboy practices and cane his erring servants, a light admonition by African standards, whether Boer or Bantu.

As often happens on safari, Cumming found that he was able to ask more and more from himself, that it was 'extraordinary how soon the mind accustoms itself to everything, good or bad'. Cornwallis Harris, too, had the experience and time to reflect on this point, concluding that, 'the mind ever becomes more reconciled to hardship and suffering than the body'. Only once does Cumming reveal a moment when fright and physical fear prevail over his hardened hunting instinct. Unarmed one evening, gathering firewood along a game trail near camp, he bent low and found himself literally face-to-face with a lion hidden in the tall reeds. Giving, for the first time in his hunting career, a fearful shriek, Cumming convulsively sprang backward, as the startled lion jumped to the side, growling.

Gordon Cumming was unusual in his appreciation of the skills and character of the Bushmen, whose competence in the bush and wise use of even the smallest gifts of nature won his respect. Prodigious meat-eaters who alternately starved and gorged, in their hunting the Bushmen did not distinguish between wild and domestic animals, and so were often hunted on sight by both black and white cattle breeders. Some anecdotes indicate that, in later years, early hunting licences in the Boer Republics listed 'two Bushmen' among the allowable bag of game. Cumming was impressed to learn how the Bushmen could drive their stolen cattle across the most arid desert, where mounted pursuers could not follow. Their wives concealed water in ostrich eggs, which they carried great distances and hid along escape routes through the desert. When hunting ostrich, a Bushman would don an ostrich skin, stalking about the plain, artfully miming the gait and habits of the six-foot birds until close enough to release his poisoned shaft. Cumming observed that one must always take all the ostrich eggs one finds, for once a nest is discovered, the birds themselves will smash any remaining eggs.

Cumming himself virtually adopted Ruyter, a young Bushman who had run away from the Boers who had killed his family and enslaved him. Months later, an armed party of Boers rode into camp, and the brother of Ruyter's owner demanded that Cumming surrender the runaway. Not one to find threats persuasive, Gordon Cumming replied that the demand could not be considered, as 'the nation to which I belonged was averse to slavery'.

As the safari continued, Cumming returned several times to the frontier town of Colesberg to re-supply and to replace his dead dogs, horses and oxen. Two of his rifles exploded in the hands of his companions, including his faithful Dickson, and he was lucky to buy a fine Westley Richards double rifle. Weapons always came first. When the Hottentots stole the solder that hardened his bullets, Cumming melted down his spoons, cups, teapots and candlesticks to provide the needed hardener.

During his five years in the bush, Cumming developed his own techniques, particularly at night hunting, which he tried occasionally on horseback, after elephant, but more often from a shooting pit dug next to a waterhole. Night hunting had its risks. Once Cumming found he actually had been hunting a Boer's oxen, finally killing a brown gelding with a fine shot through the shoulder, mistaking the horse for a zebra. At night, it was an easy confusion, one later exploited in the First World War when British troops in east Africa painted army horses with black and white stripes to mislead German observers.

To save his eyes from the tearing thorns, during some chases Cumming would hold his chest flat against his horse's neck, and his head actually under its neck, thus enabling him to plunge through the fierce thorns 'like an Eton boy taking a header into the Thames'. Cumming's special quality in hunting was probably his reckless earthiness, his taste for getting in close and himself becoming another vulnerable predator among the animals. Excitable, he would be chasing buffalo, and then find himself, like a child surrounded by too many treats, shooting away at whatever came along, or stopping to drag a fourteen-foot python by its tail from a sanctuary in the rocks.

Anxious to bag a hippopotamus to feed the camp, he once wounded a large female, which then plunged about wildly in the river. Alarmed by crocodiles, but reluctant to lose the wounded animal, he leapt into the river with his knife. Trying to guide her to the shore by grabbing her tail, he found himself dragged

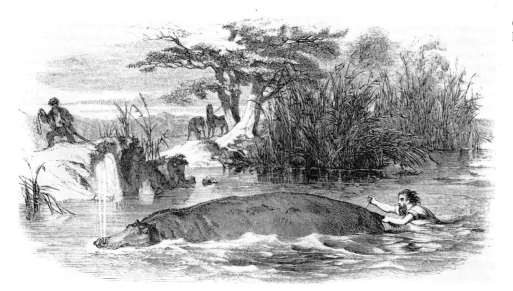

Gordon Cumming securing a hippopotamus

'as if I was a fly', as the hippo plunged and thrashed in the water. To get a better grip, he inserted his knife,

> to cut two deep parallel incisions through the skin on her stern, and lifting this skin from the flesh, so that I could get in my two hands, I made use of it as a handle, and after some desperate hard work, the sea cow continuing her course and I holding on like grim death, eventually succeeded in bringing this gigantic animal to the bank. My Bushman passed me a buffalo-hide rope, which I passed through the opening in the thick skin, and moored Behemoth to a tree. Then I sent a ball through her head, and she was numbered with the dead.

Hunting in the valley of the Limpopo River, with as many as twenty-five species of large game around him, the richest variety in the world, Cumming would shoot seven hippos or three rhinos in one day, noting the peculiar shrill scream as the rhinoceros died. He killed crocodiles indiscriminately and left their carcasses in the water as he advanced. Given to overshooting, careless about wounding animals, like other early hunters he considered Africa's game to be inexhaustible. Near the Orange River, listening to the grunts of the bushbuck, a small antelope, shortly before dawn, Cumming rose and stood on the fore-chest of his wagon. Incredulous, he saw 'the most striking scene I ever beheld, a dense living mass of springbok marching steadily along, the boundless plains covered with one vast herd, a dim red landscape of living creatures'.

Elephant hunting, 'overpoweringly exciting', was his favourite sport. Finding elephant the most difficult game to kill, he made special hardened bullets, with one part pewter to four of lead. Even then, it was often a battle, the fight lasting two or three hours from first shot to death, as he chased and fled his quarry, putting in as many as thirty-five balls from distances as close as fifteen to thirty-five yards, generally using his two-groove Dickson. A fair bull had 50 lb of ivory in each tusk, and he considered 80 lb to be exceptional. His finest single tusk was 10 ft 9 in long, and weighed 173 lb.

One of the bounties of elephant hunting was that it truly provided something for everyone, man and beast, from Cumming to the ants. Not only did the ivory make the safari self-supporting, but the destruction and total consumption of the carcass was a carnival in the bush, 'a scene of blood, noise and turmoil which baffles all description'. First, assegais removed the rough outer skin in large sheets. Then several layers of under skin were carefully stripped off and saved for later use as water bags. Next the flesh was cut away from the ribs in huge slices, before hatchets chopped through and removed each rib individually. This exposed the vast layers of fat gathered around the intestines, which were excavated with assegais by men working inside the carcass, who then passed the cherished fat to eager comrades.

Cumming found this to be a high moment, as the shouting men smeared each other from head to foot with black, clotted gore. The 'marrowy' bones of the skull were chopped in pieces and chewed raw. The remaining meat was cut into pieces, up to twenty feet long, and hung for three days to dry as biltong, strips of sun-dried lean meat that were saved for later use. As his own share of the feast, Cumming favoured baked feet and, like the epicures of ancient Rome, sliced trunk. The feet were carefully prepared in close-fitting pits filled up with hot ashes, not coals, lest they burn the meat, and then covered with a fresh fire on top.

A highland Scot who ate what his dogs ate, Cumming welcomed even locusts to his diet when game was not available. Unable to take wing in the cool night air, the swarming locusts hung from branches waiting to resume their ravaging flight in the morning. Shaking the branches over a blanket, Cumming gathered up the locusts and roasted a chewy dinner for himself and his dogs. Another day, hot and thirsty from a long chase after a female oryx, the most exhausting antelope for a horse to run down, Cumming finally shot her, and then sprang from the saddle as she fell and drank the warm milk from her teats.

Cumming's fearless ways made him risky company in the bush, although his skill and remarkable coolness generally got him through. Without his usual stud of about ten horses, and a mixed pack of perhaps twenty dogs, including greyhounds and wild mongrels, Cumming could never have survived such sport. The dogs, chasing and baying every animal from lion to elephant, distracted the game and set them up for the kill. Rhino were peculiar, in that they were never bayed, since they did not stop to face the dogs and so present an easier shot. Colesberg and Schwartzland had the hazardous privilege of being his steadiest horses, long-winded in pursuit and calm in crisis. Schwartzland was celebrated for stopping dead still in the rush of a frenzied chase if one hand was placed on his neck, thereby giving his master a steady shot from the saddle. Colesberg, however, already badly lacerated when a lion sprang on his haunches, once panicked when surrounded by trumpeting, wounded elephant, not allowing Cumming to remount as he pranced violently about. Cumming was saved only when his pointer Schwart drew off the enraged animals.

This style of hunting was riskier work for the dogs than beagling in England or coursing in Scotland. They were taken by crocodiles, eaten by lion, mauled by leopard, trampled by buffalo and accidentally strangled by the tackle of the wagon. In one brief skirmish with three lionesses, eight dogs were mauled and three killed. Cumming's best dog, horse and Hottentot were all killed on safari. In five years, Gordon Cumming lost forty-five saddle horses, seventy dogs and seventy oxen to lions, sickness and other causes. He himself accepted injuries and fever, usually malaria, as routine parts of safari life, sometimes bleeding himself with fat leeches. Like some later travellers, he complained that wounds heal badly in the bush, because of the climate and an animal diet with no vegetables. Squinting at the spoor for hours at a time, hunting near the Kalahari desert in Bechuanaland, with the 'ground as hot as the side of a stove', his unprotected eyes suffered badly from the sun. Like his dogs, once unleashed, Cumming could not restrain himself from plunging deeper into reckless pursuit, confidently facing down even a wounded lioness when his gun was

A rhino hunt, by Thomas Baines

empty, addressing her in a clear, commanding voice, certain that his only chance of safety was extreme steadiness.

In the course of his safari, Cumming learned not only to speak to lion, but to use magic with the Tswanas, outraging his missionary friend, Dr David Livingstone. Based at Mabotsa in the northern Transvaal, Livingstone frequently extended help to Gordon Cumming and other travellers in the interior. When Cumming was abandoned by his Hottentots, Livingstone sent four men to assist him. When the ox teams were so reduced by fever that Cumming could not move his wagons, Cumming sent Livingstone an imploring letter in a bottle, and Livingstone dispatched all his own oxen. Struggling manfully to suppress witchcraft and superstition among the Tswanas, welcoming his fellow Scot to his mission church in the bush, Livingstone was shocked by Cumming's method of improving the luck of the Tswanas with firearms. First he would ask the chief to touch pictures of animals. Then he would scarify the African's arm with a lancet, anointing the bleeding incisions with gunpowder and turpentine, and reciting incantations. If the chief now pointed the gun straight, he would say, he would kill his prey.

A hunter dining with an African chief, by Charles Whymper

Even Gordon Cumming, however, was wary of Mzilikazi and his ferocious Matabele. Arriving at the borders of the king's domain, he respectfully turned back, near where the Mokoja River joined the Limpopo. Already fearful of Mzilikazi and the ox-killing tsetse flies to the north, he heard that the disgruntled Boers wanted to capture him and his precious wagons. The Boers were not in a genial mood, surprised at being trounced by Cumming's English regimental friends at the battle of Boomplaats, one thousand men a side, on the north bank of the Orange River in 1848. This reverse forced the Boers to retreat to the Vaal River and temporarily abandon their effort to push the Bantus out of the Transvaal. Cautious for once, Cumming decided to bring his trophies safely home.

Finally returning to England in 1849 weakened by his hardships, followed home by thirty tons of Africana, including his Cape wagon, Cumming supported himself by exhibiting his renowned collection of specimens around the country, including in his travelling display his loyal Bushman, Ruyter. He enjoyed a period of eminence when his journal was successfully published in England in 1850 under the title, *The Lion Hunter of South Africa*, briefly exceeding even Dickens in sales. An immense exhibit of his African trophies was a major attraction at the Great Exhibition in London in 1851. Lecturing widely, he finally settled near Inverness, where he established a popular private museum. Anticipating his own death in 1866, at forty-seven, Gordon Cumming ordered his coffin, which he soon occupied. The Barnum & Bailey circus then added his trophies to their African sideshow. He was never again as happy as on safari, often thinking back to his days in the bush, hunting elephant in the forest by moonlight. Then he was richer than Britain's wealthiest landowner, for in Africa 'I felt that it was all my own'.

When Cumming was re-provisioning his safari in Colesberg in 1844, he met 'a dashing sportsman', William Cotton Oswell. Inspired by Cornwallis Harris's book, Oswell was on his first safari with his hunting companion, Mungo Murray. Back at Colesberg in February 1849, Cumming again met Oswell and

Murray, who were on their way to the dreaded Kalahari Desert to search for Lake Ngami with David Livingstone. Short of oxen, Oswell bought some of Cumming's best beasts, and the unwitting animals turned about and set out on an even harder trek. But the beasts were in good company.

Although Cumming and Oswell shared courage and skills, and had much in common, from education and India to physique and sport, they epitomized two different ethics, both still evident in the hunters of today. For Cumming, it was visceral, passionate sport, the thrill was in the killing, releasing the uncompromising urges of man as a primitive hunter. No matter how much he shot, the bag was never enough. Wounds and waste were of no account. One wonders what Gordon Cumming would have been like without the veneer of an elegant background.

For Oswell, the shooting was a part of the enjoyment of an outdoor, adventurous life, to be done properly, as a gentleman does everything, with a sense of standards and fairness. As later observers have commented, it is difficult to conceal one's character on safari, even from oneself. It is hard to imagine Oswell shooting a horse by accident and not seeking out the owner. Always free with his rifle and his jambok, Cumming said nothing and hoped the Boer farmer would blame the lions, though he had a different standard when the horse was his own. Cumming used his jambok not only on his own staff, but even on a Tswana chief as punishment after one of Cumming's horses was killed in a native pitfall. Unlike even Livingstone, Oswell never struck an African. Modest as such restraint may appear today, Oswell in five years shot only two female elephant, both to feed the Africans.

Researching Oswell's trail, through the writings of contemporaries like David Livingstone, the competitive explorer Samuel Baker and the author Thomas Hughes, one finds Oswell passing through their lives like a magic prince. Samuel Baker, one of the finest shots in England, was a formidable, hard-bitten man who hunted stag in the highlands using a knife instead of a gun. He bought his future wife, Florence, for £7, the price of one pound of ostrich feathers, at a Hungarian slave auction in 1859 and in the 1860s hunted with her through the Sudan and Ethiopia searching for the source of the Nile. Marching beside her lover's litter through pestilential stretches of the Sudan, Florence was one of the first white women to endure the full rigours of what might be considered early safari life, in serious company with Mrs David Livingstone and a Mrs Thompson, who took the first honeymoon safari to Lake Ngami in 1859. When Baker dismounted to approach elephant, Florence would hold his bridle, galloping to his side as soon as she heard the shot, in case a mounted chase was in order. Able and enterprising, scandalously unmarried, a victim of Dr Livingstone's characteristically petty moral criticism, even after marriage she was not received by Queen Victoria on the morning of her husband's knighthood.

Sir Samuel Baker himself was a man not easily impressed. Writing of Oswell shortly after his death in 1893, Baker described Oswell as 'full of fearlessness

Above: Samuel Baker on safari, 1864

Left: Arabs attack elephant with swords, by Samuel Baker

and kindliness, six feet, sinewy and muscular, with an eagle glance, a first-rate horseman, powerful, enduring, the perfection of a Nimrod, without a rival and without an enemy, the greatest hunter ever known in modern times, the truest friend and most thorough example of an English gentleman'. The Africans agreed. Their regard for Oswell made things easier for the travellers who followed. Oswell himself commented that the consideration that he and Livingstone tried to show to the Africans was generously returned. Livingstone, who named his youngest son Oswell, records that the blacks universally considered Oswell to be the greatest hunter that ever came into the country. The Africans were impressed by Oswell's courage in hunting elephant without dogs, which greatly reduce the danger.

A schoolboy idol, Oswell was known as 'the Muscleman' at Rugby, where generations later he was still celebrated for jumping twenty-one feet across Clifton brook and throwing his cricket ball well over a hundred yards, into the garden of Dr Arnold, the legendary headmaster. My own research suggests that, together with the author's brother George Hughes, Oswell was Thomas Hughes's principal inspiration for the Brooke brothers, the heroes of *Tom Brown's School Days* and the classic characterizations of the best of the English schoolboy. In 1894, sixty years after he himself first saw Oswell at Rugby, and twenty years before he published his classic novel, Thomas Hughes was asked to speak to the boys of Rugby the day after Oswell's portrait was unveiled in the school hall. Hughes recalled how, among the schoolboy heroes of 1834, only one boy 'stood out from the rest as Hector from the ruck of the Trojan princes, and this hero was William Cotton Oswell'.

Like Harris and Cumming, young Cotton Oswell began his career in India, where he too hunted and fell ill, on a shooting trip in the valley of the Bhavany River. Hoping to save him, the doctors at Madras sent Oswell to Cape Colony to recuperate. Recovering quickly, he was eager to hunt in Africa, for as he wrote, 'we were all bitten in those days by Captain Harris'.

From 1844 to 1851 Cotton Oswell conducted numerous expeditions in what became South Africa and Bechuanaland, including several true safaris with the sportsmen Mungo Murray and Major Frank Vardon of the 25th Madras Native Infantry, and two trips with Dr Livingstone. Even when he travelled with others, however, Oswell preferred to do his actual hunting alone, at least with no other white man, for that avoided the jealousies of the chase, added to the adventure and so improved both the hunting and the camp fire conversation. As Livingstone's first travelling companion, it was Oswell who taught the great explorer how to manage in the bush. He explicitly recognized that for Livingstone, if not for himself, these journeys were primarily explorations, rather than sporting expeditions or true safaris. In addition to providing meat and protection, Oswell gave Livingstone two things the missionary required: all the glory and none of the expense.

During the same period, other Europeans were beginning to make their way into the interior, including the greatest of the Afrikaaner ivory hunters, Jan

William Cotton Oswell, a portrait hanging at Rugby School

Viljoen and the legendary Petrus Jacobs, perhaps the most experienced elephant hunter who ever lived, but a man for whom elephant hunting was a hard-eyed business. Beginning in 1840, the English elephant hunter Henry Hartley hunted professionally for forty years, reportedly shooting 1,000 elephant and selling 50,000 lb of ivory. Livingstone himself estimated that during his time in Africa, 1841–73, 30,000 elephants were shot each year.

Drawn to exploration, appreciating 'wagon travelling in Africa as a prolonged system of picnicking', Livingstone argued to his sceptical English backers, the London Missionary Society, that 'the geographical feat is the beginning of the missionary enterprise'. The society, however, held him to a lean allowance of £100 per year (about £2,950 today), and he was fortunate to attract Oswell's money and rifle. Oswell admired the missionary's energy as an explorer and supported his determination to end the slave trade. For Oswell, the motivation was principally sport, the outdoor adventure that is the heart of every safari, with the search for unspoiled hunting grounds blending conveniently with a taste for exploration.

Oswell himself was wonderfully rich, generous and skilled in the bush. In one day, to feed his camp and a hungry village, he killed six rhinos with six bullets within one quarter mile, a record never matched. He observed that the rhino, 'a creature from out of time', had only two enemies, men and hyena. If very hungry, hyena occasionally attack a male rhino from the rear, 'eating into his bowels from behind'. More agile than rhinoceros, hyena also attack baby rhino. Most animals let their young follow along behind, but female rhino protectively guide their babies along before them with their horns. Instead of shooting the hated hyena, Oswell would unfasten his stirrup leather while chasing at full gallop, then swing the heavy stirrup over his head and kill the tough scavenger with one blow. This was a sport later practised by jackaroos in Australia against a less formidable adversary, the kangaroo.

Female elephant, pursued with javelins, protecting her young

As Oswell travelled, he made his safari welcome by supplying meat to the Africans. On safari in the Bakaa hills, shooting in the 'hunter's paradise' of the Ba-Katla valley between two distinct lines of hills that run west into Bechuanaland near the Transvaal border, he made friends with an emaciated tribe whose crops had failed, and commented that no white man would even be able to walk in their condition. Although Livingstone considered that whites generally had more endurance than blacks, Oswell was repeatedly impressed by the physical fortitude and recuperative powers of the Africans. Livingstone, however, may have mistakenly considered himself and Oswell to be representative of white powers of endurance. On his first expedition, Livingstone overheard his companions demeaning his physique. His highland blood was insulted. For days he pressed a cruel pace until the exhausted Africans changed their view.

For seven weeks Oswell hunted elephant and fed the entire Bakaa tribe of six hundred until they were strong and merry. He marvelled that they could eat 12–15 lb of meat each day. Giving a few of them some beans, he confirmed that once the diet is mixed, people need less food. Even Livingstone, when he had only meat, ate up to 8 lb of it per day. In the final day of shooting before the Bakaa tribe left Oswell for their home kraals, he shot for them 60,000 lb of elephant and hippo meat. They staggered off with strips of flesh piled in faggots, assisted by porters requisitioned from a subservient tribe.

Oswell's choice weapon on safari was a 10 lb, ten-calibre double-barrelled smooth bore made for him in London by J. Purdey & Sons. In addition, the hunter travelled with a Westley Richards twelve-bore, a light rifle and a heavy, single-barrelled rifle firing 2 oz balls. It was still the time of muzzle-loaders, and Oswell preferred the smooth-bore guns to rifles because they were easier to load in the saddle. Both the old smooth-bore guns and the new rifles, however, required that the hunter roll the ball in a linen patch, trim the corners, drop a torn powder cartridge down the barrel, ram the ball down with a loading rod and fit the percussion cap to the nipple. The difference was that the rifles, due to the resistance provided by the rifling and to a slightly tighter fit of bullet and barrel, required considerably more pressure to ram the spherical ball or conical bullet down the barrel, making it a difficult exercise on a moving horse.

Delay in reloading cost many a hunter his life, and Oswell usually fired at twenty to thirty yards instead of the seventy to eighty generally favoured by Gordon Cumming. By the 1840s, however, many hunters of dangerous game were using the early double rifles, the thoroughbred of firearms. The two barrels and two lock mechanisms gave the hunter a reliable and immediate second shot, adding a measure of safety to their sport.

On one occasion, with both barrels empty, since he had not reloaded promptly, Oswell and his horse were thrown into the air by a white rhinoceros, which killed the horse and barely missed goring Oswell, whose scalp was torn from his head. Mungo Murray later reported to Livingstone that 'I found that beggar Oswell sitting under a bush and holding on his head.' After numberless

Samuel Baker freeing the slaves, by J.P. Zwecker

charges through the bush the walnut stock of his heavy Purdey was so worn by the cuts of wait-a-bit thorns that it looked as if rats had gnawed it.

Unlike Livingstone, Oswell was an admirer of the controversial Florence Baker, and years later, in 1861, he lent his Purdey to her husband for a hazardous Nile expedition. In a desperate fight against a band of slavers, the Purdey was fired hastily with the ramrod still in the barrel. Apologizing to Oswell that the rod had not been extracted from an assailant's stomach, Baker returned the gun with a replacement rod he had carved from a thornstick.

In 1849, Livingstone, although still in pain from a lion mauling four years before, with eleven teethmarks decorating his arm, was eager to cross the daunting Kalahari Desert and discover Lake Ngami. Oswell, always ready for a shooting safari to unspoiled game country, eager to hunt where the game had never heard a rifle, agreed to pay for everything, and he knew how to do things properly. Setting off with two wagons from Kolobeng, in eastern Bechuana-land, into hard, dry country, they were attended by twenty horses, eighty oxen and supplies for a year, at an initial cost of about £600 (now £16,600). Oswell recorded the following list of supplies and expenses for a safari in 1849:

Articles, Stores, etc., required for a Trip of Ten or Twelve Months with Two Wagons and Seven or Eight Servants

Coffee, 300 lb
Salt, 100 lb
Pepper, 10 lb
Rice, one bag
Sago, 2 lb
Spices, etc.
Soap, a box
Tar, two flasks
Sugar, 400 lb
Mustard, three bottles
Meal, 6 muids
Arrowroot, 2 lb
Cheese
French brandy, two cases
Wax candles, 30 lb
Snuff, two dozen boxes
Tobacco, five rolls
Large baking pot
Smaller baking pot
3 saucepans
6 tin plates
6 knives and forks
Frying-pan
Meat knife
4 tin canisters for tea, etc.
2 kettles
2 pots
4 tin dishes
6 spoons
Gridiron
Meat axe

3 large tin dishes
Ladle
2 coffee pots
Teapot
2 lanterns
Flour sieve
Coffee mill
3 water casks
6 needles
½ lb wicks
6 tinder boxes
10 lb brass wire
Candle mould
6 beakers
Pair of bellows
Pestle and mortar
2 buckets
2 lb twine
12 knives
24 boxes lucifers
40 lb of beads
Bale of canvas
12 riems
3 saddles and bridles
6 linchpins
Spokeshave
3 axes
3 picks
Chisel
Punch
2 spare skenes

2 gimlets
Saw
3 spades
3 sickles
Cold chisel
Hammer
2 augers
Screws, nails, etc.
Thermometer
Small telescope
Sextant, etc.
Iron spoon for
 running bullets
Coarse powder, 60 lb
Fine powder, 20 lb
Caps, 3,000
Lead, 150 lb
Tin, 30 lb
Flints, 60
Muskets, 6

for boys

6 beakers
6 spoons
12 common shirts
2 greatcoats for drivers
A small tent
6 scotels
Piece of moleskin
6 jackets
12 blankets

Paid by cheque on Messrs Rutherford

	£ s. d.		£ s. d.
Mr James for wagon	37 10 0	Canvas	2 8 0
Mr James for oxen	96 0 0	Holder, for repairs wagon, etc.	12 10 0
Krommehout for wagon and span	130 0 0	Godfrey, for repairs wagon, etc.	6 9 0
Cockroft for wagon, etc.	57 10 0	Wagon box	0 12 0
Wedderburn's bill for stores, etc.	40 5 0	Wagon box	2 0 0
Ogilvie's	30 14 0	Twelve riems	0 10 0
Coffee (3 bags)	9 0 0	Mats	0 9 0
		Cartels	2 10 0
			428 7 0

Livingstone on safari, mounted on his ox Sinbad

Crossing the Kalahari was hot work, sometimes digging all day in the sand, using turtle shells as spades, to find water for the horses. Oswell soon found that the missionary, by Oswell's standards at least, could neither shoot nor ride, although he judged that Livingstone's self-reliant, persistent and imperturbable nature would have made him a fine hunter. The missionary later became accustomed to riding on the back of an ox, with a rifle across his knees and a Bible in his pocket. He was frequently mounted on his surly ox Sinbad, who enjoyed brushing him off against low-hanging vines and unfailingly kicked him when he fell. When Oswell was not with him, Livingstone was obliged to shoot frequently to feed his followers and local villagers. Sometimes as many as a thousand Africans would struggle to carve up and devour one of his elephants.

Inevitably, during years of travels in which he crossed Africa from ocean to ocean, Livingstone gained more hunting experience than did other, more dedicated hunters. Although unavoidably excited when he hunted elephant

Tswanas hunting a lion, by
Cornwallis Harris

himself, he was generally disgusted by the shooting of elephant, and in 1865
predicted their rapid disappearance. He appreciated the distinction between
proper, sporting hunting to eat and excessive shooting to kill, which Livingstone called 'the hunting form of insanity'.

Four years before he first travelled with Oswell, Livingstone received the lion
mauling mentioned earlier, one of Africa's most celebrated lion incidents. He
was attempting to assist a hunting party of Tswanas to dispose of a lion that had
killed an ox in the northern Transvaal. The Tswanas set off in their traditional
manner, so well depicted by Cornwallis Harris in 1837. Encircling the lion, each
man carried two or three assegais and a six-foot stick crowned by a plume of
ostrich feathers. The practice was to narrow the circle until the lion was close
enough for the first spear. The lion then generally charged, attacking the spear
thrower, who dodged, planting his plumed stick in the ground to distract the
lion, like a matador's cape, as the next spearmen immediately joined the fight.
Although generally no one man could destroy the lion alone, together they
could.

But in this instance the wounded lion broke through the circle and escaped
into the bush. Livingstone spotted its tail, angrily switching from side to side in
the grass. He fired. The lion charged. Standing on Livingstone's back, the lion
put one paw on his head and took his arm in its mouth, wrenching it violently.
Then the lion dragged him by the shoulder, before being driven off and killed,
leaving an injury that never fully healed. Twenty-eight years later, Livingstone's body was gutted, salted and dried in the sun for two weeks before being
sheathed in bark and carried by his followers fifteen hundred miles across Africa
disguised as a bale of cloth. Then it was shipped to London and examined at the
Royal Geographical Society in Savile Row. The old lion wound, the overlapping
end of the broken humerus, the long bone of the upper arm, was taken as
conclusive evidence that the body was indeed his. When Livingstone was buried
at Westminster Abbey in 1874, after lying in state in the map room of the Royal

Livingstone's encounter with a lion

Geographical Society, four of his pallbearers were old safari companions, including Cotton Oswell.

In his own account of the lion attack, Livingstone reports that the lion shook him, unresisting, until he was senseless, as a cat does a mouse, nature thereby sparing him pain as he went into shock. Some commentators hold that this passive behaviour can save a man, both by not provoking the animal to further violence and by sparing the body stress. Other students of the lion, however, present examples that establish the merit of resisting to the end, yelling and fighting, even stabbing with any small knife, as lions occasionally turn away or set the body down. It is unlikely that Gordon Cumming would have acquiesced as gently as Dr Livingstone. If many hunters are involved, however, there seems to be an advantage in the injured man not retaining the lion's attention, which can be difficult to lose. The Romans, Pliny records, observed that when a lion in the circus was attacked by a gang of gladiators, and surrounded by a roaring crowd of thousands, the first man to wound the lion remained the focus of the beast's anger until it died.

With the benefit of his own experience, Livingstone admired the discretion of the Bushmen lion hunters. Infinitely patient, waiting until the lion slept after feasting on a kill, then creeping to within a few feet, the Bushmen would fire a slender arrow into the groggy beast, the barb fatally poisoned with an extract they squeeze from the entrails of a half-inch caterpillar called *n'gwa*. A knowledge of nature sufficient to fascinate Livingstone, and the readers of Europe, however, was superficial and childishly obvious by Bushman standards. The Bushmen enjoyed an almost mystical integration with nature. To them, pantheistic stories, narrations, played the sustaining role that dreams have for the aborigines of Australia, providing communal continuity and refreshment for the spirit.

Livingstone's early journals, published in London in 1857 under the title *Travels and Researches in South Africa*, reveal how absorbed he had become in wildlife and the adventure of safari life. He noted how baby hippo journeyed upriver resting on their mothers' necks, peeping between the ears, and travelled on the maternal haunches when they grew heavier, presumably to avoid the waiting crocodile. He observed how buffalo butted and gored any badly wounded companion, as Oswell confirmed. He correctly predicted that white rhinoceros would be exterminated before the black, as their meat and dispositions were sweeter. He noted that the vegetable-like flavour of fried locusts varies with their diet. Measuring ostriches' strides as their speed accelerated, he calculated that they have a top speed of 26 m.p.h., while his own journeys had a pace of $2\frac{1}{2}$ m.p.h. *Sirafu* or 'driver' ants, red and vicious, attacking all in their path, bit the missionary's feet, but hyena were wont to grab sleeping men by the face.

For his food, Livingstone preferred the hump of the buffalo, the flesh of the eland and fresh eggs of the crocodile, although he deplored the slaughter of crocodile. Sharing the taste for eland, the missionary's follower Lebeole lamented that 'Jesus ought to have given us eland instead of cattle.' Some Africans favoured the rubbery meat of huge pythons, sliced into sections and carried off like logs, while, far to the west, others ate human flesh, served with bananas, the meat rather high after preservation in the earth.

On all the early safaris, tea and coffee were precious luxuries, but healthy, as they were made with boiled water, the aromas reminiscent of home, the taste killing the flavour of the water. Frequently the early hunters were lucky if they found any water, even water that Livingstone describes as 'swarming with insects, thick with mud and putrid with other mixtures'. To fight fever, presumably malaria, the missionary took one spoonful of spirits in hot water before sleeping, a modest dose by later safari standards. Occasionally at night, he would dream of English roast beef until his pillow ran wet with saliva.

In the course of their 1849 expedition, Oswell and Livingstone discovered Lake Ngami. Shallow, seventy miles long, and virtually dried out until the floods began to come down from the north in April, Lake Ngami itself was not as dramatic as Livingstone might have hoped. But it was dramatic enough for him jealously to claim, and Oswell generously to concede, that Livingstone was its principal discoverer. In most years the rain suffices to waterlog the bed of Lake Ngami and the great delta of the Okavango swamp just to the north. Then the river systems running south from what is now Angola begin to pour into the Okavango River, which empties into the swamp and its rivers, forming the largest inland delta in the world, some fifteen thousand square kilometres, a lush, independent ecosystem bordering the Kalahari Desert, itself once a vast inland lake. Perhaps 5 per cent of the moving water penetrates south through the swamp to reach Lake Ngami.

The extraordinary wildlife that inhabits Lake Ngami and the adjoining Okavango swamp region of Bechuanaland was perhaps the greatest jewel of this discovery, notably the rich bird life and the two new species of antelope. Oswell and Livingstone were credited with being the first Europeans to record the nakong and the lechwe antelopes. The lechwe, which looks like a smaller waterbuck, dark fawn in colour, with ringed, lyre-shaped horns, was first found on the Seseke plain west of the Zambesi River, but flourishes in the swampy Okavango delta. The nakong, now known as the sitatunga, is a grey-brown, amphibious swamp-dweller the size of a goat, distinguished by its elongated hooves, which enable it to skim the morasses as a camel does the desert, without sinking in, and by its defensive habit of hiding in the water with only the tip of its snout showing. Although adapted to swamp life, instead of to woodlands, the sitatunga comes from the same family as the kudu, the bushbuck and the nyala, as its two-foot-long spiral horns suggest.

After the success of their first journey together, which provided elephant for Oswell and glory for Livingstone, they shared their interests and Oswell's money again in 1851, making the first safari to the Zambesi River, which they found five hundred yards wide and thick with crocodiles and hippopotamus. With the possible exception of two Portuguese traders, they were the first white men to reach the upper Zambesi. Dazzled, moved by the sense of discovery, they considered it the most magnificent river they had ever seen. Although they did not reach Victoria Falls, just eighty miles to the east, they were amazed to find the river 'in the centre of the continent', contrary to early Portuguese maps. This safari fed Dr Livingstone's appetite for exploration and inspired him to undertake the greatest of all his adventures, the four-and-a-half-year ocean-to-ocean expedition across central Africa.

Oswell was among the first to compare the habits and sporting qualities of the heavy game, and he tended to respect elephant and buffalo more than lion. Recalling how in Madras he had seen even domesticated buffalo drive off tigers, he found the African Cape buffalo to be the 'bravest and most determined of all animals when wounded and at bay; courage is the instinct of the buffalo family'. Oswell was highly experienced with lion, and once rescued a badly injured African from an enraged, wounded lion that had the African's dog in its mouth, the lion's mane standing straight out 'as if electrified into an Elizabethan collar'.

Having had one horse killed under him by a buffalo, another killed under him by a rhinoceros and a third leapt on by a lion shortly before an overhanging bough knocked both him and the lion off the horse's back, Oswell was able to make comparisons. The lion attack underscored a key principle of big-game hunting on horseback: if you are right-handed, you must always keep the dangerous game to your left, otherwise you cannot swing your rifle all the way to the side for a wide shot. Another lesson Oswell learned was that there are many ways to die on safari. Like Baldwin, he tells a story, confirmed by other hunting incidents over the years, that when wounded buffalo are able to reach, but not to gore their human adversary, they will sometimes lick any flesh they can reach, such as a thigh projecting from under a ledge or a leg dangling from a tree, with their severely abrasive tongues until, the flesh open and dripping as the tongue scrapes and laps it, their victim bleeds to death.

Crossing the Tugela River

Oswell respectfully disagreed with Cornwallis Harris's judgement that the lion is more resolute in attack than the Indian tiger, but he cites Sir Samuel Baker's opinion that the lion delivers an even more devastating blow with its paw. Oswell, in his classic Rugby prose, invites lion fanciers 'to come with me to a desert pool some clear moonlit night when the shadows are deep and sharply cut, and the moon herself, in the dry, cloudless air, looks like a ball'. Then, he rightly says, one can watch all other animals, save the sly jackal, defer to the true king of beasts, the elephant, leaving the pool while it drinks.

The power of a lion, however, is well confirmed by other observers. Tim Davison, for example, a leading Rhodesian game warden, in the 1970s observed an old, heavy, single buffalo bull as it repeatedly drove a lioness and her two cubs away from a waterhole. Finally the frustrated lioness gave a low, grunting moan, calling her mate. At once a large, black-maned lion, perhaps 450 lb, streaked to the waterhole. As the buffalo turned, the lion gave it a single slamming blow with its paw, dropping the buffalo instantly with a broken neck. A similar incident has since been recorded at Kruger National Park in South Africa.

Oswell found the elephant to be wise and loyal, often returning to aid wounded comrades, even helping one another to escape from native pitfalls by scraping ramps down the edges of the pit and assisting the victim up with their trunks. Astonishing rock climbers, strong swimmers, with their trunks raised into the air like periscopes, able to travel fifty or more miles a night, elephant are splendid sport to pursue on foot. Like other animals, their physique varies with their habitat. He found that the drier the country, the smaller a lion's mane and the smaller the elephant. Thus mature bulls in the valley of the Limpopo River averaged eleven feet at the shoulder, although the smaller, ten-foot bulls of the Kalahari desert carried heavier ivory with a finer grain. Today there are no elephant left in the Kalahari. The last enclave of desert elephant now survives in the Kaokovelt, in the north-west corner of Namibia, near the Atlantic coast.

On his second trip across the Kalahari, in 1850, travelling without Livingstone, who had abandoned their proposed meeting place at Kolobeng, Oswell took a six-hundred-mile safari just for 'a little quiet shoot by myself', coming again to the Zouga, the river that then drained out of Lake Ngami. There Oswell found, standing massive and grey in the shade under the clumps of tall mimosa, one of the largest single sightings of the species ever recorded by a hunter under natural conditions, four hundred elephant scattered in clusters over the Zouga flats, as far as his eye could see.

The Zouga, however, was also home to two less pleasing creatures, the tsetse fly and the anopheles mosquito. The tsetse was not known south of the Kalahari, but, as Livingstone reported, had long been a problem in central and eastern Africa, north of the twenty-seventh latitude, particularly from December to April. There, in the 'fly country', domestic cattle were highly vulnerable, but horses suffered the worst, entire studs often perishing, emaciated, with their principal organs gone strangely soft. If a horse survived an attack of this distemper, however, it was 'salted', secure from future illness. The flesh of animals that die from tsetse is poisonous. Mules, goats and dogs, and most game, are generally safe from the 'fly'. The great hunter Frederick Courtenay Selous, however, later attested that he personally observed donkeys, goats and dogs perish from tsetse. He concluded, perhaps incorrectly, that the goats and dogs found surviving in fly country were the descendants of salted progenitors.

A brown bloodsucker with a grey mid-section, slightly larger than its cousin the common housefly, the tsetse proved to be as dangerous and tenacious as other African wildlife. There are about twenty species of tsetse, all belonging to the Muscidae family within the Diptera order of insects. All tsetse species gather their blood during the warmer part of the day, and all have stiff, piercing jaws that inflict a sharp stinging sensation as the fly bites. Some tsetse species regularly attack people, occasionally transmitting sleeping sickness, a variant of the disease called *nagana* that kills cattle. The flies themselves often do not outlive their victims, having a life of no longer than three months. If a female secures enough blood, she will produce fresh larvae every ten days. Eighty per cent of the tsetse that bite people are males, while most of the females take their blood from bigger game, like buffalo. Tsetse are particularly plentiful in buffalo country.

The anopheles mosquito was not recognized as the carrier of malaria until 1898, but early travellers suffered greatly, and often died, from the debilitating

Tsetse fly

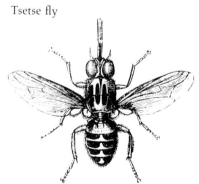

Right: Camp life, by Samuel Baker.
In the foreground is his pet
monkey Wallady

Below: Rhinoceros attacking a
horse, by Samuel Baker

'fever' transmitted by it. A chronic, acute, relapsing infection, malaria is caused by various species of single-cell animal organisms classified as blood sporozoa. An ancient and widespread infection, malaria was described by Hippocrates in the fifth century BC, and has been treated with the quinine extract of cinchona bark since at least 1700, both as a cure and as a prophylactic. Vivax or tertian malaria is the most common in Africa, and is characterized by periodic, alternating paroxysms of extreme fever and chills, anaemia and enlarged spleen, and has fatal complications. Although apes, monkeys, rats and birds can also suffer from malaria, only the anopheles mosquito naturally transmits it to humans, who may, however, give it to one another by exchanges of blood.

Virtually none of the early hunters avoided both disease and injury. Oswell himself suffered his worst hunting wound when he broke one of the rules: always respect your quarry. Hunting on foot, over-confident, letting two rhino get too close, he was attacked. Certain that if he got one, the other would charge at the smoke of the rifle, even if he himself was hidden, he fled, dodging and twisting sharply as if back on the rugby field. When the rhinoceros horn touched his thigh, he placed his rifle against the rhino's long, barrel-like head as he ran and pulled both triggers just as he was thrown in the air. Waking, groping for his wound, his fingers touched, through the open flesh, the bone of his thigh, torn in an eight-inch gash. For a month he lay on the ground, mending, sheltered under a bush, the wound bound in a rag which his men kept constantly wet, then the accepted field treatment for men and horses on safari.

Like Gordon Cumming, Oswell learned much bushcraft from the resourceful Bushmen, particularly the art of survival. Crossing the Kalahari, doing as much as seventy miles at a stretch without water, the endless flat dry landscapes sprinkled with occasional scrub and stunted bushes, mirages glimmering over the salt pans, he learned how the Bushmen survived, when they seemingly went without water for months. Oswell found that the Bushmen are geographers of the underground water systems. Boring into the desert with long poles, reaching hollows in the hard substratum, they then enlarge the boring below by gently turning the poles on the slant as the water gathers. Having created a *mamina* or sucking hole, they tie a bunch of grass to the end of a hollow reed and suck up the water. Like elephant, the Bushmen eat the bitter tsama melons of the Kalahari. Like oryx, they dig and suck the watery roots and tubers buried in the desert.

Later scholars, like Laurens van der Post, point out that the remarkably pronounced buttocks of the Bushmen store nourishment like a sponge. In 1822 William Burchell coined the anthropological term 'steatopyga' to describe these protuberant buttocks, which Colonel van der Post points out are an occasional reminder in some blacks of a distant Bushman heritage. Bushman women were favoured captives among certain Bantu tribes, due to their honey-coloured skin and delicate hands and feet.

Oswell found that the Bushmen, highly sensitive to animal life, enjoyed a refined sporting instinct, whereas the Tswanas were 'mere pot-hunters', simply

Native hippo hunting

A rhino hunt, by Charles Bell

killing to eat. The Boers, on the other hand, he considered practical but cruel hunters. Approaching a herd of elephant, wanting to bag a large number without getting too close, they would first fire their heavy roers at the front legs of the largest bulls, crippling them. Most of an elephant's weight is massed at the front, requiring thicker front legs, although their rear legs are longer. Their leg bones are solid, not hollow, holding no marrow. When an elephant walks, both legs on one side of its body move forward in unison. With a front leg splintered, the animal is unable to shift its weight and is paralysed. The Boers would then chase the other elephants, coming back later to finish off the weakened bulls.

Dismayed by the 'great cruelty' also shown by the Boers to the Africans, citing the 'evil influence and oppression they have at times exercised upon the black race', Oswell feared that, with that bad history, the time would come when 'the minority whites are almost inevitably forced for very existence to terrorize the black majority'. Oswell allowed that the Boer settlers compared favourably with English squatters in other countries, when there was no problem of race. He was uncertain whether, without a government authority to protect native rights, English settlers would behave better. The Boers, he recounts, had recently wanted the British army to suppress the Natal Zulus, who had been friendly to the British until the British abandoned them to invasion by the settlers. By 1851, the Zulus defeated, the bloody job done, the Boers wanted the British out of Natal.

Livingstone, although he himself occasionally caned his porters when they were uncooperative, identified forced labour as the essence of slavery and considered the frontier Boers to be slave-owners. In return, he was despised by them. The Boers considered the British to be the protectors of native land claims, and resented the activities of British missionaries, traders and hunters. When Livingstone was absent from his mission in Kolobeng in 1852, a commando of four hundred Boers, with eighty-five wagons and a cannon, attacked the Tswanas there, enslaved two hundred children and destroyed the stored property of several English hunters, killing the African guardians. They sacked Livingstone's house, tearing up his books, destroying his medicines and later auctioning his stolen furniture and clothing to pay for their expedition. The Tswanas had originally welcomed the Boers, knowing them to be enemies of the hated Mzilikazi, but they soon told Livingstone that 'Mzilikazi was cruel to his enemies, and kind to those he conquered; but the Boers destroyed their enemies, and made slaves of their friends.'

Slaves on the march, by Thomas Baines

Like Livingstone an ardent abolitionist, Oswell was shocked to meet, at the Chobe River, near the Zambesi in northern Bechuanaland in 1851, Africans who had been selling other blacks for clothing and trinkets to the Mambari slave dealers, gangs of half-caste Portuguese. Slavery and elephant hunting had been African enterprises since at least the first century AD, when a Greek writer recorded that Africans were selling ivory and slaves to Arab traders in exchange for wine and iron implements. Oswell noted that the Mambari slave dealers encouraged tribal raids, their own supporting guns making the difference. Then they would enslave the losers, and their black allies would seize the cattle.

With the Royal Navy tightening the anti-slavery blockade on both coasts of Africa, however, Oswell considered that only two things kept the slave trade alive: the use of slaves as porters to carry ivory to the Arab trading centre on the island of Zanzibar, and the refusal of France to let the Royal Navy search French vessels for slaves. Protecting commercial interests in the name of sovereignty, the United States then also limited this 'right of search', despite the international anti-slavery convention that allowed it. While other nations permitted the Royal Navy to impound their flag vessels if they were found fitted out for the slave trade, the United States only permitted seizure if the vessels actually contained slaves when searched. This legal nicety encouraged American slave ships, when pursued, to throw their living cargo into the sea to avoid seizure.

William Charles Baldwin, by Joseph Brown

Back in England in later years, long married, with five children, troubled about the future of the game and the people he loved, William Cotton Oswell wrote about Africa only months before his death in 1893. Conceding that he was a young man in his safari days, that it was exciting work, and that he was feeding hungry men, he confessed to his fellow hunters in his contribution to the Badminton sporting library that he felt 'sorry now for all the fine old beasts that I have killed'.

Oswell's own approach to one's personal conduct on safari has endured, even today, as the standard for the best of the professional hunters. As Cotton Oswell's son wrote:

> It was his creed that a man should be able to bear any pain, trouble, worry or privation, without murmuring; act in any emergency, go out in any weather, walk any distance, eat anything, sleep anywhere; and he was unmerciful to petting, coddling, or talking about one's self.

One year after Oswell left Africa in 1851, and before Livingstone began his expedition to the Zambesi to 'discover' Victoria Falls, a new hunter arrived in South Africa, drawn by Gordon Cumming's book, *The Lion Hunter of South Africa*. William Charles Baldwin, a restless Englishman pondering whether to make an outdoor life in America or Africa, came upon Cumming's new book 'in the very nick of time'. He sailed for Natal in 1852, bringing 'my little all, consisting chiefly of guns, rifles, saddles and seven deerhounds'. Baldwin returned safely home eight years later. His hardy deerhounds did not. Bred for generations to heighten their hunting instincts, they did not long survive the lavish opportunities that overwhelmed them in Africa.

Baldwin was blessed neither with Oswell's fortune nor his physique. He was 5 ft 2 in tall, 8 st (112 lb), once reduced by malaria to 5 st 10 lb (80 lb). Carrying a 14 lb elephant gun, he was obliged to earn his way in order to support the safari life he desired. Never a top shot, his friends remarked that, 'Baldwin's trouble is he cannot see over the long grass.' Although not a hunting guide in the sense of the later professional paid safari hunters, he lived by his bush skills, shooting for ivory, skins and meat, whatever was required to maintain his independent life. Between 1852 and 1860, he undertook pioneering safaris through what became Botswana, Zambia and Zimbabwe, twice crossing the Kalahari to visit Lake Ngami.

On his first safari up the east coast, hunting for hippos at St Lucia Bay, collecting ivory, making long whips and jamboks, and storing melted lard in hippo bladders, eight of Baldwin's ten white companions died of malaria. Thereafter he travelled mostly with Africans. He learned to admire the honesty of the Zulus, the camp-fire humour of the Hottentots and the courtesy and craftsmanship of the Amatongas, particularly their skill in fabricating water-tight grass baskets holding nine gallons of beer. But he also occasionally administered 'a little wholesome chastisement with a rhino jambok'.

In 1860 he became perhaps the second white man to see Victoria Falls, and the first to come upon it from the east, an accomplishment he celebrated by carving his initials in a tree, just under Livingstone's, on an island in the Zambesi. He travelled to the mile-wide falls by moonlight, hearing from ten miles away the thundering water as it crashed a thousand feet. He arrived just before daybreak, exhausted, drenched by the mist that rained about him, as the dawn sun illuminated the eternal rainbow.

More personal and confiding than other Victorian journals of Africa, Baldwin's records more than fortitude and sporting observations, although it has its share of those. He gives the feeling of early safari life, the sense of isolation that comes with the freedom, the fear that accompanies the excitement, the combination of violence and beauty that are life in the bush. His diary, written as a record for his brother, a minister in England, provides the detail of survival and improvisation in a life 'miserable enough at times, but a roving, careless, wandering life that has charms for me'. It was a lonely life of illness, risk and hardship. He often subsisted on Zulu milk and beer, sleeping in mud under a wagon, at night fending off 'villainous black ants' and the rats that ran over his face, one night listening to hyenas cracking the bones of his horse Sweep.

Above all, it was hard work. Just maintaining his twenty-seven-year-old wagon, binding it together with rhino skin and green hides, soaking the wheels in rivers so the parched wood would expand again to meet the metal rims, was a constant preoccupation. Dealing with the languages and conflicting demands of the Boers, Bushmen, Hottentots and Bantus was also difficult and time-consuming. Each day he developed new tricks, greasing his guns with oil from

Zanjueela, Boatman of the Rapids. A Zambesi river scene by Thomas Baines, 1863

the kori bustard, making a torch brilliant with crocodile fat, fashioning splints for a broken arm with the back of a book and the lid of a tea-chest.

Often the game hunted the hunter. One buffalo pursued Baldwin relentlessly through a series of bush encounters until the man finally finished the old bull with a 'settler'. Another day, desperately fleeing a wounded elephant, the chase so close that the elephant's trunk swung over his horse's hindquarters, even his goatskin trousers were shredded to rags by what the Boers called *wag 'n bietjie*, wait-a-bit thorns. In a famous incident painted by the artist Joseph Wolf, Baldwin and his exhausted horse Ferus were pursued by a man-eating lion, which the Bushmen had begged him to kill. The lion leapt upon Ferus, hitting Baldwin's shoulder and nearly dislodging him. Another day he rushed into a river to recover a shot goose, sharing the bird with a crocodile that ripped it from his hand, leaving Baldwin with the legs, back and entrails. Besides his heavy elephant gun, he often used a two-grooved Witton rifle, 'the most perfect weapon I ever handled', generally firing a conical bullet with $\frac{3}{8}$ oz of powder. His favourite gun was his old Burrow seven-bore, which he carried for ten years, always relying on its exceptional accuracy and force.

For everyone on safari, the day's reward was an evening feast, with the blacks chasing bites of roasted flesh with mouthfuls of raw innards and clotted blood. When lucky, Baldwin began his day with a breakfast of cold bush pig, ram kidneys and mushrooms, and ended it by the fire with stewed eland marrow, pumpkins and sea-cow stew, a rhino hump baked in a hole, pickled buffalo tongue, or, the finest treats, buffalo kidneys or elephant-trunk steak. Lunch was not served. But fearful of a late chase, Baldwin might stuff a dried eland tongue into his pocket, once setting off with a giraffe tongue slung from his belt and hanging down to his ankles.

Climate and health often intruded to push aside every other concern. At times the ground was so hot that the dogs danced as they drank at the muddy waterholes, the air so hot that the metal heel-plate of his gun was too painful to put to his shoulder and the bacon melted in the wagon. One night was so cold that he used his stirrup leathers to bind together the legs of his greyhound Hopeful, beating the animal until it lay still, and then holding it all night on his chest like a blanket, 'the warmth of his body saving my life'. In the Kalahari, where Baldwin often avoided the parching heat by trekking by moonlight, the stocks of his guns shrank and the wagon's frame withdrew from its fittings. Water, carried in six giraffe bladders, grew so precious that he drank from the stomach of a quagga, followed Namaqua partridges and turtle-doves until they drank, and at night lay death-still, listening for frogs.

The worst ordeals were the ague, flaming fever and deep chills of malaria. This ravaging illness struck many hunters season after season, and even the survivors rarely recovered fully. Each hunter was his own doctor and surgeon. Baldwin tried Dover's powder, pheasant broth, or quinine when he was lucky. Seeking to vomit bile, he mixed weekly emetics from calomel, tartar and laudanum, an ingredient based on opium. For open wounds, he favoured a wet tobacco leaf as a dressing. Amusing himself with Raffler, a hypochondriac Hottentot, Baldwin fed the enthusiastic patient nauseous mixtures, but even castor oil blended with mustard and warm water did not deter Raffler's appetite for medicine. The horses suffered with the men. The value of a horse in the north depended on whether it was 'salted' (had already survived the tsetse country north of the Limpopo River). The first sign of horse sickness was a swelling above the eyes. From then on the horses suffered as much from the treatment as from the fly. Bled heavily, their lives sometimes slipped away through torn veins that would not close.

In these circumstances, the pain of the hunter's prey drew little attention. Compassion was less recorded than curiosity: the striking sight of a giraffe, galloping heart-shot through the forest until its neck lodged violently in the fork of a mopane tree twelve feet above the ground, dying on its feet, or a large crocodile, alive, wedged fast in the fork of another tree, nine feet off the ground, evidently the victim of an elephant angered by the crocodile custom of biting elephants' trunks when they drink. Yet Baldwin grieved one day at his own killing of all five of a troop of eland, although famished Tswanas consumed every scrap. One day he fired so much that 'my right cheek and bone are nearly cut to pieces, and the blood at every shot runs into my mouth'. His solution was to put three pounds of lead into the stock to reduce the recoil.

In his best night of hunting, with a bit of white paper to show up his forward gunsight in the dark, Baldwin killed three buffalo, one white rhino, one quagga, one lion and one elephant. Perhaps feeling guilt at presenting this record to his clerical brother, he maintains that 'This was not mere butchery, though it looks like it. The kaffirs are more than half starved, and it was only combining sport with charity.' Baldwin also burdens his brother with the horror of enduring the

A giraffe caught in a tree

Revd Schroeder's three-hour sermon in Norwegian in a crumbling mud chapel, as the squatting Zulu congregation cracked lice and picked thorns from their feet, a far more draining experience than any but the most successful lion charge.

Early in his African career, Baldwin makes it clear that for him, as for Cotton Oswell, although companions are fine at the evening camp fire, it is best to shoot alone. His most constant companions were Lord Byron, *Martin Chuzzlewit* and his puppy Ragman, a mixed bulldog-greyhound-pointer. Ragman always 'held on like a vice, and was the best feeder I ever saw, eating huge rashers of any animal just killed, saving us the trouble of carrying food for him'. Zulus sometimes avoided that baggage problem by cutting a hole in a large piece of meat, usually an unwanted hind leg, and slipping the gory necklace over the head of the dog, so that the animal became its own porter.

Baldwin learned that self-reliance does not exclude loneliness and a craving for news from home. By Christmas Day, 1857, after six years on the trail, Baldwin was pining for the mince pies and port of England, but dining instead on 'a scrap of half-baked dough' and bits of cold, fatty rhinoceros meat. The next year finds him healthy, with 'a constant supply of good spirits', full of affection for the Africans, even appreciating his own rootlessness. But he is growing aware of his isolation, regretting that he and the Boer hunters are poor companions, because 'to me all places are alike, I have nothing to gain by pushing on, and it riles me to hear them everlastingly talking of getting home'. Finally, acknowledging 'fits of despondency', he concedes the theory that 'the colonies are only refuges for destitute social suicides'.

By 1859 Baldwin becomes desperately lonely, torn between his love of safari life and the emotional distress of painful solitude, determining in the future to trek with a companion. Several times he bought starving young slave captives, of six or eight years old, from different tribes, freeing them, fattening them up and enjoying their cheerful company as they helped around the camp. As they never cried, he preferred them to white children. Occasionally, celebrating a fine hunt, he broke the colonial taboo against drinking with his Hottentots, admiring their skilled mimicry and finding that 'a Tottie half-seas over is the most merry fellow in the world'.

Although he admired the pretty Amatonga girls, there is no suggestion of liaison. Baldwin's only allusion to his own desires is when he describes the frontier Boer custom of 'upsits', a courting practice whereby the girl whispers with her suitor as they snuggle in a chair, while her parents sleep behind a curtain, the suitor being allowed to remain so long as the single candle still burns. A suitor judges his welcome by the length of the candle, and eager lovers contrive to keep the flame burning slowly. Lying alone on the floor, feigning sleep, while two upsits proceeded in flickering shadows at opposite corners of a one-room house, Baldwin wished he was upsitting himself, considering this the best of the Boer customs. Observing Boer girls at less romantic occupations, as

Baldwin stirrup-hunting, by J. I'. Zwecker

they sharpen their knives on a stone doorstep, cut a goat's throat and peel off the animal's skin in masterly style, he found them far too manly.

Lonely as he became, however, and appreciating as he did their hospitality and extraordinary qualities as pioneers, Baldwin determined not to travel with Boers, although near the Zambesi he met the best, 'the far-famed old hunters Jan Viljoen and Pet Jacobs'. Viljoen, like many early South Africans, was of mixed French Huguenot and Boer descent. The first Huguenots had fled to South Africa in 1688. Viljoen himself had barely escaped hanging after capture by the British at the battle of Boomplaats in 1848. Hating their administration, he was none the less invariably hospitable to British travellers. Generally, however, Baldwin, like many British South Africans today, found the Boers 'hardly one remove from the kaffirs. They have no information whatever on any subject but waggons and oxen, never read a book of any sort, and are perfectly ignorant of what every child in England knows.'

Baldwin also became somewhat discouraged by the strife among the Africans, particularly the Zulu conflicts in which King Panda's sons, Cetshwayo and Mbulazi, fought for his throne at the battle of Tugela River. There the stench of corpses hung in the air for twelve miles along the wagon route, and Baldwin frequently found a single spear pinning the body of a mother and the child on her back. Panda himself had killed seven of his brothers, and was calm when his sons fought to be his heir.

By 1859, Baldwin's Hottentots were terrified that he might lead them to the hunting grounds of the dread Mzilikazi. The Maccalacas they travelled amongst were too scared of Mzilikazi even to mention the king's name.

By the late 1850s Mzilikazi and his Matabele had completed their final trek and were well established in their new settlements north of the Limpopo River, in what became Rhodesia. Having been twice defeated by Boer commandos in 1837, they were driven from the Transvaal, wandering in two separated columns of impis, cattle, women and children, attacking lesser tribes as they proceeded. The Boers now claimed virtually all of Mzilikazi's old kingdom in the Transvaal, the northern Orange Free State and Bechuanaland. After lean months walking about the Kalahari and the desolate saltpans of northern Bechuanaland, in 1840 the Matabele had settled in the wooded regions and grazing lands north of the Limpopo. There Mzilikazi built his royal kraal, creating Matabeleland and slaughtering the pastoral Mashona, who on occasion retaliated by cutting off the legs and arms of captured Matabele girls. Over a century later, in 1979, the Mashona finally recovered control of their country from both the Europeans and the Matabele, taking power in Zimbabwe in the election that followed the end of white rule.

By 1860 Baldwin had also wandered far enough. Even he was exhausted, and tired of his lonely state. He had travelled 15,000 hard miles. Having amassed over 5,000 lb of ivory, but lost all of his trophies when a wagon driver left them hanging in trees in order to make room for more tusks in the wagon, it was time to go home.

On 24 April 1860, Baldwin started to make his way south from the region of Victoria Falls. Unable to find large numbers of elephant, he was passing through Matabeleland and what is now Zimbabwe's Hwange National Park, one of the greatest elephant reserves in the world. Unknown to Baldwin, on that same day, six hundred miles to the south, there took place the largest one-day hunt in the history of Africa. As much as any single day could, it marked the end of the first generation of the old white hunters, and the beginning of the elegant safari, when local professional hunters escorted privileged Europeans on organized hunts into the bush.

In 1860, Bloemfontein was the capital of the Orange Free State, a Boer republic spread between the Orange and the Vaal rivers. The republic was established in 1854 when the British government, declining further colonial responsibilities, renounced its sovereignty over the area and abandoned the natives to the Boer settlers, who, Baldwin reports, in 1857 adopted the local custom of killing the women and children of defeated tribes. The Transvaal had received a similar independence in 1852. To celebrate the visit of Prince Alfred, the 'Sailor Prince' and the second son of Queen Victoria, the proud Orange Republic organized a vast hunt on Hartebeeste-hoek farm five miles from the capital. A levy of a thousand Barolongs, a Sotho tribe once much abused by Mzilikazi, was recruited to drive game inwards in a vast circle, with three hundred pack oxen standing by to bear the carcasses.

Eventually 20,000–30,000 animals were hemmed in by the human cordon. There were no elephant and buffalo, or lion and rhinoceros, for in 1860 these were already extinct in the Orange Free State. There were vast herds of light plains game, wildebeest, zebra, blesbok, hartebeest, ostrich, springbok and bontebok. As larger and larger herds stampeded desperately about in the dust, thousands charging through the lines into the plain, several Barolongs were trampled to death in the confusion, while the assegais and rolling fire of the hunters killed a number of animals variously estimated at 300 to 5,000. Properly tanned, an antelope skin fetched about fifteen shillings. The battle was painted by the artist Thomas Baines, after the fleeing animals swept past his house in the adjoining valley.

Returning to the confinement of Victorian England, where the tales of African game were now stirring even the thinnest blood, Baldwin and the other old hunters missed Africa with every sense. Recalling his safari life shortly before he died in 1893, half a century after he walked with Livingstone, Cotton Oswell wrote:

> There is a fascination to me in the remembrance of the free life, the self-dependence, the feeling as you lay under your caross that you were looking at the stars from a point on earth whence no other European had ever seen them; the hope that every patch of bush was the only thing between you and some strange scene – these are with me still. Were I not married with grandchildren, I should head back into Africa again, and end my days in the open air. It is useless to tell me of civilization. Take the word of one who has tried both, there is a charm in the wild life.

3. 'I MEAN TO BE LIKE LIVINGSTONE'

Frederick C. Selous

Late on a sunny January after-noon in 1867, England's worst ice-skating tragedy struck at the Ornamental Water in London's Regent's Park. To clear water for the birds, park keepers had broken some ice along the banks. As a boy of fifteen skated across the centre of the lake, cracks splintered sharply through the thawing ice. Five hundred panicked skaters fled desperately back and forth across the cracking surface, unable to reach shore as slabs of ice broke loose, tilting skaters into the water and closing over their heads. Three thousand spectators watched friends and relatives struggle and die before them. A few bystanders entered the water, hauling out bodies and swimmers. Three rescuers were themselves pulled under the ice by drowning men. Others threw oars and branches to frenzied skaters.

Ignoring the hysteria, the boy stood calmly on his skates, looked carefully about him, and lay down spreadeagled on his dwindling patch of ice. Unnoticed as the winter afternoon darkened, as death and rescue occupied the crowd, the boy planned his route and slowly crawled crab-like from slab to slab, until he reached an island and then hobbled across and skated on unbroken ice to shore. Meanwhile, the first bodies were carried to the nearby Death House of the Marylebone Workhouse. Among the survivors, the worst cases were rushed to the tent of the Royal Humane Society and dipped in a warm bath, three at a time, with their clothes on. Finally, after a week of quarrying the ice, diving and dragging the water with hooks and fishing nets, finding hats, a walking-stick and bodies stiff as trees, the count of the dead reached forty-nine. But Frederick Courtenay Selous, fifteen years old, survived. In time, repeatedly drawing on the same alert instincts during a lifetime of hazard in the bush, he became the greatest of all the white hunters.

Lions on the veld, by Cornwallis Harris

Already at thirteen, with the African diaries of Gordon Cumming and Charles Baldwin filling his imagination, Selous had chosen to sleep on the bare floor at boarding-school, explaining to his headmaster that 'I am going to be a hunter in Africa and I am just hardening myself to sleep on the ground.' The Selous family was related to the Scottish eighteenth-century Abyssinian explorer James Bruce, and Frederick Selous's brother later recorded that Frederick was born with an elemental determination to live an outdoor life in Africa.

Some nights young Selous would scramble from his dormitory window down a rope, then climb the nearby oaks and elms, studying the forest and collecting rooks' eggs for his friends. Canon Wilson, a housemaster at Rugby School, was advised to reject young Selous due to his nocturnal trespassings in private forests and his run-ins with angry gamekeepers. But the Canon, aware of similar tales concerning Rugby's William Cotton Oswell, liked what he heard, welcomed the lad and asked what he wished to become. 'I mean to be like Livingstone,' the boy replied.

Selous did not change his ways at Rugby. He would hide a small pea rifle on his poaching trips, with the thick detachable barrel slipped up one sleeve and the stock concealed under his jacket. He learned to catch young pike in a canal, stunning them as he fired into the shining waterlilies and then gathering the fish with a long stick. Aware that herons were nesting fifteen miles from the school on an island in a lake, he learned that they were early hatchers. Making his way across country one bitter March day, he stripped, swam through a fringe of ice and raided two nests high in a tall tree. Then he swam back with eight large blue eggs secured in his sponge-bag, which was clenched in his chattering teeth, an achievement that earned him the classic Rugby reward of writing out the fourth Georgic of Virgil, some sixty-three lines for each heron egg. He also learned about Oswell, whom Selous later called the 'ideal of the roving British gentleman'.

One Sunday an enraged gamekeeper chased Selous to the door of the Rugby chapel, helping the boy to arrive on time, with his top-hat in one hand and a sparrowhawk's eggs in the other. Writing home at fourteen, he appealed for two slingshots, lamented that the pelts of his meticulously skinned water-rats had been eaten by an unknown creature and praised Livingstone's new book on the Zambesi. A well-bruised schoolboy boxer, Selous was the youngest boy to win a rugby cap, relishing the wild games, twenty a side, fought without the restraint of modern rugby. Violent shin-kicking, known as hacking, was permitted then, as the side with the ball hacked it through by kicking the opposing shins as hard as possible.

Schoolboy blood sports aside, Canon Wilson soon saw in Selous 'the fire and the modesty of genius'. He never forgot the extraordinary acuity of the boy's senses. When others could barely make out birds flying in the distance, Selous discerned exactly what the kingfishers were catching and carrying. When Canon Wilson was surprised to find Selous searching for a nightingale nest that the canon himself had discovered, Selous explained that he had heard the canon speak of it across the noisy dining-hall, for he 'could disentangle voices, and listen to one, as a dog can follow one scent among many'.

The son of a prosperous family of Norman émigré Huguenots, after leaving Rugby at seventeen, Selous was sent to the Continent to learn languages and prepare for a career as a doctor. First he was bored in Switzerland, then apprehended poaching honey-buzzard eggs in Germany and finally he studied in Austria, where he caught two elusive purple emperor butterflies in the rainy hills above Salzburg. Returning to England, Selous realized that a doctor's life was not for him.

Instead, Baldwin's hunting tales kept drawing him to Africa, and for three months he studied medicine as a useful preparation. At nineteen he sailed for Natal, with £400 and a fine Reilly double breech-loading rifle, fresh and eager for the lifetime of adventure that would challenge fiction. He was 5 ft 9 in tall and weighed 12 st (168 lb). Throughout a life that found him warmly welcomed both in Matabele huts and the White House, he could never resist the call of the African bush. Even late in life, lulled in England by wounds, marriage and retirement, he could not stay away.

By the time Selous first arrived in South Africa in 1871, the land of Cornwallis Harris and Gordon Cumming was changing rapidly. The Afrikaaners were settled in the Transvaal and the Orange Free State. In 1870, across the Limpopo River, Mzilikazi's son Lobengula had founded the town that became Bulawayo, the name derived from the Matabele word *bulala*, to kill. With the discovery of gold and diamonds, new waves of immigrants were spreading north from Cape Town, pressing both Boers and blacks. Many Bantu tribes were beginning to suffer the dispossession, loss of traditional structure and economic subjugation that would be their future. And the big game was being drastically thinned out across large areas of southern Africa.

Even in the 1850s, Charles Baldwin had lamented that he was too late for the great days of elephant hunting, when men like Petrus Jacobs, who shot more lion than anyone in history, could axe the ivory from five hundred bulls in a lifetime. By 1870 elephants were virtually extinct in the Transvaal, and even the most resourceful ivory hunters were struggling to make a living in South Africa. The best elephant hunting had moved gradually to the north-east, where the animals still flourished and generally carried heavier tusks than the southern elephants. As early as the 1850s, 30,000 elephants were killed each year in what became Kenya, Tanganyika and Uganda, according to estimates derived from the old trading and auction records. By 1880 the number was 60,000–70,000. Generally these elephant were taken by black hunters armed by the Arab traders with rough muzzle-loaders, the men hunting in large gangs, with many wounded elephant surviving, carrying the bullets until they died a different death. The tusks were sold through Arab traders in Zanzibar, generally ending up at the London ivory auctions, before being carved up for after-dinner service as billiard balls.

Determined to hunt elephant, but with his double rifle stolen as soon as he reached the Kimberley diamond fields after a four-hundred-mile wagon trip from the coast, Selous paid £12 for two elephant guns of the type used by the Boer hunters. Crude and heavy at 12.5 lb, these smooth-bore single-barrel muzzle-loaders were manufactured by Isaac Hollis of Birmingham and fired a spherical bullet weighing four ounces. The bore of a gun is determined by how many of its shots total one pound in weight, and Selous always referred to these as his 'four-bores'. These weapons were not the Purdeys, Hollands and Rigbys carefully crafted for gentlemen sportsmen. These were sturdy common guns built to get the job done, and were used by both black and Boer elephant hunters. In addition, Selous was equipped with a small double-barrelled shotgun, and an inferior double rifle by Vaughan that fired its bullets across each other's paths. After paying £300 (about £7,400 today) for a wagon, oxen and five horses, his pockets were nearly empty, and for powder the young hunter could afford only 'the common trade powder that is sold to the Kaffirs in five-pound bags'.

A south African village scene, by G.F. Angas

Travellers pointing out the route,
by Henry Butler

In April 1872 Selous set out from the Kimberley diamond fields with two hunting companions, crossing the Vaal River and trekking north, aiming for the main wagon track to the interior. Like Cornwallis Harris thirty-six years before, he was struck by the beauty of the old missionary town of Kuruman, and admired the dark-leaved orange orchard that Livingstone's father-in-law, the Revd Moffat, had planted in Harris's day.

On the way north to the Limpopo, Selous suffered the first of many safari injuries. As he removed cartridges from a small box of loose gunpowder in a side case on the wagon, his friend Dorehill turned to Selous with a pipe in his mouth, scattering smouldering tobacco into the powder. They were badly burned by the explosion and, to prevent the disfigurement that often follows gunpowder wounds, the two men rubbed a spicy mixture of salt and oil into their skinless faces, which could not bear exposure to the sun for a fortnight afterwards. In this condition they lingered for a few days with Livingstone's celebrated disciple, the Tswana chief Secheli, who served them tea from a silver pot and inquired anxiously about the reported indisposition of the Prince of Wales.

As they moved north towards the new homeland of the Matabele, however, the country, the game and the Africans all grew wilder. For the first time in his twenty years Selous encountered an outdoor adventure that exceeded his ability. Galloping wildly through thick forest after his first giraffe, separated from his companions during a one-hour chase, reins in one hand, rifle tight in the other, he nearly broke his right leg when his inexperienced horse smashed him off against a tree. Stunned, lost, alone except for his horse, without food or materials for starting a fire, on a freezing moonlit night, Selous began to learn the art of survival in the bush. He was still what he later called 'a tyro in forest lore'. Ripping a scrap of linen from his shirt, he dampened it slightly and tore open one of his three remaining cartridges, rubbing the gunpowder into the linen and igniting it with the firing cap of his rifle. Despite repeated tries with the powder of all three cartridges, the grass kindling would only smoulder and not flare and burn. Using his claspknife to cut grass for a bed, a comfort he learned from reading Baldwin, Selous tried to sleep, but instead lay awake in the cold listening to the howling hyena, 'the most mournful and weird-like sound in nature'.

Early the next morning he remounted and searched all day for his companions, finally again cutting some grass, and lying down shivering and hungry in the crisp light of the full moon. The second night his horse, although hobbled, made off as he slept. In the morning, on the third day, Selous hung his saddle on a branch, shouldered his empty rifle and walked until sunset, again without food or water. On the fourth day he came on an old Bushman holding a giraffe's intestine full of water. This the man tried to sell to Selous, until interrupted by a small boy, who sold Selous a calabash of goat's milk and a large gourd of water in exchange for his claspknife. The next day the Englishman found his wagon and companions, and reflected on his first lessons in the bush. Twenty-five years later, in 1897, with the heads of six of his lions decorating the speakers' platform, Selous was to tell this tale to the wildly cheering boys at Rugby. Nearly a century later, in 1985, the Rugby Natural History Society was renamed the Selous Society.

Crossing the Limpopo, Selous was at once impressed by the Matabele, as he paused at their frontier kraal while messengers hurried to Lobengula requesting permission to proceed. The Tswanas had been dressed in ragged trousers and old shirts, but the handsome Matabele still wore only the spare girdles that Cornwallis Harris had described, and the young hunter remarked on the naked beauty of the Matabele girls, who had a high reputation for virtue among the European travellers.

Arriving finally at the royal kraal of the Matabele in Bulawayo after walking and riding over a thousand miles from the coast, young Selous was asked by Lobengula what he meant to do in the land of the Matabele. 'I said I had come to hunt elephant,' Selous wrote later, 'upon which the king burst out laughing, saying "You are only a boy, have you come to hunt tiny antelopes?"' Selous conceded that he had never yet seen an elephant, and Lobengula joked that the elephants would drive him from the country. But the son of Mzilikazi granted permission. When Lobengula rose to end the audience, his followers crouched low, crying out the king's praises, 'Oh, prince of princes! Thou black one! Thou bull elephant!'

Like his father, who had died in 1868, Lobengula was tall, robust, impressive and handsomely suited to his role. Selous found that Lobengula, when not clad in dirty European clothing, looked admirably 'like what he is, the chief of a savage and barbarous people'. Fear, humour and arbitrary execution were the tools of his statecraft. Tswanas and Mashonas knew the cost in slaughter if they failed to offer their scheduled tribute. Provided that they respected his authority, Lobengula was generally receptive to British hunters, traders and missionaries, and graciously offered to take Queen Victoria as a wife.

In 1866 Mzilikazi had permitted the first two safaris of European elephant hunters to hunt in Mashonaland to the north of Matabeleland. One party was led by the Englishman Henry Hartley, and the other by Jan Viljoen and Petrus Jacobs, who together bagged 210 elephant in one season. Greedy, trading for ever more tusks, Viljoen betrayed Mzilikazi by bartering five guns with a Mashona tribe. This proved to be an expensive trade for the vassal Mashona tribe, which an annoyed Mzilikazi soon destroyed in consequence, killing the men and seizing the women, children and cattle in traditional fashion. The European hunters found much of Mashonaland infested with belts or zones of tsetse fly, and as the elephant retreated to safer country, the hunters were obliged to go after them on foot.

In the curious way that some of nature's creatures form unwitting alliances in protecting each other, Africa's largest animal was now protected by one of her smallest. Persecuted to near extinction as far north as the Limpopo River, the elephant had retreated north to the fly country, where the tsetse kept horse and farmer at bay. During the hunting season, from May to December, Jan Viljoen and the other Boer ivory hunters were accustomed to hunting on horseback from base camps, where their wives, servants and many children lived by the wagons in wattle and daub huts, bringing the domestic amenities of farm life to the bush. Often the families suffered with the hunters. When Martinus Swartz died of malaria while on safari in 1877, ten members of his family died with him. As they were not inclined to leave their families or to hunt elephant on foot, and knowing the Matabele resented them, most Boer hunters preferred to avoid the fly country to the north.

The British hunters, too, whether sportsmen or professional ivory hunters, did their work on horseback. Even when mounted, and supported by dogs and Africans, it was hazardous and tiring enough. But hunting elephant on foot added dangers and exhaustion to the chase. Other animals added unpredictable risks, and the advantage of speed and range shifted to the quarry. Finding and pursuing elephant on foot with unreliable, single-shot weapons was not for the lazy, fearful or incompetent. It meant trekking to the elephant country, walking up to ten hours a day to find the herds, stalking the large bulls and then running after them for miles to kill them. Every year the elephant grew more wary, avoiding their traditional water holes, seeming to sense the coming of the hunters, growing harder to find. They are capable of travelling many miles when wounded, and often the chase had no end. But Selous, and a few others, were prepared to play the game on foot.

Eager to accept the king's generosity, Selous soon set off into the fly country, accompanied by one young African carrying his blanket and spare ammunition, and by Cigar, a former Cape Colony jockey and experienced Hottentot elephant hunter. It was a lean safari. Selous's four-bore guns were far inferior to the double-grooved rifles used by Harris, Oswell and Cumming in earlier years. Carrying not even coffee, tea or meal, they lived on native corn, water and what meat they shot, beginning a saga of foot safaris that became African legends.

Selous was twenty, light-hearted, alive with a sense of freedom, already hard
and whipcord fit when he started walking north carrying his muzzle-loader,
with a leather bag filled with powder and a pouch containing twenty four-ounce
bullets. In a lifetime of hunting and studying game on three continents, he
never changed. A companion described Selous at sixty-five, when he was cut
down by a German sniper in Tanganyika, at the end of another long march, with
his field-glasses in his hand and his rifle at his side:

> He wore a double Terai grey slouch hat, slightly on the back of his head. Khaki
> knickerbockers, with no puttees, bare legs, and shirt open at the neck, with a knotted
> handkerchief to keep the sun off, and a long native stick in his hand. He had a rooted
> objection to wearing a corked helmet. It was impossible to forget the impression he
> made. He was straight as a guardsman, with a broad deep chest, a beautiful healthy
> look in his face. He was adored by the men. Most went sick and died like flies. He was
> cheerful as a schoolboy.

In the three years after he left Lobengula's kraal, Selous killed seventy-eight
elephant, all but one on foot, often reloading his heavy gun as he tore through
the bush at top speed, drawing handfuls of gunpowder from the open leather
bag swinging by his side. Intensely observant, analytical and yet highly
instinctive, Selous learned from each safari. Like Sherlock Holmes emerging
from a crisis in a crowded room, his mind analysing a thousand details when
everyone else recalled only chaos, so Selous after a wild hunt reflected on his
field observations. When other hunters thought only to weigh the ivory or
measure the trophy, Selous recalled how the elephant enjoyed the yellow fruit
of the macuna trees, and the way the butterflies glided in the uneven light as he
advanced quietly through the acacia forest. Soon Lobengula developed a
different view of the hunter's ability, saying to another English hunter, 'Selous
is a young lion.'

Studying the condition of the bruised leaves scattered along an elephant
track, concluding that the animal had recently passed, Selous would strip down
to what he called 'nice light running order', his trousers off, wearing only a long
cotton shirt, his felt hat and shoes. He soon learned that wounded elephant
soldier on for miles until they drop, holding to a long, swinging walk, a pace that
requires a pursuing man to run, reloading as he goes and then steadying himself
to shoot again as he controls his gasping breath. He found that even between the
eyes a four-ounce ball, hardened by zinc and quicksilver when he made his own
bullets, was frequently not enough, failing to find the brain if not penetrating at
just the right angle. He considered a good lung shot often better than a heart
shot, which can leave an elephant more capable of one last desperate attack.
Generally, he aimed first just behind the shoulder, confident then of hitting a
vital organ.

After participating in many close engagements, Selous knew from the pitch
and frequency of an elephant's screams exactly when it had overtaken and
stamped on its enemy. He himself was once crushed under the chest of a

Above left: Selous as a young hunter

Above right: A narrow escape, Mashonaland, 1878

wounded cow elephant that had dropped to its front knees after ramming and goring Selous's horse. Stunned, struck by the strong smell of the elephant above him, covered in its blood, Selous crawled away. With one eye injured and the skin rubbed from his chest, the hunter recovered his rifle and killed the wounded animal.

Selous developed great respect for the scent, intelligence, sense of family and resourcefulness of elephants, their ability to climb precarious steep trails, and to cool themselves by reaching into their mouths with their trunks and drawing water regurgitated from their own stomachs, showering their shoulders as they move on. Observing a large herd of two hundred elephant, he noted that elephant, like people, move more slowly when in large numbers than they do when alone. He found little danger in creeping up to shoot a solitary bull. Sometimes, like many young hunters, he shot too much, occasionally five elephant in a day, caught up by the excitement, needing the tusks to finance his safaris, once even confessing that since the elephant were so scarce he had to shoot even the smaller ones. The ethic of the day was the pursuit of ivory, with thirty pounds and more considered a fine tusk, and he learned the remarkable variation in tusks taken from the same animal, and how a tusk may lose ten pounds when it dries. Hunting without horses or wagons, the ivory itself was a burden. If no carriers were available, caches of tusks were carefully buried for later recovery. After a hard chase in the hills, he once cut the head off an elephant and rolled it down the steep hillside before axing out the ivory.

Selous learned much from Cigar, coming to appreciate the Hottentot's skill as a teacher in the bush, and his generosity in always allowing the Englishman to take the first shot, a critical advantage as the elephants were then generally standing peacefully. Selous preferred to hunt with Cigar than with Boer hunters, for Cigar was a gentleman in never claiming animals that another hunter shot. Although Selous considered Cigar to be the finest foot hunter he ever knew, Cigar had been trained to hunt elephant on horseback by William Finaughty, a pioneering ivory hunter of the old fraternity of frontier rogues. Cigar taught Selous Finaughty's old tricks, and the lore was passed on from hunter to hunter.

Finaughty himself began hunting elephant in Matabeleland in 1864, eight years before Selous, later hunting north in Mashonaland, and finally abandoning the chase in 1870 when the elephant retreated to fly-infested country, precluding hunting on horseback. On one safari, Finaughty's party lost fourteen of seventeen horses to the tsetse, all within thirty days. Shooting five hundred elephant in five years, Finaughty was blessed to be hunting in unspoiled game country, once galloping beside a herd of three hundred giraffe, the most glorious sight he had ever beheld, and once, he reported, dazzled to find the south bank of the Simukwe River near Bechuanaland literally black with thousands of elephant. On most hunts, Finaughty's tusks averaged 45–50 lb each, and ten elephant was his largest one-day bag.

Reminiscing to a Rhodesian newspaper editor in 1911, recalling these scenes after sixty-eight lively years, with an experienced face that reminded people of the Duke of Wellington, Finaughty said he had never been lonely in the veld, but he complained that modern African sportsmen did not appreciate the hardship of hunting in the old days.

Just imagine what it was to carry all day in the blazing sun a heavy old muzzle-loader with your powder loose in one jacket pocket, a supply of caps in another and your bullets in your pouch. Add to this that the gun kicked one's shoulder with almost as much force as the bullet struck the elephant, and you can believe me that it was no child's play. The recoil was so great that I was more than once knocked down by it. On two occasions I was taken completely out of the saddle. One's shoulder was literally black and blue after a day's elephant shooting . . . In the two finest months of my life, I shot ninety-five elephants on the Umfuli River in Mashonaland, the ivory weighing 5,000 lb.

William Finaughty, aged seventy

When Finaughty first called on Mzilikazi in 1864, he found the old king still greedy and alert, and suspicious lest Finaughty be a Boer. Carried about by four burly wives in an armchair given him by the Revd Moffat, his legs paralysed by gout, thick mealie beer always at his side, the old Black Bull Elephant of the Matabele was still genial with English hunters, and in unqualified command of his people. Ever crafty, Mzilikazi had recently agreed to buy a trader's wagon in exchange for ivory. When the European began to empty the wagon, the king objected, saying that he did not take out the insides of a bullock when he sold it. Finaughty appreciated Mzilikazi and admired the Matabele. He particularly enjoyed hunting elephant with parties of young warriors, sometimes loading them down with more meat than they could carry.

Finaughty long remembered the annual Matabele harvest celebration, the Inxwala, or First Fruits ceremony, when he reportedly saw 25,000 Matabele warriors dance about the camp fires at night, shaking their assegais, and stamping their feet to the war drums, while 540 oxen lay dead, butchered for the feast. When Selous first attended the three-day Inxwala celebration five years later in 1873, he estimated four thousand warriors in the three-day dance, tall and magnificent in their war dress, in capes and head-dresses of black ostrich feathers, and girdles of swinging leopard tails and monkey skins, the *indunas* or officers with bonnets of otter skins and waving crane feathers. On the third day, with his warriors standing about him in a semicircle six deep, chanting, stamping in unison and beating on their shields, Lobengula danced quietly, every bit a king. Then NiNi, the king's favourite sister until he ordered her execution, danced with her brother. Hugely fat, pausing winded with her hands on her thighs, she was richly hung with beads, brass amulets and silver chains. In 1888 the artist-explorer Thomas Baines, himself a fine hunter and by then a keen gold prospector, depicted a more modest Inxwala ceremony, painting himself and his white companions into the scene.

On one occasion William Finaughty saw Lobengula's fierce father use dancing for a different purpose. When a two-thousand-man impi returned exhausted and humiliated from an unsuccessful raid on the Mashona, the king, whose tribe's survival depended on dominance over the more numerous

The Inxwala, or First Fruits ceremony, by Charles Croonenberghs, 1880. Both Selous and Finaughty attended these ceremonies. Note the artist himself in the foreground

Henry Hartley finds gold. Henry Hartley shot an elephant at Hartley Hills in 1865. It fell on a quartz reef with visible traces of gold and was later painted by Thomas Baines

Mashona, made the defeated men dance, unfed, for four days and four nights, each man knowing that to stop was to stop for ever, as some did.

Finaughty, a thoroughly professional hunter himself, took pleasure in reporting the misfortunes of an early safari mounted by three amateurish English sportsmen in 1864. Barred at the frontier by Mzilikazi because they had brought Zulu servants from Natal, they camped in the fine lion country near the Maklautsi River in the north-eastern corner of Bechuanaland. For two months they were besieged by lion in the thick, seven-foot-high *zareba*, or thornbush enclosure, that the Zulus built around their wagons. Their last horse was killed by the lion that drove off their oxen. Roaring close by every night, each day the lions prowled near the camp with increasing confidence.

Abandoned by the Zulus, who feared the Matabele, and too scared to return on foot by themselves, the inexperienced English hunters were too frightened to emerge from the zareba, even to examine the besieging lion shot by Finaughty after he found the wagons. With the loan of a span of oxen that hauled both their wagons lashed in tandem, the party finally set off for the south. It was tales like theirs that made apparent the need for professional safari guides, the white hunters who were to dominate the last century of the African safari.

Other celebrated hunters of Finaughty's day were Henry Hartley and George Wood, whose calm pulse, Selous said, was the same during a lion charge as at breakfast. Colonial legend relates that Hartley discovered gold in Mashonaland in 1865 when he shot an elephant whose tusk scratched open a quartz reef as it collapsed, revealing shining ore. Although Hartley is credited with shooting twelve hundred elephant in thirty years, Finaughty disliked the Hartley style of hunting. Not forgetting that he himself bagged seven elephant in a week in which Henry Hartley and his three sons got two, he complained that instead of each man going after his own elephant, the Hartleys bunched together, all shooting at one animal until it was down, and then going after another. But Henry Hartley, at least fifty and crippled by a club foot, was then hunting for tusks at an age when his Victorian contemporaries considered it exercise to stroke an ivory cue ball.

A rather ungenerous commentator, Finaughty apparently resented the celebrity soon enjoyed by Selous, to whom he once sold an expensive salted horse, and he was careful to emphasize that he had trained Cigar before Selous even arrived in Natal.

But the 1870 safari was his last, as Finaughty abandoned the chase rather than hunt on foot in the fly country. Always enterprising, he became a trader, later looting the farmhouses of European settlers when they were abandoned during a Matabele uprising. Despising the Boer hunters, Finaughty called Afrikaans a Hottentot language, and named his finest hunting horse Dopper, a name given to a puritanical sect of the Dutch Reformed Church, due to their baptismal custom of 'dopping', or immersing in water. Finaughty enjoyed playing rough pranks on the Boers, and in 1875 enraged them by smuggling two antique ship's cannon across the Transvaal to Lobengula in exchange for ivory. As he retreated to fireside nostalgia, the old hunter's one regret was that he had sold his sturdy elephant gun, which went on to wound two subsequent owners. Still unused, his cannon today adorn the entrance to the Bulawayo museum.

Although even hard cases like William Finaughty and the old Boer hunters found elephant hunting on foot to be too gruelling and too dangerous, to Selous it was refreshing, a wild mixture of freedom and exhilaration, the essence of his lifelong expectation. Noticing one day how well his wounds healed on safari, he commented that, 'There is nothing, I should fancy, like elephant shooting on foot to keep the blood in good order.'

Hearing the shrill, clear trumpeting of a bull elephant as it drank at a pool in the night, Selous sat alert listening in the dark. Priming his guns as soon as the early light filtered across the camp, he snatched a few mouthfuls of grilled meat from the fire, bolted his strong camp coffee, and started for the water. Finding the fresh tracks of a dozen giant bulls, the impressions of their pads still moist in the mud, some 'regular old teasers' with footprints two feet in diameter, he followed them across the park-like game country and rolling hills of Matabeleland, south of Victoria Falls, as the elephant fed on the succulent machabel trees, stripping the bark, and leaving an easy trail. Then they moved faster, through harder, dry country. Selous's Matabele tracker Minyama took up the spoor, removing his sandals for stealth when they found warm dung, and always mindful of the wind, both men knowing that an elephant's keen sense of smell compensates for its poor eyesight.

Marvelling often at the elephant's remarkable ability to avoid detection, its massive form somehow dappled in the shadings of heavy country, its movement strangely silent as it eased through the bush, sometimes first revealed by the rumbling of its intestine, Selous was always thrilled by Minyama's whispered words, 'Nansia incubu!' ('There are the elephant!') Suddenly he saw them too, huddled together in the shade, thirty yards off, 'gently flapping their huge ears in a sleepy, contented sort of way, all unconscious of the deadly enemy that lurked so near'.

First checking the favourable wind blowing from the elephant, sending four men up hillsides to drive them back should they flee, then creeping to twenty feet, with two gunbearers close behind, Selous searched for the finest tusks. Crowded together, the bulls offered only a fair shot. Spotting a fine long tusk, he fired, instantly taking his second gun. But the massed bulls roared off through the dense bush, panicked, cutting a path like a wagon road, with Selous flat out after them. Very fast runners downhill, but only moderate uphill, the elephant slowed to climb, the wounded animal dropping heart-shot after a hundred and fifty yards. Suddenly driven back down by the Africans, the herd crashed downhill, frantically taking stones, bushes and trees with them. As they flashed past him, Selous took a snap shot at a passing shoulder, at once grabbing back his reloaded first gun.

Slowing to a half-walk, half-trot, the wounded bull lagged behind, with Selous running hard to catch up for a side shot, carefully staying downwind to avoid a charge. Catching the scent before Selous could get alongside, the bull stopped, turned, and with ears extended and trunk stretched straight forward, prepared to charge. Struck in the chest by another four-ounce bullet, the elephant fell on to its front knees, and then recovered and walked slowly on. Just then four more passed, moving downhill, forty yards off, and Selous shot another, hitting it high in the shoulder. Wheeling, receiving a second shot, the elephant shook its head, flapping its giant ears, and 'surrendered up his tough old spirit'.

But the second, wounded bull had turned on a pursuing African, who had wounded it twice more. As the man bent low following its spoor, the elephant charged from behind a bush. Chasing the hunter so closely that the man's back was sprayed with blood from its trunk, the elephant finally slowed, and after a third chase was killed by Selous.

The first bull carried only a single tusk of 53 lb, a deprivation more common to cows than bulls; the second, kneeling bull, two even tusks of 42 lb each; and the third, two fine teeth of 55 and 57 lb. Altogether, an ivory bounty for Selous, and meat enough for many villages. By the 1880s, one 40 lb tusk would fetch £20. Celebrating that night, roasting his favourite cut, the heart, which Selous preferred to the feet or even the upper trunk, the twenty-two-year-old

Englishman enjoyed his camp, as the Matabele gorged on the fattiest meat, white as lard, and then sang and danced naked before the high log fire, finally acting out the day's hunting glories in wild pantomime.

An elephant hunt

Thoroughly candid about his days of heavy shooting, Selous later recorded that he soon regretted as 'dreadful' the killing of those elephants he shot only for their tusks, when there were no Africans clamouring for the meat. Like most hunters, Selous became more sensitive about some animals than others, calling it a grievous sin to shoot rhinoceros, lumbering and stupid, unless in real need of their meat. He documents the dramatic decline in the rhino population in Matabeleland between 1874 and 1877, and regrets that the Swedish explorer C.J. Andersson shot eight rhinoceros in a single evening in Bechuanaland. Like elephant, rhinoceros are burdened with a fatal possession. About 1880 rhinoceros horn began to have commercial value in Europe as knife handles, as it does today in Arabia. As ivory grew scarce in parts of Africa, traders supplied this new vogue. In the early 1880s a single Arab trader armed four hundred Matabele hunters with guns to hunt rhinoceros.

One missionary told Selous that before 1860 game was so plentiful in southern Matabeleland that buffalo and rhinoceros drank two hundred yards from his doorstep, and natives begged him to drive elephant from their cornfields. By the 1870s the big animals were gone.

The Matabele, too, grew concerned about the game. Pressed by his councillors, in 1883 Lobengula held a trial of four European hunters, including Selous. This may have been the first trial of European hunters by an African authority for the offence of excessive shooting, a procedure perhaps not repeated until after the end of colonialism a century later. For three days the Europeans sat on the ground in the rain, before a semicircle of Matabele councillors, while Lobengula heard the cases. Makwaykwi, one of the king's indunas, accused Selous of killing hippopotamus without returning their bones to the river, thereby risking a drought, charging, 'You, Selous, have finished the king's game! You are a witch! You must bring them all to life again, all, all! Let them walk in at the kraal gate, the elephant, the buffalo, the elands!' Selous said he would do so, if the induna would stand there to count the lions. Knowing who was the braver man, the Matabele laughed, and Lobengula was pleased to let the hunters off with fines, assessing an outraged Selous at £60 (about £1,700 today). This added a new risk for the early safari hunters, and in its way anticipated the game fees of a later period.

But even with the Matabele, Selous had a reputation for perfect honesty. When he denied killing hippopotamus, Lobengula believed him. Occasionally too trusting himself, Selous once bought a slave's freedom by paying 320 cartridges to his Portuguese owner, who advised Selous to tie up the man each night. Selous left him free, and the man stole a valuable elephant gun. Despite this lesson, a friend of the hunter's later said, 'He was the easiest man to cheat, but no one dared to do it.'

In his own accounts of his safaris among the Matabele, Selous neglects to describe his visit to Lobengula's harem, an omission remedied by the diary of Walter Montagu Kerr, an Englishman for whom 'golden Africa was the dream of my youth' and who succeeded in his ambition to go on safari with Selous himself. Kerr describes a highlight of the 1884 safari, Lobengula's ladies, lounging, drinking beer and eating meat, attended by their slaves, immensely heavy and perfumed with small balls of rolled wild flowers and herbs, beaming and 'gracefully basking their symmetrical forms like seals in the sun'. The queens' houses were tidy, with polished black floors made of crushed ant heaps, ox blood and cow dung, all worn smooth by kneeling slaves as they rubbed round pebbles over the surface, spitting on the small stones. At the Inxwala feast Kerr was distressed to see the flesh cut from living oxen. Kerr concluded that 'the vengeful morality of the Matabele would take an archbishop to exemplify'. But when the Englishmen left Lobengula, the friendly king said, 'Go well, sons of the sea.'

Although Selous generally hunted on foot, he occasionally rode when he was not in the fly country. Once his horse was knocked over by a charging elephant, and on another occasion his mount was chased for seventy yards with a leopard at its heels before Selous pulled up sharply and dropped the cat with a fast shot. Near the Nata River in 1874, Selous was lucky to survive when a buffalo 'pitched my horse into the air like a dog', and charged the fallen hunter, who rolled quickly but took a damaging blow to his left shoulder. A wounded buffalo would have stayed to finish the job, but the unhurt buffalo trotted off, leaving Selous to shoot his maimed horse.

Animals were not the only hazards in early safari life. Many hunters were injured by bursting rifles, or by their prey when weapons misfired. Once, chased through the bush by a cow elephant avenging her mate, his shirt and belt torn from his body by thorns, Selous grabbed his four-bore elephant gun from his gunbearer. The man had loaded the powder twice. The shock of firing lifted Selous off the ground, shattering the stock against his face and sending the broken gun yards past his shoulder. Another accident destroyed a tear duct and left a three-quarter-inch-long chip of wood lodged at the back of his nose. One year later, while strolling along Bond Street with the great naturalist Rowland Ward, Selous coughed up the chip of wood. He also endured malaria, fevers, ripped tendons when his horse broke its back plunging into a hunting pit, a broken collarbone from a rhinoceros hunt, and a brain concussion during an eland chase.

With medical help unobtainable, sometimes hunting with a party of Matabele for four months at a time, Selous used his early medical training, and learned tricks from the blacks and the Boers, who successfully dressed lion wounds with fresh milk and castor oil, although Selous preferred to cauterize these with a strong solution of carbolic acid. Field medicine was a routine part of his safari life, treating his gunbearers, pushing in the intestines of his dog Blucher and sewing up his flank after a leopard mauling, syringing out the cuts of lion claws on his horse's hindquarters, and setting his own left collarbone in camp, when he found it sticking up in a point under his skin after his horse fell during a rhinoceros chase. For weeks his shoulder ached in the cold nights, the bone not properly set, disturbed each day by hard rides with the reins in his left hand, his right burdened with a rifle.

Selous tried to understand the medical reality that lurks at the core of even the most far-fetched medical superstition, recording the proven effectiveness of a snake-stone brought from India, which drew the venom from snakebites. Like his contemporaries, Selous considered that malaria came from a feverish miasma that hung in the air in certain regions. Finaughty coped with malaria with a bracing diet of gin and mutton broth taken every four hours. Selous, however, drank only tea and champagne, usually tea, and for malaria he preferred Warburg's fever tincture.

Reports of Selous's escapes captivated H. Rider Haggard, a young English diplomat posted in South Africa in the 1870s. Haggard went home to become the first important African novelist, in 1885 creating from Selous's exploits the fictional hero Allan Quatermain, the great white hunter of *King Solomon's Mines* and other novels. Haggard's romantic works, including *Allan Quatermain*, *She* and *Nada the Lily*, in turn became a magic inspiration for generations of young Englishmen, turning their interests to the adventures of empire. In the long English winters, controlled by the disciplines of boarding-school and bound in by Victorian and Edwardian convention, the freedom of Africa, with its warm horizons and impossible animals, became a bright magnet. To Haggard's young readers, Allan Quatermain was the image of the hardy English gentleman, tough and honourable, capable and adventurous.

By 1881 Selous was himself a successful writer, with the publication in London of A Hunter's Wanderings in Africa, the account of his first eight years in the bush. The first important African hunting book since Baldwin's African Hunting and Adventure in 1863, it was immediately popular, although Selous's candid listing of all the game he shot drew criticism from early conservationists. Defending himself, Selous maintained that he shot only to feed himself and his men, but gradually he himself adopted more restrained shooting standards, as his trips to England exposed him to criticism, and even to ridicule in Vanity Fair, and to the growing conservation ethic. In later years he often declined to shoot even at tempting targets.

A key development in the reduction of game in the last quarter of the century was that by 1875 the breech-loading rifle was in widespread use, permitting even mediocre hunters to secure large bags. The smaller game was also now being shot out to support the commercial trade in hides. In the three years from 1878 to 1880, one dealer in the Transvaal exported nearly two million skins of springbok, wildebeest and blesbok, a large 200 lb antelope with a purplish gloss.

Selous's reputation earned him his first work as a paid safari guide in 1887, taking three English clients lion hunting in Mashonaland, and discovering the limestone caves and blue subterranean lake at Sinoia. The following year he was again hunting in Mashonaland, and some Barotsis, angry that Selous would not barter gunpowder for ivory, threatened that 'You will live two days more, Selous, but on the third day your head will lie in a different place from your body.' His camp attacked at night, Selous escaped across Mashonaland, through three hundred miles of largely hostile territory, on foot, generally alone and armed only with a knife. For Selous, travelling mostly by dark, it was again the boyhood adventure of the lonely forest at night.

In 1890 Cecil Rhodes engaged Selous to lead four hundred British pioneers into Mashonaland, to forestall the Portuguese, whose slave dealers and military posts were moving in from the east and north, where Portugal had had a colony since 1505 in what became Portuguese East Africa, now Mozambique. The first white man to travel and shoot in Mashonaland had been the Portuguese Antonio Fernandez in 1511. Selous considered the Portuguese to be decadent colonialists, poor hunters and corrupting in their dealings with the Africans. Despite his scorn for the Portuguese, the only individual woman whom Selous ever admitted to admiring, in the twenty years covered by his African journals, was a languid Portuguese quadroon he observed boating down the Zambesi, reclining on mats under a canopy of bent saplings thatched with grass.

Accustomed to paying his African bearers at the end of a safari, Selous was offended that the Portuguese had lied to the Africans so much that they demanded to be paid in advance. But the game was plentiful, for the Portuguese had little taste for hard hunting. Although Portugal was officially opposed to slavery, Selous was disgusted to find that both slavery and serfdom flourished in the Portuguese territory.

Throughout the Portuguese reaches of the Zambesi valley, he found that the Portuguese, who were often carried about the bush in litters, employed Shakunda tribesmen to enslave Batonga girls for their use and sale, generally paying an old musket or its equivalent for each girl. In 1882 Selous himself had observed as many as nine blacks bound by the neck on one heavy chain, five feet between each, as they laboured at building a house. One Portuguese trader offered Selous young slave girls in exchange for the hunter's ivory. The Portuguese government had divided the land into *pracos*, or districts, often rented out to Goanese, who then extracted all they could from the serf-like blacks on their land, using black slave dealers as their surrogates, and compelling the chiefs to pay annual tribute either in corn and gold dust, or in women and children.

On their side of the Zambesi, the Matabele also still had slaves, frequently Bushmen. Like the Tswanas, the Matabele killed adult Bushmen and enslaved the children. As Mzilikazi did with Truey, Lobengula used young girls as presents, giving them to his vassal chiefs. Occasionally he had old women slaves thrown to the hyena. In much of Africa, among both blacks and Europeans, the British aversion to slavery was a virtual eccentricity. The Boers, Selous reported, continued to revile the British for the culminating wrong of freeing their slaves.

Slavery was slow to die in Africa. In 1890 it was still necessary to hold an Anti-Slavery Conference in Brussels. Slavery flourished in Abyssinia, now Ethiopia, until at least 1910. The last slave caravan is reported to have crossed Portuguese East Africa, Mozambique, in 1912. In 1907 Germany was still issuing decrees regarding the terms of slavery in German East Africa, where slavery was not terminated until 1918.

Due perhaps to his trial and fine in the sea-cow incident, Selous now felt no personal obligation to Lobengula, who denied Cecil Rhodes's request for permission to send wagons through Matabeleland to the north. At Lobengula's request, Selous rode fast to Kimberley to invite Rhodes to Bulawayo to parley with the king. Rhodes would not come, and Selous succeeded in confusing the Matabele as to the intentions of the pioneer column as it moved north in 1890. Skirting Lobengula's domain to the east, the eighty wagons trekked north, strung out over two miles, struggling along the route that Selous had cut several weeks before. Each day one of Selous's five scouting parties rode twenty miles back along the path of the wagons and then circled round towards the Matabele border, watching for the dreaded impis.

Finally the caravan was safely past the thickly forested Matabele territory and into the more open country of Mashonaland. Having hunted across much of Mashonaland, enjoying the cool nights of its high plateau, 4,000 feet above

Lingap, a Matabele warrior, by
Cornwallis Harris

sea level, Selous considered the well-watered valleys and verdant mopane
forests to be the finest land he had seen in Africa, entirely fit for British
settlement, the more open country largely deserted due to forty years of raids
by the Matabele. Tribal raids were a way of life in much of Africa, and the
Matabele were the best at it. In 1883 Selous met one Matabele veteran, just
returning from a gruelling eight-hundred-mile march across the Kalahari
Desert to Lake Ngami and back, who also had been with the impi that
Cornwallis Harris had observed as it returned from fighting the Boers at Vegkop

in 1836. Displaying the rough wound on his stomach where a Boer muzzle loader had shot him, the old veteran described the battle to Selous.

On the 1890 pioneer expedition Selous launched the country that became Rhodesia, later Zimbabwe, building the 460-mile 'Selous Road' through the bush from Bechuanaland and creating a chain of forts all the way to Fort Salisbury, now Harare. By the time the Matabele finally fought, and fought bravely, in 1893 and 1896, it was too late. Like the elephant, the impis gave way before European firepower. For the next eighty-five years Rhodesia was dominated by British settlers, until white rule finally ended in 1979.

By the 1890s Selous was financing his own travels and safaris with his writings, following the success of *A Hunter's Wanderings* with *Travel and Adventure in South-east Africa* in 1893 and *Sunshine and Storm in Rhodesia* in 1897. In 1894 he married in England, taking his wife for a time to live on his farm near Bulawayo, but eventually living mostly in Surrey, and travelling to hunt in Transylvania, Wyoming, Norway, the Yukon, Iceland and other habitats. But safari life always called him back, and in 1902 he made his first expedition to East Africa, careful now not to shoot any animal, such as rhinoceros, of which he already had a good specimen.

During his visits to England Selous acquired the latest in hunting weapons, often as gifts from the great London rifle makers, Holland & Holland, Purdey and Rigby. When a new ·450 rifle was delivered to him in London one hour before he left for Waterloo station to catch the boat train en route to Africa, permitting him no time to test the sighting and cartridges, Selous called for the maid to order a cab to stand by for immediate departure. Then he opened his bedroom window, leaned out with his rifle overlooking Regent's Park, aimed at a chimney-stack one hundred yards distant, and squeezed off five fast shots. Approving the pattern of hits with his fieldglasses, he cleaned the rifle and went to the cab, acknowledging to the curious crowd that he, too, had heard shots. In the field in Africa, he frequently used a ·450 Express by Henry of Edinburgh and his favourite 'light' rifle, a ·450 single barrel Metford B.P. Express by Gibbs of Bristol. For elephant he might use a 540 g bullet driven by seventy-five or more grains of powder, the bullet itself hardened and solid, not hollow.

By the turn of the century the global hunting fraternity recognized Selous as the greatest outdoorsman of his time, a reputation certain to attract the adventurous Assistant Secretary of the Navy in the United States, Theodore Roosevelt. By 1897 the two men had developed a rich, personal correspondence, with Colonel Roosevelt unusually deferential, as he wrote to Selous about the difficulty such men find in balancing the 'two hearts', love for family and love of the outdoors. As his four sons grew, Roosevelt would gather them in the evening and read aloud favourite passages from Selous's *Wanderings*. A lifelong scholar of sporting literature, Roosevelt encouraged Selous, telling him, 'nobody can write the natural history of game as you can'.

At the President's suggestion, Selous finally gathered together his unpublished notes on African game and with the benefit of half a century of wildlife observation, in 1908 published *African Nature Notes and Reminiscences*, parts of which Roosevelt himself edited. Not only did this work become a reference book of game lore, but it gave Selous the forum for presenting the scholarly, frequently controversial side of his interest in wildlife. He rejects the conclusions of other hunters as to the alleged hostility and danger of rhinoceros by analysing in detail the hunting experiences they relate, explaining how the rhinoceros were themselves first threatened. He is not convinced that the old Boer hunters really understood the animals around them. Interested in meat and money, as a British sportsman might be interested in a trophy, they developed no scientific knowledge of the animals, caring little about a dead rhinoceros, except whether it was fat. At the same time, Selous was generous in admiring the knowledge and observations of certain hunters, like A.H. Neumann and the colonial administrator Sir H.H. Johnston.

Most of all, Selous admired the Bushmen, the finest naturalists, trackers and gunbearers in his experience. Selous learned to consider the Bushmen highly intelligent companions, able to travel eighty miles on foot in two days, and at their best in the bush when neither starved nor sated, but when their tracking skills were sharpened by moderate hunger. He envied their omnivorous intestinal tolerance, the ability to relish decomposing meat and rotting ostrich eggs. He admired the bark boxes, lined with gum, in which they stored poisonous caterpillars to keep the toxins fresh for their deadly arrows. Knowing hunger, he respected their forethought in hanging old hides on branches as larders for a day when even leather would be a welcome feast.

Perhaps uniquely, Selous lived so much with the Bushmen that he learned the secret of how their bushcraft became so superior. The answer began in infancy. Given small tortoises to play with, two-year-old children learned, as a game, the art of tracking animals across traceless stone. As the released tortoise crept off across the rock, the children crawled after in pursuit, learning to follow the little reptile by the imperceptible claw marks it leaves as it crosses the stone.

Like many great hunters, Selous lived too close to the land not to respect those who were part of it. After many years in Africa, living for months on his own among the Bushmen, Selous stated that his original disrespect for them was foolish and ignorant. Although he abhorred the rapacity of the Matabele, he learned their language and admired their skills and courage. He became intolerant of white arrogance, concluding in *African Nature Notes* that, 'Whenever I was told, as I often was in South Africa, that all natives were black brutes who could not understand kindness, I always knew that the masterful gentleman or fair lady had no kindness in their own natures.' His regard for the Boers varied, admiring their marksmanship, hospitality and pioneering energy, and judging that the British government was hard on them, but he wrote to his mother that 'mentally they are the most ignorant and stupid of all white races, and have not one tenth the courage of the Zulus'.

When Selous himself advanced opinions on wildlife, they were meticulous deductions, derived from field observations and from the collating of gener-

Colour painting of Frederick C. Selous. Presented to Rugby School by Judge Thomas Hughes and Charles Marshall, both old Rugbeians

ations of information. Presenting a brief study of the waterbuck, for example, Selous would describe its variations in its different territories and habitats, listing its names in Latin, Afrikaans, English and seven African languages. Denying that there were distinct subspecies of lion and rhinoceros, as other hunters claimed, Selous gathered nine specimens of horn, carefully measuring each and having it precisely drawn.

In explaining why Selous is the best of African naturalist writers, President Roosevelt concludes that it was Selous's combination of experience, observation, analysis and power of expression. The President, having heard and told many wild hunting yarns across much of the world, trusted Selous. In his Foreword to Selous's *African Nature Notes*, written in the White House in 1907, he lauds Selous and dismisses the 'delusion that the average old hunter knows all about animals'. This fallacy, Roosevelt argues, is equally misleading as regards Boer and black hunters in Africa and white and Indian hunters in the United States. Not only do few hunters combine observation and articulation,

No. 1.—Lion killed on the upper Hanyani river in Mashunaland in June 1880.

No. 2.—Lion killed on the Umzingwani river near Bulawayo in Matabeleland in September 1887.

Three drawings of lion by Selous, taken from *African Nature Notes and Reminiscences*

No. 3.—Lion killed on the Botletlie river, near the Makari-kari Salt-pan, in May 1879.

but many exaggerate their own experiences. As Selous wrote, 'animals shrink before the tape measure'. The President, himself immersed in intense naturalist debate in advocating his position that an animal's colouration is not greatly influenced by its protective needs, welcomed Selous's supportive conclusions.

Having read the available literature, dreaming of a safari of his own, Roosevelt was particularly impressed by Selous's notes on the lion, which he considered the best commentary on the subject. Selous himself killed only thirty-one lions in his lifetime, the largest over eleven feet long, nose to tip. Selous considered himself an experienced, rather than an excellent hunter, and often said that he was not a top shot. His distinction as a hunter, however, was in his endurance, his unique sense of nature and his broad knowledge of bushcraft.

Insisting that 'I never killed an animal for mere sport', Selous killed lion occasionally for the skins and occasionally to protect his camp, and sometimes for the meat, to which he was more partial than most hunters, for he considered it like veal, pale and free of smell or taste. Hunters rank lion trophies by the fullness and blackness of their manes, and Selous quarrelled with the old notion that different shades were different subspecies, for he made a study of siblings of different colours. He attributed the differences in fullness principally to climate, warmer weather inhibiting larger manes.

Selous was convinced that lion, lovers of darkness, are the most dangerous game. He understood their habits, knowing a charge is certain once a tail rises straight in the air, like a bar of iron. When charging, lion come in low, ears flat, generally not leaping, nor striking with their paws, but biting, usually with their forepaws barely off the ground. Alternating idleness and ferocity, hungry lion are not picky eaters, occasionally even eating a lion carcass. Lazy, they often eat the remains of shot game, returning to feed at night on festering meat that has become a seething mass of maggots. Yet lion eviscerate their own kills as neatly as a butcher, first ripping open the animal where the skin is thinnest, where the thigh joins the belly, then cleanly removing the stomach and bowels before eating the other entrails. Alternately, they tear open the anus, and devour the soft flesh of the buttocks in large lumps with the skin attached. Occasionally they pull out the entrails, roll them in a heap and cover them with sand to preserve them for a later meal.

Always setting the record straight, Selous denounced the critics of the artist Sir Edwin Landseer, who in 1867 unveiled his four giant bronze lions at Trafalgar Square. Landseer was ridiculed by London critics for placing his lions' forelegs in an unnatural position, straight out like a dog, but the hunter confirmed that this is indeed the correct position for a lion on the alert, before its forelegs are either drawn in under its chest prior to attacking, or turned with the paws inwards like a cat's if in repose.

On the other hand Selous scoffs at Livingstone's report of feeling no pain during a lion mauling, having nearly tested the point himself, and having observed directly the sufferings of those who did. Old Petrus Jacobs told Selous that the lion wounds in his thigh hurt him throughout his life, and that during his mauling every scrunch was brutal pain. When attacking horses, lion rarely leap on to their backs, but instead clasp each haunch in one paw and attempt to drag the horse down, often leaving bone-deep gashes when the talons cut in as the horse breaks free. One long night in Bechuanaland, Selous lay waiting for light enough to shoot, as he listened to three lions tear the flesh and crack the bones of his horse Bottle, occasionally squabbling over a favoured piece. Finally Selous could discern the ivory foresight of his rifle glimmering in the grey light. Then he looked up, directly into the greenish-yellow eyes of a lion, lying just twelve yards off, resting near the open body of his horse. He made a bad shot and all three cats escaped.

The eyes of a wounded lion, remarked by so many hunters, burn with a fierce, scintillating light, Selous said, unimaginable by one who has never seen them close, savage with a 'wondrous brilliancy and a furious concentration', even retaining their flaming yellow glitter for hours after death. Despite this, once wounded, lion often have less vitality than many African animals, sometimes dropping when an antelope with a similar wound would continue. But unpredictably daring when hungry, swift as death, at up to 450 lb the strongest animal for their size and weight, sometimes using their own smell to drive game to ambush, able to kill even small elephant, 'lion possess two requisites for terrestrial happiness – good appetite and no conscience'.

Enervated by the confinement of his eight-year presidency, Roosevelt in the White House planned the ultimate hunting adventure, an African safari so long that it would become not a holiday, but a life of its own.

This ambition was stimulated by Selous's visit to the White House in 1903. Selous spent time rock climbing, riding and swimming across the Potomac with the President. In the evenings the President asked the hunter to relate African hunting tales to the Roosevelt children. Selous brought the old stories to life, bending down and acting out the parts of lion and elephant. Years later Roosevelt observed, 'There was never a more welcome guest at the White House than Frederick Selous.' After hearing Selous's narratives first-hand, and studying all his writings, the President concluded that, 'Probably no other hunter who has ever lived has combined Selous's experience with his skill as a hunter and his power of accurate observation and narration.'

From the White House, on 20 March 1908, the President wrote to Selous, asking his assistance in organizing what he had decided would be his chosen alternative to a third term in Washington. Selous set to work, planning the great Roosevelt safari that began in April 1909.

As he lived on into the twentieth century Selous became a living transition, bridging the periods of discovery and colonialism, narrowing some of the gaps between African and European sensibilities, embodying the new awareness of the passing of the game and the need for conservation, initiating a scientific approach to the study of African wildlife, and himself making the change from pioneering hunter to paid safari guide. He personally participated in the development of the African safari from the lands of its origin in South Africa and Bechuanaland, up through Rhodesia, Mozambique and central Africa to east Africa, where the safari came to flourish in Kenya, Uganda and Tanganyika. Specifically, his organization of the Roosevelt safari launched the booming trade in American safari clients, which became the financial core of the safari business.

The First World War found Selous, at sixty-three, living quietly in Surrey with his wife, writing and managing his private natural-history museum. Frequently he undertook hunting and egg-gathering trips for his collection of birds' nests, taking up again his old boyhood interest. Immediately, he was alarmed by the menace of the Schutztruppe, the well-prepared forces waiting in German East Africa. Determined to serve, Selous undertook a rigorous physical examination designed to assess insurance risks, and passed magnificently. Then he had a Member of Parliament present his application for African duty directly to Lord Kitchener himself. Kitchener at first decided that Selous was too old, not wanting to be responsible for the death of the legendary hunter, but Selous persisted and became intelligence officer to the Legion of Frontiersmen, the special African unit officially listed as the 25th Royal Fusiliers.

An unconventional outfit, rather like Teddy Roosevelt's Rough Riders in the Spanish–American War, the Frontiersmen banded together veterans of the French Foreign Legion with a Honduran general, a lighthouse keeper and music-hall acrobats, Texas cowboys and Russian émigrés. After disembarking in Kenya's Indian Ocean port of Mombasa in May 1915, they were reviewed by a controversial, aggressive officer, Colonel Richard Meinertzhagen. A veteran safari hunter, Meinertzhagen immediately neglected the men standing in review to discuss with Selous the Nakuru hartebeest, and the subtleties of breeding Harlequin duck in Iceland.

East Africa was a hard campaign. Under the brilliant General von Lettow-Vorbeck, several thousand professional German soldiers led Schutztruppe companies of highly trained *askaris*, or native troops, from what is now Tanzania. Often the worst casualties did not come from combat. Entire British regiments virtually dissolved from malaria, dysentery and prostration. Selous's

Captain Frederick Selous, DSO shortly before his death

The Last Trek. The artist, Sir John Millais, used his friend Selous as the model for a dying hunter

battalion had left London 1,166 strong. On Christmas Day, nineteen months after they had landed at Mombasa, only sixty of the original force remained fit for duty. But immune to fever, heat and fatigue, Selous was still, as Theodore Roosevelt wrote, 'hardy as an old wolf, after a life as full of hazard and romantic interest as a Viking of the tenth century'.

At sixty-four Selous led an amphibious attack across Lake Nyanza, took not a day off duty in over a year in the field, and led patrols of exhausted men forty-five years his junior through heavy swamps. When others collapsed after long marches, Selous would set off alone into the bush with his butterfly net. An exhausted officer complained, 'When Selous falls out, no one else will be left standing.' In September 1916, at the age of sixty-five, he was awarded a DSO for 'conspicuous gallantry, resource and endurance'.

His final safari, hunting German field companies instead of elephant, found Selous trying to encircle General von Lettow-Vorbeck at Behobeho on the Rufiji River in January 1917. Raising his fieldglasses to his striking blue eyes, he was shot in the head by a German sniper. Instantly berserk, Selous's old gunbearer, Ramazan, charged the German lines, killing the sniper and several officers and askaris around him. As Selous said when he left Rugby as a boy of eighteen, 'If I can't get good shooting and fishing in this world, I'll get it in the next.'

4. *CAMERAS, CORDITE AND WOMEN*

Changes on Safari

While Selous stalked sable antelope and elephant on the high plateau of Lobengula's domain in Mashonaland, Winston Churchill, at eleven, lay awake in Brighton reading Rider Haggard's *King Solomon's Mines.*

Mesmerized by the adventures of the white hunter Allan Quatermain, Churchill in 1885 wrote to his mother from his Brighton prep school imploring her to send him all of Haggard's books. A lonely boy who adventured by reading and arraying his lead soldiers, young Churchill was so captivated by Quatermain that his aunt Leonie took him out of school to meet Haggard. The author then sent the boy the companion novel *Allan Quatermain*, also drawn from the adventures of Selous, and Churchill wrote to thank him, finding the second book even more thrilling.

Seven years later, Winston Churchill's father, Lord Randolph Churchill, was himself on safari in Mashonaland. Dying of syphilis, his marriage to the American beauty Jennie Jerome long cooled, his political career in disarray, no longer parliamentary leader of the Conservative Party, Lord Randolph sought to recover in the bush what he had lost in Westminster. Hoping to restore his health and rebuild his fame and influence, he prepared for a long safari, planning to fill the press with accounts of his observations and exploits, to be presented best by his own pen. For Lord Randolph, like some who followed him, the safari was not so much a wilderness hunting adventure as it was a stage, a set on which to earn attention and applause.

One of the first truly lavish safaris, the expedition helped to make such trips part of the Anglo-Saxon leadership culture, particularly after Lord Randolph wrote about his safari in the British newspaper the *Daily Graphic*. There it competed for attention with the serialization of Thomas Hardy's *Tess of the*

Opposite: Camp life in the Gold Coast, 1910

123

Lord Randolph Churchill steps ashore in Cape Town, 1892

D'Urbervilles, and earned him perhaps the highest fee yet paid to an English journalist, £100 per article.

As he recorded his safari for the English press, Randolph Churchill was generous with his criticism, sparing neither the London purveyors who packed his goods in fragile cases, nor his shipboard chef, nor the Boers he antagonized as he travelled. But he was careful to spare Cecil Rhodes, who, over maps in London, had helped him plan his safari.

Randolph Churchill's reactions to Africa were what one might have expected from his party's leading proponent of Tory democracy, Benjamin Disraeli's political philosophy that combined three principles in a strangely durable mixture: the welfare of the working man, the advancement of the Empire and the preservation of English traditions. Appalled by the indignities suffered by the black diamond miners at Kimberley as they were probed for smuggled gems at the end of their workday, Lord Randolph expressed a view that provoked a national uproar when it was published in London during his safari. The hardships of the miners, he wrote, were endured,

> to extract from the depths, solely for the wealthy classes, a tiny crystal for the gratification of female vanity in a lust for adornment essentially barbaric. Some mitigation of criticism might be urged if the diamonds only adorned the beautiful, the virtuous and the young, but this, unhappily, is far from the case, and a review of the South African diamond mines brings me coldly to the conclusion that, whatever may be the origin of man, woman is descended from an ape.

Only too aware of the excesses of women and Afrikaaners, Lord Randolph on safari did not deny himself a few indulgences. In addition to his personal light spider coach, the overloaded transport consisted of four heavy Cape wagons, three lesser wagons and a Scottish cart, all attended by fourteen transport drivers, two herd boys, four grooms, four cooks, a surgeon, an officer of the Bechuanaland Border Police, an army safari manager, several African servants and three white domestics, including Churchill's dedicated personal servant, Thomas Walden. Even four Cape wagons, enough to have supported several

Boer families for years, were barely sufficient, each loaded to incapacity with impractical luxuries, altogether twenty tons of freight, including tinned meat and pressed vegetables from London, twenty-four rifles and shotguns, and a piano that later drew ridicule from Churchill's delighted enemies.

Like Cornwallis Harris and Selous before him, he also bore gifts for the king of the Matabele. By 1891, Mzilikazi's son Lobengula was old and heavy, although he retained the cunning and greed of his youth. Well advised before he set out from Cape Colony, Lord Randolph brought many presents. Most splendid was an outsize gold and red wheelchair, crowned with an umbrella, custom-designed to let the gout-ridden king hold court in greater comfort.

The safari laboured slowly up-country across the Transvaal and north to Fort Salisbury in Mashonaland. As they journeyed, Churchill hunted on horseback

Randolph Churchill and the professional hunter Hans Lee encounter a troop of lions in Mashonaland

with the veteran safari hunter Hans Lee, highly pleased with the ·500 double Fraser he used for all heavy shooting. He was not preoccupied, however, with securing a large bag, and did not distinguish himself in the field, although he got his share of quail, duck and pigeon. He enjoyed hard gallops after antelope, but often lost his quarry, occasionally bagging a roan antelope or hartebeest. He wrote candidly about an encounter with a pride of perhaps ten lion, when Lee did all the shooting. 'The idea of galloping at full speed on a second-rate horse through thick bush, chased by a lion,' he admitted, 'was singularly unpleasant to me.'

Although characteristically difficult and disgruntled for much of the time, he came to appreciate the charm of the bush, finding that it gave 'the soundest sleep at night, the best of appetites for every meal, the clear head, the cool nerve, the muscle and wind as perfect as after an autumn in the highlands'. Gradually he involved himself in the details of safari life, personally managing the cooking staff for a few days and flavouring the soup with Harvey or Worcester sauce, before eating with 'a zest only the African hunter knows'. His greatest delight, however, came from the exhilarating freshness of early-morning canters with Hans Lee, as the morning light spread the landscape before them and the startled game bolted across the bush.

Frequently, while Churchill rode off to hunt, the groaning wagons were mired to their axles and stores were jettisoned by the trail. In time the straining mules and horses began to suffer from the tsetse fly, falling short of breath, discharging torrents of mucus, and in a few hours suffocating in agonizing spasms as a yellow fluid filled their bronchial tubes. Applying himself to the problem, distraught at the death of his favourite hunting pony, Charlie, Churchill insisted that the best way to save the animals from this sickness was to brush the inside of their nostrils with tar and give them two wine glasses of gin a week, although he himself preferred champagne at the end of a dry day on safari. But even a half bottle of gin, mustard poultices and the forced inhalation of burning sulphur failed to save many of the mules and horses. London's *Daily Graphic* later sent a reporter to Paris to consult Louis Pasteur about this medicinal horse cocktail, which Churchill mixed with just enough quinine to cover a shilling. The French scientist declined to comment.

Finally Churchill came to realize that his safari was still over-burdened, that unneeded equipment provided more strain than comfort, so at Fort Salisbury he held a four-day auction, to the amazement of the hard-bitten local settlers, who bought Lord Randolph's excess eau-de-cologne and other luxuries at triple the London prices. He was particularly pleased to sell his surplus trade beads, the white-eyed red ones favoured locally, for twenty-four times the price he had paid for them in Kimberley. Despite the lavishness of his own expedition, Churchill estimated that £2,100 (£67,400 in today's currency) should cover the cost of a reasonable six-month safari, including £100 a month for the native staff.

During his safari Lord Randolph did much to aggravate problems with the

Boers, who called him 'de Lord'. Some commentators thought his performance damaged rather than enhanced his reputation at home. But young Winston was enthralled by his father's trip and scornful of his political enemies, frequently writing to ask for details of the chase and begging for a small antelope head to decorate his room at Harrow. The boy would not forget Lord Randolph's harsh criticism of the Boers for treating the Africans as less than human, and his prophetic conclusion that, 'upon the pages of African history the Transvaal Boer will leave a shadow, of a dark reputation and an evil name'. Not surprisingly, as the safari proceeded to the north, the Afrikaaners burned Churchill's effigy in the streets of Pretoria, the capital of the Transvaal Republic.

After the end of his six-month, 2,500-mile safari, Churchill again passed through Cape Town, in December 1891, staying as a guest of Cecil Rhodes. When friends asked why he stayed with Rhodes when he did not enjoy his host's company, Lord Randolph exclaimed, 'My dear fellow, it's the only place in this God-forsaken country where I can get Perrier Jouet '74.'

Churchill's grand tastes were a harbinger of what was to come, as a different breed of hunter was drawn to the camp fires of Africa. His expedition was not only lavish, but was the first of the great celebrity safaris, and it came at a time of many transitions, which collectively did much to change the character of the typical safari. As the turn of the century approached and the long Victorian era came to an end, changes in safari life reflected developments in the faster, modern world beyond Africa. Women, cameras, conservationists and cordite, the new smokeless explosive, all made their appearance in the bush, and things changed. So, too, did the hunting grounds, as the Suez Canal made the east coast of Africa more accessible, colonial advances opened up new territories and economic development reduced the game in the old ones.

In 1885 less than 10 per cent of Africa was colonized by Europe. By 1914, over 90 per cent of Africa was claimed by Europe, and only Liberia and Ethiopia were independent. As east Africa* developed shortly after the turn of the century, Nairobi increasingly became the centre of safari life, for the growing town was a congenial place and gave access to the diverse habitats and game of the region. As Kenya's distinguished paleontologist Louis Leakey explained years later, east Africa is nature's richest garden. 'Because there was always some optimum area,' he wrote in 1969, 'the creatures of east Africa evolved with less natural disturbance than in many other places, and today enjoy an almost unbelievable variety of habitat.'

By 1900, it was no longer the day of the lonely eccentrics, the pioneer, unpaid hunters who lived for the free, wild life of the hunt. The new hunters were visitors, essentially on a sporting holiday, and many needed local experts to plan their expeditions and lead them in the field. Some, despite Randolph Churchill's

---

* The term east Africa is generally used to include the territory of those countries now called Kenya, Uganda and Tanzania.

The Earl of Scarborough by a
baobab tree in Gambia, 1890

disdain, were women, and often far better in the field than he. Gradually the
white faces at the camp fires came to represent two different worlds, as overseas
clients paid a new breed of African professional hunter to introduce them to the
bush.

Since Cornwallis Harris first made the analogy in 1839, hunters have
observed that a safari is like a ship going to sea, self-contained and surrounded
by an ocean of nature. A few hunters, opening up the sport in west Africa, even
tried to combine the two, hunting from their yachts along the mouths of the
rivers Niger and Gambia near the end of the century. The Earl of Scarborough's
shooting party, hunting along the coast while cruising on the *Lancaster Witch*
in 1890, lost one shipmate to an elephant. Unable to reload quickly after his
paper cartridges had been soaked by rain, the hunter was lanced by a tusk that

Right: The Earl of Scarborough's party on board the *Lancaster Witch*

Below: Canoeing in a swamp, Gambia

entered his chest, pierced his lungs and came out at his back. Lord Scarborough never forgot the scene that night, 'The little log hut close to the beach in which we laid him, lit by lanterns, thronging crowds of excited natives without, and the thundering surf behind, showing up white in the darkness.'

Sailors have long held that having a woman aboard brings along another passenger, bad luck, and some hunters have borrowed this attitude. Samuel Baker, however, was not one of these. His wife may have been the first in the long tradition of women hunters on safari. In the 1860s Florence Baker shared, and sometimes led, her husband's safaris in the Sudan and what became Uganda. Said to be the first European woman ever to visit central Africa, Florence Baker was staunch and durable on safari, whether sharing elephant hunts along the Nile, emerging from a malarial coma to find her grave being dug, or helping her husband outface bands of black and Arab slavers.

Florence Baker was not, however, the first woman to go on safari, although her predecessors may not have hunted. The early Boer hunters were often accompanied by their wives and children, at least to their base camps, and David Livingstone's wife, Mary, occasionally travelled with him between 1845 and 1852. When Baldwin was hunting near Lake Ngami in 1859, his party encountered the wagon of a Mr and Mrs Thompson, who were on a honeymoon safari from Cape Town. The shimmering heat of the Kalahari desert, however, was too much for the oxen, and the wagons were unable to pause for conversation. But women in the bush were a rarity until at least the end of the century, and the hunters' diaries tended to record their appearances. Selous, for example, noted that in 1882 he met a Mrs Dorehill on safari, whom he thought to be the first English lady to visit the interior of Mashonaland. Six years later, Selous met a Mrs Thomas, 'a plucky young Englishwoman', on a shooting trip to Victoria Falls with her husband, both under the escort of a professional white guide and hunter.

All these enterprising women, and others, however, were essentially accompanying a man's safari, and generally were not taking an active part in the sport itself. An early exception, in her entirely independent initiative, was Mary Kingsley, a scientifically minded Victorian spinster anxious to exercise her latent abilities. Mary Kingsley first set out for west Africa in 1893, and her travels were principally zoological and anthropological adventures, rather than safaris in the sense of hunting expeditions, but they showed other women that they, too, could survive and enjoy safari life. Inevitably, as with the Bakers and Livingstones, the daily realities of nineteenth-century wilderness travel in Africa were similar to those of shooting safaris. There were many ways to die, and as Rudyard Kipling said of Mary Kingsley, 'Being human, she must have been afraid of something, but one never found out what it was.'

Unlike Lord Randolph, Mary Kingsley travelled light, with a black portmanteau and one long waterproof sack containing blankets, boots and books. A lady, her jungle outfit consisted of a high-necked white blouse, a heavy black skirt, tall lace-up boots and a cummerbund, which served as a towel when she bathed

Above left: Florence Baker, 1865

Above right: Mary Kingsley, c. 1895

in the dark, swampy rivers. Sometimes not even removing her sodden boots at night, lest they shrink beyond use, she found her Victorian outfit strangely practical. Plunging one day into a fifteen-foot game trap, the thick folds of the long, full skirt cushioned her from the twelve-inch ebony spikes on which she fell.

About her cummerbund she wore a revolver and a heavy bowie knife. The latter came in useful when the pistol was soaked after long marches through slimy waterways. The knife's large un-hinged blade took no time to open and gathered no rust, the crescent depression behind the point being always sharpened to a fine edge. As to the revolver, Mary Kingsley concurred with the man who was asked if you needed a hand-gun in Carolina: 'You may be here one year, and you may be here two and never want it; but when you want it, you'll want it very bad.'

Making her way through what became Sierra Leone, the Gold Coast, Gabon, the French Congo and Cameroon, Mary Kingsley came to relish the peculiar beauty of the wet jungles of west Africa. The land itself was so fertile that it was said an umbrella, planted in the evening, would bear leaves by the morning.

Instead of travelling by Cape wagon or horseback, Kingsley journeyed on foot and by flat-bottomed pointed canoe, a small fire glowing in the bow on long trips, protected in a calabash filled with sand. Shadowy mangrove swamps fringed the dark, tropical rivers, punctuated by lakes of ink-black slime, occasionally obliging Kingsley and her party of six or eight black retainers to slosh along for hours. Dreading crocodile, often up to their chins in thick swamp, they would finally stagger up a muddy bank to find frills of leeches garlanded about their necks 'like astrakhan collars'. Drawing off the bloated leeches with handfuls of coarse salt, they were then plagued by flies attracted to the bleeding sores.

In time she learned to see. As Randolph Churchill remarked, it is incredible how an untrained eye cannot discern even large animals in the bush. A serious naturalist, Mary Kingsley became truly aware, almost like a Bushman in the superficially desolate Kalahari, or Selous in the bush of Mashonaland, able to appreciate the complex life in each scene of the twilight forest, as out of the blank gloom before her eyes a world gradually grew, a society of 'snakes, beetles, bats and beasts'.

Most fascinated by the rich life of the African darkness, she spent long nights in a canoe, sometimes gliding soundlessly with a sheet for a sail, sometimes slapping an African companion with a paddle to remind him that a tired limb hanging over the side was sweet bait for cruising crocodile. Her proudest moment came when an old hunter, a member of her favourite tribe, the cannibalistic Fans, exclaimed, 'Ah, you can see.' She learned, too, about the 'mind-forests' of the wild tribes, that unless you spend time alone with them, making a patient, respectful study, you cannot perceive how they think and what they are.

Mary Kingsley marvelled at the hunting skills of the Fans, as their trained dogs, bells tinkling about their necks, drove the delicate grey forest antelope into the spider-web vortices of their incredibly fine nets. She was dismayed, however, by the unsporting Fan method of hunting elephant. A village would encircle a herd with barricades of felled trees and vine ropes and then drug them with poisoned plantains and surround them with fires. Finally the hunters would remove the gorilla-skin sheathes from the flint locks of their muskets and fire ceaselessly into the panicking animals. Ivory was so precious in west Africa that men killed for one tusk. Sometimes the tusks were hidden in the ground until they grew dark with rot. Generally the Fan divided their ivory among the hunters, who eventually sold it, together with balls of rubber gathered in the jungle, to the black and white traders who plied the west coast of Africa.

Although some creatures, such as elephant, antelope and pygmies, seem to grow small under the jungle canopies, others grow larger. Mary Kingsley carefully measured a python of 26 ft, a crocodile of over 22 ft, and a gorilla 5 ft 7 in tall. She found gorillas horrifying in their appearance, but she observed that no animal could match them at going through the bush, as they swung from vine to bough at an incredible pace in a 'graceful, powerful, superbly perfect hand-trapeze performance'.

In 1900 Mary Kingsley died of enteric fever near Cape Town, while nursing prisoners during the Boer War. Seven years later, two thirty-year-old, well-born English cousins, Agnes and Cecily Herbert, came to Africa for adventure. Both fine shots, they had planned their expedition carefully, and were well advised and well armed by an experienced uncle. On their own, they undertook a four-and-a-half month shooting safari to the rocky deserts and blistering hot bush of Somaliland, to the north-east of Kenya.

Setting out south to the Ogaden region from Berbera on the Gulf of Aden with forty-nine heavily laden camels, they soon learned that on safari intelligent planning is never wasted. With each chest meticulously packed and labelled with its listed contents, little time was lost in camp. Practical, an experienced housekeeper, Agnes had the tent ropes made of cotton, expecting that the usual hemp cords would be too elastic. As they progressed, the women astonished the men they came across, both Somalis and Europeans. The Somali men were accustomed to leaving their wives scraps of meat from their own meals, and to burying their women under the light protection of thorn branches when they themselves were interred under hyena-proof stone mounds. To an English hunting party, the ladies made most embarrassing rivals. The Englishmen, two sporty Indian Army officers whom the ladies met after their Pacific & Orient steamer left them in Aden, were quite taken with the Herberts, but found it disturbing that the women sometimes outshot them in the field.

Agnes Herbert's diaries, like the account of Mary Kingsley, reflect, with witty good humour and a generous spirit, the weight of Victorian presumptions, as the women themselves are surprised by how well they manage. With ease, Agnes Herbert concedes her moments of tears and fear, her failures in the field, her inadequacy at pig-sticking and shooting from the saddle. But she and Cecily always get the job done, stopping charging rhino, going after wounded lion and leopard, braving armed Somalis, and stitching up each other's wounds when they are injured by lion, oryx and aardwolf, a striped creature the size of a large fox or jackal that is something between a dog and a hyena.

Calmly coping, the Herberts see themselves more as acting with the steadiness expected of their nation, rather than as women stridently asserting the competence of their gender. They recognize, with affection, that all men, especially hunters, are selfish liars. A spirit of rivalry ignites in them when they hear the old Indian Army warrior admonish the younger, who fancies Cecily: 'Look here, if you are not careful, we shall have those two girls trying to tack on to our show. And I won't have it, for they'll be duffers, of course.'

Vexed, feeling shirty, dubbing the male safari 'the Opposition', the ladies declined to hunt with the men when the two caravans met by accident in the field, refusing even to visit the opposing camp to examine its inferior trophies, lest the men boast of some success. One wonders how Agnes and Cecily would have responded to Randolph Churchill. They did confess to selfish dismay at what is annoying on safari even today, finding that the vast bush is not all one's own, even though one is oneself a guest in it. In fact, the women had finer weapons, better trophies and a happier camp, managed with the help of Clarence, a skilled head Somali known to their uncle. Habituated to dealing with servants, contemptuous of the sloppy, familiar way that Clarence's recent American client had behaved with the men, the ladies ran a trim ship. They carefully recruited staff from several tribes, knowing that friction among the men was more tolerable than conspiracy.

Like the wagons, porters and canoes used as safari transport in other countries, camels, too, brought their own problems. If loaded unevenly, they developed sores, which drew first flies, then maggots, and finally the merciless attentions of sharp-beaked rhinoceros birds, or tick birds, which neatly picked both maggots and flesh from the wounds. Normally advancing at two and a half miles an hour, the philosophical animals would stay down after collapsing in wet country, waiting too patiently to be unloaded. Annoyed by flies, they would roll with their packs. Angry, they fought each other, opening wounds with nasty bites that required the application of searing-hot stones to close them.

But at night, as the land cooled, the grunting of the camels came to be a lullaby, and Agnes Herbert left open the fly of her tent, a twelve-bore hunting pistol loaded by the bed, as she enjoyed the dark and the dawn, and listened to the wild life beyond the zareba. After early-morning tea, served before the tent in an enamel cup with tinned milk from the Army & Navy Stores in London, her favourite moment was breakfast, shared with Cecily and the insects of the table before the day grew fiercely hot. Unlike Mary Kingsley, the cousins wore knickerbockers, gaiters, stout English shooting boots and khaki safari jackets, the wide pockets busy with string, knives and other handy aids. When particularly delicate stalking was required, Mary would remove her boots and hunt in her stockinged feet.

For ascending trees the cousins had equipped themselves with spiked climbing irons, which their Somalis used with delight, going up like woodpeckers. No safari brings everything, however. Finding a cool pool in a rocky basin of the Hawiya desert, they had to make Victorian bathing costumes from Somali *tobes*, or robes, amazing the men with their pale skin and golden hair, for their faces and hands had turned mahogany brown.

After a difficult day, or when they cut open their carefully cured warthog to find it teeming with maggots, the greatest comfort was soup, whether rhino-tail or mulligatawny, made from Lazenby's cubes. When other restoratives and medicines failed, they turned to the two drinks used even by Selous, tea and champagne. Down to their last gallon of water in the parching reaches of the Marehan desert, suffering from sunstroke, they sipped their way through a bottle of warm champagne, then paid the traditional price with a frantic thirst. When a camel-man fell ill, writhing on his mat, they forced 'the everlasting remedy, champagne' between the Muslim's set teeth, and he died where he lay.

The safari suffered two additional casualties, the flight of their rebellious Somali butler, and the death of the Baron, Agnes's gunbearer, who was

Army & Navy Stores catalogue, 1900

No. 84.   **White Drill and Khaki Canvas Shikar Helmet.**
On Green Felt 13/6

Lady's White   **Shikar.**
On Green Felt 12/6

Lady's Pith.
Covered White or Drab Felt   14/6

No. 60.
Gentlemen's Drab Felt 17/6

Gentlemen's Pith.
Covered White or Drab Felt ... 14/6
Covered Drill....................... 8/6

No. 58.
Gentlemen's Drab Felt   17/6

Children's Pith Helmets,
5/6

No. 58.   **White Drill and Khaki Canvas Shikar Helmet.**
On Green Felt 13/6

Gentlemen's Single Terai.
In Drab only 10/0

Tennis Hats, Soft.
White, Cardinal, Gray, 1/0, 1/6, 2/0

TRESS & Cº'S FAMOUS HELMETS
THE "SHIKAR"
White Drill or Khaki on Green Felt.............................. 13/6

Boating.
White Drill 2/0

Lady's Terai (for Tropical wear).
Drab 18/0
Light Brown 18/6
White............... 21/0

1913.
Black, Dark and Light Brown,
and Drab, 9/0

Soft Clerical.
1st quality... 9/0 | 2nd quality... 8/0

Multiform or Lounge.
In Drab only 5/6

The " Ferdinand."
Black, Dark and Light Brown
and Drab, 9/0

Gentlemen's Double Terai.
Drab 18/0
Light Brown 18/6

Lady's Pith Evelyn.
Covered Drab and Fawn
Silk, 10/6
Covered White or Drab
Felt, 14/6

Soft Karachi.
In Drab........................... 8/6

"Graham."   8/6
Light Brown and Drab ....

trampled and gored by a black rhino in thick thorn country. Agnes was deeply distressed by the Baron's death, and so angry over the butler's flight and thefts that she pursued him relentlessly on camelback. Finally sighting him, she fired one long warning shot with her ·500 double-barrelled hammerless ejector rifle and brought the offender back to camp along with the Winchester ·35 he had stolen. But in time the deserter fled once more, on a faster camel, and was never seen again.

Agnes Herbert's favourite animals were black-backed jackal, oryx and Somaliland's biggest antelope, the greater kudu. She complained that the country was already largely shot out, both by Somalis and Europeans, and was no longer the old-time sportsman's paradise that it had been in the 1890s. Saddest of all, there were no longer any elephant whatever. Clarence told her of the hunting days of his youth, when his father's tribe in the Gadabursi region would kill several elephant a week for the ivory. Never touching the meat, they rode the animals down in open country, slashing their hamstrings from horseback with long, double-edged swords. For lion, the Somalis carried barbed spears. Keeping the flight straight with a trembling of the blade derived from knocking the spear against the palm, a Somali could pierce his quarry at seventy yards.

More candid than most hunters, and perhaps more sensitive, Agnes Herbert 'often wished when I was flush with success, and I saw my beast lying dead, that I had not done it'. Like many trophy hunters, once she had a specimen of each, she grew tired of the killing and passed more and more time lying down, watching, sometimes wondering if the day would come when it would suffice to stalk, and perhaps photograph, without shooting. She accepted the necessity for controlled, limited hunting to conserve game, but regretted the inevitable loss of 'elemental romance' in the freedom of the hunt. When Clarence brought her a baby oryx he had taken from its mother, she put the timid creature across her saddle, and gently left it where it had been taken, observing from a distance until the mother returned. But back in England, often aching for the wilds, Agnes retained the trophy hunter's taste for ornament and animal furniture, taking her tea from an oryx-hide tray, and delighting in her rhinoceros table, the hide top polished like clouded amber, mounted on the animal's four legs.

Agnes Herbert was by no means the first African hunter to be distressed by the loss of wildlife to excessive shooting and settlement, or the first to consider the alternative of photography. The distinguished global sportsman Edward North Buxton was probably the first widely recognized shot to convert from hunter to photographer–conservationist. Buxton had hunted so well and so widely that no hunter could belittle him when, about 1890, he began to take the position that a camera might be more sporting than a rifle. By 1906 he was advocating a comprehensive programme of wildlife conservation throughout the British empire, through much of which he had hunted. By that date the first hunting restrictions were already in operation in Kenya.

Cecily and Agnes Herbert

Lamenting the virtual extermination of the Somali elephant by the time of his safari there in 1896, Buxton said he 'would as soon shoot a horse as an elephant'. Returning to London, he was instrumental in having the British colonial administration protect the remaining elephant in their retreat in the Gadabursi Mountains of north-western Somaliland. On the same safari, to be sure, Buxton used his Mannlicher to bag ten different species of antelope, all used both for the pot and as trophies. Delighting in the stalk, he especially enjoyed hunting greater kudu, remarking that only ostrich were more elusive, as the birds had learned the value of their feathers in the Aden market. Limited by his skill and equipment, a finer shot than photographer, Buxton's better pictures were camp scenes, not animals, and he had them meticulously reproduced in England by the Swan Electric Engraving Company before publishing them in *Short Stalks* in 1898.

Distinguished field photography began earlier, with the Crimean War in 1855, when Roger Fenton took memorable photographs of individuals and post-battle scenes near the Black Sea. During the United States Civil War in the 1860s, the potential of outdoor photography came to public attention through the work of Mathew Brady, who required several railway carriages to transport his equipment from site to site. It is not certain who took the first photograph on safari in Africa, but in 1863, Professor Fritsch, a German explorer on safari in Cape Colony succeeded in taking the first recorded photograph of an African wild animal, using a dry glass-plate negative. In 1888 Selous reported that Monsieur Coillard, a French Protestant missionary who accompanied the hunter on a safari to Barotseland on the upper Zambesi, into country which is today part of Zambia, brought with him his 'photographic apparatus'. Apparently Coillard had already taken interesting pictures of native customs and the landscape of the Zambesi valley, but Selous makes no reference to any pictures taken on safari.

Writing later, in *African Nature Notes and Reminiscences* in 1907, Selous comments that ornithological photographs are misleading as to the detectability of bird nests, for in the field the nests are far more difficult to spot than photographs suggest. Disappointed, he concluded, perhaps too hastily, that, 'I rather distrust the camera as a true interpreter of nature.'

In 1896, while Selous was in Matabeleland assisting in the suppression of the Matabele rebellion, a young German, C.G. Schillings, was getting his first taste

Self-portrait of C.G. Schillings

C.G. Schillings's large format camera

of the veld in German East Africa, the Tanzania of today. A hunter himself, he deplored the excessive killing and destruction of wildlife. Fearful that the heavy game could not last long, he determined to preserve it for ever on film. Three times he returned to Germany to perfect his technique and equipment, experimenting at the Goerz Optical Institute at Friedenau, the source of perhaps the finest optics of the day. Appreciating that over half the life of the bush was nocturnal, Schillings was intent on creating first-class wilderness photographs by day and by night. Plagued by malaria, heart disease and impractical flash apparatus, both his health and equipment failed him on his early trips to Africa. But he had learned to study the bush closely on his first safaris, astonished by the 'degree to which civilized man has unlearnt the use of his eyes and ears'.

Outdoor flash photography was originally based on the ignition of powdered magnesium, which was first suggested in 1865. By the 1880s powdered magnesium was being mixed with various chemicals to increase the actinic power of the light and to accelerate the flash. Some of the volatile compounds, containing such materials as gunpowder and gun cotton, were extremely dangerous. In time a mixture of powdered magnesium and potassium chlorate became the most popular compound, the length of the flash varying from one twenty-fifth of a second to half a second, depending on the mixture used. The technique was called 'flashlight photography'. In a sense, the duration of the artificial flash came to perform the function of daytime shutter speed. Having mastered these new techniques in Germany, and refined his own apparatus, C.G. Schillings, well prepared at last, was determined to record Africa's fauna as they lived by day and hunted or died by night. In 1903, he set out on the first of the grand, truly professional, photographic safaris.

Limited to working in black and white, without the benefit of high-speed film and modern telephoto lenses, photographers at the turn of the century were also gravely encumbered by the bulk of their equipment and by the time required to set up and work. Due to the immense size of the negatives, however, it was possible to achieve a degree of detail not available in contemporary thirty-five-millimetre photography, for the larger the negative, the more precise the detail.

Mounted on heavy wooden tripods, the wooden view cameras were generally fitted for several different backs, for film holders containing negatives varying in size from 5 x 7 in up to the 'mammoth plate' negatives of 16 x 20 in. The negatives themselves were either early film or heavy glass plates, known as dry plates, which replaced the earlier collodian wet plates. The large-format camera itself was fitted with a big lens, and the lenses generally had superior optics to those available today.

To photograph moving animals, Schillings learned to use his heavy camera like a 'photographic gun', swinging it smoothly with the movement of the target. In this way the pictured animal would be sharp, and the background somewhat blurred. Schillings himself favoured the artistic effect of slightly blurred or softened images, likening his resulting pictures to Japanese naturalist art. Under field conditions, he found it impractical to calculate each exposure time. Instead he learned to work instinctively, like a deft shooter, allowing just enough exposure to secure a clear impression.

The negative was then developed in a makeshift darkroom tent, in order to determine whether the picture was successful, and to retain its undiminished quality. The developed dry-plate negative was then printed on to either silver bromide paper, or albumen paper, which was coated with a solution of salt and beaten egg whites to impart a smooth protective gloss. The total photographic process, like early flashlight photography, was difficult enough to execute under ideal laboratory conditions. In the field, particularly on safari, each picture was a challenge. In camp every evening, Schillings was careful to make duplicate negatives of his more successful pictures. He then shipped the duplicates back to Germany as rapidly as possible. Once home he could make new prints on either carbon or silver bromide paper.

African creatures of every size conspired against the photographer. The developing and printing process required the use of chemicals and water, but the water available was often cloudy and alive with organisms, even tiny fish. Fierce black ants gnawed the wooden camera. A mongoose stole the lens cap and hid it in an ant-hill. Hyena carried off the linen sandbags that hung from the flashlight tripod. Rhinoceros and crocodile harassed the porters.

Transporting scores of wooden chests containing glass plates, chemicals, cameras, tripods and related equipment, all of it both heavy and fragile, was a serious undertaking even by rail in Germany. In the mountains and swamps of German East Africa, it was a daily epic. The straggling caravan of 170 porters, supporting their sixty-pound loads either on their heads, their shoulders or on long poles, was charged by rhinoceros in thick thorn country and threatened by crocodile as it crossed shoulder-high rivers. But Schillings had learned much from his earlier safaris, and travelled with his own taxidermist, surgeon and

Schillings's safari camp with
photographic supply boxes

askaris. Frequently Schillings on safari moved with complete double sets of photographic supplies, in case loads and porters were lost in the rivers. When he set out for brief expeditions from his base camps, he moved with thirty bearers, the men immediately behind him carrying his camera and guns.

Schillings's safari camp was a lively place, at times like a little kingdom, as the taxidermist William Orgeich and his assistants worked on the skeleton of a giraffe and the baby rhinoceros Fatima played with its inseparable companions, two goats that often sat on it like a cushion. Then a live hyena might be carried into camp slung on a pole, while the baby ostrich scrabbled about in their pen made of negative crates, and Schillings himself delicately mixed the explosive powder for his flashlight. On some evenings, setting up his night camera before laying out its string triggers in the bush, he would have his men act out the parts of lion or leopard as he carefully adjusted his preparations.

But C.G. Schillings, relentlessly pursuing his work, was not always the ideal sportsman. As a pioneering experimental photographer and as a collector of specimens, both dead and alive, for German museums and zoos, he often employed ugly methods, such as heavy metal traps, on a large scale. Having set up the stand for his magnesium flashlight, he would tie up an ox or donkey as bait, generally using an animal that was already suffering from tsetse or some

'While a lioness killed the ox with a terrible bite on the neck, a maned lion drew near. This is the only photograph in my book that has been "retouched". The negative was imperfect and has been retouched on the left side.' From C.G. Schillings, *Flashlights in the Jungle*

other infirmity. Near by might be his 66 lb iron traps, manufactured by R. Weber in Germany. With them he caught, and then generally killed, thirty-seven lion, forty leopard and 121 striped hyena. For the skins, and to feed his large camp, Schillings also hunted with his 8 mm rifle made by Altmeister Reeb of Bonn. To reduce the quantity of game killed, he kept his men on a diet that was at least half vegetable matter.

Like the hunters, collectors, scientists and photographers who followed him, Schillings justified his own wildlife depredations in his own terms. A sincerely ardent conservationist, appalled at the 'tragedy of civilization' that had already destroyed most of the heavy game in southern Africa, highly critical of the Boers, he advocated regulated hunting and the setting aside of large game sanctuaries. Intensely patriotic, assertive of his nation's claims in Africa, he called Mt Kilimanjaro 'Germany's highest mountain'. Yet he greatly admired Britain's early efforts to preserve the African fauna, particularly the creation of an animal preserve along the line of the Uganda Railway. Repudiating the German assumption that all wild animals must be exterminated before whites could settle in a region, he concluded that, 'we may take English ideals of sport as our example, as well as the regulations drawn up by English authorities for the protection of the animal world'.

Although Schillings would shoot cow elephant in order to capture their young, he was deeply upset by the agonized, human expression of a shot baboon. He worked hard to collect specimens for zoos, for he believed that live animals were essential to educate and influence people regarding the value of wildlife and its preservation. He carefully supervised forty bearers as they transported a spotted hyena to the coast in a 330 lb iron cage. Often he respected animals more than he did the people who found them so strange. He denied that mankind was intrinsically superior to the rhinoceros, which he credited with highly developed instincts and a remarkable memory for terrain.

By the time Queen Victoria died in 1901, a loose network of international conservationists was trying to preserve the game in Africa, Europe and the United States. Generally the leaders of this effort were themselves active hunters, like Buxton in England, Theodore Roosevelt in the United States, Schillings in Germany, and Selous and Sir Harry H. Johnston in Africa. They knew each other's works and reputations. President Roosevelt, for example, wrote in praise of Schillings's work on behalf of wildlife. Schillings gave similar credit to Buxton. Before her death, Queen Victoria herself identified with this trend, by lending her sponsorship to the Anti-Osprey Movement, which was working to make illegal the killing of the little egret for its plumes. The Queen declined to admit into her presence any woman wearing 'osprey' (i.e. little egret) plumes.

In Africa itself, the first conservation efforts were initiated by government, notably at the Cape, where both the Dutch administration in the seventeenth

Elephants' tusks in one of the workrooms of an ivory factory in Germany. There were a number of other such factories in Europe and America. Photograph by C.G. Schillings

century and the succeeding British government sought to restrain hunting. The first private initiative came when a group of hunters assembled in Durban and formed the Natal Game Protection Association in 1883, coincidentally just nine days after Africa's last quagga died in its cage in Amsterdam. The last buffalo in Natal had been exterminated twelve years previously. In 1900 the first International Conference for the Protection of Wild Animals, held in London, forbade the export of any elephant tusk weighing less than 10 lb. Over the preceding ten years, the tusks of 185,000 elephant had passed through the Antwerp ivory market. From 1888 to 1902, over seven million pounds of elephant ivory changed hands in that market, the average tusk weighing 18·7 lb, and most of it coming from the Congo.

Harry Johnston, an active figure in the final suppression of the slave trade in East Africa, and the High Commissioner of Uganda in 1900, was perhaps the most influential of the early conservationists in British Africa. He believed the 'ravages of European and American sportsmen to be one of the greatest blots on our twentieth-century civilization'. Johnston considered photography to be the sportsmanship of the future. His attitude helped to launch the enduring relationship between conservation and photography, both as an alternative to hunting and as a tool for public education. He accepted as appropriate the death by rhino charge of the German hunter Dr George Kolb, who in three years in German East Africa killed 150 rhinoceros, 'each one a far more interesting mammal than himself'.

Like Buxton, Schillings and Roosevelt, Johnston believed that hunting and the taking of animals for scientific purposes should be part of a broad scheme of conservation. But he wanted hunting to exist within enforced limits, and deplored attempts to exterminate some animals in order to increase the number of game animals, the way owls and weasels were sacrificed to pheasant in England. Writing in his introduction to Schillings's *Flashlights in the Jungle*, Johnston considered the egret and the sable to be 'as aesthetically important as the well-dressed woman'. He ridiculed the notion that 'the destruction of African fauna is part of a fashionable man's education'.

Even as individuals and governments were launching efforts to preserve Africa's game from the Cape to Somaliland, the last of the great elephant hunters were also going about their work. Between 1893 and 1925, Arthur Neumann, James Sutherland and Karamojo Bell killed over 2,000 elephant, in a total of about sixty years of hunting in nine countries. The introduction of cordite in 1889 came just in time to help. This efficient, smokeless explosive, made from gun-cotton and nitroglycerine, and named for the cord-like appearance of the gun-cotton, delivered a high velocity from a small charge. The result was smaller calibres, with lighter rifles firing slender bullets with a flatter trajectory and greater range, speed and accuracy. The new rifles, such as the ·256s, ·275s and ·303s, were lighter and easier to handle than the old ·450s and ·577s, but some traditional hunters judged that the new weapons did not have the same stopping power as the old elephant guns. The smaller and faster the bullet, the greater its penetrating power, to the extent that sometimes they wasted impact by passing entirely through the animal.

The combination of cordite and repeating actions, allowing multiple high-velocity shots from an easily managed gun, finally tilted the balance in favour of the hunter, permitting amateurs to take the field with more confidence. The new bullets included full metal-jacketed lead 'solids' for dangerous, heavy game, designed to penetrate deeply and smash bone, and variations of hollow bullets and 'softs', with lead showing through at the top, intended to stay in soft-skinned animals and mushroom expansively. A few hunters adopted the practice of setting out with a soft bullet in barrel No. 1 and a hard in barrel No. 2, prepared to reload with whatever was required.

The introduction of less expensive repeating rifles, such as the Henry rifle, made everyone a potential big-game hunter after 1870. With the advent of the improved Mauser-action magazines, the transition from Selous's single-shot four-bore elephant gun, firing a quarter pound of lead, to the elegant two-shot double rifles, and finally to lightweight repeating rifles, like the ten-shot ·303, was now complete. Most African professional hunters, however, have continued to prefer heavier-calibre double rifles to magazine-fed rifles, due to the superior reliability, balance, mechanical silence and speed of use of the double rifles. There are virtually no reported instances of a top-grade double rifle, such as those made by Holland & Holland and other leading riflemakers, ever failing to fire due to a fault in the weapon itself.*

As he opened up new hunting country in northern Kenya between 1893 and 1905, Arthur Neumann's preferred weapon for elephant was an old ·577 double rifle by Gibbs. Typically, as he hunted to the east of Lake Rudolph and in the wild forests of the Mathews Range, Neumann himself would carry his Gibbs Lee-Metford single ·450, exchanging it for the heavier rifle if time permitted. When his ·577 was disabled, Neumann acquired a heavy ten-bore Holland & Holland, firing the traditional smoky, black-powder cartridges. He always preferred solid lead bullets over newer sophisticated models employing steel cores or points, for he observed that the lead was stripped off on meeting bone, leaving the light steel with little momentum.

James Sutherland, hunting south of Kenya in the thick country of Portuguese and German East Africa, chose different weapons. At times he himself did not carry a gun, a habit which occasionally endangered both him and his gunbearers, who sometimes dropped the weapons to speed their flight. One gunbearer carried Sutherland's ·318, ideal for light and soft-skinned game, firing Westley-Richards's patented expanding copper-capped bullets. This rifle and bullet combined the velocity of the modern small-bore with some of the shock-giving quality of the old larger bores. The expanding bullet would stay in the animal, instead of passing through it.

* Double rifles are still made today. For £27,000, one can buy a new ·375, ·465, ·470 or ·577 from Holland & Holland.

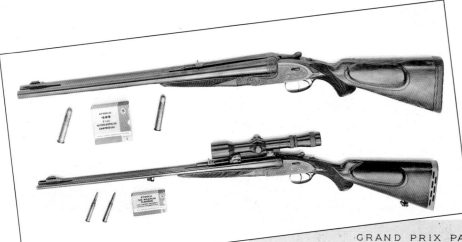

From small-bore double to the largest 600-bore: a 240-flanged Holland & Holland royal-model double-barrelled rifle complete with its telescopic sight and a royal-model double-barrelled rifle by Holland & Holland weighing 16 lb, with a barrel length of 22 inches. Both are colour-hardened finished.

Below: Rare 600-bore double-barrelled big-game rifle which W.W. Greener made for the famous photographer and naturalist Marius Maxwell. This unique rifle is carved with elephants in deep relief. It is interesting to note that Maxwell ordered a second pair of barrels to interchange with this rifle.

GRAND PRIX PARIS 1900.

BY SPECIAL APPOINTMENT TO

BY SPECIAL APPOINTMENT TO
H.M. THE KING OF ITALY.

H.R.H. THE PRINCE OF WALES.

BY SPECIAL APPOINTMENT TO
H.M. THE KING OF PORTUGAL.

HOLLAND & HOLLAND,
LTD.
Gun & Rifle Manufacturers,
98, NEW BOND STREET,
LONDON.
ESTABLISHED 1835.

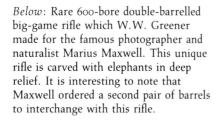

A rare and massive late-nineteenth-century four-bore black-powder breech-loading big-game rifle by Thomas Bland. Loading 14 drams. The barrel is clearly engraved and has an interesting inscription.

Crocodile taking Shebane, New Year's Day, 1896

Sutherland's other gunbearer carried the hunter's stopper for the thick-skinned, heavy game, for elephant, rhinoceros and buffalo. This was a 13 lb Westley-Richards double ·577 with a 750 grain lead bullet. He found that ·600 bore rifles were too heavy, weighing 16 lb, and had insufficient penetration, whereas lighter calibres lacked the killing power of the ·577. Sutherland's one modern preference on his double rifle was a single trigger, permitting greater speed between shots and eliminating the old problem of injured trigger fingers.

Both Neumann and Sutherland were keenly aware that the days of the great free elephant hunts were coming to an end. Feeling that he had started too late, bitterly defensive about his killing, Neumann justified his shooting entirely as a personal economic necessity. The ivory was required to pay for his adventures. As a hunter, he suffered from fits of nerves and a tendency to flinch. Shooting small cows and bulls because 'even smallish tusks were better than no ivory', Neumann thought nothing of taking hasty snap shots at vanishing targets. He would not pause to finish a disabled cow as he dashed past to wing another. He noted that, going after heavy bulls, one could not get away with the sort of sloppy shooting that sufficed against cows.

Neumann used a similar approach in collecting the ivory. Rather than relying on skill or supervision in carefully extricating the ivory with axes, he avoided injuring the tusks by waiting several days to let the face of the animal decompose around them. As on the rough-edged safaris of Gordon Cumming, there were casualties. One wounded cow pinned Neumann to the ground by stabbing a tusk through his bicep. His gunbearer Squareface was taken from camp by a lion, as Neumann fired into the darkness. In the morning he found the remains. On New Year's Day, 1896, as the hunter sat in his camp chair by a river, lacing up his boots after a refreshing bath, before drawing on the gloves he always wore on safari, there came a chilling scream. He turned to see the last moment of his camp servant, Shebane. Gripped like a fish in the beak of a heron, Shebane was caught in the jaws of an immense crocodile, its long head raised above the water before it disappeared with the man.

Noting that his tusk-bearers were proud to carry the 100 lb tusks that were too long or heavy for the donkeys, Neumann did not restrict his porters' loads to

147

the 60 lb limit that was then mandatory in British Africa. When his men, unsupervised, failed to refill their water bottles, he denounced their 'stupidity', forgetting the British military dictum that there are no bad men, only bad officers. But he enjoyed hunting elephant with the crafty Dorobo of northern Kenya, fascinated by their falling javelins, poisoned darts and appetite for warm blood. Honey lovers, the Dorobo refused to pay more than ten working beehives for a good wife. Neumann gave a Dorobo chief, who had solicited a charm to improve his hunting, a well-chosen verse of Shakespeare, illustrated with the sketch of an elephant.

> I bought an unction of a mountebank,
> So mortal that, but dip a knife in it,
> Where it draws blood no cataplasm so rare,
> Collected from all simples that have virtue
> Under the moon, can save the thing from death
> That is but scratched withal; I'll touch my point
> With this contagion, that, if I gall him slightly,
> It may be death.

> *Hamlet* IV, vii.

Superstition is a universal element of hunting, as James Sutherland also learned. In Nyasaland, now Malawi, the hunters' wives were never safe from it. Sutherland's African companions believed that if a dying elephant grabbed a tree as it fell, then it was certain that the wife of the man who fired the first shot was an adulteress. This was always found to be true. Knowing this, the hunter would dash home, testing all his wives by the ordeal of poisoning. Since African women then performed much valuable work, indeed nearly all of it, from agriculture to home construction, the poison was administered to the household fowls, each wife having a surrogate champion.

An enterprising medicine man himself, Sutherland recovered from an elephant tossing with liberal doses of an emulsion of whisky and olive oil. When his tracker's thigh was ripped open by a buffalo, he honed a needle from a sliver of bamboo, unravelled twill from his khaki shirt and stitched up the wound. Humane, he was shocked by the bartering of slave women that continued in Portuguese and German East Africa in 1910. He himself assaulted one slaver and released a slave girl and her companions. A Yao chief sent Sutherland a present of three slave girls, soliciting in exchange a barrel of gunpowder and medicine to improve his hunting. Instead Sutherland sent the man a bolt of blue calico cloth and advised him to take two cold baths a day and to consume a great deal of tobacco, his own regimen on safari.

Sutherland himself hunted for the joy of safari life, for the bird songs that woke him in the forest, the sense of danger on the stalk and the demands it made on him. As he sailed again for Africa after a brief visit to England, Sutherland flung his morning coat and silk hat into the sea, desperate once more to 'peel from his mind the trivial veneer of civilization and to brood upon the elemental heart of life'. To do this was expensive, and the elephant paid the price. Although expressly conscious of an elephant's pain, he would shoot under all circumstances, even when the animal slept, deeming that action to be 'absolutely on a par with the taking of a bullock's life for food'. Yet he considered it scandalously unsporting to hunt lion with dogs, or for three armed men to go after one lion.

Like other thoughtful men who sometimes carry their sport to excess, Sutherland sought for rationales, and the assertive morality of the preserva-tionists made him uncomfortable. He believed the creation of game reserves would increase the number of game and bring 'calamity' by multiplying the tsetse flies, which were then thought to breed in their dung. The matter, he said, reduced itself to one simple question. 'Is Africa going to serve as a colony for surplus European populations, or as a collection of big-game reserves?'

Although some considered that Neumann was the greatest elephant hunter of his time, and Sutherland claimed that his own bag of 447 bull elephants was the largest in history, neither man knew his rifles or his elephant as well as Karamojo Bell. Not for Bell the frantic snap shots of Neumann or Sutherland's stampeding wounded bulls. Spurning their heavy ·577s, he shot with surgical precision. Karamojo Bell killed over 800 bull elephants with a five-shot ·275 (7 mm) made to order by Rigby in London with a reliable Mauser bolt action and a foresight bead of gleaming warthog ivory. Named after the Karamojan hunting grounds in north-eastern Uganda, which he opened up, Bell loved that wild region as 'country where a man could still slit a throat or grab a native girl without being badgered by alien law'.

A Scot who went to sea at thirteen, Bell as a young boy was riveted by the tales of his countryman Gordon Cumming. The dream of his youth was to hunt elephant on the African plains. At seventeen he landed in Mombasa in 1897, carrying nothing but a single shot ·303 by Fraser of Edinburgh, and a pocket-full of nickel-jacketed lead solids. With this weapon the young man earned a job as the armed escort for convoys of Indian muleteers, as they moved supplies to the forward camps of the survey parties that preceded the advancing railhead of the Uganda Railway. Occasionally he would pass the bush camp that was to become Nairobi. Hunting for his convoy, Bell learned his life-long lesson: get in close and make the first bullet count. He had little choice, for the extraction mechanism of the falling-block ·303 would jam in the heat, the spent cartridge packed tight in the chamber.

On subsequent safaris, Bell learned to value two qualities of the modern, high-powered rifle: weight and accuracy. Its light weight enabled him to carry his own weapon all day, until it became an extension of his arm, and he could raise and use it with effortless steadiness. Its accuracy made even the small bullets deadly, if properly aimed. To perfect the steadiness of his aim, Bell performed endless drills with his rifle extended in one hand. Soon he learned that a small-bore rifle is reliable only with a brain shot, for the heart and lungs

Skull of Bull Elephant killed in UNYORO, UGANDA. Sawn down middle to shew Brain. In this skull the brain measured 12" × 6". He was not very old. Tusks weighed 81

SKULL before Bisection

'Brain shot, quartering from the rear, must be directed straight for the brain as shown in the sectionalized skull.' From Bell, *Bell of Africa*

Sectionalized elephant skull showing location of brain and skull of bull elephant after skinning, both by Karamojo Bell

can absorb more punishment and take longer to bring the body down. To perfect his targeting, he studied the anatomy of the elephant as no hunter ever had before.

Sawing an elephant skull in two with a nine-foot, two-handed bandsaw, Bell studied the brain and its shelter of honeycombed bone. The cellular skull structure, later used in modern aircraft frames, combines strength with light weight, permitting the elephant's neck to support the huge head and heavy tusks. Carefully Bell assessed the relative vulnerability of the different routes to this target, learning the precise angles that give sure access to the elephant's ten-pound brain, roughly the size of a loaf of bread.

Practising in the field until his 'subconscious aimer' took over, he used the ear root and the eye to plot the location of the brain. To do the job quickly and cleanly, with less pain to the animal and more safety for the hunter, he got in close, thirty yards, and aimed always for the brain itself. The alternative was more dangerous. In thick thorn bush, when a man can barely move, a six-ton elephant cuts through like an icebreaker, covering a hundred yards in ten or eleven seconds.

Proud of the finality and silence of his technique, Bell knew 'nothing more satisfying than the complete flop of a running elephant shot in the brain'. In this way Karamojo Bell, using various rifles, killed over a thousand elephant in twenty years of hunting, covering over 60,000 miles on foot from Abyssinia to Liberia. In 1909 Bell was pleased with the ivory he bagged hunting in the Lado Enclave, the personal shooting preserve of Belgium's King Leopold II, tucked between the Anglo-Egyptian Sudan and the Belgian Congo. It had been agreed in the Anglo-Belgian Agreement of 1894 that six months after King Leopold's death the Lado territory would pass to the Sudan. In the six months after the King died in 1909, as the Belgian administration withdrew, there was a vacuum of authority in the Lado, with no restrictions on the excellent elephant hunting. Ivory hunters and ragtag adventurers poured in from across the world, with the greedy abandon of a gold rush. The old hands knew how to make the most of it.

Normally, elephant hunting was a lonely and Spartan profession, but in the Lado a wild camaraderie arose, with the hardy mixture of fraternity and rivalry of a Klondike mining camp. The departing Belgian authorities had long been celebrated for their camp revels, but now even Bell was impressed by their efforts to drain their stores of alcohol. Preparing for the alcoholic stress of the evening, the Belgians would have a dozen raw eggs set at each man's place in the mess tent. Each diner would then direct his servant to prepare his eggs to order. The English guests were astonished when some Belgians, already enjoying limitless rough wine, would crack the raw eggs over an early course and mash them through the food. Having helped himself to a serving of red beetroot, rich with uncooked eggs and vinegar, Bell was astounded to find that the beetroot was in fact raw buffalo flesh.

It was the Belgian custom to drink until insensible, following the wine with

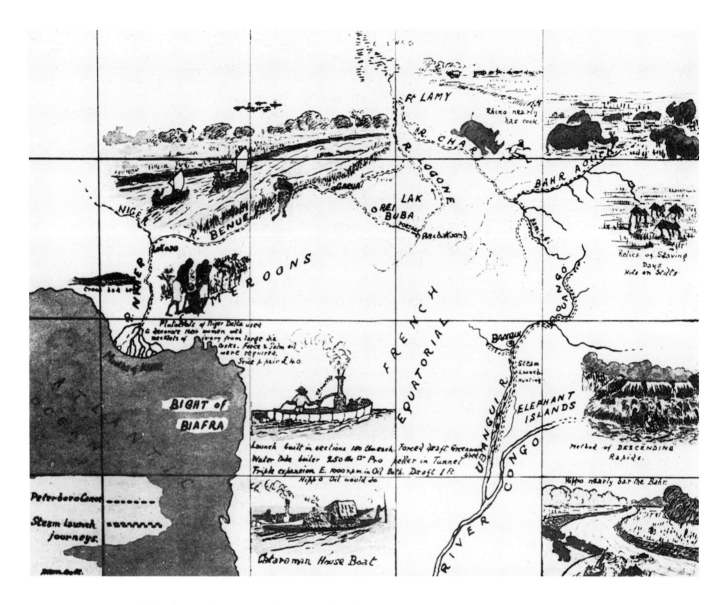

Map showing areas west of the Nile where Karamojo Bell hunted

beer, whisky and absinthe, with every white man finally either on or under the table. Peering through the mosquito netting that hung down from the sides of the dining tent, the Africans seemed not at all surprised to observe the *chef de poste*, a personage whom they usually saw when his presence dignified public floggings, fall flat along the table across the food. After one such celebration, fresh, still fit and thirsty after weeks in the bush, drinking for England, Bell rose to his feet. He walked slowly to the locker of another hunter, removed the man's final bottle of curaçao, and drained it with the other survivor, a hardy Dane.

When the Lado passed to the Sudan in 1910, Karamojo Bell tried west Africa. In Liberia in 1911 he was disappointed to find pygmy hippos, small elephant, and the descendants of freed American slaves, who were enslaving local Africans on their plantations. On the Ubangui River in French Equatorial Africa in 1912 he assembled a steam launch brought from England and hunted the elephant-haunted river islands. Always it was the ivory. On his most profitable day, shooting in the Sudan, he collected 1,463 lb of ivory from nine elephant slain in the seven-foot swamp grass near the Pibor River. That earned him £900 at Hale's auction rooms in London.

To hunt as he did, averaging two shots an elephant, often killing with one perfect shot, Karamojo Bell had to study his prey. He never ceased to do so. He noted how elephant swing their heads from side to side as they flee, enabling them to watch their pursuers without pausing. He studied their diets, and the animals that attend them, whether the black-faced vervet monkeys that pluck the unchewed tamarind seeds from their fresh dung or the hateful one-inch stinging flies that drive them into the mud. When parched, he drank the pure water that flowed from their stomachs after a careful spear thrust. This water came from the same ten-gallon tank that the elephant draw on when they bring the water up into their throats and then shower themselves with their trunks. He learned that elephant enjoy green bamboo shoots as people do asparagus, relishing them for their deep moist roots. He watched them eat salt and earth, and then discovered by surgery that elephant use these to scour out the large maggot-like worms that infest their intestines.

Bell came to admire the stately old bulls, sometimes sixty years old or more, recognizing these gentlemen not just by their heavy ivory, but by their hollow temples, sharp spinal ridges and folded corrugated skin. Studying the scarce

Sketch by Karamojo Bell

remains of elephant in country where at times the horizon was jagged with twenty-five lumbering animals, he learned why there are no elephant cemeteries. The ivory is taken by natives, and the bones soon disappear, 'weathered away, gnawed down, dragged off, burned, disintegrated'. He was sceptical, too, of the legend that leeches so inflame the insides of an elephant's trunk that the animals beat their trunks against trees until they swell and cause suffocation. Most of all, Bell learned that there are no rules about elephant hunting, that the great animals are truly unpredictable.

Unlike most white hunters, including the Herbert ladies, Bell always welcomed African women on his safaris. He attributed the usual prejudice against them to Victorian ignorance, for he found the women to be stronger and more enduring than the men. He said they made his camps cheerful, and kept their men busy with beer and wife-beating, and away from dangerous mischief with local natives. When the women quarrelled, the camp headman issued hippo-hide whips to the disputants, who flailed until the tears came, but never aimed at breast or face. Camp justice was served in a different way for the men, with the combatants fighting either with stout sticks or with Bell's four-ounce boxing gloves. Immediately forgotten, the bouts soon gave way to feasting and hunting.

In the mornings, the 'donkey men' were up at 2.30, loading their beasts with tusks, each sewn into an animal hide, dried to shrink around it. At 5.00 a.m., tea and biscuits, fresh shorts and a hunting shirt were brought to Bell's spacious sleeping tent. Before sun-up he was off, hunting in the unspoiled quiet ahead of the safari, perhaps with one man carrying a calabash of sour milk. At about 5.30 the safari followed. Each day Bell shot to feed 150 people. Elephant walk at six miles an hour, and Bell reckoned that his average elephant cost him seventy-three miles of walking and running. The days were so hard that he walked through twenty-four pairs of shoes a year and his feet were always raw with blisters. Their soles worn down despite giraffe-hide sandals, none of his men could last more than four months on the trail, and some worked in one-month shifts. Bell himself came to favour crêpe rubber soles with soft leather uppers, a form of desert boot that appeared in his later years.

Back in camp, his two personal tents afforded him a bathroom with a canvas bath, a veranda, Jaeger rugs and a large camp-bed with linen sheets and mosquito nets. Close as he got to elephants and to his Africans, Bell found that after a chase he preferred his own favoured camp drink, a split of champagne, to the Karamojan favourite, a quart of golden, liquid eland fat. Sometimes Bell regretted that he could never be as festive as his merry companions. But, rolling a cigarette from his Dutch shag tobacco, he always found good company in *The Pickwick Papers*, 'the only contact with civilization that I ever found pleasurable'.

The return of a Karamojo Bell safari, among the last of their kind, was a spectacle even in the ivory centres of east Africa. Sparkling in brightly beaded robes, a hundred men paraded to the ivory market, proudly bearing the teeth of

180 elephant. Escorted by Bell's six armed askaris, the donkey men kept 180 donkeys in order. Each of the great 100 lb tusks, so hot that it blistered the shoulders, its empty nerve hole filled with the bearer's belongings, was carried by one of the thirty-one picked Karamojan porters. Blood-red ostrich feathers and the manes of giraffes, lions and baboons bedecked each man's head. Averaging one elephant per day over the six months of hunting on a fourteen-month safari to Uganda and the Lado Enclave, Bell returned with a hoard of treasure. The magnificent Karamojo tusks averaged 53 lb each, the Lado tusks 23 lb. The total cost of one safari was £3,000 (about £90,600 today), of which the wages were £600. The ivory sold for £9,000. In today's money, the safari realized a profit of £181,000.

Thinking back, Karamojo Bell considered solitary rambles with a gun to be the joyful essence of hunting. But the heart-stop always came when he found fresh tracks of the great bulls of northern Uganda. 'It is as if all one's senses had been half asleep and had just awakened fully,' he wrote. 'Speed, hearing and sight become intense. Never could I prevent my pulse beating faster. It is because nothing is ever the same. Anything can happen at such close quarters. The feel of the rifle in one's hand sends a thrill through the body.'

Long after his first safari, no longer a tyro, now trained by the gunsmith Fraser himself to follow a bullet in flight with the naked eye and never to flinch, Bell experienced a highpoint of his life. While he was on an extended safari, his new custom rifle arrived from Edinburgh, finding him at last after many adventures. It was a slim Mannlicher-Schoenauer ·256, reworked in Scotland. With the barrel shortened and the action machined down, the carbine weighed a clean five pounds. The bluing, stocking and sighting were executed by a master, Daniel Fraser himself.

I shall never forget the unpacking of that ·256 in the wilds of the African bush, the ripping open of that tin-lined case that looks so incredibly small. There, wrapped in greaseproof paper, lay the oily little rascal. Out in the hot sun it was but a moment's work to strip off the mercurial grease Fraser used for protecting his steelwork on tropical voyages. What a thrill just to handle it.

Eager as a schoolboy, Bell filled the magazine with solid Steyr cartridges, Austria's best, and his belt with a mix of solid and soft-nosed. Following his habit, he checked each cartridge case for flaws and kept the breach empty to suit the need. Leaving camp with his gunbearers, stealing through a wild orchard, he discovered a party of elephant browsing on the heavy fruit. As he paused, planning his shots, his eyes instinctively searching out the paths to their brains, he caught the scent of Africa. Wild flowers mingled with 'elephant dung, urine, and the buzz of countless insects, making a quivering jelly of the air, quite intoxicating to the hunter'. That day the new Fraser killed twelve fine bulls with one brain shot each. But a new century was beginning. Never again would a hunter in Africa bring down such a bag.

5. BWANA TUMBO

Theodore Roosevelt on Safari

Braced on the cowcatcher of an American Baldwin locomotive, its prow battered by a night-time crash with a rhino, Frederick Selous and Theodore Roosevelt crossed the Kenya plateau. The former president found it an intoxicating vista of bush and open forest, alive with ostrich, zebra, impala and cantering giraffe, 'literally like passing through a vast zoological garden'.

Leader of the wild charge up San Juan Hill during the Spanish–American War, one eye blind from a boxing injury, a future candidate who, on his way to hospital with an assassin's bullet lodged against his right lung, was to harangue a campaign crowd for fifty minutes, Teddy Roosevelt was at home with adventure. But at the end of it all, his 1909 safari was the highpoint of his private life, when he felt most intensely what he called 'the hidden spirit of the wilderness'.

For Theodore Roosevelt, as for the old hunter on the cowcatcher beside him, the adventure of Africa was the inevitable conclusion to a boyhood passion for wildlife. Like young Selous, Roosevelt was first seduced by David Livingstone's *Missionary Travels*. He was fascinated by the depiction of the lion dragging off the dazed missionary. Like Winston Churchill, Roosevelt was also drawn by the African romances of H. Rider Haggard. As a skinny lad of eight Theodore Roosevelt founded the Roosevelt Museum of Natural History in his bedroom in New York City, launching the collection with the skull of an Atlantic seal he had found displayed outside a fruit store on Broadway. He kept four pet mice, 'red-eyed velvety creatures, very tame for I let them run all over me'. At eleven he penned essays on ants and fireflies. By then the museum's collection numbered over 1,000 specimens, many labelled in Latin, and his young cousins were proud to serve as official anatomist and conchologist. The museum boasted a library, and a bank balance of $27.

By the age of thirteen, in 1871, Teddy Roosevelt was taking lessons in taxidermy. Already, like young Selous at Rugby, he was immersed in

President Theodore Roosevelt and Frederick Selous on a cow-catcher, Kenya, 1909

157

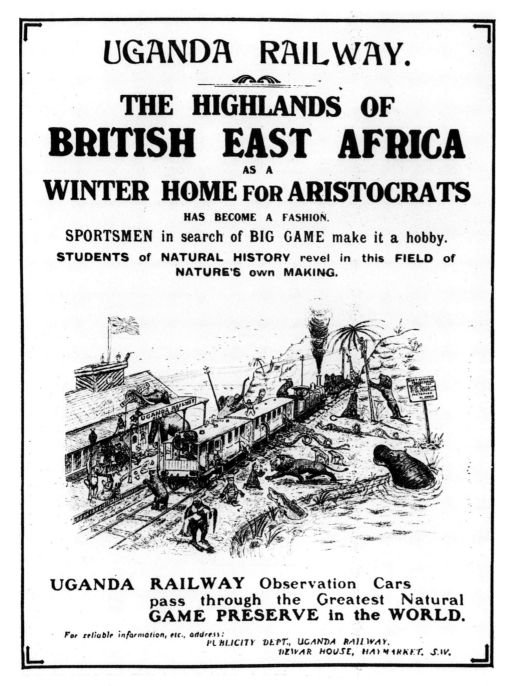

UGANDA RAILWAY.

THE HIGHLANDS OF
BRITISH EAST AFRICA
AS A
WINTER HOME FOR ARISTOCRATS
HAS BECOME A FASHION.
SPORTSMEN in search of BIG GAME make it a hobby.
STUDENTS of NATURAL HISTORY revel in this FIELD of
NATURE'S own MAKING.

UGANDA RAILWAY Observation Cars
pass through the Greatest Natural
GAME PRESERVE in the WORLD.
For reliable information, etc., address:
PUBLICITY DEPT., UGANDA RAILWAY.
DEWAR HOUSE, HAYMARKET. S.W.

Poster for the Uganda Railway

ornithology, keeping detailed notebooks of his bird sightings. At fourteen he stuffed and mounted the crocodile-bird and the lapwings he collected when the Roosevelts visited Egypt. A proper Yankee, in Alexandria he haggled in the market for a quail for the museum, cutting the asking price in half. Outside Cairo he shot a warbler for his collection, 'the first bird I ever shot and I was proportionately delighted'. He was using his first gun, a twelve-gauge pinfire Lefaucheux made in Paris, a temperamental weapon that frequently jammed shut, requiring a blow from a brick to open it. From then on he never stopped, even shooting a red-tailed chat off a column of the Rameses temple at Thebes.

158

Best of all, the family passed two months on an Arab sailing vessel, going up the Nile, the boy shooting birds with his father in the sandy bogs and palm forests along the river banks. Back on board, seated on the deck with his scalpel and arsenic, surrounded by curious barefoot sailors, the fourteen-year-old would skin and stuff his Senegal doves and hooded crows.

Thirty-seven years later, Theodore Roosevelt returned to Africa to hunt and collect specimens for a different museum, the Smithsonian Institution. This time he was more heavily armed, and a great deal heavier on his feet.

Recognized in Europe and America as the pre-eminent conservationist of his time, the President was also a keen hunter. Roosevelt loved nothing better than hunting pronghorn antelope in the Dakota Badlands. A student of bird songs, he listened to the melody of the Missouri skylark with more concentration than he gave to many senators.

By the time Roosevelt left Washington for his visit to east Africa in March 1909, he had created fifty-five wildlife refuges, expanded America's national parks, created his country's monument system, organized national and international conservation conferences, and generally provided the founding momentum for the conservation and environmental movement in the United States. More than anything, he popularized a sensibility, a respect for nature, a sense of trusteeship for the wilderness at a time when the phrase 'man against nature' still evoked a thrill of conquest.

As Governor of New York, Roosevelt advocated that the state should ban the use of bird feathers in articles of apparel, seventy years before the same principle was applied to the skins of leopards and cheetahs. He demanded that the Grand Canyon should for ever be spared from all development, and believed that 'Wild flowers should be enjoyed unplucked where they grow. It is barbarism to ravage woods and fields.' He was proud to share the camp fire of the inspirational environmentalist John Muir in the temple of the giant sequoias at Yosemite. 'Camping with the President was a remarkable experience. I fairly fell in love with him,' wrote Muir, the founder of the Sierra Club. 'I never had a more interesting, hearty and manly companion.'

Contemptuous of the timber barons who were destroying his country's woodlands, Roosevelt rejected the fraud that allows greed and destruction to masquerade as inevitable economic progress. He more than quadrupled the acreage of the nation's public forests and built the United States Forest Service, which came to administer one twelfth of the land of the United States. Although he hunted grizzlies in British Columbia and longhorn sheep in the Rockies, he probably saved more habitat and wildlife than any individual in history.

Still, it is fair to say that Roosevelt's personal hunting was sometimes sadly inconsistent with his statements and public policies. As a twenty-five-year-old, anxious to bag an American buffalo 'while there were still buffalo left to shoot', Roosevelt in 1883 boarded a train for the Badlands of the Dakota Territory. He carried a ·50 calibre English double rifle by Webley and a heavy Sharps ·45 buffalo gun that fired $1\frac{1}{4}$ oz of lead.

These were the final days for the hunted remnants of the vast, shaggy brown herds of American buffalo, or bison, as Teddy Roosevelt later insisted they be called. A few days before his arrival, the Sioux, their hunt sanctioned by the federal government, had slaughtered perhaps the last great herd in the Dakotas, said to be five thousand head. Now native hunters and white sportsmen were busily hunting down the remaining pockets across the western states.

After six days Roosevelt finally found his first buffalo. Impatient, inexperienced, a mediocre shot with bad eyesight, he chanced a long shot, hitting the animal poorly at 325 yards. Gamely he followed the bull until after dark, finally losing the wounded animal for ever in the dim moonlight. As he was to demonstrate a quarter of a century later in Africa, it was a lesson he never learned. He continued to take long shots under difficult conditions. But in a few days, hunting to the west in Montana, he finally killed a fine bull, 'his glossy fall coat shining in the rays of the sun'. As President, twenty-five years later, Roosevelt paid his debt to the buffalo, authorizing three sanctuaries, including the National Bison Range in Montana.

Long before he sailed into Mombasa in April of 1909, Roosevelt's energy as a hunter had aroused reactions varying from admiration to mockery. His hunting adventures were cartooned in the press and ridiculed by Mark Twain. As President he grew defensive and rarely hunted. Accustomed to holding the high moral ground himself, Roosevelt had no patience with his moralizing critics. He enjoyed deriding the notion that animals lived in a blissful state of nature, emphasizing instead that theirs was naturally a life of violence and iron cruelty. 'Game butchery,' he said, 'is as objectionable as any other form of wanton cruelty or barbarity; but to protest against all hunting is a sign of softness of head, not soundness of heart.'

Although he had bitter, animal-loving detractors both before and after the safari, most observers accepted the conclusion of the wildlife photographer C.G. Schillings. An increasingly fierce critic of heavy shooting, Schillings wrote in 1907 that 'President Roosevelt has always been one of the foremost pioneers in the movement for the preservation of wildlife in all its forms.' Schillings's friend Sir Harry Johnston, however, visiting the United States before the President set out, remarked, 'If I had my say, I would present a telephoto camera instead of a rifle to the President.'

For many, then and now, Roosevelt epitomized the apparent Jekyll and Hyde dilemma of the hunter-conservationist. In Europe, Africa and America, the most effective conservationists have often been the most dedicated hunters. It is difficult for non-shooters to accept this reality. They will not believe that serious hunters truly love and protect the creatures they kill. In fact, most hunters and conservationists share a love of nature. Critics of hunting often assume that the conservation efforts of hunters are merely self-serving, limited to prolonging their own depredations. This is an error both as to physical results and attitude. More interesting, it fails to perceive the inspiration of hunting. The protection of an animal or an acre also preserves the creatures that interrelate with it, including people. Hunters and fishermen everywhere, like Theodore Roosevelt and Frederick Selous, actively support conservation and environmental programmes from which they will never personally benefit.

The more complex error of perception, however, relates to the inner motives of hunters and fishermen. Why do people protect animals? Why do they hunt and fish, apart from the need for food? Why do they not simply enjoy wilderness and wildlife without killing?

Throughout most of mankind's experience, during the thousands of formative years of the Paleolithic era, man was a hunter. Hunting was man's first organized endeavour, his first craft and the central subject of his earliest art. Although in an earlier period parts of man's body, such as his molars and intestines, evolved to support him as a gatherer and grain-eater, the body and mind he has today largely developed as the body and mind of a hunter. His appendix, for example, once a large, essentially herbivorous organ, shrank to its present size, its function largely lost. Man required intelligent skills to obtain meat, and as he learned to hunt, his body and his instincts adapted.

The history of man's evolution from a primitive non-meat-eating primate to an armed, organized carnivorous hunter is a complex and contentious subject, rich in paleontological and anthropological debate. Dr Louis S.B. Leakey's discoveries of giant fossils in Tanzania's Olduvai Gorge, in the Serengeti National Park, establish east Africa as the last home of the giant animals of prehistory, and the nearby tools establish the proximity of early hunting man. Robert Ardrey, in *African Genesis*, concludes that the high veld of east Africa was 'the main stage for the dramatic emergence of man from the animal world', where we descended from carnivorous apes. 'We learned to stand erect in the first place as a necessity of the hunting life,' Ardrey explains. 'We learned to run in our pursuit of game across the yellowing African savannah.' Finally, man became what he is, 'a predator whose natural instinct is to kill with a weapon'.

In *The Naked Ape*, Desmond Morris studies man as a hairless ape from the analytical, comparative view of a zoologist. He finds that 'we are vegetarians turned carnivores', primitive predators whose forest-ape ancestors became ground-living hunting apes. Today we are prisoners of this 'carnivorous evolution', and our innate hunter's aggression now seeks such hunting substitutes as work, sport-hunting and gambling, outlets for the 'challenge, luck and risk so essential to the hunting male'.

The relationship between hunting and man's nature is inescapable. The more removed we become from nature, the deeper our need for our lost natural environment. Hunting and fishing are the most intense form of man's integration, or re-integration, with nature. In the fullest sense, hunting may be considered a return to basics, for it reactivates man's dormant physical senses. For many hunters, some of whom today use a bow and arrow, a hunt is more satisfying and more fair to the extent that it is conducted on a more equal basis with the animal, a more primitive basis, relying on fewer people, less sophisticated equipment and less transport.

Like it or not, the possibility of a kill at the end of the hunt brings an intensity of the senses that is not available on a non-shooting stalk. Thirst, fatigue and even pain are ignored during a hunter's chase, much as they would be during the heat of battle. This is not true of a hike, or a walk with a camera. Carried out, however, with the discipline of a true hunt, in silence and with mental and physical tenacity, a non-shooting stalk comes closest to the pleasure of hunting, if it is done without the incompatible distractions of photography.

The photographer is concerned with light direction, a clear view of the animal and, above all, a retainable object for the future. The hunter or stalker must be concerned with wind direction and a protected approach. He is committed to the present. You can have a brilliant day's hunting with no trophy, and even no shooting, but the photographer must have a picture. The photographer benefits from a tamed, accessible animal that will appear wild, but the hunter wants truly wild, elusive game. Much of even the best game photography is done from vehicles, itself an abandonment of the intimacy of the chase.

The visceral fulfilment of hunting explains why, even when it is not essential for food, it has been one of man's most pleasurable and sought-after activities. This is why the privileged have made it their chosen recreation, from Pharaoh Rameses II with his hunting chariot in 1270 BC, to Chairman Lenin with his powered hunting sled in 1920. In ancient Macedonia, in Victorian Bengal and in contemporary Hungary and Tanzania, the big game has been reserved for the privileged, whether by position or by wealth. In the United States, where hunting is more democratic than it is in Europe or Africa, there are today more than 17,000,000 licensed hunters.

As the Spanish philosopher Jose Ortega y Gasset expresses it in *Meditations on Hunting*, 'man is a fugitive from nature'. He can re-enter it by hunting. As a sport, hunting gives him a primitive renewal, a refreshment, reopening his instincts as 'the hunter's soul leaps out and spreads over the hunting ground like a net'. As one hunts, realities like terrain, wind, light and smell become not background conditions, as they are in hiking or photography, but active, moving participants in the tension between hunter and hunted, until 'the hunter feels tied through the earth to the animal he pursues'. In the final stalk of the best hunts, the hunter often imitates the animal, bending, running and crawling on its track. He moves, as if in a dance, in harmony with the wind and the cover, in what Ortega y Gasset calls a 'mystical union' with the game.

The best of the educated hunters, like Selous and Roosevelt, understand and feel this as they hunt. Some express it when they write, as Theodore Roosevelt did in his three books about the final days of wilderness hunting in the American west. Often these hunters are blessed with a rare intimacy with nature when young, and as they grow older they remain youthful. Intimate with nature, these hunters work to preserve it. Revelling in the detail of natural history, as Roosevelt did even in his last hospital bed in 1918, they seek to preserve the wilderness that they sense and understand more than other people.

In our own day, Britain's Prince Philip, the Duke of Edinburgh, carries on the tradition of the responsible hunter-conservationist. Like Roosevelt an effective world leader of the environmental movement and an active champion of species and habitat preservation, as President of the World Wildlife Fund, Prince Philip is a keen bird shooter and occasional deer hunter. When he is challenged by environmentalists who have little experience with either wildlife or the economic realities of habitat conservation, Prince Philip replies that, although 'There are anomalies and contradictions in the simultaneous conservation and exploitation of game, yet, paradoxically, therein lies their security.'

For many environmentalists, protecting animals is a moral imperative, but for some hunters it is also sensual. Frequently, at life's end, as they approach what Teddy Roosevelt called 'the rifle pits', the intensity of their memory turns to nature. Often they come to regret, as Roosevelt sometimes did, their own excessive shooting. When Roosevelt declined an easy second campaign for the presidency, and instead determined to go on safari, he was expressly conscious that time was limited, that the longer he delayed and the less young and active he was, the less close to nature he would be in the field. As he had said earlier, 'I am fond of politics, but fonder still of a little big-game hunting.'

The President planned his safari with loving care, using Frederick Selous and Edward North Buxton as his principal advisers. To make the safari a success, he deliberately used foresight and planning as substitutes for the lost physical prowess of his youth. Unable to get about well himself, as he explained in a letter to Selous, he brought his twenty-year-old son Kermit to replace him in the hard chases. After a twelve-year correspondence with Selous, he knew that the old hunter would understand his requirements, but he was disturbed when Selous and Buxton disagreed on a key point.

Buxton, experienced with Somali headmen, recommended that Roosevelt 'leave the Cook tourist element behind and trust to the native', hiring a 'black *shikari*' to undertake the day-to-day management of the safari. Selous, taking offence, scarcely a Cook tourist himself, disagreed. He knew that the huge safari would employ men of various tribes and would pass through different regions as it made its way north from Nairobi through Uganda to the Nile. Like many white hunters, Selous apparently thought that African hunters can be incomparable on their own terrain, but that they are less adaptable elsewhere. Accordingly, looking for men with a broad knowledge of Africa, he recommended Kenya's two most experienced professional hunters, R.J. Cuninghame and William Judd. The President took Selous's advice, and Cuninghame prepared to direct the expedition, which he organized with the help of Nairobi's premier safari outfitter, Newland & Tarlton.

Lord Cranworth, a director of N & T and a distinguished Kenya pioneer, who came out to the colony in 1906 for sport and profit, described the period from 1908 to 1914 as 'the palmy days of big-game shooting'. Newland & Tarlton put the safari together, and R.J. Cuninghame won high marks from his demanding client. Some suggest that Cuninghame was the model for the illustrations of Haggard's Allan Quatermain. Still others believe that the character Quatermain was based on Alan Black, an old hunter famous for leaving no trace whatever when he left camp, breaking even his wooden pipe matches into tiny fragments. But Cranworth, who knew them all, concludes that 'it was in fact that splendid hunter, Selous'.

Exhaustive preparations for Roosevelt's safari proceeded throughout 1908 and 1909 in Washington, London and Nairobi. The President enjoyed the work, fussing over the equipment, obsessive about each detail of his weapons. He invited African experts to the White House, notably the American hunter-photographer Carl Akeley, who once strangled a wounded leopard with his hands. Roosevelt had already lunched with Rider Haggard in Washington in 1905, and was to correspond with the writer after his return from Africa. He was proud to welcome the celebrated Colonel J.H. Patterson, the English engineer who killed the man-eating lions that feasted on the Indian railway coolies at Tsavo as the railhead moved west from Mombasa. Altogether perhaps twenty-eight Indians and a hundred Africans were killed by lion as they laboured to build the Uganda Railway across Kenya to Uganda. For a time in 1898 all work stopped until the man-eaters were destroyed.

The introduction that Selous wrote for Patterson's *The Man-Eaters of Tsavo* authenticated the details of that incredible story. Roosevelt had a boyish interest in the fastidious way the lions ate their kills. First their abrasive tongues licked the skin off their victims. Then they sucked the blood from the bodies before starting to eat them, feet first. On one occasion, the lions were driven off before they got to the coolie's head, which was sent back to the railhead camp for identification. The two colonels had much to discuss at the White House, swapping hunting tales and discussing weapons late into the night.

R.J. Cuninghame, known to the Swahilis as Bwana Medivu, 'the Master of the Beard'

As his light rifle, Roosevelt selected for African use his favourite thirty-calibre, bolt-action Springfield Sporter, custom made and adapted from the Springfield military rifle that normally carried a bayonet below the barrel, and specially mounted with a flattened Rocky Mountain Buckhorn sight. For heavier work he ordered a pair of the western classic, the Model 1895, lever-action ·405 Winchester. When the makers failed to satisfy the President's specifications, Roosevelt angrily returned the rifles, outraged that the narrow notch sight was 'the poorest rear sight ever used for game . . . It was entirely useless to send them out to me in such shape.'

Finally Winchester returned the perfected rifles, and the President hurried to the basement to test-fire them on his White House firing range. For his old campaign in Cuba, he had been equally fastidious, equipping his Rough Riders with the latest military rifle, the Krag bolt-action carbine. Roosevelt's concern about gunsights was partly provoked by his bad eyesight, a problem aggravated by a haemorrhage of the retina of his left eye, a boxing injury suffered in the White House in 1904. Although he kept it secret, and misled people by wearing ordinary spectacles, by 1908 the President had no sight whatever in his left eye.

Despite his patriotic preference for American weapons, Roosevelt delighted in his heaviest rifle, possibly the finest rifle ever made, a Royal grade Holland & Holland, double barrel ·500/450 Nitro Express. Never too busy for such

Right: Lord Cranworth coming ashore, Kilindini harbour, Mombasa, 1906

Below: Mombasa, 1906. Scene with the lawcourts and trolley lines. Trolleys were a principal means of transport

refinements, the President himself drew the design for the gunsight on his White House notepaper. Intended to stop the heaviest charging game, this rifle was commissioned as a present for Roosevelt by fifty-five English naturalists and sportsmen. Given to him to honour his work in establishing public parks and forests in the United States, 'in recognition of his service on behalf of the preservation of species', the rifle's donors included Buxton, Lord Curzon, Lord Lugard and Selous. Nearly eighty years later, firing this magnificent double rifle while on safari near the Ruvu River in Tanzania in 1986, I found it still in perfect condition.

Financed largely by Andrew Carnegie, and by the President's proposed writings, the $75,000 safari ($950,000 in 1988 currency) was also sponsored by Washington DC's Smithsonian Institution, often known as the National Museum. Annoyed by public criticism, Roosevelt repeatedly emphasized that he would not 'do any butchering', but would shoot to collect specimens for the Smithsonian and the American Museum of Natural History in New York. Like Randolph Churchill, he financed the expenses of Kermit and himself by journalism, writing articles for _Scribner's_ magazine, later to be published in book form as _African Game Trails_, for which he received a fee of $50,000 and a 20 per cent royalty on the book. In 1910, _African Game Trails_ was declared the 'Book of the Year' by New York's _Herald Tribune_.

The need to preserve thousands of skins and heads added enormously to the scale and cost of the safari, the largest ever mounted in Kenya. To assist with its scientific mission, the safari included three professional field naturalists recommended by the Smithsonian, two of them skilled in taxidermy. Although warned that the President was not an easy man, they all came to be impressed by his kindness, unfailing good humour and courage on safari.

After a tumultuous public send-off in New York harbour as the President set sail on the steamship _Hamburg_, he finally arrived in Naples on 5 April 1909 for his rendezvous with Frederick Selous. There the two men boarded another German vessel, the _Admiral_, for Mombasa, enjoying the mixed crowd of planters, missionaries and traders that shared their ship. Roosevelt was particularly impressed by 'the fine set of dashing young Englishmen' going out to join the colonial administration, feeling that he knew them already from the pages of his friend Rudyard Kipling.

Each day, as the _Admiral_ steamed south across the warm, smooth waters of the Red Sea and the Indian Ocean, Roosevelt and other hunters would gather around Selous on deck to hear his tales of Africa. Then the President would tell one of his favourite frontier stories, 'Cold Turkey' or 'Hell Roaring Bill Jones'. As a response, several passengers published a shipboard journal, _The Lookout_, its name a play on the weekly magazine _The Outlook_, for which the President was a contributing editor in New York. In a farewell letter to Roosevelt, _The Lookout_ lamented, 'How shall we miss that deck circle where under sunny skies we spent hours enthralled. Your tales will live for ever in our memory as our most precious reminiscences in the sear and yellow twilight of our lives.'

Loading Theodore Roosevelt's safari supplies, New York, 1909

Finally arriving off Mombasa on the night of 21 April, the *Admiral* garlanded from stern to bow in coloured flags, Roosevelt and his son debarked in a surf boat in cascades of driving rain, their heavy khaki clothes soaked through. Once the boat grounded, they were borne ashore in chairs carried by Africans. Then they were welcomed by the acting Governor of British East Africa, Sir Frederick Jackson, Africa's leading ornithologist and a close friend of Rider Haggard. Jackson provided his private railway carriage for the ride inland.

Kenya's white population welcomed the visit as recognition of their achievement in building the colony, and as a magnet to draw future visitors and capital, a point emphasized by the editors of Nairobi's *East African Standard*, as it urged the settlers to be on their best behaviour because 'the whole civilized world is watching'. The paper noted with approval the President's stated intention to abide by British East Africa's game laws.

The Uganda Railway from Mombasa to Nairobi was a suitable introduction to east Africa, providing the blend of adventure and luxury that made colonial life seducing. From the train he studied the spectacle of nature on the Athi plain, where the Swiss psychologist Carl Jung had been moved to say, 'This is the stillness of the eternal beginning, the world as it has always been.' After a day

Roosevelt and Selous on board *The Admiral*, 1909

with Selous on the cowcatcher bench, and a handsome dinner with Selous and Jackson, Roosevelt spent a comfortable night in the Governor's state coach. Only ten years earlier, workers and travellers on the same line had their rest interrupted by lions raging through the carriages.

Roosevelt himself met a survivor of an incident involving an Italian, a German and an Englishman, who in 1899 shared a sleeping-car as it passed the night at a siding near Tsavo. With the door open for a breeze, the German had climbed into an upper bunk, the Italian was stretched out on the floor, and the Englishman sat by a window, watching for a particular man-eating lion that his companions had come to shoot. The Italian woke to find the hind feet of the lion braced on his body as the animal reached up to kill the dozing Englishman. The German jumped from his bunk, falling on the lion, which took the Englishman in its mouth and leapt through the open window to complete the meal outside.

When Roosevelt's train pulled up at the little bush station of Kapiti Plains, the array of porters and tents suggested a small military expedition about to depart. Lined up at the station were *saises* (or grooms), gunbearers, tent men, fifteen uniformed askaris, and 265 Swahili porters in khaki shorts, blue puttees and blue jerseys. As Roosevelt stepped from the train, the porters cheered in greeting, 'Jambo, Bwana King, ya Amerik!' 'Hello, Mr King of America.' Behind the men were eight large tents for the hunting party, a mess tent, a skinning tent and fifty small tents for the Africans, all ranked behind a large American flag. It was not enough. In time the safari grew to 500 porters.

Each porter cost $4.50 a month. Under the Colony's game licensing system, when Roosevelt arrived each elephant cost $85 and each rhino or hippo $15, with a hunter limited to two of each. It was unlawful to shoot cow elephants, or bulls carrying less than 30 lb of ivory a side. Leopard and lion, still considered pests, required no licence.

The President was fortunate to be well financed, but he soon grew concerned. After only five weeks on safari, he wrote to Andrew Carnegie, indicating that without another $30,000 the scientific expedition could not be completed. Carnegie responded by cable, 'Rest easy. I will arrange.'

Once on the march, the safari caravan was often strung out over a mile, led by the flag and Africans playing a tin drum and an antelope-horn trumpet. Then came the 'tail' of porters bearing sixty-pound loads, including hundreds of animal traps, sixty barrels containing four tons of fine salt for curing skins, a long beam scale for weighing game, tins of Boston baked beans, and the President's 'Pigskin Library', *Paradise Lost*, *The Pickwick Papers* and fifty-seven other favourites, all specially bound to endure hard use. In the heat of the afternoons, when the safari paused, Roosevelt would rest and read under a flat-topped acacia tree, or sit with a book by the body of a dead beast while he waited for the skinners.

Despite the paramilitary organization of the President's safari, experts like Lord Cranworth felt that by 1909 caravan porters were managed on relatively sloppy lines. A man of high standards in everything, Cranworth recorded in

Roosevelt's tent in Kenya

From a photograph by Theodore Roosevelt

My boma when
I was camped

Above

T. R.

Kenya Chronicles that he himself had only once been able to afford a safari truly done in the grand, princely style. Used to rough western camping, however, the President considered his own safari to be luxurious, attended as he was by two tent servants, two saises and two gunbearers. To men habituated to the rich trappings of sport in India, however, as Cornwallis Harris had remarked seventy years before, African safaris were relatively lean.

Cranworth's own safari headman, Chandi, was a man of the old school, who ran camp and caravan without compromise. Chandi's estimate of a sixty-pound load exceeded that of the porters by about twenty pounds, and Chandi's opinion always prevailed. Tents were raised and lowered when notes were sounded on a bugle. Loads were laid out in precise order, and then lifted and set down only at a blast on the bugle. However long the march, there was no rest at the end. The instant their loads had been put down, the porters cleared brush and divided up into wood parties, water parties and latrine parties. Cranworth observed that the early safari pioneers had 'studied their comforts and reduced their attainment to a fine art'.

Safari near Lake Victoria, 1910

Roosevelt himself covered much of Kenya on horseback, usually on his stout sorrel Tranquillity. His ponies did not carry a light load. As he himself put it when deciding to face a lion where he stood, instead of remounting, 'an elderly man with a varied past which includes rheumatism does not vault lightly into the saddle'. Thanks to his sedentary life in Washington, the President earned the native nickname 'Tumbo', the Stomach, and was known among camp boys and porters as 'Bwana Tumbo'. In his own account of the safari, Roosevelt preferred to report that his camp name was 'Bwana Mkubwa', or Great Master. Kermit was known as 'Maridadi', the Dandy. The use of two names by the safari staff was an old custom. William Cotton Oswell reported that, in the 1850s, his African companions called him Tlaga, or On-the-Lookout, to his face, whereas behind his back he was known as 'Mfupa', or Bones, owing to his leanness.

Roosevelt often hunted with Cuninghame, 'lean, sinewy, bearded, exactly the type of hunter and safari manager one would wish for'. Occasionally he hunted with William Judd, a powerful man reputedly able to carry a mule on his shoulders. Some years later Judd was killed by an elephant that stamped on his face, a fate Judd had anticipated in a dream one night before, but mistakenly thought involved his friend J.A. Hunter. Disturbed, Judd had sought to warn Hunter to be careful. Kermit generally hunted with Leslie Tarlton, a wiry little Australian said to be the finest rifle shot in the colony.

On his first day's hunting, the President wounded a bull wildebeest at 400 yards, and a cow wildebeest at 350. Both were hit too far back, well behind the heart, and galloped out of sight, but Kermit, a spirited horseman, killed the bull after a hard, seven-mile ride. The cow was hunted down shortly before sunset by Sir Alfred Pease, soon to be the Roosevelts' host at his farm at Kitanga.

They were expensive guests. Visiting Washington, Pease had invited the President to stay at his hunting lodge, which he was then obliged to build when Roosevelt accepted. Pease himself was a man after the President's own self-image, equally at home with the powerful or in the bush, independent, tough and literate. They became sound friends, and Pease later dedicated his classic *The Book of the Lion* to 'the Honourable Colonel, Theodore Roosevelt'.

Pease had a deep regard for lions. A diligent student of their habits and history, he was impressed that the ancient Chinese and Egyptians succeeded in training lions as hunting and battle companions. Two weeks into the safari, Roosevelt had some hunting tales of his own, killing six lion while hunting with Pease at Kitanga.

Roosevelt wrote that it was 'the king of all sports' to hunt lion the way Pease did, galloping the animal down on horseback and then killing it on foot when it charged. Faster than a greyhound, at over 40 m.p.h., a charging lion can cover the last hundred yards in four or five seconds, although they rarely charge from over sixty yards. A shot in the heart may not stop it in time. Only a brain or vertebrae shot will do, and Pease did not want to lose a guest. The President, however, was protected not only by his expert companions, but also by his gold-mounted rabbit's foot, the gift of the heavyweight champion John L. Sullivan.

Cartoon drawn on the Roosevelt
safari with participants' signatures

Roosevelt's early lion kills were slightly messy. After unwittingly shooting a cub, he wounded his first big male at thirty yards, then missed, then wounded it again. The animal finally collapsed when Sir Alfred, Kermit and Roosevelt all fired together. Karamojo Bell would not have considered it sport. After shooting vainly at another from very long range, Roosevelt and Kermit shot from horseback at 150 yards, both missing, before Roosevelt steadied his Winchester on the shoulder of Simba, his sais, and wounded the lion. Two more shots and it was dead.

As the safari progressed, the President did better, making about half his kills at ranges of over 200 yards. He used his heavy Holland ·450 to hit, if not always to stop, buffalo, elephant and rhino. Occasionally the dangerous game was stopped by the professional hunters. During the safari the President and Kermit bagged 512 animals of over eighty species, including 17 lion, 11 elephant, 20 rhinoceros and 10 buffalo. Altogether the expedition collected and shipped home to the Smithsonian 4,900 mammals, 4,000 birds, 500 fish and 2,000 reptiles. Some of Roosevelt's specimens are still on display, and not all the original packing cases have yet been opened. In 1882, the Smithsonian welcomed 622 specimens from young Roosevelt's boyhood museum, including his Nile bird skins.

While the Smithsonian naturalists were preoccupied with their traps and taxidermy, skinning mole rats and snaring elephant shrews, curious little creatures with tiny upright trunks, Roosevelt was often absorbed by the bird life. Kenya contains over one thousand species of birds, more than any country outside the Amazon basin, and ornithologists have counted as many as a hundred species in a single day. Roosevelt paused to study the eared owls as

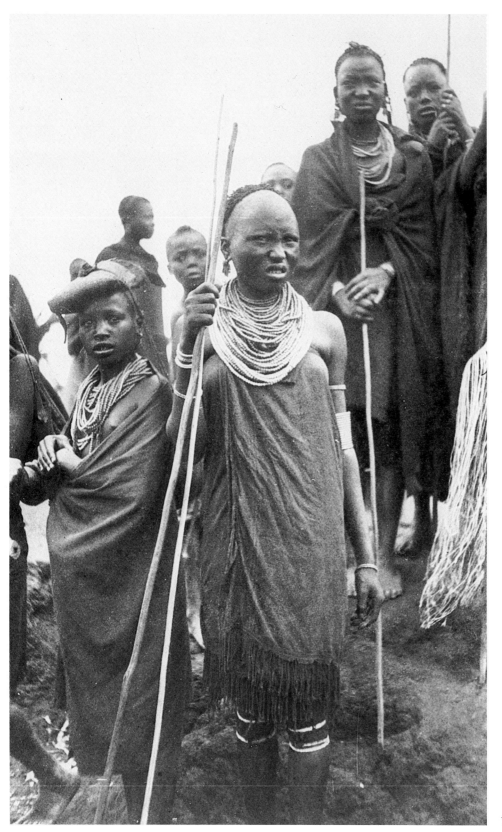

Young Kikuyu

they rose from the reeds, and the strange ways of the red-billed hornbills. The female hornbill is walled into a tree hole with mud, saliva and dung regurgitated in pellets by the male, who feeds her and the chicks through a tiny slit until she finally breaks out with her large, curved beak. Roosevelt admired the zigzag flight of the flappet lark, and the cunning of the weavers, which tie grass in knots over branches, building globe-like suspended nests with narrow entrance tunnels. The song of the flame-coloured pippits reminded him of his old companion, the Missouri skylark.

Although he preferred the wildlife, mishaps and adventures of life on safari, Roosevelt also enjoyed Nairobi. It was just his taste, an energetic combination of sophistication and wild-west adventure. Sometimes the elegant horse races of the afternoon were followed by the nocturnal gunfire that welcomed the visits of leopard and lion, as zebra and hartebeest stampeded through the town. Where else could he dine with three men each of whom had been mauled by a lion?

Hunting extensively in four countries, the Roosevelts enjoyed a rich diversity of companions, terrain and game. They shot with the finest hunters of the day, including Cuninghame, Judd, Pease, Tarlton, Delamere, Berkeley Cole, Quentin Grogan, Harold and Clifford Hill, and Philip Percival. In Kenya they travelled through the land of the Masai, Wakamba, Kikuyu, Dorobo, Samburu and Nandi. Roosevelt was impressed by the Nandi as lion hunters and the Dorobo as elephant hunters, and by the Masai, 'as graceful and sinewy as panthers'.

Philip Percival's wagon on the Theodore Roosevelt safari, 1909

Always energetic and eager for the morning, in Kenya he hunted hippo at Lake Naivasha and elephant in the mountain woodlands of the Aberdares. He hunted white-eared kob, a very dark brown, mid-sized antelope with heavy horns, in the papyrus marshes of the Sud along the White Nile, and sitatunga and giant eland in Uganda, in terrain so hot that a rifle barrel was untouchable and the ground crippled the feet of the porters. In the Lado the safari required new porters, unknown to the headmen, so Cuninghame required each to wear a numbered tag about his neck, made from the specimen labels sent by the Smithsonian.

As the Roosevelt caravan moved north, it was shadowed by another safari, a substantial expedition financed by the Associated Press. Roosevelt had dreaded the attentions of the press when he planned his safari, but most of the papers were content with reports from Naples, Mombasa and Cairo. The AP, however, determined to provide its syndicated newspapers and readers with prompt coverage of the greatest safari in history, was careful to select a resourceful reporter who would be congenial to his subject. It chose Captain W. Robert Foran, formerly of the Indian Army and the British East African Police, an enterprising man familiar with the terrain.

Foran became friendly with Roosevelt on board the ship to Mombasa and the President permitted Foran to keep himself informed, in order to preclude inaccurate stories in the press. Foran's safari hung back at a respectful distance, as the Captain stayed in touch through runners and tapped into the Uganda telegraph line to get his stories out. 'Rex' was the codename for the President's expedition.

As the safaris pushed across Uganda towards the Lado Enclave, Foran became seriously ill with a hernia or stomach abscess. The President offered the services of Colonel Edgar Mearns, the ornithologist and physician assigned by the Smithsonian. An operation was performed successfully under canvas, without anaesthetic. Never squeamish, Roosevelt acted as male nurse while Mearns made the incisions, the President holding the bandages and chatting with the conscious patient. In his own lengthy account of the safari, however, Roosevelt never once mentions Foran's name.

Hardy himself, the President hunted when every other white man on his safari, except Kermit, was down with fever or dysentery. For five days he himself suffered attacks of fever, a recurrence from his old Cuban campaign. As a result, his hand shook when he raised his rifle to bag a hippo. Interested, too, in the political and social conditions as he travelled, the President commented that, unlike the Kenya highlands, Uganda could never be 'white man's country'. Despite this limitation, the children at Uganda's Church of England mission received the President with the 'Star Spangled Banner', recited phonetically from their text:

> O se ka nyu si bai di mo nseli laiti
> Wati so pulauli wi eli adi twayi laiti silasi giremi . . .

Foran and Cuninghame arranged for the President to hunt in the Lado Enclave with one of the last great elephant hunters, Quentin Grogan. Brother of the famed 'Cape-to-Cairo Grogan', who walked much of the length of Africa to win a lady's hand, Grogan was an expert in the Lado, and his assignment was to help Roosevelt bag white rhinoceros in their famous refuge. When the presidential party arrived in the Lado by Nile steamer in January 1910, Grogan was fresh from a great bush banquet. Celebrating New Year's Eve, 1909, eight elephant hunters assembled at Koba as guests of John Boyes, a seaman shipwrecked on the African coast in 1896 who came to be recognized as the King of the Kikuyu.

The hunters had gathered in the hope of meeting President Roosevelt, and Grogan found it a more congenial evening than the extraordinary egg and wine orgies of the Belgians. When Theodore Roosevelt arrived a week later, he judged the waiting men to be 'a hard-bit set, these elephant poachers. There are few careers which make heavier demands upon the daring, the endurance, and the physical hardihood of those who follow them.'

Both in his articles and in his unpublished memoirs, Grogan is unusual in admitting his fear as a hunter, specifically his dread of hunting at night and his terror of lions. The impossible speed and carnivorous ferocity of a lion frightened him far more than the tramplings and gorings that could be the price of a good elephant hunt. Elephants, of which he killed eighty, also alarmed him,

Roosevelt returns from a day's eland hunt

Quentin O. Grogan in Uganda, 1911

particularly when he found himself surrounded in tall bamboo, barely able to make his way, while the animals cut through like locomotives. Spotting fresh elephant tracks, or steaming dung, Grogan was at once tense with excitement, his stomach leaping, his imagination racing, almost panicked, until his nerves steadied to the chase. A careful shooter, Quentin Grogan did not fire at the finest bull he spotted: a towering animal which carried tusks so long and heavy, approaching 200 lb a side, that it was obliged to hold its head high so the tusks did not drag on the ground.

A charming gentleman, who had the hard shafts of Sudanese male bamboo fashioned into walking-sticks by Briggs in London, Grogan frequently hunted alone with the President, who described him as 'about twenty-five, a good hunter and a capital fellow. We were great friends.' For his part, Grogan liked Roosevelt more every day, growing very fond of 'the old man', whom he found to be as excited as a schoolboy as he tramped for hours through tangled six-foot grass. Grogan had only two complaints. He thought young Roosevelt 'about as dull as anyone could be', and he deplored the lack of alcohol at the President's camp fire. Grogan used to plant Sutton's vegetable seeds whenever he thought he might return to a camp, for he believed that the lack of a proper diet was the reason why so many hunters 'have gone west'. Always taking proper nourishment, Grogan himself lived on into the 1960s, the last of the old elephant hunters, complaining impatiently about the decline of colonialism and the 'dreadful commercial disease called tourism', asking himself in his memoirs, 'Why does man spoil everything in the name of progress?'

In his memoirs, Grogan records that the President became very candid when they hunted alone, particularly when they rested under a tree during the heat of the day. One afternoon they discussed the painful difficulties of race relations in the United States. It was a time when lynchings were not uncommon and the progressive President, a close friend of the American black leader Booker T. Washington, was concerned about racial oppression and the protection of individual rights. Grogan asked him, 'If by pressing a button, you could eliminate all the negroes in the United States, would you press it?' Roosevelt replied, 'I would jump on it with both feet.' Without a button, asked Grogan, what was the solution? 'As far as I can see, integration is the only answer.'

Two years later, when Grogan wrote to the American hunter after he had been wounded by a pistol shot during the 1912 Bull Moose presidential campaign, Roosevelt replied, 'I did not mind the shooting at all. It was not the kind of incident that would disturb even a second-rate elephant hunter.' Then, after his signature, the President characteristically reminisced, 'I often think of our hunting days together, and wish I could live them over again.'

As the safari came to an end, steaming down the Nile for Khartoum on the way to Cairo in March of 1910, Teddy Roosevelt recognized some familiar birds, reminders of his boyhood expedition thirty-seven years before. His old victims, the crocodile plovers, desert larks and green bee-eaters, rose to greet him. He found it painful taking leave of his personal retainers, with whom he had shared so much fun and adventure. He had been touched several times to detect affection in their dealings with him and Kermit, and he always kept a special place in his heart for the men with whom he shared the trail, whether in the Badlands or the Sudan. As he kept his diaries, he carefully mentioned every man by his African name, and wrote more about their personal qualities than he did about his elegant European hosts.

Writing shortly after he returned home, Roosevelt justified the heavy safari shooting in terms of science and meat for his vast retinue, protesting too much in his narrative that he and Kermit shot only from necessity In fact he shot Cape buffalo at the age of fifty much as he had shot Dakota bison at twenty-five, for what he called 'the strong eager pleasure of it'. Nor can it be justified on the theory that it was the accepted standard of the day, for even his contemporary white admirers in Kenya were sharply critical.

Most distressing was the President's greatest abuse as a hunter-conservationist, the killing in the Lado Enclave of nine white rhinoceros, including four cows and a calf, and the wounding of two other calves. A student of the subject, he knew well that these animals already had been exterminated in southern Africa and were virtually extinct in most of east Africa.* The President himself wrote that no African animal is 'in danger of imminent extinction, unless it be the white rhinoceros'. His licence allowed for six, and he wanted two family groups for museums, with a calf for each. He and Kermit shot approximately one third of all the white rhinoceros that they were able to find, so impressing the locals that to this day the site is known as Rhino Camp.

Roosevelt's first white rhinoceros was asleep when he shot it, and as it rose he was struck by its resemblance to Cornwallis Harris's artful drawing of many years before. The naturalist in him was intrigued by the distinctive qualities of the square-mouthed white rhino, six feet tall, with long, barrel-shaped heads, once known to hunters as Burchell's rhinoceros. He observed that they were grazers, not browsers, feeding only on grass, and generally did not leave their dung in heaps. He noted, however, that both types of rhino are three-toed ungulates, or hooved animals, of the tapir or horse family, with one predominant toe. The hippopotamus, also an ungulate, is of the cloven-hooved family, like the cow or pig, with two principal digits.

He observed that the tick birds that accompany the rhino also vary. The black rhino in Kenya are hosts to the cow heron, a type of white egret. The Lado's white rhino had as their watchmen the black-legged, yellow-toed egret, which deposited their whitewash liberally on the shoulders of their massive companions, even perching on a dead calf.

Roosevelt's friend Lord Cranworth, a keen but restrained hunter himself, deplored 'the slaughter which he and his party perpetrated', later asking, 'Do those nine white rhinoceros ever cause ex-President Roosevelt a pang of conscience or a restless night? I venture to hope so.'

One feature of Roosevelt's hunting that did not impress the Kenya sportsmen was his habit of taking shots at, and occasionally wounding, animals at long distances, particularly as he had bad vision and a slow horse, and was not a reliable shot. The President's basic tactic was to spot the game and start shooting. He frequently fired at distances exceeding 300, and occasionally 400 or even 500 yards. He missed one lion at over 600 yards. Even at the end of his safari, when his shooting and sensibilities had improved somewhat, Roosevelt fired off more than two magazines at a retreating bushbuck. Often he relied on what he called the 'Ciceronian theory, that he who throws the javelin all day must hit the mark some time.'

The President often seemed impatient with the careful stalks on foot that are generally required for a close, sure shot. As Cranworth put it with affection, 'Colonel Roosevelt's bulk and conversational powers somewhat precluded him from tracking.'

* At the present time, the survival of the white rhinoceros is principally due to conservation efforts in South Africa, where over a thousand have been exported from Natal in recent years for reintroduction in other habitats.

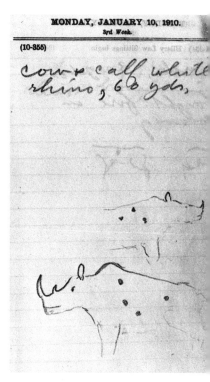

Page from Roosevelt's 1910 diary showing where he hit cow and calf white rhinoceros

Page from a letter written by Roosevelt on safari

Frederick Jackson found the President to be charming, alive with what the British always consider to be naïve American candour, and altogether the most interesting man he had ever met. But he found Teddy Roosevelt's account of buffalo hunting with a fusillade from 'backers-up' at two hundred yards, as three animals finally dropped and the wounded fled, to be 'most unpleasant reading'. Jackson himself was famed for patient, tireless stalks to close range, and for his rigorous personal rule that it was a disgrace to lose a wounded animal. He scorned telescopic sights and hunting lion with bait. Jackson was astounded by the President's statement about his wounded wildebeest, that 'as ammunition was of no consideration, I continued to shoot at long range until it disappeared over the brow'.

When Frederick Jackson himself wished to hunt the elusive bongo, he designed special dark clothing for camouflage in the forest, and carefully blackened his face and hands. At 500 lb and 4 ft at the shoulder, bongo are the largest of the forest antelope. Wary and unapproachable, they are a favoured quarry of experienced hunters. During his interminable bongo stalks, Jackson in his lifetime never once fired a shot. Although he spotted several among the shadowy branches, their large ears and striped rufous coats giving them away as they bent to eat the lower vegetation, he never had the opportunity for a clean shot and would not risk a wounded animal.

The Roosevelts also hunted bongo, learning that they require long stalks on foot in thick country. Patience, fitness and good eyesight are useful qualities in their pursuit. The President did his sporting best for ten days, but never saw a bongo. Kermit, hunting with the pioneer Kenya settler and sportsman Berkeley Cole, wounded one that got away, then fired at a small patch of striped chestnut hide lurking in the trees, killing a baby, and finally wounded two others, securing a female.

The professional hunters themselves generally shared the strict hunting ideals of men like Lord Cranworth and Jackson. But, then as now, they tended to indulge and protect their clients up to a point, permitting a degree of hunting abuse they would never tolerate in themselves or their sons. Thus profit and hospitality bent the rules, particularly if the hunter was eminent or if tolerance appeared to be in the country's interest. There is no record of Cuninghame, Judd or Grogan ever restraining the Roosevelts, and they personally remained loyally discreet about the excesses, as professional hunters tend to do today. Grogan, indeed, writes that every hunter sometimes breaks the rules, and so, as with many moral issues, the question of degree raises its fuzzy head.

Sir Alfred Pease considered that wounding big game lightly was dangerous to the hunter, and unfair to the animal if it survived. After dismounting, he favoured shooting charging lion at twenty-five yards, a fine drill, as a rushing lion comes in at incredible velocity and can leap over twelve yards in its last bound. After considerable study and experience, Pease concluded that no hunter ever loses his nerve after a lion begins to charge. There is not time, and the effort to survive takes over automatically. Even if the lion is literally on top of the hunter, Pease recommended resisting to the end, citing a friend who, unlike Livingstone, struggled as a lion dragged him away by his shoulder, stabbing the lion three times with a small knife. The lion then dropped the man and went off to die. The man survived.

In his book on lion, Pease spoke for the best of the colonial hunters, expressing not merely love of adventure and the hunt, but respect and understanding for natives and animals.

> The generation to which I belong has seen Africa yield up her secrets. I have loved the chase not only for its own sake, but even more for where it has taken me. I possess memories I would not exchange for all the wealth and distinction the world can give. I love these years in Africa as I do the shade of palms and the sound of waters after the dust and toil of a desert march. You go out to Africa to see savages, and you find them only on your return.

Pease, and other top hunters who shared safari sport with the President, all respected his courage, youthful enthusiasm and love of the country. Lord Cranworth said the President conquered not only the animals, but 'the heart of everyone with whom he came in contact'. The Englishman blamed the shooting excesses on the President's need to satisfy his publisher by getting a record bag, and on American hunting attitudes. The American concern for results instead of method is a point of distinction that English sportsmen make even today. Cranworth found the sporting President very perceptive, particularly when he asked, 'Cranworth, are you quite sure your country is big enough?'

Lord Delamere, the leader of the white settler community and the brother-in-law of Berkeley and Galbraith Cole, was charmed by Roosevelt, who was his guest for ten days at Delamere's splendid farm, Equator Ranch. The President saluted his enterprising host as a 'leader in the work of taming the wilderness, of conquering for civilization the world's waste spaces. No career can be better worth following.'

Altogether, Teddy Roosevelt revealed much of himself on safari: his remarkable energy, his need for both privacy and display, the demanding self-image that required him to justify his own excesses, his sense of family and history, and his admiration for men who choose a life close to the wilderness, men 'with a little iron in their blood'. First among these was Selous. Much of the President's character emerges in his correspondence with Frederick Selous, and in the safari writings of the two men. Perhaps nowhere else does Roosevelt expose so clearly his melancholy, his need to be respected by the manly characters whose company he always sought, and his wish to be remembered not as a killer of animals, but as a lover of the natural world around him.

The desire to establish one's manly credentials in the field, and specifically to be respected by one's professional white hunter, is often the most important trophy a client seeks on safari, and Roosevelt was no exception. Later white hunters came to perceive that this manly affirmation is a valuable commodity to be sold to their clients, in some cases with great skill and profit.

Fifty years later, the President's grandson Kermit Roosevelt, going on his own safari with his own son Kermit, studied Selous's books and the hunter's correspondence with Teddy Roosevelt. Returning from Africa, Kermit Roosevelt wrote, 'Frederick Courtenay Selous was, next to TR, the most memorable figure I came to know in Africa, although he, like TR, had been dead for forty years. Selous's books, and the letters he and TR exchanged over the many years of their friendship, gave me a deeper understanding of TR than anything else.'

For years Roosevelt had ridden and hunted the most beautiful retreats of the American west, but he came to love the bush as he did the Badlands. He compared the scattered thorn bushes to sage-brush. He delighted in the deep-green wild fig trees that dappled the hills, in the scented yellow blossoms of the thorny mimosas, and in the sweet peas on which the ostrich fed. Few men can have come to Africa as prepared as he was to relish the nature and the sport. A lifetime of fascination with every form of wildlife, forty years of reading, hunting and specimen-collecting from Alaska to Egypt, and many a camp fire had all prepared him well. As interested in his first oryx as he had been in the seal's skull on Broadway forty-two years before, Roosevelt retained his boyish enthusiasm for nature.

> I cannot describe the beauty and unceasing interest of these African rides, in the wild, lonely country, through the teeming herds of game. It was like retracing the steps of time for sixty or seventy years, back in the days of Cornwallis Harris and Gordon Cumming, the palmy times of the giant fauna of South Africa.

One of the few regrets expressed by Roosevelt about his grand safari was that he did not shoot on his fifty-first birthday, 27 October 1909. There is no record of whether he lost weight on safari. Roosevelt always enjoyed evidence of his hardy rigour and self-discipline, and he records that he denied himself at midday, condemning 'the parlour or drawing-room sportsman' who eats an elaborate lunch. But he relished his tea and gingersnaps upon returning to camp, waiting hungrily for his favourite dinners of elephant-trunk soup, oryx tongue and ostrich liver. He was particularly fond of heart, especially giraffe and ostrich, and one evening had fun toasting slices of elephant heart on a pronged stick over the fire.

Perhaps most of all, Roosevelt loved the end of the African day, heading back to camp as 'the red sunset paled to amber and opal and all the vast, mysterious African landscape grew to wonderful beauty in the dying twilight', then riding in by moonlight, the bush shining about him like silver, with lion pelts swinging from poles as the Africans chanted and his camp fire sparkled in the distance.

6. NAIROBI

Home Port

The Rift Valley, Kenya

When Teddy Roosevelt arrived in 1909, Nairobi was a wild ten-year-old, alive with an exotic frontier spirit that blended European, African, Asian and Arab influences in one booming village. The first outpost of civilization was the Norfolk Hotel, built in 1904, where the manager of the Boma Trading Company, accustomed to skirmishing with Abyssinian brigands and bartering donkeys and beeswax on the northern frontier, would enter the dining-room on his mare and jump over a dinner table without disturbing the silver.

Already the town brought together the wildness of Dodge City, the commercial enthusiasm of a young Shanghai, and the abandon of Brussels the night before Waterloo. Goanese merchants and Masai spearmen mingled with land-hungry settlers from the Transvaal and the House of Lords as rickshaws, camels and ox-carts tangled in the open street, alternately thick with red dust or deep in mud. For the rest of the century, the character of Nairobi, and what it represented, would be part of every African safari.

Ten years before, in 1899, the railhead of the Uganda Railway, having struggled three hundred painful miles from Mombasa, had reached the swampy flatland of the Nairobi River, named for the Masai word for cold, due to its source in the chilly waters of the Aberdare range. It was the last opportunity to place a railyard on the flats at 5,500 feet before the track scaled the Kikuyu escarpment and then plunged down on its way north-west to Lake Victoria. Already the chief engineer, George Whitehouse, had planned the station, the repair yards and the location of the town centre, building his own bungalow on a hill, with rows of tents laid out on the plain below. Soon Indian traders and railway coolies were sharing the new town with English adventurers and employees of the Imperial British East Africa Company, and with the local Kikuyu and Masai. Their common language became Swahili, a mixture of

185

'The Lunatic Line', the Uganda Railway

coastal African dialects influenced by Arabic, Portuguese and English. The root term *sawahil* means 'coasts' in Arabic.

Known as the British East Africa Protectorate until 1920, in 1900 the land of Kenya was thought to be a useless region that had to be crossed in order to reach what became Uganda, then widely recognized among missionaries and empire builders as the jewel of east-central Africa. There the British took control in 1895, the same year that the Kaiser declared what is now Tanzania to be German Crown Land. It was the time of the Berlin Conference of 1884–5, when, with a colonial arrogance that seems incomprehensible today, fourteen powers met in Europe to divide up Africa.

The Uganda Railway, the 'Lunatic Express', was designed, at first, to make Uganda accessible and to incorporate it firmly into the British sphere of influence. Nearly 15,000 workers were brought from India to build it. The railway's surprising cost, £8m, and the expense of maintenance, soon made the

Settler wagons crossing the Njoro Plains, c. 1908

A settler wagon

British administration look for new revenues to support it, and that meant developing a Kenya economy to nourish the railroad. That in turn meant white settlers, and in 1903 the first arrived. Until that year, less than one dozen Europeans were cultivating land in the vast territory of Kenya, over four times the size of England.

Characteristically, British colonial policy was ambivalent. Contrary to anti-imperialist legend, there was no coordinated purpose by British government, commerce and religion to expand British territory and power. From the arrival of the first settlers in 1903 until Kenya received full independence sixty years later, the white settlers in Kenya, like their cousins in Rhodesia, were at sharp odds with the colonial authorities. Generally, the government sought to preclude racial conflict by restricting the acquisition of land by Europeans and Asians. The policy problem, expressly recognized from the beginning, was to balance settler ambitions with native rights. This inherent conflict, focusing on land, is not quite dead today, and continues to influence issues of game and habitat that are at the core of the safari business.

At the centre of European settlement was a lion hunter from Somaliland, Hugh Cholmondeley, the third Baron Delamere. A hot-tempered Eton dropout without the money to sustain his extravagant sporting tastes, Delamere first went on safari in Somaliland with several other young bloods in 1891. They were escorted by a professional white hunter who complained to Delamere's trustee about the youths' profligacy and intemperance. But the hunter admired young Delamere's hard stalking and his courage with lion. Thereafter the young man returned yearly, poorer but more skilled, hunting on his own, until in 1894 he was savaged by a lion that seized him by the leg. Abdulla Ashur, Delamere's Somali gunbearer, threw himself on the lion and was mauled in turn before Delamere, his leg broken, recovered his rifle and drove off the animal. As the injured men lay in camp that night, they were kept awake by a roaring din as a pack of hyena finished off the wounded lion. Like most lion wounds, the infected leg festered and grew black as the young hunter made his way back to Berbera. Twice each day he stopped the march, lancing the wound with his knife to drain off the poison. For the rest of his life he wore a special boot to reduce a painful limp. The incident taught Delamere respect for both lions and Somalis. Later, when at sea, an English ship's captain once abused Ashur as he came on deck. Enraged, Delamere knocked the captain overboard into the Gulf of Aden.

Back again in Berbera in 1896, Delamere set out to the south with a doctor, a photographer, a taxidermist and two hundred camels. He was determined to cross the untracked southern desert of the waterless Haud, the Ogaden and Gallaland, and proceed through hostile Abyssinia to Lake Rudolph in northern British East Africa. Not much changed since the days of Cornwallis Harris, the Abyssinian slave dealers and hunters of the 1890s considered a rhinoceros to be worth four men, a lion ten, and an elephant forty. Many lions and hardships later, Delamere in 1897, at twenty-seven years old, emerged from his desolate sandy trek into the green, park-like highlands of central Kenya. They were to be his life.

Before him was a paradise of clover-sprinkled fields, clear icy streams and cool cedar forests rising 5,000–8,000 ft above sea-level, and in the distance the bamboo thickets, snowfields and glaciers of Mt Kenya, 17,000 ft at its peak. As Elspeth Huxley expressed it in 1935 in her evocative biography, *White Man's Country*, the highlands seemed to Delamere a modern Eldorado, the 'promised land, the realization of Rider Haggard's dream of a rich and fertile country hidden beyond impenetrable desert and mountains'.

Fortunately, much of the highlands and other regions of Kenya best suited to Europeans were virtually empty, with a population of under one person to the square mile, one fiftieth of the density of Nigeria at the time. Unlike the Cape in the seventeenth century, there were no Bushmen. The rare Masai that sometimes wandered in the highlands were relatively recent immigrants,

Lord Delamere, third left, in Somaliland, 1897, after hunting warthogs

thought to have raided down from the north a century or a century and a half before.

Occasionally, there were also small groups of Dorobo, primitive survivors of clans displaced by the Kikuyu and Masai. The term Wandorobo, given to various remnants of Kenya's earliest tribes, was the Masai word for 'miserable people'. In 1900 all the Masai in the country numbered less than 50,000. The tribe was dedicated to grazing and cattle raiding, holding the belief that god had originally given the Masai all the cattle in the world, a generous allotment since a bride cost only three heifers and two bullocks.

Each young Masai warrior, or *moran*, elegant, idle and proud, his slender frame and lean Nilotic features glistening red with ochre and animal fat, was required to blood his spear with a dead enemy. Nomadic stockherders, who hunted lions in spearing hunts rather like the Tswanas of Cornwallis Harris's day, the Masai preferred the lower plains to the high country, and there were no native dwellings whatever in the land found by Delamere.

For a time, under the British governor Sir Charles Eliot, European settlers were encouraged to take up farms of 640 acres, one square mile, or grazing lands of 5,000 acres at nominal cost. At first there were few takers. Some settlers made special applications to secure larger properties at higher prices. The total land made available for European settlement, essentially unoccupied at the time, was less than 10 per cent of the country. By 1914 there were 6,000 settlers, most struggling with little capital, arriving at their wild plots on mule wagons piled with tin bathtubs, bags of seed and rifles, like nineteenth-century pioneers in South Africa and the American west. Although there was never the heavy fighting that characterized efforts to occupy native lands elsewhere in Africa and America, nothing was easy. Supplies were precious, markets were distant, labour was scarce, and the inviting bush was thick with hidden enemies, the exotic diseases that struck people, animals and crops.

Delamere, mortgaging himself to the bone by pledging his Cheshire estates, borrowing and scrounging wherever he could find a pound, accumulated two great properties totalling 142,000 acres, Equator Ranch and Soysambu. Both were located in the Rift Valley, the giant fault in the earth's crust that runs from Mozambique to the Red Sea. He held the 100,000-acre Equator Ranch on a ninety-nine-year lease at an annual rental of one halfpenny per acre, some £200 (£6,400 today), at the time considered excessive, in addition to an obligation to invest £5,000 (£160,500 today) in its development. Equator Ranch was in totally unoccupied land west of the Masai country. Delamere finished assembling Soysambu in 1906 by acquiring land from other settlers. Each transfer of over 5,000 acres had to be approved by the Secretary of State for the Colonies in London, and Soysambu was the last large assemblage approved by the government.

Masai warriors

On these estates Delamere and his wife lived for years in mud and grass hovels, rising at 5 a.m., checking the herds and crops, cutting open dead sheep to identify the killing diseases, importing and testing varieties of wheat to create strains impervious to rust fungus, laying irrigation pipes, building a motorized plough from the ruins of railway equipment, establishing Kenya's first sawmill and refrigerated meat-packer, and importing bulls from England, rams from New Zealand and seeds from Australia, endlessly testing, breeding and refining to create the animals and crops that would survive in Africa.

As he struggled, Delamere learned a tolerant affection for the Masai who pilfered his cattle, and for the game that ate his crops and killed his sheep. Giving up hunting as a sport, shooting only to eat, usually the Thomson's gazelle that provided his daily Tommy chops, Delamere made his farms into game sanctuaries.

The Masai became his stockmen, grazing their cattle with his, occasionally stealing a few for their own herds. By day they carried the umbrellas he gave them against the sun and the rain, standing stork-like on one leg, the other foot braced against their knee. By night they wore the black greatcoats Delamere had made for the cool highland darkness. Like some other old hunters, Delamere came to favour the company of his African companions to that of most Europeans, typically passing the evening before a fire chatting with the Masai herders who squatted around him in his hut, some sitting on the seat removed from his mule buggy. With no door and holes for windows, Delamere's simple huts did not intrude on the African landscape. As the men spoke of cattle and lions, Lady Delamere's china and Georgian silver sparkled in the flickering light, the mahogany sideboards and oak tallboys resting at crazy angles on the packed earthen floors.

Pioneer life soon made the Delameres practical and resourceful. Requiring bonemeal as a fertilizer to help vines grow up the side of the hut at Equator Ranch, Delamere had a deep hole dug at the base of the plants. Elspeth Huxley records that he then led a sick ox up to the hole, drew his revolver and shot the animal so it fell neatly into the waiting grave. The vines flourished.

Other problems were harder to solve. Sheep, imported and then crossed with native ewes, suffered and died from lung sickness, foot rot, intestinal worms and large grubs that bred in the sinus cavities behind their eyes. All Delamere's Hereford cattle, and many others, died from viral pleuro-pneumonia, redwater tick fever, blue tongue, East Coast fever and other afflictions. Lion and Masai took their share. While Delamere grappled with these adversaries, assisted by a shepherd and a dairyman he had brought from England, and guided by scientific tests he directed in Nairobi, Lady Delamere struggled to breed pigs, chickens and ostrich.

Soon Delamere and the other new farmers began to participate in the inevitable conflicts between wild game and farming and ranching. Just as the giraffe ripped down the telegraph line along the Uganda Railway, so rhino swept through the 150 miles of wire fencing imported by Delamere. Some antelope would leap even a five-foot fence to get at the crops. Hippopotamus trampled irrigation pipes and devoured the precious lucerne grass brought from England. Worst of all, it became evident that the domestic cattle were being ravaged by the brown ticks and various parasites whose natural hosts were buffalo and other game.

At the same time, planting and fencing, irrigation and the domestic use of waterholes, upset the movements and feeding habits of the wild animals. British East Africa's early game laws strictly limited the shooting colonists could do on their own farms. The white settlers resented these restrictions as bitterly as many African farmers do today. In 1905 Delamere himself was prosecuted for shooting animals that were eating his crops. He was fined, but his public outrage secured a relaxation in the law to permit farmers to shoot zebras and other animals known to damage their crops.

Nearly a century later, these same difficulties, relating to land use, disease and water, are today the crux of one of the two threats to the survival of Africa's wildlife: the land hunger of a growing population. (The second threat is poaching.) Lord Delamere was among the first to perceive the need to plan a balance between game preservation, limited hunting and development.

As early as 1900, at the time of the international wildlife conference in London, Delamere suggested the creation of a game reserve at Baringo in the Rift Valley. After this was accomplished, he developed a more sophisticated proposal. The Masai do not eat game, existing on the blood and milk of their cattle. Occasionally they feast on cattle or eland, which they regard not as wild game, but as 'god's cattle'. Roaming vast areas as they moved their herds, the Masai were habituated to killing lions and less warlike Africans. To protect both game and Masai while freeing other land for development, Delamere conceived the notion of combining inalienable Masai land with game preserves, an idea that has since led to the preservation of both wildlife and Masai customs over vast reaches of Kenya and Tanzania.

Occasionally, however, the lion and leopard grew too numerous and destructive for even Delamere's taste, and he would use his old safari skills to cut down on the toll of the predators. Often his guests, anxious to bag lion, would do the job for him. So in 1912 Delamere invited the American sportsman and motion-picture photographer Paul Rainey to Soysambu with the famous pack of lion dogs that Rainey kept on his farm at Naivasha. Hardened bear hounds brought from America, the pack was divided into two groups: swift hounds trained to course a lion until it was bayed, and a rough pack of thirty mongrel fighting dogs for the finish. The coursing hounds were first trained on the spoor of a captured lion cub, which was then retrieved in a wagon, while its salivating pursuers were rewarded with a generous feed of raw meat. Many Kenya hunters considered the lion pack to be an unsporting method of hunting. It transferred the risk from man to dog, and the shooting tended to be relatively unchallenging, as the lion was typically preoccupied with a circle of snapping dogs, instead of charging the hunter.

Having bagged twelve lions in fifteen days at Soysambu, Rainey returned to Naivasha, where a lion finally won. After other hunters had declined to help, Rainey had hired the dashing Austrian hunter Fritz Schindler to assist him in photographing a lion charging at his crank-operated movie camera. Schindler, renowned for his spotless white breeches and gleaming boots, for his daring and his womanizing, became the first professional hunter to be a casualty of photography. After the hounds bayed the lion in thick cover, Schindler rode his white polo pony cautiously into the bush to draw out the lion, confident that his mare was adept at turning fast and breaking into a hard sprint.

But the lion was faster. Bursting from cover, the cat struck a massive swinging blow at the haunches of the horse, knocking it to the ground. Schindler landed on his feet with his double rifle in his hands, but his shot missed and the lion seized him by the stomach, shaking him like a rat and then casting him down to die. Rainey and his surviving hounds soon returned to America, having killed seventy lion in one year, more than twice as many as Selous in his lifetime.

Although Delamere himself, like many experienced hunters, found less and less pleasure in shooting animals, he himself became a fixed part of the agenda for every important visitor to British East Africa, and when they came to visit him, they expected to hunt. In 1907, the young Secretary of State for the Colonies, Winston Churchill, went pig-sticking with Delamere at Soysambu. Young Churchill enjoyed the 'neck or nothing' gallops across hidden stones, holes and lacerating thorn-scrub. Churchill had none of the lust for killing that stimulated certain hunters, and was rather pleased not to shoot a lion, wryly noting that 'Nothing causes the colonist more concern than that his guest should not have been provided with a lion.'

As the sport went on and the Delameres were building their farms, other settlers, with far less capital and experience in the bush, also came to British East Africa for profit and sport. Lord Delamere's brother-in-law, Galbraith Cole, was a determined sheep farmer who settled on the high plateau above the Rift Valley in 1903. Like a Voortrekker in 1836, he took his wagons apart at the bottom of the Mau escarpment, carried them up by hand piece by piece and then, at 10,000 feet, reassembled them at the top. The Cole brothers, rarely absent from any account of Kenya's early days, had a dashing spirit and an energy for friendship that made them popular figures in the widely dispersed settler community.

Another well-respected pioneer and sportsman, President Roosevelt's friend Lord Cranworth, came ashore in Mombasa in 1906, 'full of excitement and loaded with ignorance', having practised rifle shooting at a wooden lion at home. Searching for a home site on his plot in the highlands, he let five lion make the choice for him. Lying on an eminence, shaded by a fig tree, the lion surveyed a stretching vista of green hills gradually rolling up to the slopes of Mt Kenya. Deciding that if it pleased the lion it should satisfy them, the Cranworths began building their first grass hut near Makuyu as the lion grunted in the bush and zebras barked on the plain behind them.

Left: 'The Inseparables'. Tanganika and Bokari, Lord Cranworth's camp assistants, 1906

Below right: Lord Cranworth's game licence for 1906

Bottom: Lord and Lady Cranworth with a heavy morning's bag of oryx, 1906

Above left: The cookhouse and all attendants, 1906

Above right: Shadrack picks the ticks off Lord Cranworth, 1906

Below: A Cranworth safari crossing the Iam River, 1906

Then they settled down to the gruelling work of building a sisal plantation, Cranworth shooting for meat and his wife growing vegetables. With an estimated 14,000 antelope on the 25,000 acre property that Cranworth owned with three partners, it was many years before he faced a butcher's bill.

Above left: Berkeley Cole in his customary kit, 1906

Above right: White Rhino Hotel, Nyeri

One of Cranworth's partners, Donald Seth-Smith, had also arrived in 1906, straight from Oxford, with £250 and limitless tenacity. Pioneering neighbours, business partners, hunting companions, fellow soldiers, there was little that these two men could add to friendship. Seth-Smith's letters home to his father in 1907, written at night in his tent or wagon, provide a remarkable sense of what the first days were like. Optimistic, driven to make a go of it, bursting with the enthusiasm that each day in Kenya was the beginning of a new opportunity, Seth-Smith drew his father into investing in agriculture, timber, engines and buildings. When his father sent two bicycles from England, Seth-Smith reminded him to 'send no lamps as, due to the lions, one does not patronize night travelling'. Betting their families' English assets on the future of Kenya, risking more and more, Cranworth and Seth-Smith stretched each day with gruelling work. Increasingly, hunting became their practical recreation. Half a century later, when Cranworth wrote Seth-Smith's obituary, he recalled that 'in a country of sportsmen, I have known no better, with a profound knowledge of bird and beast'.

Always hungry for cash to finance the farm, young Cranworth launched a transport business, rented out a primitive shooting-lodge, traded ivory and grew rubber in Uganda, practised journalism in Nairobi, imported coffee from

German East Africa, rented huts to trainee settlers, and cultivated flax and wattle. Before the First World War, he organized Kenya's first motorized shooting safari in a 15 h.p. Napier. Among his least successful efforts was the White Rhino Hotel at Nyeri, which Cranworth founded with Berkeley Cole. The bedrooms were infamous for their paper-thin walls, which often provided feasts of scandal for the lively bar crowd. The White Rhino foundered on the old chit system of British clubs, working on the theory that a good drinker deserves credit. But at the White Rhino, unlike Boodle's or White's in London, the drinkers cheerfully signed their names and moved on.

When Delamere and the other Kenya pioneers needed recreation or cash, they either went on safari or went to Nairobi. Ivory, lion skins and clients were profitable, and a safari was merely an extension of their normal life on farm or ranch. They would no more be without a gun than without their boots, and it was a natural step from shooting lion to protect one's cattle to hunting lion with well-paying clients. When the coffee failed or the rams died, it was the wild animals that paid the bank loans. Ivory brought 25s. a pound in east Africa in 1910, and lion skins fetched £1 each. Many farmers took to professional hunting for several months a year, raising cash and enjoying the life, as the clients paid them to do what they liked best. Lord Cranworth, more enterprising still, became a principal in the first safari outfitter, Newland & Tarlton, which by 1914 was the largest employer in Kenya. Some government officers even blamed the safari business for the labour shortage, as the hunters paid double the usual native wage and drew off the most willing workers.

As they hunted and farmed, the pioneers recorded, in their diaries and letters, the wildlife experiences that enhanced their days and became part of the vast inventory of Kenya's safari lore. Cara Buxton, who came out on safari in 1910 and then stayed on as a settler, was fascinated by an old hyena that the Africans thought walked on its hind legs at night. Hyena are elevated in front by their longer forelegs, and it turned out to be simply a very large specimen, walking in the usual way. An American, Max Fleischman, photographed a female rhinoceros as it was slowly dragged into the deep water of the Tana River and killed by a giant crocodile, an incident about which Selous and Roosevelt later corresponded.

Seth-Smith's brother, Martin, in the course of his long foot safaris, developed the practice of stopping a lion with a heavy ·577, and then finishing it with a light Mannlicher ·256, aiming at the tip of the nose so that the bullet penetrated into the neck. Once his gunbearer, who carried snuff in an old ·577 cartridge stopped up with a cork, loaded the right barrel of the ·577 with the snuffbox during the pursuit of a wounded lion. When the snuff failed to fire, the hunter confirmed the virtue of a double rifle by stopping the lion with his left barrel. Martin Seth-Smith was a student of cheetah, noting that they kill by pace, running down their quarry to exhaustion, whereas leopard kill by stealth. Having much in common with the dog family, cheetah have non-retracting claws, unlike cats, lion and leopard.

Left: Safari lunch at Rumuruti, 1914

Below: Bringing in the ivory

Bullocks rolling the High Street, Nairobi, 1906

After the isolation and exertion of life in the bush, whether on safari or farming, the hunters and farmers descended on Nairobi with the explosive enthusiasm of sailors hitting port. There was little time for play on an African farm, although Delamere found recreation at Equator Ranch in racing his buggy against passing railroad trains. Drawn at bouncing, frenzied speed over the rough ground by his grey American trotter, it was a jarring amusement for a man who had already suffered three spinal concussions from a variety of adventures. The real races, however, were in Nairobi. Since the first race meeting on an afternoon in July 1900, the Nairobi races have been the centre of the country's social life. As the horse trainer and aviatrix Beryl Markham recalled, writing of the early race meetings in her autobiography *West with the Night*, 'the little hotels filled, the streets humming, each day the grandstands mottled with the costumes and the colour of a dozen tribes and peoples'.

Much of the excitement of race week was gathered at the Norfolk Hotel and at the Muthaiga Club, which Berkeley Cole founded in 1913 so he might have a place where his drinks would be properly served. Like the later safaris, Kenya was now beginning to provide a pleasing blend of hardship and luxury, as the Muthaiga offered its croquet course, polo stables, Goanese chef and European chauffeurs. The Muthaiga's sturdy rooms, 'none so elaborate as to make a rough-handed hunter pause at its door, nor yet so dowdy as to make a diamond pendant swing ill at ease', were the refuge after long hunts, lean crops and strained meetings at the bank. As Beryl Markham went on to remark, these were the 'rooms in which the people who made the Africa I knew danced and talked and laughed, hour after hour'. Much of the social life also revolved around sport, not only hunting, but also polo and cricket. Randall Swift, a farming neighbour of Lord Cranworth, occasionally left his sisal plantation at

Manica Road, Salisbury, Rhodesia,
1910

2 a.m. and walked forty miles to Nairobi for a few sets of late-afternoon
tennis. Golf was less popular, as the rough was thick with ticks, an occasional
rhinoceros reduced concentration and one player was mauled by a lion on the
fairway.

As the first president of the East African Turf Club, Delamere during race
week occasionally put aside his holster and outsize sun helmet for wild white-tie
dinners. Lord Delamere and his friends retained the English schoolboy's taste
for smashing things up, whether hurling billiard balls at antelope heads on a
club wall, playing rugby in the hotel bar, or shooting out street lamps outside
government buildings. He and his companions, however, had little tolerance for
another British tradition, closing the bar early, particularly after a long, thirsty
day that began with a pre-breakfast, hell-for-leather jackal hunt, and included
cricket and cock-fighting. When the manager of the Norfolk sought to end one
party, Delamere remarked, 'Oh, damn the fellow, let's put him in the meat
safe', and acted on the suggestion.

Whether in Nairobi, at home or on safari, Kenya's Europeans tended to
develop an unusual relationship with the Africans who worked with them. The
relationships were based on far more than paternalism or exploitation, although
there was much of both. The Europeans, both at work and on safari, depended
on the Africans not just for labour, but for survival, whether for their livelihood
on the farm, or for life itself in the bush. Each race complained endlessly of the
other, but in Kenya often almost cheerfully, and more than sometimes with
affection and respect. In time, of course, each race tended to indulge in its own
amnesia. Many Africans came to forget that the Europeans brought an end to

A photograph of Victoria Falls,
taken by Lord Cranworth when he
visited Rhodesia in 1907

Lord Cranworth and Lord
Wodehouse with their trophies

famine, slavery and perpetual tribal war. Too many Europeans forgot that they had not 'built the country' on their own, and that Africa, after all, belonged first to the Africans, as Winston Churchill reminded his readers in 1908.

Consistently, from Selous to today's top professionals, serious European hunters have acknowledged their gunbearers with respect and affection. The inescapable reality of the relationship, of employer and assistant, tended to diminish as danger mounted, and even to vanish in the fraternal intensity of life-and-death crisis. Then the priorities of trust, survival and ability left no room for position and race. But back in camp, each generally went to his separate fire, and at home the gunbearer often became the favoured servant, his special role never forgotten. Cranworth's gunbearer Kiriboto, the 'Flea', was an unflinching henchman, '100 per cent honest, trustworthy and loyal, and 120 per cent brave . . . who could not run away if he tried'. As silent in the household as he was on the trail, Kiriboto would steal up on a reading house guest and snatch the book from his hand, explaining in his quiet, deep voice, 'The Lord wants . . .' Kiriboto never finished the sentence.

As Nairobi grew in the untrammelled years before the First World War, hunting increasingly became a profession, and many a hunting farmer or ivory hunter became a 'professional white hunter', a man paid to escort clients in the bush. A common Kenyan fallacy is that professional white hunting originated in British East Africa in about 1900. In fact it began years before in Rhodesia, South Africa and Somaliland. The term 'white hunter' is thought to have been originated by Lord Delamere, who employed two men to control the predators on his land. One was an Abyssinian. The other was the early professional hunter, Alan Black. To distinguish him from the Abyssinian, Delamere referred to Black as the 'white hunter'.

In Kenya itself, the origin of professional safari hunting is often credited to Clifford and Harold Hill, cousins who arrived from South Africa in 1904 to make their fortunes farming ostrich and selling the feathers to European haberdashers. In South Africa ostrich were by then so rare that a good cock cost £200, but in Kenya they still flourished. Kenya's ostrich are taller and about fifty pounds heavier than those of southern Africa. Capable of running at 38 m.p.h., the males weigh over 300 lb and stand almost 8 feet tall. The colonial government gave the Hills a farm at Machakos, to serve as a buffer between two hostile tribes, the Wakamba and the Masai. Clifford Hill grew fond of his ostrich, noting that their expressive eyes were the most beautiful in the world, although he found that domesticated males became strangely vicious and can kill a person with their big toenail.

But ostrich were even more popular with the lions than with the ladies, and as the ostrich multiplied so did the predators, who tirelessly raided the Hills' bird pens. Not yet hunters themselves, the Hills were armed only with old Snider military rifles. Circumstances, however, soon made them into determined lion hunters: finally one lion broke into the pens and killed twenty birds, and two

Clifford and Harold Hill with a hunting party

neighbouring farmers, George Grey and Alfred Pease, who was President Roosevelt's hunting host in 1909, joined the cousins in hunting down the offending lion. When it burst from a *donga*, a gully thick with bush, Grey galloped after it, going in too close, instead of dismounting to shoot from a safe range. Pease always recommended dismounting at 200 yards. As Grey leapt from the saddle to shoot at 90 yards, his aim unsteady from the gallop, he missed two shots and the lion charged home. Before the other hunters could come up and kill the beast, Grey was hideously torn and mauled, dying five days later in cruel pain, after whispering to his friends that the blame was all his own.

Soon the Hills became celebrated lion hunters. After taking many friends shooting they finally made a business of it, which led some later Kenyans to believe that they were the first professional white hunters. But about the same time a young Scotsman was also learning the trade.

Leaving his native parish in disgrace at eighteen after a stirring friendship with an older lady, J.A. Hunter was sent off to Africa in 1905 by an embarrassed father, who revealed his affection for his departing son in the best British manner. Wishing him to be armed like a gentleman, he handed him a gun instead of embracing him. 'Son,' he said, 'you may take the Purdey.'

After three months on the decaying Limuru plantation of his cousin, a man so Scottish that a farthing 'screamed for help' when it passed through his fingers, in 1905 Hunter got a job as an armed guard on the Uganda Railway. Keeping an old · 275 Mauser in the chopbox with the food, Hunter would lean out the train window to bag lion and leopard. Then he would pull the alarm brake and leap out with a young African to skin the animal. After a time he trained the conductor to toot the whistle twice when he saw a lion and three times for a leopard. Soon, with lion skins at £1 each, Hunter was at it full time.

Above: Ngorongoro crater from the rim, Tanzania

Left: Ostrich on the veld, by Cornwallis Harris

Then young Hunter, a keen reader of Selous, led two American clients south on the first paid safari to the Ngorongoro crater in German East Africa. Rising 9,000 feet from the flat, hot plains of the Serengeti, Ngorongoro is a vast extinct volcano, fifteen miles across, the centre green with grass cropped short by thick herds of eland, giraffe, Thomson and Grant gazelle, zebra, reedbuck, ostrich and duiker. On later safaris Hunter pleased the Masai by hunting the large black-maned Ngorongoro lion that were preying on the cattle, finally hunting with a pack of 'kangaroo hounds' and shooting several hundred lion. The moran then told him that the crater was his. Lion were so plentiful that they were considered a dangerous nuisance, and J.A. never contemplated that they would become a valued game animal.

Hunter's Ngorongoro clients, victims of 'American trigger itch', shot until their guns were too hot to hold. Determined to bag a record head and enter their names among the world's princely hunters, they began each day by studying Rowland Ward's *Records of Big Game*. At night they slept with revolvers tied to their wrists. Their dawn studies led J.A. to observe that 'At that hour a bowl of porridge looked far sweeter to me.'

Above: A German safari in central Africa in 1909

Left: A German safari in the Sudan, 1912

Finally, after days of scanning the crater with fieldglasses, the Americans found their trophy. A record impala, with horns over the critical thirty inches. One client fired, regrettably dropping a different buck grazing just near by. Back in camp, the desperate client asked Hunter if he would consider 'steaming these horns to stretch the ferrules and get a record'. Hunter declined, learning early the truth of the white hunter's saying, 'It's not the wild beasts that are the problem. It's the clients.'

The clients, however, enjoyed the sport. As Cranworth later recalled, the years 1908–14 were a time when 'princes, peers and American magnates poured out in one continual stream'. As Donald Seth-Smith wrote to his father in December 1907, regretting that his Christmas plum pudding had not arrived from England, 'The country is crawling with big-game shooters. Thirty more parties are coming in the next boat or two.' Newland & Tarlton had three hundred clients in its peak year just before the First World War.

No visitor contributed more to the safari boom than did Theodore Roosevelt. An admirer of the British Empire, and a supporter of the 'Manifest Destiny' doctrine that welcomed a continental expansion of the United States, Roosevelt was impressed by the work of Kenya's pioneers. Speaking to a welcoming dinner in Nairobi in 1909, he declared,

> You young people are doing a great work of which you have every right to be proud. You have brought freedom where there was slavery. You are bringing health where there was disease. You are bringing food where there was famine. You are bringing peace where there was continual war. The time is coming when the world will be proud of you.

Not all the new safari clients came to shoot. The Hamburg zoological firm of Carl Hagenback organized a seven-month animal-collecting safari in 1911 that gathered for shipment to Europe 8 giraffe, 11 hippopotamus, 2 rhinoceros, 34 ostrich and many antelope. Buffalo Jones, the old plainsman whom President Roosevelt had appointed as game warden of Yellowstone Park, came to rope buffalo and rhino, bringing ten American cow ponies and hard-twisted lassoes of Russian hemp. Jones was said to be the man who defeated 7,000 competitors in the Oklahoma land rush by repeatedly leaping on to a fresh galloping horse running side by side. He and his assistant cowboys captured a rhino and a lion, losing three dogs and roughing up a few horses in the process. The safari was managed by the Boma Trading Company, filmed by the pioneer safari photographer Cherry Kearton, and welcomed back to Nairobi at a rousing dinner at the Norfolk.

In 1910 the Duke and Duchess of Connaught enjoyed one of the earliest grand, classic safaris, hunting elephant with Philip Percival and lion with the Hill cousins. Accompanied by a lady-in-waiting and an equerry from the Scots Guards, the safari employed 2 Somali headmen, 8 Somali shikaris or gunbearers, 15 askaris, a Goanese head cook, 3 Swahili assistant cooks, a Swahili baker, 5 Kikuyu 'mule men', 10 Kikuyu saises and a Masai head sais. The *East*

African Standard described it all as 'a simple camp life'. A typical seven-course dinner began with buffalo-tail soup followed by fresh barbel as the fish, proceeding through mutton cutlets with vegetables, roast guinea-fowl, stewed apples, and giraffe marrow-bones as a savoury, followed by cheese and coffee. Reportedly wines and spirits were taken only in moderation, and brandy and champagne were kept in reserve as medicine. The only exceptional luxury on the Connaught safari was thought to be the use of china and glass instead of enamel and aluminium. Seeking to avoid the vast caravans of the Roosevelt safari, supply bases were set up in advance along the route, with pack mules and donkeys conveying in the goods as needed.

Many of the early safaris had a higher cost in health and injury than in money. In 1913 the basic £50 licence entitled a client to kill or capture 2 elephant, a buffalo, 2 rhino, 2 hippo, 2 zebra and nearly 200 gazelles, antelopes and other species. Lion and leopard required no licence because they were classed as vermin. For a total of £350–500, including licence fees, a client could enjoy a six-week safari. Some hunters, however, never came back, like the veteran sportsman Gerald Longden, whose distraught wife returned to Nairobi from the Belgian Congo without him. After felling a mighty bull elephant with 150 lb of ivory each side, she reported, he was gored by a cow whose tusk passed through his back into his intestines, resulting in a slow and painful death after three more days in the bush.

Nairobi's leading newspaper also warned safari clients against sunstroke and tropical depression, the first symptom of which is a longing for 'the shady side of Pall Mall'. Recommending toilet vinegar and talc against the unmentionable irritations of prickly heat, it suggested smoked goggles and bathing the eyes twice weekly with sulphate of zinc. If the eyes became excessively sore, they should be 'touched with a very soft camel hair brush dipped in the little phial of castor oil commonly provided for the purpose in the medicine chest'.

By 1913 the motorcar was in active, if not common, safari use in the bush, not just for transport as Lord Cranworth had first used it earlier, but as a substitute for pursuit on horseback. Clement Hirtzel, an early Kenya pioneer, took Childs Frick of New York chasing lion on the Serengeti Plain, and soon made it a regular business, guaranteeing to spot seventeen species of game in a fortnight. Hirtzel worked with a specially fitted-out Ford, designed to be used at night as a sleeping compartment.

While J. A. Hunter and the other early professionals were learning the safari business, and Delamere, the Coles and Cranworth were working their farms, other new hands began to arrive. Some came out as shooting clients drawn by reports of President Roosevelt's grand safari, and then bought their own farms or plantations. Many were settlers eager to find fortune and adventure. No matter what tales they heard before they left home, all were astonished by the lavish game, the sparsity of human life in the bush, and the exhilarating sense of freedom that Africa gave them.

Above: Pitching camp in Kenya, 1907

Right: Duke of Connaught with attendants and lion during his east African safari, March 1910

Below: Duke of Connaught's safari menu, March 1910

H. The Duke of Connaught's
Safari.
tish East Africa.
10th March 1910

MENU.

Eland Tail Soup
Eland Steak
Roast Guinea Fowl
Fruit Pudding
Eland Marrow on Toast
Coffee

Sir Henry Hesketh Bell, Governor of Uganda, with his trophies, 1908

While studying at Oxford, the second son of the Earl of Winchilsea heard the legends of British East Africa. Confiding to a friend that he felt constrained by the Victorian code that lingered on in Edwardian England, young Denys Finch Hatton declared, 'England is too small. Much too small. I shall go to Africa. I need space.' In 1911, at twenty-three, Denys Finch Hatton stepped ashore in Mombasa's Kilindini Harbour.

At once, he was at home. The African sun, by itself, was a welcome he craved, hating, as he did, the cold damp of England. Within four weeks he was on his way back to London, making arrangements to settle in Africa. Already he had journeyed to Nairobi by rail, stopped at the Norfolk, become friendly with Berkeley Cole, visited the highlands, and bought a farm at Eldoret. The scent of the cloves and lush flowers in Mombasa, the galloping game on the Athi plain near Nairobi, the relaxed high spirits of the town itself, and the aloof elegance of the Somali and Masai all drew him. But most of all, he was drawn by the freedom of the life.

Even at Eton, where he spread a quiet magnetic attraction, Finch Hatton had shown the easy athleticism, effortless talent and sense of reserve that defined him. Lean, six feet three, with a strong nose and handsome, balding head, Finch Hatton gracefully combined the intellectual and the athletic. Witty and musical, he quickly became as famous for his courage with lions as he had been for leading his side in Eton's brutal Wall Game. As the *Eton College Chronicle* put it, 'When charged, he rises to the occasion.' Carefree, always somewhat remote, Finch Hatton seemed to give others a chance by never trying too hard himself, for as Lord Cranworth remarked, 'nature presented him with more gifts than were the fair share of one man'.

Denys Finch Hatton

Less than a year after Denys Finch Hatton had returned to Kenya, while he was occupied with farming, trading and shooting, a young Danish lady arrived in Mombasa to marry her cousin. Her fiancé, the Swedish Baron Bror von Blixen, met her by boat in the sparkling surf of Kilindini Harbour, and they were married the next day. Even in Scandinavia, before either of them had ever left Europe, the cousins had been united by the dream of life in Africa. 'Between us we built a future in our imagination,' Bror Blixen wrote twenty-two years later, and 'the promised land which hovered before our eyes was called Africa.'

As a boy, Blixen had hunted on family estates in the south of Sweden, always preferring a rifle to a book. Tough, congenial and poor, suited only to a hearty outdoor life, he was fortunate to find a wife whose family agreed to finance a farm in Africa. His bride, Tanne Dinesen, later known as Tania to her British friends, and finally as the writer Karen Blixen or Isak Dinesen, was raised in the romantic tradition by a father whose passions were writing, hunting and war. From him she learned a hunter's regard for observing the detail of nature, and a high respect for personal independence, the ability to be unattached. Both were to serve her in Africa.

On the nineteen-day voyage from Naples to Mombasa, sailing, like Roosevelt and Selous before her, on the *Admiral*, Isak Dinesen became friendly with the German officer who was to be Africa's greatest military figure since Mzilikazi, Paul von Lettow-Vorbeck. It was January 1914, and the colonel was on his way to Dar es Salaam to take command of the troops waiting in German East Africa. She agreed to buy in Kenya ten Abyssinian breeding mares for the German cavalry, and to go on safari with von Lettow in August, but that proved to be a busy month for the German army. Never a jealous man, Blixen invited von Lettow to dine with Isak Dinesen and himself at the Mombasa Club on their first night together in Africa.

When Blixen first took her to the farm in the Ngong Hills, twelve miles from Nairobi, the land itself not yet cleared for planting, 1,200 Kikuyu workers cheered a greeting. The Ngong Hills were named for the Masai word for knuckles, which the four main hills suggest from a distance. Within weeks the Blixens were absorbed by their farm, and by the fine sport that was so incredibly accessible. First the rich red earth had to be turned up, then each young coffee plant, six hundred to the acre, carefully set in by hand with its taproot free and straight. Too soon, the Baron increasingly turned his attention to the sport, spending his time hunting, drinking with friends and flirting with the ladies, well knowing he was too charming, too blue-eyed and too broad-shouldered to refuse. Isak Dinesen often shared the hunting, but became first preoccupied, and then obsessed, with the 4,500 acre coffee farm, just too high, at 6,000 feet, for the proper balance of rain, temperature and soil.

But Isak Dinesen was soon committed to the farm, and mesmerized by the Ngong Hills, whose aspect changed like the sea with the mood of the weather against the violet sky. 'Everything you saw made for greatness and freedom', the immense views over the vast dropping cleft of the Rift Valley, the iron-like figures of buffalo darkening the luxuriant greens of the ridges, and, at night, the lions, speaking like the 'thunder of guns in the darkness'. It was, she wrote, 'a landscape that had not its like in all the world', the spiced scent of the grass 'so strong that it smarted in the nostrils', the air at midday 'alive over the land like a flame burning'.

By early June 1914, 600 acres of coffee seedlings were in the ground, the heavy rains had come, and it was nature's turn to do the work. The Blixens went on safari for a month with nine servants and three mule wagons. It was Isak Dinesen's first time under canvas, her first experience shooting big game, and her first opportunity to appreciate her husband at his best. She found safari life as exhilarating as champagne. On safari in July in the Masai country to the south-west, she lost herself to Africa, astonished by her own appetite for shooting. Blixen, a natural instructor, gave her a ·256 with a telescopic sight and trained her to stalk in close, making the most of every cartridge. After one chase, she admired the spare sinewy body of a lion, its muscular secrets exposed under the skin as its pelt was cut and drawn back by the skinners.

Like her father, Isak Dinesen seems to have found a parallel between hunting and loving, relishing the ritual of the pursuit, as Judith Thurman points out in her fine biography. In Africa, in the feudalism and naturalism of colonial living, she found a basis for the romanticism she shared with her father. Thirty years later, having apparently caught syphilis from Blixen, childless, divorced, her lover dead, she remembered it all, concluding, 'If I should wish anything back of my life, it would be to go on safari once again with Bror von Blixen.'

Just back from her first safari, Isak Dinesen was searching for von Lettow's mares when war came to east Africa on 4 August 1914. It was an awkward time, for Sweden was known to be sympathetic to Germany, and Kenya's Scandinavians at once fell under suspicion. Meeting at the Blixens' bungalow, the leaders of the Scandinavian community decided to support their new country, unless Sweden actually went to war on the side of Germany. Bror Blixen promptly bicycled into Nairobi to report for duty, signing up with Bowker's Horse and finding a characteristically exotic scene as Kenya's Europeans took mobilization into their own hands. At the time there were approximately 7,000 Europeans and 2,500,000 Africans in British East Africa, and 5,300 Europeans and 7,650,000 Africans in German East Africa.

Hunters, farmers, traders and transport riders poured into Nairobi, heavy with pistols and double rifles, filling the hotels, setting up tents, improvising uniforms and organizing like boy scouts into flamboyant units like Ross's Scouts and the Lancer Squadron, which thundered through Nairobi with steel-tipped bamboo spears and pennons fluttering. With elements of only three professional battalions of the King's African Rifles available, the war in Africa soon became what Lord Cranworth called 'a grand season for incompetents'. The east African campaign, it appeared, was to become the ultimate game of capture the flag.

The safari skills of the hunters, however, served the British well as the men took the field. As with virtually every enterprise, Delamere took the lead.

Recognizing the danger that von Lettow's Schutztruppe posed to Kenya's vulnerable communications system, with the railway running within forty miles of the German border, Delamere, his white hair flowing to his shoulders as he worked in the bush, organized Masai scouting parties to patrol two hundred miles of unguarded frontier. Top hunters like William Judd, Donald Seth-Smith and the American Charles Cottar took responsibility for key sectors as von Lettow, anxious to strike before British reinforcements arrived from India, probed the border. Bror Blixen served Delamere as an intelligence officer, being responsible for communications between Delamere and Nairobi. Blixen used motorcycles, native runners, heliograph stations and carrier pigeons, but the birds, taken by hawks, often failed to make it home.

As the Germans penetrated Kenya, the colony became the only part of the British empire to be invaded by the enemy in the First World War. Under the resourceful General von Lettow-Vorbeck, 2,200 professional soldiers led the Schutztruppe, meticulously organized into mobile, independent, German-officered field companies, each with its own cobbler and each armed with eight times the machine-gun strength of comparable British units. They were supported by a few companies of Arabs and by reserve companies of German farmers who had prepared for the war by drilling in rifle clubs.

Von Lettow permitted his askaris to march with their women and children, and his Arabs to march with their boys. The German askaris were carefully selected from martial tribes like the Manyamwesi. Many were hardened veterans of years of warfare in German East Africa, where they had helped in the brutal suppression of tribal rebellions against compulsory labour and other practices of the early German colonial period. In Kenya, where relatively little force had been used to establish a colony, the King's African Rifles lacked such training.

In addition to the African camp followers, at least one armed white woman marched with the Schutztruppe, and she was to become east Africa's first professional woman hunter. The redoubtable Margaret Trappe, whose husband Ulrich served in the Schutztruppe, abandoned her family farm near Mt Meru in German East Africa to soldier as a mounted courier for von Lettow, occasionally crossing British lines armed with her Mauser rifle and Parabellum pistol. She was so skilled in the bush that the Africans claimed she could milk female elephants, and European hunters said she was able to call hippos from the water. Von Lettow, however, embarrassed by propaganda that he was using a female combatant, finally directed her to surrender to the British. After the war, to help support the new family farm near Momella, Margaret Trappe conducted safaris as a paid white hunter. On one occasion, boasting to her male hunting companions that she could do something they could not, she wrote the word *pumbavu*, meaning idiot in Swahili, in chalk on the back of a rhinoceros.

The German forces faced mixed troops from Britain, India, Kenya, Rhodesia and South Africa. The blacks of Kenya were far less martial than their southern counterparts, with the exception of the Masai, who did not take to regimental

Above: General von Lettow-
Vorbeck leading the Schutztruppe
through the bush, Tanganyika,
1914

Right: Schutztruppe machine-gun
nest at Latema-Reata, 1916

training. In time, to compensate, the British imported battalions from five colonies in west Africa. Most made splendid soldiers and some enjoyed an unearned reputation for cannibalism. Occasionally, men of the Gold Coast Regiment amused themselves by encouraging anxiety among their German prisoners, letting it be known that they were short of fresh meat and dancing around their captives brandishing woodcutting knives. Troops from the Belgian Congo, now Zaïre, sometimes assisted the British in operations around Lake Tanganyika to the west, and the Belgian officers were frequently concerned lest their askaris exhume and dine on their dead adversaries.

Both sides benefited from the assistance of professional hunters, the Germans using civilian sharpshooters armed with sporting rifles, such as Hollands and Rigbys, occasionally firing soft-nosed expanding bullets. It was unconventional warfare in the truest sense. The Germans, hunting game as they skilfully evaded the British on foot through four countries, dragged the ten 4·1 inch guns of the sunken cruiser *Königsberg* through the bush, each remounted on wheels at the German railyards at Dar es Salaam. The ship's crew were added to the Schutztruppe, trained in bushcraft and taught Swahili. Many of the *Königsberg's* old shells were adapted to use as land mines. When von Lettow finally surrendered in Northern Rhodesia shortly after the war ended in Europe in 1918, the *Königsberg* was still represented by fifteen sailors and a one-legged officer, out of an original crew of 323.

The sinking of the *Königsberg* in 1915, the first major British achievement of the campaign, was largely the work of the notable Afrikaans elephant hunter, Pieter 'Jungle Man' Pretorius, recruited by the British to locate the 3,400 ton ship as it lay hidden in the mangrove jungle passages of the Rufiji River. A

SMS Königsberg

master in the bush, slipping easily through the screen of German positions that surrounded the warship, Pretorius seized two villagers to guide him to the cruiser, her hull now painted jungle green and foliage concealing her long guns.

Kidnapping the local village headman, Pretorius accompanied him to the vessel, where the man's son now worked as a coal stoker. Disguised as an Arab trader, his skin already nut-brown from sun and malaria, Pretorius spied out the condition of the vessel. Then, disguised as a native fisherman, the hunter made hundreds of soundings with a pole, many in view of the ship herself, in order to determine how British ships could reach her. Needing shallow craft that could outgun her in the river, the British then towed two monitors, flat-bottomed gunboats with a four-foot draft, from the island of Malta to the Rufiji River. Assisted by aircraft spotters, the monitors did the job. The wily Pretorius later became chief scout to General Jan Christiaan Smuts, the new commander of the British forces in east Africa.

Although regular army officers took charge of field operations after the early days, the British hunters remained active throughout the war. Sometimes the troops watched the sky as Flight-Lieutenant Karamojo Bell, the fabled elephant hunter and perhaps the finest rifle shot in Africa, flew low in an ageing 60 m.p.h. biplane, his front cockpit empty to give his rifle a clear field of fire as he hunted German askaris. To camouflage the two grey horses he used scouting, Lord Cranworth painted zebra stripes on them with iodine and found that they blended nicely into the bush. Celebrating St Andrews Day, the Eton holiday on the fourth of June, Cranworth shared a bottle of champagne and a small fire with three other Etonians, including Finch Hatton, 'my brother officer and the man with about the most impressive personality I have ever known'. Frequently the hunters shot to feed the troops. Once Cranworth was asked to carve up a single hippo into rations for a thousand men. In one two-week period, Delamere supplied the army with the bodies of 1,200 Thomson gazelle.

The arriving British, South African and Indian regiments dissolved from illness as they struggled in the bush and swamps. As one German officer had predicted, 'A white force would be nothing more than a walking hospital.' Even the 2nd Rhodesian Regiment, a tough lot, experienced in Africa, suffered only thirty-six battle deaths, but 3,100 cases of malaria, and 7,500 casualties from such illnesses as guinea worms and burrowing insects called chiggers. Taken in water, multiplying in the body, and boring into the legs or scrotum and other organs, guinea worms had also plagued the old hunters. Once the worm breaks the skin from the inside, it can be wound carefully around a small splint, a few centimetres each day, until it is drawn from the body. The military animals also suffered. In one two-month period, 19,000 horses died, mostly from tsetse.

Over 200,000 Kenya Africans toiled in the Carrier Corps, providing the transport that slowly helped to give the British an edge. In an east African army in which nearly 500,000 men served, Frederick Selous's regiment, the Legion of Frontiersmen, was the last white unit to survive in the bush. Cranworth observed that the regiment was too tough to manage, except in battle. He had

Red Cross ambulance ox wagon, 1914

seen them marching in to the attack, 'in rags, shaking with fever, emaciated and white beneath the tan, yet full of an incredible determination'. After its final battle, fifty men were left standing out of a total wartime complement of two thousand. Never ill, Selous himself was the wonder of the unit, both for his endurance and his moral spirit. One young officer wrote of Selous, 'Anything mean or sordid literally shrivelled up in his presence.'

In his final action near the Rufiji River, having already been awarded a Distinguished Service Order, Selous was trying to encircle von Lettow's troops. Finally shot down by a German sniper, the old elephant hunter, part of Africa dying with him, was buried beneath a tamarind tree in what is now the Selous Game Reserve, the continent's largest wildlife sanctuary. Before the war the Kaiser had urged German youth to model themselves on Selous. After his death von Lettow, who said he once spared Selous when he had the old hunter in his sights, remarked that both sides mourned.

The war, as they sometimes do, drew on reserves of energy and resolution that are rarely used. Even the relaxed Elizabethans, Berkeley Cole and Denys Finch Hatton, extended themselves, although Finch Hatton seemed to find the whole exercise more tiresome than exciting. Berkeley Cole, close to the Somalis and deeply attached to the Somali mistress he maintained conveniently near the Muthaiga Club, organized eight hundred sometimes mutinous Somalis into

Donald Seth-Smith

Below: Pony camouflaged as zebra for Cole's Scouts, Tanganyika border, 1914

Bottom: Cole's Scouts watering

Donald.
aug. 1917.

Cole's Scouts, with the assistance of Cranworth and Finch Hatton. Donald Seth-Smith took soldiering in the King's African Rifles as seriously as farming at Makuyu. He won a Military Cross for gallantry, and was in a trench on the ridge near Selous when the old hunter was cut down.

For her part, Isak Dinesen during the war learned how to run a safari, organizing and leading convoys of ox-wagons from Bror Blixen's relay station at Kijabe to the East African Mounted Rifles camp at the border. Anxious to join her on one brief leave, Blixen once walked eighty-six miles in two days to find her, a serious stretch even for that durable philanderer. Dinesen later recalled that the wartime expeditions truly made her feel part of Africa. Undistracted by her farm or personal life, she was closer to the animals and the land than she ever was again. Other European women, like the remarkable unmarried pioneer Cara Buxton, ran as many as five farms during the war. Although less celebrated than Isak Dinesen, she was a better shot and a better farmer. During her pre-war safaris, Cara Buxton, like the Portuguese planters and officers in what is now Mozambique, occasionally travelled in a porter's chair called a *machilla*. During the war, however, she was constantly in the saddle, organizing labourers, checking crops, shooting leopard that attacked the sheep, hunting for meat, and fighting bush fires that threatened the farm buildings.

As the end of the war approached in Europe, von Lettow after many battles abandoned his base near Mt Kilimanjaro and retired through Portuguese East Africa, where the Africans welcomed him as a deliverer from the cruelties of the Portuguese. The Schutztruppe found their Portuguese adversaries so ineffective as to be little more than a convenient source of resupply. Bone-thin with malaria, several toenails removed to extract the chiggers that his cook cut from his feet each day, his spectacles broken and his good eye cut by elephant grass, seven times wounded, von Lettow was blessed with a handsome present on Christmas Day, 1917. His men presented him with a bed, clean sheets, roast pork, wine and cigars, all the unwitting gift of the Portuguese.

Schutztruppe morale was high to the end, the Africans and Germans hardened comrades, routinely marching fifteen to twenty miles across hard country in six hours, with half-hour stops every two hours. The Germans made bandages from bark, and resisted malaria by sipping the foul-tasting 'Lettow schnappes', a quinine drink made by boiling bark. A typical lunch on the march was hippopotamus fat spread over rough bread made from boiled rice and any available grain. Shortly before they surrendered in Northern Rhodesia, the men feasted on the flesh of eight hippopotamus. Thirty-five years later, at the age of eighty-three, von Lettow was to return from Germany to Dar es Salaam. His veteran askaris, waiting at the dock, carried him through the town on their shoulders.

When the 'Kaiser's War', as some settlers called it, finally ended in November 1918, over 90 per cent of the troops on both sides were black. Fifty thousand men had died in the east African campaign, most of them blacks unfamiliar with the demands of Balkan nationalism. Nairobi celebrated as African regiments

General Paul von Lettow-Vorbeck

paraded and Europeans danced in the streets. In the Ngong Hills an immense bonfire signalled against the sky.

Finch Hatton, as peace came, was taking flying lessons with the Royal Flying Corps in the Middle East, where he developed a close friendship with a young American officer, Kermit Roosevelt. They shared a love of poetry and discussed old safari days in Kenya. When Kermit Roosevelt was short of books, Finch Hatton buzzed him from the air and dropped a copy of *Plutarch's Lives*. Then it was back to Nairobi, and the safari boom that followed the Great War.

7. VINTAGE YEARS

1919–39

Essentially British, the white hunters who survived the First World War were a hardened lot whose friends and brothers had disappeared in the mud of France and the swamps of Tanzania. Of Denys Finch Hatton's Oxford generation, it has been said, with only some exaggeration, that more died in France than in England. Virtually all of Finch Hatton's best friends from Eton and Oxford had perished by 1916, including two brothers, the Grenfells, who died in different actions on the same day. From Selous's old school, for example, 2,700 Rugbeians were serving by that year, of whom 900 received military honours, including twenty-three DSOs and two Victoria Crosses. Of all countries that participated in the war, Kenya and Rhodesia had the highest enlistment rates, in the case of Kenya over 85 per cent of all European males of fighting age. Some fought in Africa. Many went to France. Few families were unscarred. It required a charmed life to survive big-game hunting, and the war, and still be a young man in 1919.

It did not take long, however, for the Roaring Twenties to come to Africa. New clients and new settlers soon brought new energy, the clients prepared to buy lavish adventure, the settlers hungry to build a new life. Nairobi's hotels, outfitters and taxidermists enjoyed a second boom, and the old hunters trained the next generation of professionals. The first non-British hunters joined the profession, including the Americans Charles Cottar and Al Klein. Trucks and safari cars replaced the lines of porters of pre-war days. Game laws grew more stringent. Hunting became more and more of a business. Clients came to expect not merely trophies, but high times, an African extension of the privileged life that entertained them, or bored them, in Biarritz and St Moritz, in the West End and Newport. The Norfolk, although a little rough for some, became an extension of the Savoy and the Ritz. Like polo and yachting, safaris combined excitement with luxury.

Above: Donald Seth-Smith in his car with a dead lion

Opposite: Mt Kilimanjaro

For the brief period from 1919 to 1939 a grown man, in the absence of other credentials, could identify himself with pride as a yachtsman, a polo player or a big-game hunter. Each involved a bit of testing, but not too much. Big-game hunting could indeed be dangerous, but generally for the professional, not the client. It was the white hunter who went into the long grass and finished the job. Losing a client was unheard of, even injuries were rare. It was the code of the Alpine guide: if only one man comes down the mountain, it must be the client. The best client did not just pay his bills, however. He was the one who hunted cleanly, understood the ethic, respected the Africans, was courageous but not foolish, and slept with the right woman.

Norfolk Hotel, 1927

The new settlers were different, particularly the rush that arrived with the Soldier Settlement Scheme in late 1919. These British veterans were not all of the country-gentleman standard of Kenya's early leading settlers, and many did not have a long background in field sports. But they were industrious and committed to making a life in Kenya. One thousand and thirty-one farms were allotted at low prices under the scheme, following clamorous public drawings held in London and Nairobi to choose among thousands of eager applicants, their names and numbers drawn from revolving drums. By 1925 the land officially 'alienated' to whites totalled 12,000 square miles, and the land secured in native 'reserves' totalled 48,000, in a country of 240,000 square miles. New land went into cultivation. The high forests were cut back for tea and coffee. Flax and maize grew over the hills. Sheep and cattle spread across the plains. Once again the troublesome lion and black rhino were killed and driven back, and a new generation of European boys grew up on the edge of the bush with a rifle in their hands.

For men like Bror Blixen and Denys Finch Hatton, who even before the war had preferred the excitement of safari life to the toil of the farm, professional hunting soon became an easy choice. In March of 1919, well before he took out his first client, Denys Finch Hatton took the wife of his friend Bror Blixen on safari. It was an experience from which Isak Dinesen never recovered. Like Blixen, Finch Hatton shared with her the magic of life on safari, but beyond that, and in relation to it, he opened for her a life of the spirit, of ideas, self-expression, intellectual taste and finally, later, the urge to create.

Blixen was a gregarious rogue, a man's man and a lady's man, delighted to drink and seduce all night, and stalk and shoot all day. As one of his clients once warned another, when on safari with Blixen it was best to bring an extra woman so that he would be too busy to sleep with your wife. Finch Hatton, although comparably athletic and attractive, was essentially alone, discreet and cerebral. He and Berkeley Cole, Dinesen felt, were exiles from another, more graceful age. Reciting Shakespeare, Coleridge and the Old Testament by the camp fire, teaching her Latin and Greek, singing madrigals, encouraging her to tell tales as she invented them, Finch Hatton taught her that, as she later said, love should be the companionship of another mind.

Baron Bror von Blixen and Isak Dinesen at home in the Ngong Hills

In their complex intimacy, Denys Finch Hatton and Isak Dinesen were never more close than when they hunted lion. At the end of one night-time kill, she wrote, they were silent, without a need to speak. They understood their unity. When they hunted together, she remembered twenty-five years later as she wrote *Out of Africa*, they were always lucky with lion. She and Finch Hatton related hunting to seduction, apparently in the belief that both aim at securing possession of the essence of another creature.

At dawn on New Year's Day, 1928, driving hard on the track to Narok just before dawn, they suddenly passed a dead giraffe bull, which, from its high smell, had apparently been shot three days before. As they went by, a feeding lioness raised her wet face from the carcass. Finch Hatton stopped the car. Isak Dinesen's Masai neighbours, prohibited by the government from bearing spears, had asked her to shoot marauding lion, and she urged Finch Hatton to take the shot. He complied.

When they passed again a short time later as sunrise flared, they found a fine male lion, evidently the mate, standing upon the giraffe, his mane ruffling gently in the wind. Some dispute the details, but Dinesen wrote that she made the kill with Finch Hatton's heavy double rifle, 'the shot a declaration of love', leaving her 'aglow with the plenipotence a shot gives you, because you take effect at a distance'. Then, with the lions skinned, as Finch Hatton and his gunbearer Kanuthia paused after their work, the two lovers sat in the grass near the three dead animals and breakfasted on almonds, raisins and a bottle of Bordeaux.

Finch Hatton on safari believed not in luxury, but in meticulous planning, the avoidance of difficulty and discomfort. The founding principle, he thought, was derived from knowing the precise utilization rate of a single tin of sardines. Once you understood that one pound of tea lasted one man a fortnight, it all fell into place. The daily need for stores could then be projected and supplies gathered and loaded into the Dodge car and two Chevrolet trucks that Finch Hatton used for long safaris. Then it would be the standard drill for serious professional safaris, with fresh laundry every day, eight-foot-high tents, and hot baths and drinks waiting in camp as the sun went down.

When Berkeley Cole and Finch Hatton visited Isak Dinesen at the farm in the Ngong Hills, however, they expected a higher standard of luxury and conversation, much of which they provided themselves. It came to be understood that Finch Hatton would keep the farm supplied with books, gramophone records and cigars from Benson & Hedges in London. Berkeley Cole, even when the bank was hounding him for his overdraft, furnished the wine. With a shared taste for Château d'Yquem and Chambertin, the three drank well. The two men were astute members of the Muthaiga Club wine committee, and Finch Hatton once visited Paris to buy for the club's cellar. When Cole stayed at the farm, each morning at eleven he took a bottle of champagne to the forest, complaining that it saddened him when the Baroness did not provide her best Danish glasses for such moments. Finch Hatton also defined himself with elegant eccentrici-

Isak Dinesen outside her farmhouse with her staff, 1929

ties, covering his bald head with faded blue bowlers made in London by James Locke. The servants called him Bedar, the Balding One. Studying the ease with which the Masai stood for hours on one foot, he had boots made by Peals in the shape of the Masai feet, with a square toe and perfectly straight along the sides, to the astonishment of a friend who saw him wearing them, brilliantly polished, outside Harrods.

Both men found the Ngong farm a civilized refuge. Slight, red-haired and precisely erect, Cole was haunted by a weak heart and a precarious coffee estate. Finch Hatton, always valuing freedom first, carried to its extreme the English gift for privacy, of personal non-disclosure. The perfect witness, he never volunteered information. He asked friends to destroy his letters. He explained to his possessive lover that he visited her for pleasure, not for commitment. A lonely life on safari suited him well. Once, as Errol Trzebinski records in her thorough biography *Silence Will Speak*, after days of travel, an anxious courier, the last in a chain of runners, finally reached Finch Hatton deep in the bush with a note wedged in a forked stick, 'Do you know the address of George Robinson?' Scribbling the single word YES on the back, Finch Hatton sent the runner home.

A relaxed man himself, Bror Blixen accepted his wife's romantic arrangements as the sort of thing he understood. At times he and Finch Hatton shared a room at the Club, each using it when the other was on safari. Occasionally he would introduce the Englishman as 'My friend, and my wife's lover, Denys

Finch Hatton.' Safari life was the one thing that all three shared. Isak Dinesen herself was irritated by the friendship of her two men, considering it unnatural, annoyed that love for her was insufficient to force them apart. In time the relationship grew still more Byzantine as Isak Dinesen's young friend Beryl Markham, the daughter of Lord Delamere's horse-trainer, had affairs with both Blixen and Finch Hatton.

Like Isak Dinesen, Beryl Markham was brought up by her father to have a manly independence and a zest for the wilds. Raised in the bush, learning to hunt with a spear with her African companions, Beryl Markham grew up with a sense of self-containment that permitted her to discard lovers, and even a son, as easily as she slid off the back of a racehorse or took off for Newfoundland on the first solo trans-Atlantic flight from east to west. Even for Isak Dinesen, she cannot have been an easy rival. Long-legged, feline, blonde, and with a face that reminded admirers of Greta Garbo, Beryl Markham had a dash and detachment that few forgot. If the tales are true, Beryl Markham could use a spear like a Masai moran, ride like an Irish jockey, fly like Charles Lindbergh, seduce like a houri and write better than Ernest Hemingway. Only her writing has been questioned. Lacking both scruples and education, Beryl Markham is thought by some to have borrowed the literary talents of one of her husbands, Raoul Schumacher, in order to produce *West with the Night*.

Beryl Markham

While the involvement of Blixen, Dinesen, Markham and Finch Hatton is recalled today with a charming aura of intellectual romance, a more fashionable and sordid style of social adventure is thought to have characterized the life of Happy Valley, an area of rich estates above Gilgil in Kenya's Aberdare Mountains. There, alcohol, drugs, infidelity and murder brought corrupt excitement into the idle lives of a few rich and occasionally titled families as they flirted across the line from exuberance into decadence. In *White Mischief* James Fox presents a dramatic account of the mystery that still surrounds the greatest of the Happy Valley dramas, the roadside murder of Josslyn Hay, Earl of Erroll. A rabid philanderer, and at the time the lover of a married woman called Lady Diana Broughton, Hay had so many enemies that it was difficult to identify the one who had killed him. A spoiled combination of vanity and decadence, his perverse pleasure was to borrow a few quid from each husband he cuckolded. Lady Diana, five times married and divorced, was blamed for introducing shorts as a women's fashion in east Africa.

For a time, Kenya provided the Happy Valley set, and some safari clients, with an exquisite atmosphere of indulgence. In a sublimely un-English climate, without the constraints of life in Europe or America, they were blessed with the luxuries of cheap land and cheaper servants. With the entire colony as one extended shooting estate, with polo and naked Africans visible from the same veranda, surrounded by an exoticism that made it easy to feel the abandon of a perpetual costume party, the Happy Valley set danced in a fantasy. But for some safari clients, as these personages were pointed out across the bar at the Muthaiga Club, they added a scandalous glamour to the excitements of Africa.

Interior of a settler's home in 1920s

To present the Happy Valley set as representative of Kenya's settlers, however, is historical perjury. As Lord Cranworth put it, 'their existence means nothing to the real life of the colony.' The colonists had neither the time, the money nor the character to live a Happy Valley life. Most of the settler-hunters did, however, know how to enjoy a well-deserved drink. When they drank, they drank. At one party in 1926, Delamere's two hundred guests consumed six hundred bottles of champagne. Sir Frederick Jackson said of Selous that the old hunter would never have been so abstemious had he been brought up in east Africa, instead of to the south. But by the time the Earl of Erroll's friends staggered home at seven in the morning with their dresses and black ties hanging loose, Beryl Markham would be completing a check of her stables, Lord Delamere was examining the mouths of sick cattle with his Masai herders, and Galbraith Cole was at work among his merino sheep. They found determination more useful than decadence.

It is perhaps equally misleading to present Bror Blixen and Denys Finch Hatton as the two finest professional hunters of their day. They were indeed accomplished and respected, perhaps also the most elegant white hunters in European terms, and certainly the most celebrated in later writings. But they themselves were the first to respect the superior experience and the mastery of bushcraft of men like R. J. Cuninghame, J. A. Hunter and Philip Percival. None was a finer shot than Hunter.

What survives most of the great white hunters today is the odd cloudy snapshot, a few letters or diary pages and, best of all, but perhaps least accurate,

The Rift Valley

Opposite: Philip Percival as a young blood

the tales still told around the camp fire of how, like Oswell and Selous, they lived and hunted when Africa seemed young. Shortly before his death in 1950, Donald Seth-Smith in 1948 began to collect manuscripts from many of the old-time hunters, including Philip Percival, intending to publish a book on the changing condition of Kenya's wildlife. His son, today's crack professional hunter Tony Seth-Smith, made these unpublished manuscripts available to me for the preparation of this book.

Tony Seth-Smith's mother, a pioneer lady of the hard school, left several hunting accounts drawn from her own life. One afternoon in 1926, hunting alone on Suswa Mountain, a rugged extinct volcano above the Rift Valley, she was charged by two rhino, one of which she had wounded with an old ·450 double Rigby. One rhinoceros hit her, scraping the length of her body with its horn and scalping her before tossing her in the air and trampling on her, breaking three ribs. She made it down the mountain, climbed the Rift escarpment and flagged down a train before collapsing in Nairobi hospital. Today the offending rhino horn hangs in Tony's house, with her dried scalp still on it.

Left: Donald Seth-Smith's future wife, Kathleen, after being scalped by a rhino

Below: Hippos by Donald Seth-Smith, 1933

Right: Kathleen Seth-Smith's safari staff, including, on the left, the gunbearer who drove off the rhino that attacked her

Below: Kenya's first six-wheel vehicle, 1927

J. A. Hunter, fortunately, also left a written record of his safari days. In a tradition that still continues, he was always generous with less experienced hunters, like his friend Denys Finch Hatton, whom he largely trained. Hunter himself had been taken on his first lion hunt by Donald Seth-Smith, on the edge of the Kapiti Plains at Kilima Kiu, the 'Hill of Thirst' in Swahili. There Seth-Smith frequently galloped lion with Alfred Pease and the Hill cousins. Galloping lion in open country, the sport that killed George Grey and many others, had its own strict code. It was understood that only light rifles would be used, ·256s (6·5 mm) or ·275s (7 mm). When the pursued lion, angry and tired, finally stopped at bay, the form was to leap off and face the lion as it charged, preferably kneeling or sitting for a good shot. Dismounting at a range of two hundred yards, as Pease recommended, gave the hunter a few seconds in the event of a charge. When lion were hunted on foot in thick country, they generally charged from thirty yards and there was not time to sit. Accordingly, the hunters used heavier, double rifles with less long-range accuracy but more stopping power.

The last time that J. A. Hunter and Finch Hatton hunted together, in 1931, they were after two lion that were killing cattle in the Masai Reserve in southern Kenya. A moran complained that the lion jumped on the back of his cattle, forcing their heads down with a massive paw until the desperate, galloping animals fell and snapped their necks. Spotting the lion just ahead, Finch Hatton, described by J. A. as one of the bravest hunters he ever met, loped towards them. As the lions reared up to strike, Finch Hatton raised his double rifle and killed both so fast that it sounded virtually like a single shot.

'Good effort,' Hunter observed.

'I'd take any chance with you behind me, J. A.,' Finch Hatton replied.

Shooting often on government game control assignments, killing rogue elephants wounded by other hunters on Mt Kenya, or clearing buffalo, rhinoceros and lion from agricultural areas, Hunter probably shot more heavy game than any other modern hunter. When J. A. first started hunting lion for a living in 1906, there were about forty professional lion hunters based in Nairobi, of whom over half were brutally mauled at least once. In half a century of African hunting, Hunter killed over 350 buffalo, 1,000 black rhinoceros, 1,400 elephant and hundreds of lion. Shooting elephant on control work, the government paid the hunters with one tusk from each pair, granting the hunter the right to buy the other for one shilling a pound.

With hunger and tribal warfare at an end in colonial Kenya, the African population began to increase dramatically in the 1920s. As different tribes expanded to cover more territory, the Game Department asked professional hunters to cull the wild animals. At the request of the Wakamba, Hunter was once assigned to reducing the black rhinoceros in the Machakos district, where he killed 163. Later in life he served as a game warden, becoming an active conservationist, particularly protecting the rhinoceros, and turning his bush skills against the white and black poachers. Like his successors, he distinguished

Samburu country, Kenya

between occasional poaching for survival by local natives in a hard year, and large-scale commercial poaching directed to the markets in Nairobi and Zanzibar.

When he looked back over his experiences, analysing his adventures with animals, Hunter decided that, as a general rule, if hunted in a sporting manner, without bait, leopard were the most dangerous game. Typically charging from perhaps ten yards away, leopard give no warning, whereas lion generally growl and stiffen their tails. Until reduced by massive poaching in later years, leopard were plentiful, for the females have a gestation period of only three and a half months, and have litters of one to four cubs. Hunter noted that elephant, being the most intelligent, had learned and changed the most, retreating from the open country, becoming far more dangerous as they grew wary, hiding in the forests, often knowing more about guns than the clients who pursued them.

Leopard, however, did not change. As one of the few animals that sometimes kill for the pleasure of it, leopards have retained their ferocity and invariably attack when wounded. A rushing leopard, blazing fast and stretched to the full, up to nine feet long from nose to tip of tail, presents a narrow target weighing perhaps half as much as a lion. It can be so difficult to shoot that Hunter himself, although a deadly shot with either his ·500 Holland & Holland or his favourite Jeffreys ·475 No. 2 loaded with a 480 grain bullet and 85 grains of cordite, preferred to pursue the wounded animal with a twelve-gauge shotgun loaded with heavy shot.

Crafty, given to ambush, particularly enjoying the flesh of dogs and young baboons, leopard even entered houses to get at domestic pets. Going after them on foot requires the hunter to study each tree as he advances, for, unlike lion, leopard often lie pressed flat on a limb, waiting to spring, sometimes betrayed only by a long dangling tail. An unwounded leopard will generally let an unaware hunter pass beneath, but should their eyes meet, the cat attacks instantly.

On one safari, Hunter's honeymooning clients were asleep in their tent, their Alsatian watchdog resting by their bed, when a leopard crept in and seized the dog by the neck. Thrashing about violently in the tent, the dog was saved when its spiked brass collar injured the mouth of the leopard. Returning the next night to finish the job, the leopard was killed by Hunter's gun trap. Hunting once in the Masai Reserve, Hunter's companion was charged by a leopard in one twelve-foot spring from behind a boulder, 'nothing but a yellow flash of light', so fast that the man could not raise the rifle. Hunter fired a 'snap-shot', as if bird shooting, breaking both the leopard's shoulders as it fell dead on his friend. Contemplating his many escapes, Hunter considered that his boyhood training, firing at waterfowl as they darted across the Lochar Moss in Dumfriesshire, saved his life many a time.

Leopard talons are so infecting and putrid with decaying meat that even cattle tend to die from the scratches. Hunter had many farmer friends who had lost an eye or part of their face to leopard while defending their livestock. A leopard often leaps for a man's face, fastening its teeth in the neck, clawing for the eyes, and working against the body with the rear talons, a more general assault than that delivered by most lion charges. Old Masai lion hunters taught J. A. that a lion's most dangerous weapon against people are its dewclaws, the curved, sharp and retractable claws on the inside of each foreleg, corresponding to a person's thumbs, with which a lion will slash and disembowel. Disagreeing with Alfred Pease, Hunter recommended submitting quietly once in a lion's power, for the animal is often satisfied with chewing on an arm or thigh before making off. Resistance is futile and dangerous. Buffalo, on the other hand, unlike rhinoceros, he found to be cruel and vicious once wounded, always seeking to kill a wounded man.

Gunbearer Mkamba and leopard,
Kenya, 1926

On one game control hunt in the mid-1920s, shooting at the request of the
Masai and the Game Department to cut down the overpopulation of lion that
had developed as the Masai herds increased and the Masai stopped lion hunting,
Hunter killed eighty-eight lion and ten leopard in three months. The Masai
were so pleased that they offered to purchase J. A. from the Game Department
for 500 cattle, enough to buy over 150 hard-working wives. A skilled professional could make a fine living hunting, with a good black-maned lion skin
going for £20 in Nairobi, leopard skins at £4, buffalo skins at £7 for shields,
rhino horn at 30 s. a pound, and ivory at 24 s. a pound, or £150 for a fine sixty-
pounder. For sale as jewellery to the Indians, Hunter also collected a boxful of
floating bones, the small unattached, curved bone found in the shoulder muscle
of every lion.

The old professional hunters like J. A. generally had three types of informal
students: the next generation of professionals, their clients and their own sons.
Their sons did not receive the discreet assistance and flattering assessments
expected by most clients, but they learned the trade. Gordon Hunter, J. A.'s
eldest son, recalling the old days one afternoon at his coffee farm at Thika,
described to me how his father introduced him to the sport, never forgetting the
demanding standard that the old hunter required of him. J. A. himself believed

237

that every hunter passes through three stages: first nervous, then cocky and foolhardy, and finally learning to take only acceptable risks.

When Gordon was eight, J. A. gave him a ·22 and began teaching him in the bush, often with a Waliangulu tracker or with his gunbearer Saseeta, who carried a bag of ashes for testing the wind. At sixteen, a devoted reader of *King Solomon's Mines*, confident in the bush, Gordon once shot in a day all four topi permitted by his licence. Reddish-brown antelope, up to four feet at the shoulder, topi are extremely gregarious, although the males are intensely territorial during the mating season. Annoyed at his son's excessive shooting of topi, J. A. told him next time to go hunting with only two bullets, one for coming home with. Hunting for his first elephant the same year, Gordon went shooting with his father at Samburu near the coast. Spotting a fine bull, with 85 lb tusks, the boy prepared to fire his ·404 at forty yards. 'You bloody well won't,' J. A. whispered, slowly stalking in with him to ten yards. Always silent at the end, using hand signals, Hunter observed that his son was scared and shaking. Pulling Gordon's neck hairs sharply in a prearranged signal, he stopped him from shooting until the boy steadied. When the bull fell to Gordon's shot, the other elephant stampeded and his father dropped a second heavy tusker.

Above all, J. A. taught his son, and his clients if they would learn, to be calm in the bush. 'Keep your cool,' he would urge. 'If you get windy, take a smoke. Then do it.' In the field, Hunter himself seemed to have no nerves. Gordon remembers watching a charging elephant come to fifteen feet away, as his father fired, concentrating calmly as another man might if driving a motorcar and then hopping aside as the elephant 'fell on J. A.'s footprints'. Like a surgeon or a general, Hunter always studied the situation carefully before he began, learning the land, but finding wisdom also in native lore, in what some white men regarded as barbarous superstition. He taught his son, as the Dorobo had taught him, that one should not destroy a snake that crosses one's path, lest the day's hunting be a failure, a lesson that Gordon's experience confirmed. Like a buffalo or rhinoceros with tick birds, Hunter relied on birds as his scouts to educate him. Different birds served as various indicators, clues to habitat and wildlife.

J. A.'s clients, who inevitably included Rothschilds, Schwarzenbergs and maharajahs, received more gentle instruction than his son Gordon, though they tried his patience both on the trail and in camp. Frequently, game-control work came as a relief to Hunter, particularly after an American client spent his evenings sobbing in his tent whenever an actress in Paris failed to respond to the daily cables the man sent from Nairobi via the camp's radio. Unlike Bror Blixen, the Scottish hunter did not satisfy all the demands of his female clients, who, he said, could be more dangerous than the animals. Hunter learned the lesson early. One of his first clients was a French count, who believed that each man should do what he did best. Hunter collected the trophies. The Frenchman drank. One night the Countess raised the flap of J. A.'s tent and seated herself on his cot in a lace nightgown, holding a beer glass of whisky in one hand.

'Countess,' J. A. inquired, 'where is your husband?'

'Hunter,' she replied in annoyance, 'you Englishmen ask the strangest questions.'

Another client was a well-known German baron, not much of a hunter, and desperately jealous of his ravishing wife, who was a keen sportswoman. Anticipating the worst, the baron brought a reliable male chaperon, an ex-major in the German army. The baroness was not permitted to hunt without the major, who had the distinctive heavy tread of a German soldier, unwittingly saving the life of many handsome trophies as he forced his way through the bush after the baroness.

One evening at supper she told her husband, kicking Hunter under the table as she did so, that the next morning they proposed to hunt in a donga so thick with bush that a party of three would be dangerous. The major, however, was not deterred. They found no lion, but as Hunter went ahead to drive a large warthog towards the baroness, he heard her scream. Running to her side, J. A. found her naked to the waist, covered in vicious red safari ants. To remove the ants, he scraped her body with the dull edge of his hunting knife. Just as she buttoned up, the major came bursting through the bushes. When the two left him, Hunter sank to the ground, trembling as if he had just survived a rhino charge, certain that a few more seconds, as he put it, would have cost him his licence as a professional hunter.

While some women clients were stalking their hunters, however, others found better sport out of camp. In 1923 Vivienne de Watteville, twenty-four, and her Swiss father Bernard, set out on foot from Nairobi to collect specimens for the Berne Museum. They were underfinanced. To economize they had no vehicle and no professional hunter. They went on safari with a gunbearer, headman, cook and skinners, with thirty porters and six donkeys for transport, hoping to buy two riding mules on the trek.

The safari's purpose was to collect animal skins for mounting in group scenes, particularly the skins of an elephant, giraffe and white rhinoceros. It started badly, with de Watteville missing his first shots, to the contempt of the hungry porters and the embarrassment of his gunbearer, Kongoni, a leader in his profession who was used to the high shooting standards of his former client, Prince William of Sweden. Soon, however, when Bernard bagged his first lion, Kongoni danced around the carcass, for the first time using English as he exclaimed, 'Good luck, my boy!' After a few weeks, as they grew fit and the safari proceeded north-east across the Tana and Thika Rivers, they settled into a comfortable routine, with de Watteville shooting to secure specimens and food for the camp, and Vivienne responsible for cleaning, curing and preserving the skins.

Determined to get an elephant skin early in order to ensure the expedition's success, de Watteville shot a fine bull at dusk by a pool in the Meru forest near Mt Kenya. Skinning even a small animal requires that the work be done swiftly lest the carcass begin to spoil and the skin no longer come away cleanly. If any flesh whatever remains attached to the skin, the skin itself will rot through, but if the work is done hastily, it will be cut. To preserve the skin in one piece, it is necessary to cut an even centre slit along the belly, extending up the rest of the body. One additional cut is made inside each foot, running up the inside of the leg to meet the central cut at the groin and chest. The work, even for a moderate-sized animal like an oryx, is both heavy and delicate. If the job is not done carefully, and the skin thoroughly dried, the skin will begin to 'slip', as it loses firmness and the hairs come out.

De Watteville's bull died on a slope in the dark, wedged between the hillside and a tree. Digging out the ground under the elephant, levering it with heavy poles cut from the forest, and hauling on ropes, Vivienne de Watteville and the entire safari party finally muscled the huge body on to its back, its legs already bent rigid from rigor mortis. Working all night by hurricane lamps, slitting from the very tip of the trunk on down the entire length of the elephant, they kept the immense skin in one piece. The whetstone sang all night, for the tough skin, in places an inch thick, soon dulled the knives. Wedges were driven into the mouth to prize open the jaws, clenched shut in death. The trunk itself, its rippled skin surprisingly delicate, yet each corrugation firmly attached to webs of muscle, required the most artful patience. To remove the core of the massive ears, a large cross was cut on the inside of each, and the skin was then peeled back in four pieces so that the cartilage could be removed.

Once the skin was finally free, and carried triumphantly back to camp by twenty men on a stretcher of branches, it took Bernard and eight skinners two days to scrape it clean of flesh and pare it down to a manageable thickness. Then it was spread on an elevated platform to dry, frequently requiring more scraping and stretching. The finest preservative of the time was a mixture of one part saltpetre and three parts alum, finely ground with a dash of camphor, producing a clear drying mixture for rubbing into the skin. By mistake, however, 70 lb of arsenical soap had been packed instead. Sticky, less effective, the pasty arsenic solution took longer to apply, left ridges in the skins, and seared any cuts on the hands of the workers. For two weeks they worked on the skin, each night folding it for several hours to keep the creases soft, as the skin hardened until it resembled corrugated metal. Finally twelve men stood on the elephant skin to press it flat. Then it was reduced to a parcel 6 x 5 x 2 ft and sewn up in calico dipped in arsenic to keep out rats and insects.

Sending the elephant skin back to Nairobi by truck, the safari pressed north across the Siolo Plain, where de Watteville shot an eighteen-foot bull giraffe. Unlike other animals, the giraffe seemed to retain its beauty even after death. But the reticulated skin seemed even tougher than elephant hide, although not as thick. Rubbery, fibrous and fine-grained, it defied the knife. While Vivienne took the taxidermist's honour of fleshing out the face, removing the tissue from between skull and skin, proud to satisfy her father's fastidious Swiss standards of a clean-finished job, the skinners worked on the neck and body.

Vivienne de Watteville on safari

Next it was east through hot, dry country, holding to the course of the Ewaso Ngiro as the river drained towards the Lorian Swamp, learning the tricks of bush medicine along the way. One tracker, bitten by a scorpion, crushed another and applied its body to the wound as a poultice. But Vivienne de Watteville relied on quinine powder and epsom salts as cures for all ills. Once, they faced the challenge of skinning a twelve-foot crocodile, after thirty men, hauling on a rope attached to its leg, succeeded in dragging the thrashing, wounded animal from the river.

On the edge of the Lorian Swamp they learned to respect the leaden, adhesive richness of wet black cotton soil, which is rock-hard when dry and glue-like if wet, as it adhered to their boots until they could not walk unless they repeatedly scraped them clean. Contrary to reports, game in the region was scarce, the lion so hungry that they devoured one of the camp's canvas bathtubs and broke into the zareba to attack the mules. Killing one marauding lion, which was reckless with hunger and an old spear wound, they found its belly held only grass. Another lion left scraps of canvas and three nails in its droppings.

Making their way south-east, buying pack camels and trekking by night in the cool moonlight, and then gliding south by dugout canoe on the Tana River, they finally arrived at the old Arab slave-trading port of Lamu. Then the second leg of the safari began, hunting forest hog and bongo in the Aberdares, crossing

Lake Victoria into Uganda, and unsuccessfully chasing mountain gorilla through the bamboo tunnels of a volcano taller than the Jungfrau, in what is today Burundi. Denied permission by the Belgians to hunt gorilla in the Congo, the de Wattevilles walked north towards President Roosevelt's old base, Rhino Camp, securing special permission to kill one white rhinoceros for the Berne Museum.

Elephants on safari in the Belgian Congo, where, uniquely in Africa, they had been trained as pack animals

One evening in the Congo, after de Watteville hunted lion while his daughter rested in camp, fever-struck, she heard him return, calling out for water. Then he entered her tent with the words, 'The lion has got me this time.' His clothes shredded, blood running down from his body, only his head uncut, de Watteville remained conscious for three hours, directing the surgery, while his daughter washed him, cutting away the lacerated tissue and forcing raw crystals of permanganate into the thigh wounds that would not be staunched. The bone of his right forearm stripped bare to the elbow, he wondered aloud whether she might save it.

Later the cook told Vivienne de Watteville that her father had wounded a lion, his nineteenth, accompanied by a lioness and cubs. Pursued into a reedbed, the lion turned, reared up and cuffed the hunter down without harming him. As the lion bolted away, de Watteville rose and fired again. The lion dashed back, pinning him to the ground and furiously rending him. Jamming the rifle muzzle under the lion's jaw, de Watteville killed it. In the lion's death its talons contracted into the hunter's body, forcing the man to tear them out one by one before he could rise. Then, for two hours, he walked back to camp, where he soon died.

Resolute, Vivienne de Watteville at once took charge, leading the safari, having her father's unfinished task before her, the men more loyal than ever. Already she had acquired on safari both a sense of true freedom as she became part of nature and the feeling that 'real physical fear is a glorious thing'. By now, too, she had learned her father's hunting lore, knowing that a single blade of grass near the muzzle can deflect a bullet, and that the real joy comes before the kill. Persisting, she collected the species to complete the Berne collection: buffalo, waterbuck, bushbuck and, finally, a white rhinoceros. After the safari came to its end, sailing north on the Nile from Rhino Camp, more expressive than most male English hunters, Vivienne de Watteville wrote that she had learned a love for the bush, 'a love so deep and vibrating that it flows in upon one's consciousness continually, given by the trees, the sky, the very earth you walk upon'.

The same day that Bernard de Watteville killed his magnificent male bongo on the Kijabe Escarpment, 12 April 1924, an American couple, Martin and Osa Johnson, gazed down upon Kenya's Lake Paradise, the goal of their own remarkable safari. For de Watteville, the day had marked the end of his greatest hunt, seven weeks of silent stalking at 9,000 feet, tracking bongo in the cool forests of the Aberdares, the forty-foot bamboos sighing as they tossed and stroked each other in the wind, their feathery tops forming a cloudy canopy overhead. The most elusive game, like bongo, mountain nyala and greater kudu, compel their hunters to give the time to learning their natures, and de Watteville had become an accomplished student. His study of the drinking habits and diet of the bongo finally yielded his prize, an old bull with amber-tipped spiralling horns 31 inches long, given to browsing on ten-foot tall green shrubs with nettle-like leaves and knotted pinkish stalks.

For the Johnsons that same day was the beginning of four years at Lake Paradise, dedicated to recording on motion-picture film what they considered to be the last days of Africa's vanishing game. They were not the conventional safari clients, interested in large bags and easy trophies. For years they had used photography to finance a life of adventure, finding themselves more at home in Borneo than in their native Kansas. At the urging of the animal sculptor Carl Akeley, the director of New York's Museum of Natural History, they had first come to Kenya in 1921, going on safari to Lake Paradise. An unknown lake at Marsabit near the Kaisut Desert, Lake Paradise was revealed to them by Boculy, their Warusha gunbearer. The son of a legendary elephant poacher, Boculy was at first reluctant to share this spoon-shaped sanctuary, three quarters of a mile long, the glistening centre of an extinct volcano, cradled by wooded banks rising steeply 200 feet above its shores. Numberless animals drank in the shallows about the lake, as cranes and egrets bowed elegantly among the water vines and blue African waterlilies. Inspired, naming it Paradise, the Johnsons took photographs and determined to return fully equipped for a sustained safari to create the finest filmed record of the game of east Africa.

Left: Osa Johnson in a sedan chair, 1924

Below: The Johnsons' two Sikorsky aircraft

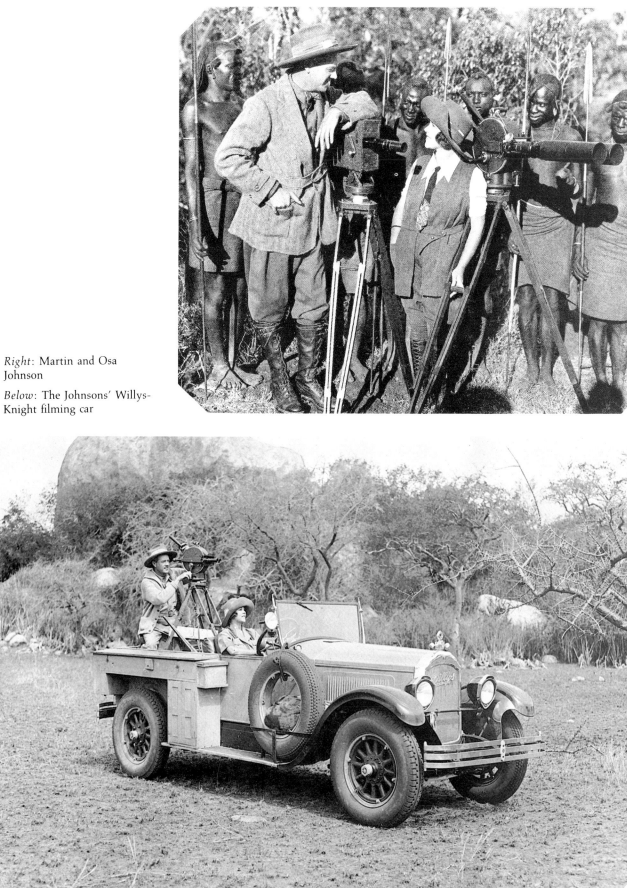

Right: Martin and Osa
Johnson

Below: The Johnsons' Willys-
Knight filming car

Short of money, they went to Rochester, New York, to solicit support from George Eastman, the founder of the Eastman Kodak Company. Hearing them briefly, but without the time to study their pictures, Eastman replied that he never invested in private enterprise. As her husband brooded on the train ride home, Osa Johnson stood up, forcing him to descend at Albany and go back again to Rochester. Once more Eastman admitted them, 'his eyes like pieces of blue ice with the sun on them', Osa Johnson wrote, 'his patience tied up tightly with thin white string'. Hearing them out, examining the pictures of Lake Paradise, he gave $10,000 towards the cost of the safari, and the right to use his name to raise more.

The Johnson expedition that left Nairobi in 1924 was a triumph of safari logistics. Not only a complex array of supplies, including bags of building cement and containers of developing acid, but vehicles themselves were shipped from America. Six Willys-Knight cars with custom-made safari bodies were uncrated and assembled in Nairobi. In addition, the cavalcade comprised four motor lorries, five mule-drawn wagons, four ox-carts and two hundred porters with sixty-pound loads. Thirty-five other Africans served as gunbearers, supervisors and personal servants. Most fortunate, they were to be escorted by Blaney Percival, a leading naturalist who had recently retired after many years as game warden of Kenya.

On their 1921 expedition, the Johnsons had been badly prepared for the arduous travel across the hot, jagged lava fields of northern Kenya. Desperate, fearing his collapsing men would perish of thirst if left behind on the searing rocks, Martin had even commanded his headmen to use whips to keep his porters on their bleeding feet. In 1924, the second Johnson safari was almost too well prepared. Although their transport was American, much of their equipment came from England. London had now become a rear-base for many safaris, and not only for the splendid weapons made by Holland & Holland and other top rifle makers. Fortnum & Mason and the Army & Navy Stores furnished the outfitters' supplies. Rowland Ward meticulously updated the documented records of big-game trophies, which they had first published in 1892. The legends of the great hunts were kept alive at spirited dinners of the Shikar Club, where hunters from around the Empire gathered to discuss sport and conservation.

The Johnsons' tents, chairs and other camp equipment were all made to order by Benjamin Edgington of London. Both Johnsons were dressed in Solara safari outfits, tailored in Nairobi from cloth made in London, the fabric interlined with a red and purple weave to deter Africa's ultraviolet rays. Electric fans, crates of Heinz soups, live chickens and boxes of Kansas watermelon seed shared the wagons with Kalowatt, a pet gibbon ape from Borneo that often ate at the Johnsons' table using a tiny fork. Once in Nairobi, the eighteen guns and twenty-one cameras were all carefully checked out. Each lens had been made to order by Bausch & Lomb in Rochester or Dallmeyer in London. By the time the Johnsons reached the Ewaso Ngiro River and Blaney Percival met them in his

Boculy, the Johnsons' tracker

worn Model-T Ford, its body literally held together by baling wire, they had learned, as Randolph Churchill had in 1892, that luxury is itself a burden.

But at Lake Paradise, five hundred miles north of Nairobi, after hacking their way through the forest, with fifty men cutting a trail with *pangas*, axes and crowbars as they advanced, the Johnsons established a base camp that had no rival. With logs, vines and thatch they built their cottage, its chimney's firebricks made from clay. Near by were storehouses, gardens, a corral and a camera laboratory. As a concession to Africa, the cabin logs were set upright in native village fashion instead of horizontally as on the American frontier. The wooden packing cases soon became smooth floors. The cabin exteriors were stuccoed with a pink surface made from one half clay and one half elephant, rhino and buffalo dung. One day each week Osa Johnson checked the entire camp, seeing that every hut was swept and scoured.

Frequently the Johnsons, following Boculy, ventured along the game trails that crossed the forest. Boculy, an elderly, bony, wizened man with a jaw disfigured by an elephant encounter, had a mystical understanding of the great beasts. Widely admired even by the hunters of other tribes, frequently walking on his own for sixty miles without water, he was known to all as the 'Little Brother of the Elephants'. Like a Frenchman on his boulevard, Boculy was at home on the centuries-old, hard-packed elephant trails that criss-crossed the virgin forest, knowing the avenues that took the elephant to waterholes and forest feeding grounds in the dry season, and to desert and plains during wet weather.

After many trips to Africa, and years spent in the bush, Martin Johnson later concluded that Boculy had no equal at endurance or bushcraft. When other Africans lost the track, Boculy would proceed with his shambling, crablike gait, his sandals artfully made from old tyres, dressed in faded khaki breeches and puttees, proud in a tattered blue shirt of the King's African Rifles. Muttering to himself, twitching his monkey-tail fly swatter, inhaling snuff, he studied bits of mud that had been pressed between the toes of his quarry, knowing the different types of mud that elephant, rhinoceros and buffalo prefer for their baths, able to deduce precisely their numbers and pace of march.

Johnson learned much from Boculy, especially to read the signs that animals leave as they pass through vegetation. A flattened blade of grass, he learned, requires three hours to pull itself erect. Its intermediate angles, allowing for variables, can be read like the hands of a clock. But the sharp hooves of buffalo cut the grass, instead of pressing it down as an elephant does. Looking at the tallest branches, Boculy would observe where giraffe had neatly eaten off the tender buds, leaving the branches undisturbed, whereas elephant would strip the bark and break the limbs, often pulling down entire trees just to reach a few juicy branches. Like the finest trackers, Boculy possessed a remarkable gift of sight, being able to discern creatures that Johnson could barely find with his fieldglasses.

Each day Johnson worked with one or more of his ten motion-picture cameras, five of them specifically designed for game photography by Carl Akeley. Two were mounted together, one taking simultaneous slow-motion pictures. Another was fixed on a heavy unipod bolted on to a Willys car. Others were operated by remote control, with wires and an electric motor. Frequently, Johnson experimented with wide-angle, portrait and diffusing lenses. Each evening Bwana Piccer, as he was called, or Master Picture, worked in the laboratory among his drying drums, storage cases and developing vats, patching his films together in 200-foot lengths, stored in tins sealed with paraffin wax. Like Schillings twenty years before, Johnson found that clear water was a precious essential. Each day 800 gallons of water were hauled up from Lake Paradise by mule, and then repeatedly filtered through charcoal, sand and cotton. Due to the impossibility of getting colour film back to a proper laboratory for exposure and development within the requisite seven days, the Johnsons worked in black and white. The result of his work was several hundred thousand feet of film for New York's Museum of Natural History, and a successful commercial film called *Simba*, released in New York in 1928.

While Johnson was preoccupied with photography, Osa fished, made bitter-plum jam, picked wild spinach and asparagus, and planted watercress and sweet potatoes for the elephants on their route to Lake Paradise. Osa Johnson, 5 ft 2 in tall, vain and mettlesome, also did most of the shooting, once saving her husband as she brought down a charging lion, which fell dead thirteen feet from his tripod.

From time to time the Johnsons took lengthy safaris from their base camp, travelling with about fifteen men, perhaps a dozen of them carrying photographic equipment when out filming, each trained to rush to Johnson's side with the needed apparatus when he called out a certain number. For night photography, he would set trip wires across game trails. When a wire was disturbed, a dazzling flash of magnesium powder illuminated the night as a camera snapped automatically and the temporarily blinded animal blundered about. As the Johnsons worked, hunting only to eat, and never shooting at Lake Paradise itself, they came to know the game as few foreigners do, learning, in particular, a respect for the dignity and family loyalty of elephant. Once they were amazed to observe four cows teaching their calves how to trumpet in different tones. Occasionally, however, the Johnsons were disrespectful to the animals, particularly for an idea Johnson had for a film to be called *African Golf*. This involved using the mouths of hippos and crocodiles as golf holes, and the side of an elephant as a bunker, all scenes that the Johnsons actually photographed. As I have been unable to view *African Golf*, it is difficult to describe these scenes convincingly, and the foregoing must pass on vicarious authority.

One morning in 1925 Osa Johnson was astonished to receive a runner bearing a message from the Duke and Duchess of York, who were to be the future King George VI and the 'Queen Mum' of later years. They invited the Johnsons to travel south to meet their safari. Osa Johnson at once selected vegetables from her garden, loaded her Willys and set out, with her husband following in the camera car. She, however, floundered to a halt in the Ewaso Ngiro River, where her car stuck fast in a deep hole. From across the river an African swam out with a rope, and the members of another safari pulled and heaved until her car climbed the bank. It was the royal party, out hunting with Pat Ayer, a leading Nairobi professional hunter. Sharing lunch by the river, they all discussed elephant lore and photography, until the Duchess exclaimed, 'I hear something singing.' When her husband asked what it was, she replied that it was probably a mosquito singing 'God Save the King'.

The visit of the Yorks to Kenya, their first trip together to any country in the Empire, aroused considerable attention both in Britain and Africa, with journalists speculating whether the Duchess would wear shorts in the bush, and the Duke remarking that London's safari outfitters had offered him enough 'gadgets to exterminate every kind of game between Mombasa and the headwaters of the Nile'. Before setting out on safari, they celebrated Christmas 1924 in Nairobi, where European and Indian schoolchildren lined up separately on two sides of the tea pavilion and sang 'Land of Hope and Glory' for the Duchess.

Soon after the Johnsons returned to Lake Paradise, they enjoyed the long-awaited visit of their benefactor George Eastman. A spirited seventy-three-year-old, Eastman was attended by his personal physician and by the distinguished white hunter Philip Percival, the brother of Blaney Percival. Philip Percival was one of the earliest professional hunters, having started in 1910 after he helped the Hill cousins on the lion hunts of President Roosevelt's safari. Prior to that he was an ostrich farmer, learning much about the game while scouting for ostrich nests on the Kapiti Plains during the nesting season. The best time for finding ostrich, like game spotting, was at dawn and dusk, when the female and the male ostrich changed the guard, the darker male birds always taking the night shift. Ostrich eggs, each weighing five pounds, were stolen and raised in incubators. Occasionally, too, Percival and a gang of Africans would rush a nest with hatched chicks, scaring off the parents and grabbing the young birds as they squatted down. Contrary to ostrich mythology, the ostrich hunters learned that ostrich do not put their heads into the sand, but that they do actually protect themselves best when they put their heads against the sand, thereby lowering and reducing their profiles.

The most valuable ostrich plumes, in the golden days of feather fashions after 1900, were the thirty pure white plumes found in each underwing of a mature male between two and thirty-five years old. These sixty feathers weighed one pound, which sold for as much as £25 by 1925, by which time it was illegal to rob ostrich nests in Kenya.

The Hill cousins, also retired ostrich farmers, taught Philip Percival to hunt lion, and he agreed that galloping lion on the open plains was the finest sport, and not one for amateurs. The Hills and Philip Percival made a speciality of finding lion for clients who had failed to bag one on safari. They charged £25 for a one-week safari if they got a lion, and only £10 if they failed. They never

Above: The Duke and Duchess of York at a camp table, Kenya, 1924

Left: HRH The Duke and Duchess of York with a hunting companion, Kenya, 1924

Right: The Duke of York's safari car being pulled across the river at Archer's Post, northern Kenya, 1924

failed. The safaris were lean, consisting of three Europeans on horseback, a bullock wagon for transport, a few dogs, and Philip Percival's gunbearer Kieti, who preferred safari life to the Percival farm, where the hunter's son rode on Kieti's back while he polished the floors.

Scouting for lion on one hunt, Philip Percival's grey pony was pursued by an infuriated lion which finally pulled even with the horse. The horrified Percival watched the lion's shoulder blades pumping as he himself rode for his life. Finally, Percival confessed in his unpublished hunting notes, the lion desisted when Percival's terrified screams made it clear that he was not a zebra. His worst moment in lion hunting came, however, when a reckless porter rushed too close to a wounded lioness, thinking it was dead. The lioness seized the porter by one arm, and the man resisted violently, provoking the lioness further and giving Percival a difficult kill shot. Thereafter Percival agreed with J. A. Hunter and always recommended passive behaviour when seized by a lion.

Out with Philip Percival in 1926, Pop Eastman, as he was known on safari, was in experienced hands. Although he was well-armed for heavy game, with a

Kieti, Philip Percival's head safari man

new pair of Westley Richards ·470 double rifles, Eastman was a better cook than shot, taking great delight in squatting over a Dutch oven in camp, baking his superb huckleberry pie. So impressed was Percival by Eastman's lemon tarts and corn bread, that he offered him half his own monthly salary, £150, if he would stay on and become his safari chef.

Always an inventor, Eastman soon contrived a new form of safari shower-bath, a blessing to later clients. Seated in his zinc bathtub, he manipulated a clothespeg attached to a hose that regulated the flow of warm water from a suspended canvas bucket. A man of varied experience and travels, Eastman wrote that the greatest thrill of his life was the day he killed his first lion, running it down in a Buick and then hitting it in the groin with his 9·5 mm Mannlicher from 125 yards, before finishing it at 100 yards. Later, moving north from Lake Paradise, the safari acquired camels, the entire party consisting of 7 whites, 61 Africans, 5 mules and 28 camels. Each camel could carry 300 lb, 60 lb more than a good pack horse, and five times as much as a man. Later the safari moved south to the Serengeti Plain in Tanganyika, where Eastman, again

Camels in northern Kenya,
Eastman safari, 1926

George Eastman blowing an ostrich egg for a breakfast omelette. Before cooking it he weighed the contents

running down his quarries by Buick, bagged a rhino with his ·470 and later prepared a flawless ostrich-egg omelette, after carefully piercing the eggshell, and blowing out and weighing its contents.

In the letters he wrote on safari, Pop Eastman recorded some candid observations, concluding that Philip Percival, although excessively happy-go-lucky, was a 'splendid fellow, absolutely staunch and reliable in an emergency'. For his part, Percival considered that the wonder of the safari was Osa Johnson. Eastman wrote that Percival hated the sight of a woman in camp, but was captivated by this particular one, whether she was fishing, shooting, driving or cooking.

After four months on safari, Eastman returned home late in 1926, leaving the Johnsons to finish their work at Lake Paradise. With the ambivalence of many homeward-bound visitors to Africa, Pop Eastman wrote that he looked forward to returning to a country where 'the inhabitants are not unspeakably filthy and mosquitoes are not allowed to spread disease'. But as he boarded the train for Mombasa, he grumbled, 'Back to the world of fraud and pretence.'

The following year the Johnsons also left for home, eager to work on their films, but knowing they would miss Africa. Their greatest sadness before departing was the death of their pet gibbon. Playing on the roof of the Norfolk Hotel, Kalowatt had swung on to an electric wire, dying as smoke rose from his hands and the current held him fast. As a crowd of Africans laughed below, Johnson knocked several men down, including a doctor who came running from the hotel. That night the Johnsons buried Kalowatt in the forest ten miles from Nairobi, the body secure in the tin dress case of a British officer. Back in the States, preparing his memoirs, Johnson reflected on all the difficulties of the four-year safari. The most insoluble, Bwana Piccer concluded, was 'the workings of the native mind'.

Opposite above: Eastman safari group, 1926

Opposite below left: Eastman safari, the cook, Kisoroni, and his equipment

Opposite below right: Osa Johnson and George Eastman, baking bread, 1926

CHRISTMAS DAY MENU SPECIAL
LAKE PARADISE

*

ANCHOVIES
WILD BUFFALO OXTAIL SOUP
(with garden vegetables)
WILD ROAST TURKEY
(bustard)
WILD MUSHROOM STUFFING
WILD ASPARAGUS   CANDIED SWEET
(Hollandaise Sauce)   POTATOES
CELERY HEARTS
MIXED GREEN SALAD   WATERMELON PRESERVES
STRAWBERRIES AND CREAM
COFFEE
NUTS & RAISINS

Seeking to comprehend the distinctive attitudes and habits of the many tribes that shared their days, particularly the desert-dwelling Samburu, was an endless process. The Americans were astonished that the Africans envied none of the products of their modern civilization, other than cash and cigarettes. Accordingly, like many Europeans, the Johnsons were sometimes annoyed by what they perceived as a lack of gratitude on the part of the Africans. But the Johnsons had rapidly adopted the better aspects of colonial paternalism, caring for their 'boys' in clinics each evening and providing them with superior food and living conditions. When impatient with what he viewed as a slothful African attitude, however, Johnson would resort to his boot. American habits of cleanliness and sanitation seemed to hold no charm for the Kikuyu and Meru who shared their camps. When Johnson asked his laboratory assistant to bathe, the man replied that bathing was for hippos and that Bwana Piccer himself smelt far worse than any African, as the elephant knew well.

Comparing the hunting accounts of George Eastman, the Johnsons and Philip Percival provides a rare insight into the way white hunters and clients recall the same hunts. George Eastman, running down lion and rhinoceros in his Buick, and stepping out to make his kills, considered that he was conducting himself like a sporting gentleman. Percival, although he countenanced this conduct, found it a contemptible way to hunt. 'When the motorcar entered the field, lion hunting as a sport went out,' he wrote later in his notes for Donald Seth-Smith. Noting that lion are easy targets when they stand still, distracted and watching

George Eastman photographing a Buick in difficulty at the Ewaso Ngiro River, northern Kenya, 1926

the hunting cars, Percival wrote, 'True, the sportsman is not in the car, but for all the sport there is in it he might just as well be.'

There was no finer sportsman in Africa than Philip Percival, but like most professional hunters he occasionally found it difficult to hold his eager and unqualified clients to his own high standards. Similar compromises are still tolerated by professional hunters today, and the moral test may well be a fine question of degree and circumstance. Safari-hunting ethics have had an evolution of their own, and it may be that the best a hunter can do, whether professional or amateur, is to hold himself to the highest standard of his own time. The difficulty has generally come when times or circumstances are changing, whether the change be in weapons, laws, transport, habitat, customs or the situation of the game itself.

The introduction of cars and aircraft complicated the old standards. The intrinsic difficulties of hunting in the early days themselves made the chase inevitably sporting. Serious risk and effort, what has come to be called 'fair chase', were then unavoidable. Even more than dogs and high-powered rifles, the car changed the balance. As Philip Percival noted, 'With the advent of the motorcar, bags were doubled in half the time.' Some Kenya professional hunters, trying to make a livelihood when farming was marginal, accepted the hunting abuses of motorized transport and carried on. A few hunters, however, like Denys Finch Hatton, took up the issue of hunting from motorcars, beginning their protests in about 1927. By then the British authorities in Kenya and Tanganyika had prohibited the actual shooting of game from automobiles, and had established a system of game-law enforcement that was carried out in the field by a thin network of European game wardens or rangers and their African subordinates. In Kenya the rule came to be that one could not shoot from within 200 yards of one's car. In Tanganyika, game laws were developed partly in reaction to the over-shooting of two Americans in the 1920s, Leslie Simpson and Stewart Edward White, who between them killed 323 lion, resulting in a restriction limiting every hunter to five.

Finch Hatton, who favoured relatively light shooting combined with photography, wrote letters to the London *Times* in 1928 and 1929 protesting about the 'orgy of slaughter' on the Serengeti by motorized hunters. He quoted one American client, whose party had already driven down and shot twenty-one lion, as exclaiming, 'Let us shoot at every living thing we can find today and see what bag is possible in one day.' Particularly annoyed that such men then returned to America to be celebrated as 'big-game hunters', Finch Hatton condemned 'the methods and manners of these licensed butchers'. He himself helped his American clients, like Frederick B. Patterson, to hunt the right way, on foot and with restraint. Finch Hatton had been recommended to Patterson by the Duke of York. Patterson and the hunter first met one evening in 1927 at the Voi railway station, Patterson remarking that 'Finch Hatton loomed eight feet tall in the darkness. The grip of his muscular fist reassured me.' During the five-month safari Patterson found his hunter to be 'a true sportsman, a fair dealer with the natives, and a man fearless in the face of danger'.

Despite his ethical standards, however, like other fine hunters who indulged in dogs, bait or cars, Denys Finch Hatton had his own sporting compromise: game spotting from airplanes, a practice later banned in Kenya. Like Beryl Markham, he loved the freedom of flight as he floated over the bush in his yellow De Havilland Gipsy Moth, known as *Nzige*, the Locust. He himself pioneered the use of aircraft in spotting elephant, originally working with Beryl Markham to determine if it was possible to identify good bulls from the air, and then to stay in touch with a hunting party as it pursued the moving herd. In due course Beryl Markham learned to make a business of this work, assisting the elephant hunts of Bror Blixen with his favourite clients, like the sporting American hunter Winston Guest, who was always willing to walk fifteen miles a day after a good bull, or to help clear an airstrip in the bush by hand.

The practice was for Beryl Markham to fly low over elephant country like the Yatta Plateau, searching for heavy ivory. The bulls, however, seemed to understand the game, turning away to hide their tusks and lurking under the trees even when the cows and *totos*, the babies, remained in the open. Sometimes Beryl Markham would circle a herd for an hour, trying to assess the largest bulls. Then she would calculate the distance to camp and jot down details of waterholes, other wildlife and terrain, all before dropping her message, accompanied by a smoke signal, near Blixen's camp.

In 1928 Kenya welcomed the ultimate safari client, the future king of England. Thirty-four years old, dashing and enthusiastic, the Prince of Wales stirred Nairobi, stimulating endless gossip and social anxiety among even the most jaded members of the Muthaiga Club. At one club dinner, Kenya's Game Warden, Archie Ritchie, forced another member from the dining-room, later explaining, 'There is a limit, even in Kenya. When someone offers cocaine to the heir to the throne, something has to be done about it, particularly when it is between courses at the dinner table.'

The Prince of Wales was accompanied on his trip by his younger brother, Prince Henry, the Duke of Gloucester, who soon began his own adventure, with Beryl Markham. She was then married and at an early stage in her pregnancy. The two tall, elegant figures made a striking pair, dancing at the Muthaiga Club, racing horses at the track, riding in the hills, and going on safari together in the Northern Frontier District.

Eager to escape the colonial society he was dazzling and to get out on safari, leaving his younger brother to his own entertainments, the Prince of Wales sought to engage J. A. Hunter, but J. A. was already out with an American client. Outraged at the suggestion of a schedule change, the American protested, 'Who's the Prince of Wales? My money's as good as his.' Accordingly, J. A. declined, and the Prince went with Finch Hatton. Fit and surprisingly hardy, the future Edward VIII was a fine shot and a keen photographer. Setting out for Tanganyika, the safari consisted of two Willys-Knight safari cars, Finch Hatton's Hudson, four Albion trucks for the staff and equipment, and the Prince driving Lord Delamere's Buick.

On the first day the Prince and Finch Hatton were pursued by an angry elephant that the Prince had tried to photograph at twenty-five yards, forcing an undignified flight that did not stop until a warning shot turned the bull. Another day the Prince was photographing a rhinoceros, steadily taking pictures as the animal charged. Finally alarmed, Finch Hatton killed the beast. In a rare outburst, the Prince berated his hunter, 'How dare you shoot without an order. I wanted him right up to the camera.' 'Your Royal Highness,' Finch Hatton replied with his famous calm, 'if you, heir to the throne, are killed, what is there left for me to do? I can only go behind a tree and blow my brains out.'

With the Prince short of time and anxious to get a lion, Finch Hatton wanted Bror Blixen to lead the party in lion hunting. About to enjoy a cocktail in his camp outside Arusha one evening, Blixen was startled 'when a little man came into my tent and said, "I'm the Prince of Wales, and should like to make your acquaintance." ' Despite the jealous annoyance of Karen Blixen, the three men became fast friends, hunting lion and buffalo on foot and stopping for tea each afternoon at four o'clock, using the special primus stove in the Prince's picnic box. In due course the Prince bagged his lion, missing the first shot with his ·350 double rifle, and then killing the bounding animal in tall grass with three more shots at 140 yards. But on November 27 the news reached the safari that King George V was seriously ill, and the Prince cut short the expedition, sailing for

Prince of Wales, *right*, Denys Finch Hatton, *middle*, Miguu Anderson, *left*, on safari in Kenya, 1930

home on the cruiser *HMS Enterprise*. He had asked Finch Hatton to accompany him to England, and he wrote Finch Hatton a long letter from shipboard, reminiscing about the safari and promising to return to Africa.

Two years later the Prince of Wales was back, after writing to Finch Hatton about rifles and cameras, and complaining that, 'We are into winter good and proper now and I hate it and am longing to get away to Africa.' His brother the Duke of Gloucester, meanwhile, had continued in England his relationship with Beryl Markham, who now had a baby boy and would in due course accept a modest pension from the Duke. Frequently visiting the Duke in his apartment at Buckingham Palace, Beryl Markham once hid in a closet to avoid his mother, Queen Mary, and occasionally, as James Fox wrote, 'ran about the palatial corridors, barefoot, like a Nandi warrior.'

The highlight of the Prince of Wales's second safari was an elephant hunt, and what surprised the redoubtable Bror Blixen was the Prince's exceptional endurance. 'He makes the greatest demands on himself,' Blixen wrote in his memoirs, 'He is one of the three or four toughest sportsmen I have been out with, perhaps the toughest of them all.' On the first day of the elephant hunt near Mt Kilimanjaro, the Prince and Finch Hatton struggled twenty miles through thick bush with no success. Then the three men set off after a large bull, travelling with only a small tent and rations for two or three meals. They walked hard all day, until even Blixen was exhausted, finally camping on the open plain at nightfall, the Prince taken by the immensity of the moonless African sky, the stars sharp and bright against the dark. The next morning they were up before sunrise, on the trail again, following the elephant over hard volcanic ground for forty-two miles, the heat burning through their boots, their feet painfully blistered, the Prince uncomplaining and showing no change of expression.

On the third day, trying to keep pace after the bull, Blixen following the track, they paused as usual for tea, the food and water almost gone. When they awoke on the fourth morning, their feet were so swollen that they could barely force on their boots. At sunset they were still on the spoor, among the vegetation in the Pare foothills. Then Finch Hatton spotted the massive bull, tall and broad as a cathedral, one of the finest he had ever seen, with 125 lb of ivory a side. He beckoned the Prince of Wales forward through the vegetation for a shot. As the Prince parted the branches to take aim, he stumbled among the thorns and the wary elephant crashed off at 25 m.p.h., never to be seen again. Finch Hatton called this the worst piece of luck in his years as a hunter. Then it was a thirty-mile march to the line of the Uganda Railway.

The safari continued across Kenya, to Rhino Camp in Uganda, through the Congo and along the Nile to Khartoum. Throughout the trip the Prince was at his best, eschewing ceremony, interested in the problems of settlers and Africans, and restrained as a hunter. Advocating game preservation, he recommended photography rather than trophies. In April 1930, the Prince of Wales and Denys Finch Hatton flew home to England. Soon things changed for

Masai lion hunt, Kenya, 1920s

both men, for the carefree days were not to last. Both Europe and the safari business became caught up in the larger events of the economic crash and the coming of war. Remembering his exhilarating time in the bush, the Prince of Wales recalled in his diaries the mysterious star-filled nights of his elephant hunt, and remarked on the vitality of Africa's game, particularly one hardy Cape buffalo that, like Charles II, took 'an unconscionable time a-dying'.

Back in Africa the following year, making plans to go on safari with Donald Seth-Smith to photograph elephant, Denys Finch Hatton invited Beryl Markham to fly to Voi with him in May. At the last moment, however, she declined to join him. Returning from Voi, where he had dined with J. A. Hunter, Finch Hatton took his Locust up, hung briefly in the sky, and crashed in flames. J. A. brought the charred body back to Karen Blixen, who buried the hunter, as he had wished, among the lion and buffalo on a shoulder of the Ngong Hills. With the coming of the Depression and the Second World War, much of the carefree spirit of the old safaris was to be buried with him.

8. HAGGARD, HEMINGWAY AND HOLLYWOOD

The Safari in Fiction and Film

The image and the reality of the English gentleman hunter are at the heart of the safari ethic. Cornwallis Harris, Cotton Oswell, Frederick Selous and Denys Finch Hatton lived by this standard. Others have tried. Even hunters from different countries, like the German photographer C. G. Schillings, expressly recognize this English contribution. Unflinching courage, quiet endurance and sportsmanlike respect for the game are taken for granted by hunters of this school. One is expected to risk one's life not just for clients and gunbearers, but for an idea, and even for the animals themselves, when necessary following wounded buffalo and lion into the tall grass. Bror Blixen, a Dane, understood this code well, holding no respect for the Belgian hunters who were carried in sedan chairs through the forests of the Congo.

The beau ideal of the English gentleman hunter, the mythic African adventurer whose inspiration launched a thousand safaris, is Rider Haggard's character Allan Quatermain. Like Napoleon to French schoolboys, Allan Quatermain has served as symbol and example to generations of English-speaking boys, transporting the imagination of young Winston Churchill and bringing the romance of Africa and empire to Denys Finch Hatton's classmates at Eton. Modelled on Selous, Quatermain became the hero of fourteen novels. The earliest of these, *King Solomon's Mines*, was the first major African novel.* From the moment it appeared in 1885, Allan Quatermain's popularity was instantaneous, broad and enduring. Never out of print, his adventures have been translated into at least nineteen languages and made into at least seven

Colour poster of the MGM version of *King Solomon's Mines*, 1950

* The first significant novel based on Africa and travelling in the bush may be Frederick Marryat's *The Mission or Scenes in Africa*, published in 1845. It is based on the true story of the wandering survivors of the ship *Grosvenor*, an English East Indiaman that was wrecked on the coast of Zululand in 1782.

films. In the United States, *King Solomon's Mines* went through thirteen editions in its first year. For millions of readers, Africa became the Africa of Rider Haggard.

Haggard himself was born to a family of Norfolk squires in 1856. As a boy, he learned to shoot with an old muzzle-loader, often poaching duck and pheasant on nearby estates. He learned much about outdoor life from a neighbouring pig farmer, who gave the boy large walnuts to feed the swine. Young Haggard then made the nutshells into tiny boats. The farmer was called William Quatermain. Haggard always remembered him as 'a fine handsome man of about fifty, with grey hair and aristocratic features . . . and he always wore a beautiful work-frock'.

Like Selous, Rider Haggard arrived in South Africa at the age of nineteen. Six-foot and blue-eyed, young Haggard stepped ashore at Cape Town in 1875 as an aide on the staff of the new Lt-Governor of Natal, Sir Henry Bulwer. Soon he bought a horse, Moresco, and was hunting in Natal, like Cornwallis Harris forty years before. Much had changed in southern Africa, but Haggard was not too late. The elephant were gone, but in the Transvaal he found parts of the veld 'still black with game'. In his six years in Africa two things captivated Haggard even more than the game, however, and drove his imagination for a lifetime: the Zulus and the land, Africa itself. From this inspiration were to come over forty volumes of romantic fiction. Writing his autobiography in 1925, Haggard recalled the Africa that embraced him as a young man of nineteen:

> . . . the sparkling torrential rains, the sweeping thunderstorms, the grass fires creeping over the veld at night like snakes of living flame, the glorious aspect of the heavens, now of a spotless blue, now charged with the splendid and many-coloured lights of sunset, and now sparkling with a myriad stars, the wine-like taste of the air upon the plains, the beautiful flowers in the bush-clad *kloofs* – all these things impressed me, so much that were I to live a thousand years I never should forget them.

Natal was the homeland of many Zulu tribes, and Haggard soon learned to speak their language and to admire their character and perception. Property and rank were less important to the Zulu than dignity and courage. They had an instinct, he found, for discerning 'the base alloys in a man's metal', and he concluded that 'many an English "gentleman" would not pass with them'. In May 1876 he was privileged to attend a war dance at a royal kraal. As the heralds advanced, shaking their oxtail plumage and crane feathers, five hundred disciplined men leapt high, stamped and raised their assegais, crying out the royal salute *'Bayete! Bayete!'* It was a moment that the young man never forgot. Later he was to write four novels based on the rise and decline of the Zulu nation.

Keeping notebooks and diaries, Haggard became a keen observer of, and sometimes a participant in, the dramatic times that were unfolding around him. In 1876 he was chosen to accompany Sir Theophilus Shepstone, the Secretary

Umslopogaas from a photograph taken the day before his death, 23 October, 1897 — H. Rider Haggard

Above left: H. Rider Haggard, 1890

Above right: Umslopogaas from a photo taken the day before his death, 23 October 1897

for Native Affairs in Natal, on a four-hundred-mile journey to Pretoria in the Transvaal to examine the difficulties between the Boers and neighbouring tribes. The Shepstone expedition, in effect a political safari, was escorted by twenty-five mounted police and by Shepstone's African aide-de-camp, a sixty-year-old Swazi chief called Umslopogaas, a man described by Haggard's biographer Morton Cohen as a 'lithe black Achilles'.

Umslopogaas, his name and character soon to be preserved in many novels, influenced Haggard deeply and became the prototype for every white hunter's African companion, whether headman, tracker or gunbearer. True to image, Umslopogaas was proud, able, courageous, insightful and loyal to the death. A son of the king of Swaziland, Umslopogaas himself was described by a respectful Haggard as 'a tall, thin, fierce-faced fellow with a great hole above the left temple over which the skin pulsated, that he had come by in battle. He had killed ten men in single combat, always making use of a battleaxe.'

Twenty years after Haggard first met him, Umslopogaas was photographed the day before he died on 24 October 1897. By then Haggard had woven the old prince, and his battleaxe, into the magical fabric of Africa, depicting him for posterity as a wandering Matabele chief, a great-grandson of Mzilikazi himself. Studying the picture of his friend, Haggard wrote of Umslopogaas for the last time, 'The face might have served some Greek sculptor for the model of a dying God.'

In 1877, following Haggard's expedition with Shepstone, Britain forestalled the war threatening between the Boers and King Cetshwayo's Zulu impis by annexing the Transvaal. On Queen Victoria's birthday, 24 May 1877, the twenty-one-year-old Rider Haggard himself ran up the British flag at noon in Pretoria as the artillery boomed. When hostilities finally came with the British four years later, the Boers threatened to hang Haggard if they caught him. The young man's personal sympathies were not with the Afrikaaner settlers, of whom nearly 30,000 now occupied the Transvaal. The more Haggard travelled and lived among the Boers, the more he concluded that 'unlike the Zulu he despises, there is little of the gentleman in his composition'.

The land-hungry Transvaal farmers were surrounded by major black tribes, generally with an economy based on cattle and tribal raiding, including the Matabele, Zulus, Tswanas and Swazis, a situation quite different from that in the Cape in the seventeenth and eighteenth centuries, where it could be claimed that there were no significant resident African populations when the whites arrived. In Cape Colony itself, by 1875, there were approximately 235,000 Europeans and 500,000 Africans, with about 17,000 Europeans and 325,000 blacks in neighbouring Natal.

Although he had no legal training, in 1877 Haggard served as a travelling justice of the peace, reviewing cases and arranging settlements. Frequently he travelled about the Transvaal with a Justice Kotze, holding court from a wagon drawn by eight oxen. It became a judicial safari, with Rider Haggard and the judge shooting red-wing partridge with a fowling piece and hunting springboks and blesboks with a Martini-Henry carbine. Kotze came to enjoy 'this genial, high-spirited and romantic young man', particularly his cooking, as Haggard prepared snipe on toast while venison simmered in the baking pot. Their only trials came when the judge claimed some of Haggard's shots, and the younger hunter deferred.

As so often, it was the unexpected moments of safari life that were most memorable, dragging Judge Kotze from a swamp by his shotgun barrel and reading *Romeo and Juliet* aloud in the wagon after the axle broke in the veld. As he travelled, Haggard began to draw on his earlier diaries to write about Africa. In 1877 his first writings were published in London. His impressionistic articles 'A Zulu War Dance' and 'A Visit with Chief Secocoeni' appeared in *Gentleman's Magazine* and *Cornhill*.

Pressed by the land hunger of the Boers and by British demands to demilitarize their tribal structure, the Zulus finally confronted invading British forces in 1879, at first gaining notable success at the battle of Isandhlwana. Rider Haggard at once joined up with the Pretoria Horse. After the Zulu were defeated he left government service to marry and raise ostriches. Two years later, when the rebellious Boers defeated the British in 1881 at the battle of Majuba, Haggard could hear the guns from his land and the peace that followed was negotiated in his farmhouse. Later that year, when the Liberal Prime Minister, William Gladstone, conceded the Transvaal to the Afrikaaners,

Haggard sailed for England, dismayed at the prospects for the blacks under the Boers, convinced that 'where natives are concerned, they are one of the cruellest white races in the world'.

Back in England, Haggard soon became a lawyer, but his heart, and his imagination, were in Africa, 'since my friends were African, and Africa was far away'. After his time on safari, alive still with memories of cantering across the open bush and sleeping under the African stars, he wrote, 'I can hardly sleep in a house now. It stifles me.' Then one day in 1885, during a train ride, Haggard and his brother discussed Robert Louis Stevenson's recent novel *Treasure Island*. Haggard, recalling the adventures of Africa, said he found the book not so extraordinary a story. His brother challenged him, wagering that Rider could not write an adventure nearly so absorbing.

That evening Rider Haggard began to write, standing at the pedestal desk in his dining-room in Kensington. Allan Quatermain and Africa were alive on his pages before Haggard went to sleep that night. In six weeks *King Solomon's Mines* was completed. Safari life, hunts, war dances, tribal battles and the dazzling tableau of the African landscape came easily to Haggard, as experience, imagination and mysticism worked together in his writing.

Imaginative, but made real by the authentic detail of Africa, impossibly romantic, *King Solomon's Mines* is dedicated to 'big and little boys'. It is the tale of a great hunter, his princely African friend Umbopa, and an Englishman searching for his brother. Following a sixteenth-century Portuguese map drawn in blood, they find the fabled treasure of King Solomon, hidden in a cave by a subterranean stream deep in the mountains called Sheba's Breasts. A student of ancient cultures, Haggard describes what might be the Queen of Sheba's kingdom, the biblical land of Ophir, where Solomon secured the ivory and gold for his temple.

Apparently drawing on many inspirations, the adventure appears to be largely inspired by the Zimbabwe ruins found in Mashonaland in 1868, the word *zimbabwe* meaning temples or buildings of stone, and referring to the impressive masonry walls and towers that Selous visited and studied in the 1880s. Haggard's tale also contains evocations reminiscent of the Transvaal and of what became Botswana and Uganda. The story begins with an elephant hunt, and refers to Allan Quatermain's days as an ivory hunter in Bamangwato, in Bechuanaland, where Gordon Cumming and Baldwin hunted in the old days and where Selous killed big tuskers in 1872. Like Frederick Selous, Allan Quatermain first hunted elephant in Matabeleland with a large Boer roer, firing a 3–4 oz ball and taking powder by the handful. Quatermain, too, is trim and not tall, a hardened gentleman with a vandyke beard, a crack rifleman and unfailingly decisive, resourceful, loyal and modest. Like Selous, Quatermain is known for his veracity. 'There is no need to tell lies about hunting,' he says, 'for so many curious things happen within the knowledge of a hunter.' While Selous favoured tea or champagne, however, Allan Quatermain, perhaps more indulgent, restores himself with wine, brandy and a pipe. Both men were close to the Matabele branch of the Zulu, and both died in battle in Africa in their mid-sixties.

Selous's *A Hunter's Wanderings* had appeared only four years before *King Solomon's Mines*. When Haggard himself visited Rhodesia in 1914, his fiction had become reality, and he found place-names taken from his novels, like Allan Quatermain's Road and Sheba's Breasts.

At first several publishers rejected Haggard's manuscript in 1885, but soon it was accepted, and sold as a companion book to *Treasure Island*. An instant popular and critical success, Haggard's work was hailed by the *Spectator* as superior to the works of Jules Verne and Herman Melville. Winston Churchill was but one of many youthful admirers. One group of schoolgirls wrote to Haggard, congratulating him for creating 'a thrilling book without a heroine'. Within twelve months the book sold 31,000 copies in Great Britain. Before the end of 1885, the sequel, *Allan Quatermain*, had appeared, first serialized in *Longman's* magazine. This book was dedicated to Haggard's four-year-old son. In the dedication Haggard expresses the notion that has always been at the core of the ethic of the great white hunter:

> I inscribe this book of adventure to my son
> Arthur John Rider Haggard
> in the hope that in days to come
> he, and many other boys whom I shall never know, may,
> in the acts and thoughts of Allan Quatermain,
> find something to help him and them reach
> to what I hold to be the highest rank whereto we can attain –
> the state and dignity of English gentlemen.

Unfortunately Arthur John Rider Haggard died at the age of ten.

Rereading *Allan Quatermain* myself, after more than thirty years and many safaris, aware of the author's friendship with my own grandfather, it was easy to become entranced again with Haggard's Africa. Studying his detailed battle plan of the fight at the Masai kraal, with the wide banyan tree and the thorn bushes carefully marked by the edge of the oval enclosure, it was impossible not to be seduced once more by the details of tribal life and bushcraft, and to be drawn again by the great hunter's life. What fun it must have been for the young writer to put aside his law books and bring 'Hunter Quatermain' and the aristocratic Umslopogaas together again, after an imagined parting of twelve years. Surprised, the gaunt African prince nearly drops his battleaxe with its rhinoceros-horn handle as he cries out in Zulu, '*Koos-y-umcool!* [Chief from of old – mighty chief!] *Koos! Baba* [father]! *Macumazahn* [watchful one], old hunter, slayer of elephants, eater up of lions! Brave one, whose shot never misses, who strikes straight home, who grasps a hand and holds it to the death! Baba! Mindest thou how thou didst plant the ball in the eye of the charging buffalo?'

Soon *Quatermain* was setting sales records for six-shilling novels and Haggard was standing at his desk again, pouring out his new work *She*, a mystical romance about an ageless African queen. Written in six and a half weeks in 1886, *She* became one of fewer than a hundred books to sell a million copies in English prior to 1895. The magnetic womanly force of its heroine became for the psychologist Carl Jung a classic example of his concept of the *anima*, the image a man projects upon the woman he loves. Other Haggard heroines are remarkably complex and able for Victorian women, sometimes even skilled with a double-barrelled Derringer.

Totally abandoning the law, Haggard moved to Norfolk, where he built a model farming estate, conducted elaborate cross-country paper chases, befriended old poachers and stalked about in flowing capes with his knobbed Zulu walking-stick plotting his books, his imagination creating extraordinary tales as his mind reached back to Africa. His house, Ditchingham, was arrayed with fragments of Africa, ox-hide shields, assegais, skulls, a buffalo head, ostrich eggs, a hippo-hide whip, Zulu regalia and empty cartridge cases from the battlefield of Isandhlwana.

In time Haggard's keen admirers extended from Churchill, Jung and the schoolchildren of England to include Lord Curzon, the Prince of Wales, D. H. Lawrence, C. S. Lewis and Henry Miller. Graham Greene said that as a boy he missed a heartbeat whenever he found a Rider Haggard novel he had not yet read. Although Haggard's romances came to be considered boys' books, during his own lifetime they were fashionable among all ages. When Haggard sailed from Italy to Egypt in 1888, he enjoyed every writer's greatest pleasure, finding that nearly all his shipmates were reading either *King Solomon's Mines* or *She*.

As the First World War approached, however, Haggard became disaffected with a changing world, complaining in 1912 that 'There are two men left living in the world with whom I am in supreme sympathy. Theodore Roosevelt and Rudyard Kipling. The rest have gone.' Kipling, too, felt a special bond with his friend the President, sending him the first copy of his poem, 'The White Man's Burden', in 1898, on the occasion of the American annexation of the Philippines. Rider Haggard had lunched with the President at the White House in 1905, years before Roosevelt went on safari. Roosevelt confided to Haggard that 'It is an odd thing, that you and I, brought up in different countries and following such different pursuits, should have identical ideas and aims.'

Kipling and Haggard, as they grew older, became true friends, concerned by each other's illnesses, proud of one another's work. Remarkably, the two novelists of empire could work together, actually writing in each other's studies during the Great War. Frequently they worked in Rudyard Kipling's library at Bateman's in Sussex. There, in a haze of smoke, between two huge globes, both men wrote at the long table on Kipling's specially made blocks of pale blue sheets, pausing to discuss India and Africa, reading their tales aloud. Each man had found the perfect audience. Having followed Haggard's work from conception to completion, Kipling concluded, 'never was there a better tale-teller or, to my mind, a man with a more convincing imagination'.

H. Rider Haggard's imagination did not die with him in 1925. His books continued to sell, although increasingly as works for young people. Their influence, and particularly the thematic characterizations of the professional white hunter and the noble African, soon reached out through a new medium, the motion-picture feature film. In addition, other writers came to use the white hunter in their works, and Quatermain always seemed to establish the standard. Even a writer as characteristically American as Ernest Hemingway, for example, born in 1899, was educated in Oak Park, Illinois, in a house and a high school that strongly favoured British over American authors, and Haggard was inescapable reading.

In 1920 *King Solomon's Mines* was made into a silent film by African Film Productions Ltd of Johannesburg. Then in 1935 Haggard's *She* was released as a film, and Hemingway's *The Green Hills of Africa* was published in the United States. *She*, produced by RKO and starring Helen Gahaghan Douglas and Randolph Scott, was not the beginning of Hollywood's fascination with Africa. MGM's *Trader Horn*, an early talkie concerning a white trader who overcomes tribal hostility, contained some remarkable wildlife footage and appeared in 1931. The first of over thirty Tarzan films was released by MGM in 1932. Armand Dennis's and Lewis Cotlow's 1949 animal film *Savage Splendour* was the first full-length colour feature film made in Africa.

The first sound film in which a white hunter is the central figure is thought to be the version of *King Solomon's Mines* released in 1938 by Gaumont-British.

The IVTA version of *King Solomon's Mines*, 1920

The Gaumont-British version of *King Solomon's Mines,* 1938, starring Cedric Hardwick and Paul Robeson

Filmed in England, with only some background scenes made in South Africa, the movie starred Cedric Hardwicke as Quatermain and the distinguished American singer Paul Robeson as Umbopa. Despite a pay-scale of two shillings a day and beer, Zulu extras were difficult to procure, as they feared they were going to be pressganged for a new war in Europe. Lacking the authenticity of African footage for the major scenes, and interrupted by Robeson's gratuitous songs, the film earned a mixed reception.

Twelve years later, however, Hollywood brought Haggard's Africa to life in the 1950 version of *King Solomon's Mines.* With over 95 per cent of the final footage shot on location in Kenya, Tanganyika, Uganda and Ruanda-Urundi, the film was not only a fine safari film, but in its creation necessitated an elaborate safari that became its own adventure. Described by the *New York Herald Tribune* as the 'most ambitious location trip in Hollywood history', the film was for years the dream of MGM producer Sam Zimbalist, who was an admirer of Haggard and had been chief gaffer, or lighting man, for the 1938 film version.

Zimbalist hired Kenya's largest safari outfitter, Safariland, to manage the film expedition. Travelling 14,000 miles around Africa in five months, moving by safari car, steamboat, plane and foot, with a party of fifty-three European film-makers and some 130 Africans, including eighty-two servants, it was the largest safari since Theodore Roosevelt's. Four white hunters ran the safari

271

itself. The film for the eight motion picture cameras was stored in two refrigerated vehicles, and five additional trucks were built to order, with high frames and five speeds.

The arrival of the film's stars in Nairobi in October of 1949 was the most exciting social event in east Africa since the last visit of the Prince of Wales. Deborah Kerr and Stewart Granger arrived by Solent flying-boat at the dock at Lake Naivasha and proceeded directly to the Norfolk. There they soon impressed reporters with Kerr's baggage and Granger's arsenal. Granger was to play Quatermain. Kerr, replacing the book's character of the Englishman searching for his brother, was to play a lady looking for her husband. Both stars were ably chosen, for they were to do as well in the bush as they did at Government House and at a charity ball in Nairobi's Town Hall, where Deborah Kerr charmed the old guard and Granger undertook to bag a black-maned lion.

Working in heat exceeding 140°F on the banks of the Victoria Nile, and in an equatorial blizzard at 16,000 ft on Mt Kenya, the actors toiled in production conditions that would not suit most Hollywood stars. As one colleague put it, 'no other girl in the picture business would have taken the beating that Miss Kerr did on this safari'. _Life_ magazine headlined 'British Grit Overcomes Horrors of Savage Africa'. The blizzard scene, filmed after camping at night in Alpine conditions, with the camera frozen in the morning, was finally cut, as Zimbalist feared that audiences would not believe it possible.

The chief cameraman, Robert Surtees, whose caps were rotted from his teeth

The MGM version of _King Solomon's Mines_, 1950

The 1950 *King Solomon's Mines* on location

by the water of Ruanda-Urundi, classified the safari's problems under three headings: climate, animals and natives. The worst was climate. Torrential rains, snow, extreme heat, uneven sunlight, malaria, amoebic dysentery and two cases of typhoid fever added to the usual technical problems. 'It was all a grinding nuisance,' Surtees reported to the *Herald Tribune*, 'but as Miss Kerr never complained, none of us felt that we could.'

Umbopa's lost tribe, conceived by Haggard as one of the early northern Zulu tribes that had been a source of the southward Bantu migrations, was played by five hundred Watussi of Ruanda-Urundi, an immensely tall and dignified people who took readily to the camera. Umbopa himself, played by Siriaque, was seven feet, eight inches tall. Siriaque took his pay in goats. The Wakamba, however, were less easy to work with, losing theatrical discipline during the immense *ngoma*, or feast dance, staged for the film at Machakos, thirty-five miles from Nairobi. The old settler and lion-galloper Clifford Hill, watching in amazement as the assistant directors lost control of their vast cast and the lines of quivering young men and women came together, declared it the most impressive ngoma since the First World War. In another scene, with a hundred Masai moran recruited to charge the camera, the warriors worked themselves into the trancelike frenzy that envelops them in battle or when lion hunting. Dashing at the camera, they released their spears, two actually glancing off Surtees's sun helmet.

For many Masai extras, the production's high point occurred when an elephant, rampaging off-camera, trampled the local money-lender. Most of the movie's animal scenes, which include a stampede of 6,000 animals on the Serengeti Plain, were managed by Kenya's top animal trapper and trainer, Tom Carr-Hartley. A former professional hunter who pioneered the noosing of heavy game like rhinoceros from open trucks, learning to secure animals without injuring them, Carr-Hartley himself often raised young animals with infinite personal care. The film-makers learned a lot about wildlife, but were not reassured to hear that man-eating lion prefer whites to Africans as Europeans have more salt in their systems.

For its time, the film was expensive, with the work in Africa costing $1.8m, and the total budget approximating $3.5m. African extras were paid 30 cents a day, their salary held down by agreement with the colonial government, which did not wish to disturb the native economy. The top salary for a professional hunter, authorized by the East African Professional Hunters' Association, was then £200 a month, with apprentice hunters earning £30 monthly.

Opening to packed houses in November 1950, *King Solomon's Mines* was an immense success. Hailed by *The Saturday Review of Literature* as 'one of the most remarkable pictures ever made, a jewel of a movie', it won an Academy Award for Best Color Photography. The safari itself occupied three quarters of the film's running time, and critics saluted the brilliant wildlife footage and unpatronizing treatment of African culture. Deborah Kerr was considered fresh and persuasive in her role, as she gently stalks the hard-bitten English hunter, who, like Philip Percival, begins with the view, 'A woman on safari! No, thank you!' As they head into the bush in their Cape wagon, with the heat of the day coming on and Deborah Kerr wearing layers of petticoats and whalebone corsets, Granger loosens her clothes with the words, 'You're sealed up like a tin of peas.' White hunters, too, are human, and she ultimately gets the big game.

Some critics applauded the film's sensitivity regarding shooting, for the movie was respectful to wildlife, and did not romanticize the killing of dangerous animals. The film opens with Granger hunting elephant with clients. Spotting a herd, a client shoots despite Granger's instruction to hold fire. Wounded, one elephant is supported by two comrades, shoulder to shoulder as they assist its flight. It is a remarkable scene, for some hunters deny that elephant actually ever help each other. Granger, disturbed by the cruelty of bad shooting, calls the supportive animals 'gallant fellows'. When his client seeks to shoot another, the hunter pushes up the man's rifle, saying, 'You got yours.' Soon the wounded elephant kills one of the hunter's trackers, and he is forced to shoot it with his double rifle. True to Selous and Quatermain, the script has Granger remark, 'There are times I prefer animals to humans.'

Even as *King Solomon's Mines** filled the great screen at New York's Radio

* A fourth, undistinguished version of *King Solomon's Mines* was released by Cannon Films in 1985, filmed in Zimbabwe, starring Richard Chamberlain and Sharon Stone. A sequel, *Allan Quatermain and the Lost City of Gold*, was released by Cannon in 1986.

City Music Hall, Ernest Hemingway's Africa was also occupying Hollywood. Following his success as a novelist, the studios turned to his short stories for material, releasing *The Macomber Affair* in 1947 and *The Snows of Kiliman-jaro* in 1952. Hemingway's Africa, however, whether in the author's own life, or in books and films, is far different from Haggard's. It is not so much a land of boyish adventure and exotic romance, as another arena for self-conscious testing of oneself, like the bull-ring, war and boxing. Characteristically, Hemingway's works reveal more about himself than they do about Africa.

Ernest Hemingway first came to east Africa in 1933, at the age of thirty-four, on a two-month safari financed by the uncle of his second wife, Pauline, and attended by her and Charles Thompson, a Key West fishing companion. The poet Archibald MacLeish had declined to join them, dreading Hemingway's fame-inflated ego and his inevitably competitive approach to hunting. An experienced hunter, the writer took his shooting seriously, debarking in Mombasa with a heavy custom-made Springfield, a 30·06 Mauser, a 6·5 Mannlicher, a twelve-gauge pump shotgun and his favourite Colt Woodsman pistol.

Ernest Hemingway on safari, 1933. Philip Percival is on the left

Advised that Philip Percival was Kenya's finest professional hunter, the party waited at Percival's Machakos farm until the old hunter was free to lead them to Tanganyika. Hemingway at once reminded Percival of Theodore Roosevelt, with his broad smile, strong shoulders and poor eyesight. Percival did not know that at the age of two years and eleven months his mother had proudly recorded that young Ernest 'shoots well with his gun and loads and cocks it himself'. As a boy of eleven, already trained in woodcraft by his father, young Hemingway had been fascinated by the African mammals mounted in family groups in Chicago's Field Museum of Natural History. There the boy, dressed in his miniature Theodore Roosevelt khaki bush suit, carefully studied the warthogs and greater kudu, the buffalo and the spotted hyena, all the while imagining himself to be the ex-President on safari.

Twenty-four years later, motoring south to Arusha in a stretched safari car and two lorries, with the Ngong Hills hazy in the distance to the west, Hemingway found that nothing he had read had prepared him for the beauty of Africa. Even his beloved Montana could not compete. Percival, too, impressed him, combining English manners with that quiet hardness that Hemingway admired in the Latin peasants and blue-collar Americans with whom he often sought to relate. Years later, writing in *Look* magazine in 1954, Hemingway concluded that 'Philip Percival is the finest man I know.'

Percival, in turn, found Hemingway to be a reliable hand in the bush, and highly observant. He sometimes paid the American the professional's compliment of letting Hemingway hunt accompanied only by his gunbearer M'Cola. The gunbearer, however, understood the limitations of every client. Once, terrified at the hazards of a messy hit, M'Cola stopped Hemingway from trying to kill a lion without Percival there to back him up. From another African, Hemingway was delighted to learn a new bush trick to teach to his hunting friends in Wyoming. Slitting open the stomach of a dead reedbuck, one tracker turned it inside out, making a sack to hold the liver and kidneys. Then the man sewed this up with a thin switch and carried the bag over his shoulder on the end of a pole.

The safari finally became such a rich experience for Hemingway that he resolved to turn it into a book, unadulterated by fiction, that was designed to determine whether 'an absolutely true book' could succeed as well as a work of the imagination. The rather indulgent result was the *Green Hills of Africa*, published in 1935 as one of the author's least successful works, possibly because, like so many others, he found that the intoxication of his first safari gave him the sense that his own experience was in some way original. A similar attitude often overcomes other people too, who then compromise the sensory experience of their safari by a distracting obsession with either trophies or photography, assuming that in some sense these souvenirs are extraordinary and are more important than the underlying experience they are designed to record.

As a student of hunting, however, Hemingway was an exceptional safari client. Keen and robust, he made many fine shots on moving animals at 200–300 yards, had no difficulty facing dangerous game on foot, and bagged three fine lion. He cheerfully undertook arduous and frustrating stalks, particularly after greater kudu and sable antelope, the 'Harris buck' which Cornwallis Harris had discovered. His personal peculiarities were an excessive fear of snakes and a delight in shooting the inedible hyena. He thrilled to watch a hyena, which had been hit too far back, snapping at its own wounded stomach, finally jerking out and devouring its own intestines. He apparently used the hyena's supposed bad character to justify his own cruelty to it.

Hemingway, who years later was to kill himself with a shotgun, wrote naturally of the 'pleasant weight of the rifle' in his hand. He described a hunter's feeling before taking the luxury of a careful shot, 'freezing myself deliberately inside, stopping the excitement as you close a valve, going into that impersonal state you shoot from'. Finally there is 'the sweet clean pull of the Springfield with the smooth, unhesitant release at the end'. Candid and proud, never feeling guilt for a clean kill, but sick at losing a running, gut-shot sable bull, he confesses, 'I knew, coldly and outside myself, that I could shoot a rifle on game as well as any son of a bitch that ever lived. Like hell I could.'

As Archibald MacLeish feared, Hemingway in his mind created a competition with his friend Charles Thompson, who gradually accumulated a collection of far finer trophies. Returning to camp with a good rhinoceros, certain that he had finally defeated Thompson, Hemingway is chilled to find Thompson already in camp, with an immense rhino head leaning against a tree, the cape of its neck hanging down, its horns dwarfing Hemingway's. Days later, returning triumphant with two magnificent kudu heads, Hemingway finds his friend waiting with 'the biggest, widest, darkest, longest-curling, heaviest, most unbelievable pair of kudu horns in the world'. Hemingway, poisoned with envy, lies awake bitter all night, but is purged the next day, as Percival chides him: 'We have very primitive emotions. It's important not to be competitive. Spoils everything.'

Philip Percival himself, no longer a young hunter, less fit than in the old days, was a bit heavy on the outside, 'but inside he was young and lean and tall and hard as when he galloped lion on the lovely broken hill of Wami'. Percival was merry company, never arguing with a client at meals, but teasing Hemingway when the American got 'the evening braggies' over drinks by the camp fire, urging Pauline to 'throw a drink into the beast and he'll quiet down'. Pauline Hemingway found Percival, despite his particular distaste for American women, to be her ideal of a man. In the field Percival was strict with his clients. 'He hated to have anything killed except what we were after,' wrote Hemingway, 'no killing on the side, no ornamental killing, only when you wanted it more than you wanted not to kill it, only when getting it was necessary to his being first in his trade.'

Percival's strong character, evidently adulterated with a dash of Bror Blixen's mischief, soon found its way into Hemingway's powerful story 'The Short Happy Life of Francis Macomber', first published in *Cosmopolitan* magazine in 1936. 'Macomber' is a tale of a white hunter who keeps a double cot in his tent in case of opportunity, of a rich American client, Macomber, who passes from cowardice to courage as he finds himself on safari, and of the client's wife, Margot, a woman 'enamelled in that American female cruelty'.

Margot finally kills Macomber with her 6·5 Mannlicher as she purportedly seeks to save him from a charging buffalo. At the time, she already fears and resents her husband's new-found strength, and generations of critics have disputed whether the killing is accidental or deliberate. United Artists and director Zoltan Korda chose accident, thus permitting Joan Bennett, as Margot, to go off to a happy future with Gregory Peck, the white hunter. Most film critics condemned this decision as a distortion of Hemingway's work. The scholar Kenneth S. Lynn, however, in his perceptive intellectual history *Hemingway*, persuasively concludes that it was indeed an accident. Macomber, therefore, is truly killed not by wifely malevolence, but by his own dangerous attempt to become manly, not a rare hazard on safari. The underlying tale itself is generally held to be a Hemingway invention, and Philip Percival said he knew of no woman client who 'ever succeeded in shooting her husband as E. H. described'. J. A. Hunter, however, writing in 1952, states that 'Macomber' is based on a true incident that took place near the turn of the century.

The subject of a client losing his nerve on safari, and then recovering it, was discussed frequently by Percival and Hemingway on their own safari. Hemingway himself was always fascinated by fear and by the need to defeat it. Philip

The Macomber Affair, Hemingway's characters come to life

United Artists, *The Macomber Affair*, 1947, starring Gregory Peck, Joan Bennett and Robert Preston

Percival, mentioning no names, confirmed from experience the emotional drama of the transition to bravery. The character of Macomber was drawn from a rich young sportsman known to Hemingway. Margot was apparently a combination of Jane Mason, one of the writer's lovers, and a rich American woman who had offered to pay for Hemingway's next safari if she could join him. While in Africa, Hemingway became friendly with Bror Blixen, who later came fishing with him in Bimini in the Bahamas, and Macomber's professional hunter contains elements of both Percival and Blixen.

Hemingway's other brilliant African story, 'The Snows of Kilimanjaro', also published in 1936, was similarly bound up with his own safari experiences. The

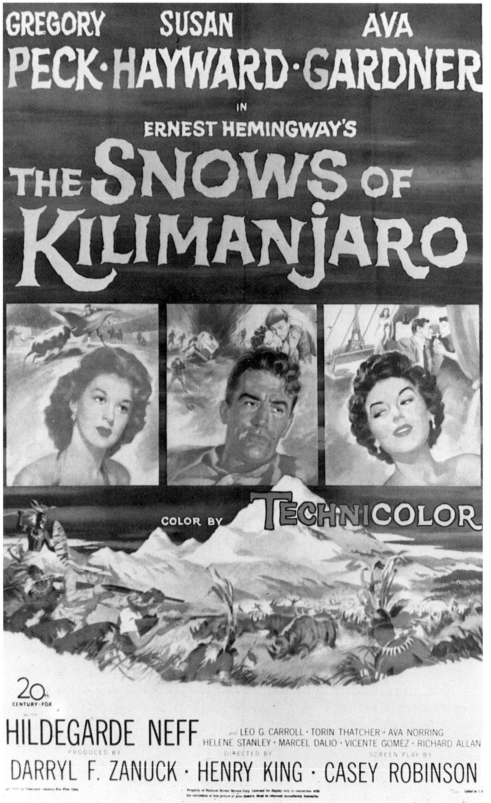

Twentieth-Century Fox's *The Snows of Kilimanjaro*, 1952, starring Ava Gardner and Gregory Peck

writer used details of camp life, bush flying and Mt Kilimanjaro itself to authenticate his brief tale of a bitterly self-absorbed, hard-drinking American writer who dies of gangrene, his leg rotting and stinking as the dreaded hyena, smelling death, lurks and whines near his tent. Once again, however, Hollywood contrived a happy ending, after sandwiching Ava Gardner and Hildegard Neff into lusty, non-African flashbacks. In due course, Gregory Peck survives his gangrene, and his guilt at sacrificing his writing to luxury, and looks forward to a full life with his rich wife, Susan Hayward.

Hemingway expressed annoyance not with the film's altered conclusion, but with the way the screenplay exploited too much of his other writings. 'When I sold you *"Kilimanjaro"*,' he exploded, cursing at director Henry King, 'I didn't sell you my entire work.' Twentieth-Century Fox and producer Darryl F. Zanuck had divided the production between six months of background shooting in east Africa and work with the stars in California, filming against the backdrop of a giant 'cyclorama', 40 feet high and 350 feet long, depicting the bush of Tanganyika and Mt Kilimanjaro itself. King was disturbed at the rhinoceros footage. The film safari had been permitted to kill only one rhinoceros, and on film it looked to the director like 'cold-blooded murder', so he cut and edited until the beast died a noble death. Only the highly trained hyena was true to Hemingway, sniffing about the tent as if waiting to avenge the thirty-five hyena actually killed on Hemingway's own safari. The hyena, however, scenting other animals on the shoes of its trainer, interrupted the filming by snapping at the man's feet, and had to be subdued with a chair. The trainer changed his shoes, and the hyena then went through its scene with Susan Hayward.

The year after Hollywood's *Kilimanjaro*, Hemingway went on his second and last safari, meeting Philip Percival in Mombasa in 1953, and once again visiting the Percival farm. By now, however, the writer's health, shooting and judgement had declined. He shaved his head, dyed his clothes a Masai ochre, hunted with a spear, and shot cigarettes out of hands with his ·22. Finally he had a fling with Debba, a very young Wakamba camp-follower, whom he described as black, beautiful and impudent, but 'absolutely loving and delicate rough'. Meanwhile he drank two or three bottles of liquor a day, and wine with his meals. To compensate for his own shooting, he claimed several kills made by his Cuban friend, Mario Menocal. At this Percival drew the line. 'Ernest,' the old gentleman protested, 'don't give me that nonsense. The whole thing has been a disgrace.' Despite awkward moments, however, Hemingway, slipping but still indestructible, managed to survive two plane crashes in Uganda and write a safari article for *Look* magazine. Philip Percival also held up well, later shooting two cattle-killing lion on his seventy-sixth birthday.

While Hemingway was on his last safari in September of 1953, Kenya's hunting world was still reeling from the largest safari in its history, the 300-tent expedition made for the MGM film *Mogambo*. A love triangle about an animal-

Hemingway on safari, Kenya, 1953

Ernest Hemingway sparring in
camp with Tony of the safari staff

trapping white hunter, a world-class playgirl and a demurely smouldering wife, the film was essentially a romantic vehicle for Ava Gardner and Clark Gable, who finally chooses Gardner and abandons Grace Kelly to her husband. Three deaths, $3.5m and a Christmas visit by a distraught Frank Sinatra, Ava Gardner's husband, were only part of the high price of this film safari. A staggering logistical achievement, beyond the resources of any one outfitting company, the safari was put together by one of Nairobi's most popular and resourceful professional hunters, Frank 'Bunny' Allen.

Although best remembered for his sparkling and seductive camp-fire charm, Bunny Allen was in fact a fine hunter. Part gypsy himself, Bunny's first hunting experience occurred at the age of five, in 1911, when a young gypsy, Piramus Berneres, took him poaching in the royal forest at Windsor. Berneres became the boy's tutor in fieldcraft, teaching him to trap hares and rabbits, partridges and pheasants. To avoid provoking the gamekeepers, they saved the deer, royal game, for special occasions. Berneres taught Bunny to think like an animal, to be hunted, not just to hunt. From him the boy learned the great lessons of silence, of stealth and of how to listen. From this came the ability to imitate precisely the noise of an animal, until Bunny could chase a rabbit into a trap by making the sounds of a stoat. An ethical hunter, Piramus Berneres always released the does. After Berneres was killed at Mons in 1914, England's first battle of the war, Bunny visited Canada with his mother, learning to hunt elk and moose with her boyfriend. Later, back home, Bunny was poaching woodpigeon near London on 11 November 1918, when suddenly he heard the cannons roar and the church bells ring as England celebrated the end of the First World War.

Sailing to Africa on the *SS Ussukuma* in 1927, Bunny Allen met Philip Percival on board, an experience Bunny, one of the last of Kenya's dwindling old guard, still remembers. In July 1986, when my son and I passed an evening with Bunny in Lamu, his blue eyes and single gold earring sparkling as we spoke, he reminisced about *Mogambo* over dinner, and about hunting over port. Sitting on a terrace by the beach, I mentioned the sadness of Beryl Markham's death only the day before. Unaware, shocked, a close friend, remembering her as 'a beautiful golden lion', Bunny was briefly silent.

He had been lucky, Bunny resumed, to come out to Africa when he did, for he saw 'the tail end of the beginning', and knew many of the old great hunters. He had his first paying client in the late 1920s, friends of the landowner on whose farm he worked at Nanyuki. In 1928 he helped provision the safari of the Prince of Wales. Then, at the Muthaiga Club New Year's Eve party in 1931, Bror Blixen and Denys Finch Hatton each gave him two clients, and Bunny Allen was in business for himself.

'The original white hunters', Bunny added, 'had to be gentlemen, either from the heart, or from school. Denys was an Etonian. Percival was a typical English squire with a fine family education. J. A. Hunter, with no education – now there was a gentleman from the heart.'

After an unusual war in the King's African Rifles, feeding his men in Abyssinia by buffalo hunting along the Omo River, and then fighting the Vichy French in Madagascar, Bunny Allen took up professional hunting again in 1946. Many of his old clients came out again, and for the first ten years, before too many people came and the hunting became more restricted, it was much like the old good days before the war. Serving as a hunting adviser to the film _King Solomon's Mines_ in 1949, Bunny earned the respect of MGM, and in 1952 director John Ford asked him to set up the film-making safari for _Mogambo_, to get it in the field and keep it supplied. 'The whole safari,' Bunny later said, 'was like running a small war.'

Bunny Allen established the 300-tent base camp on the Kagera River in Tanganyika, near where Uganda and Rwanda meet, cutting out an 1,800-yard airstrip and setting up four additional camps in four countries. The camps were kept supplied by a convoy of fifty lorries and daily DC-3 flights. The main camp was served with electricity by a generator flown in from the United States, useful for driving the X-ray machine in the hospital tent, the hair-dryers for the stars and the projector for the nightly screening of MGM films. Any African who wore shoes in camp was invited to watch the evening movies. The cuisine was said to be the finest south of Rome, and the pool played in the entertainment tent was at a high, club standard. Twenty-one professional hunters were involved in different aspects of the film safari. The animals were generally cooperative, although Bunny had to hang carcasses in the bush to keep the lions out of camp, and was once obliged to kill two rhinoceros that charged a film crew. Two Africans and one European were killed in accidents driving in the bush.

Bunny found the greatest problem was the personalities, particularly when Frank Sinatra, unemployed and disturbed to learn that his twenty-one-year-old

Bunny Allen in Lamu, Kenya, 1988

The Christmas card used by the _Mogambo_ film safari

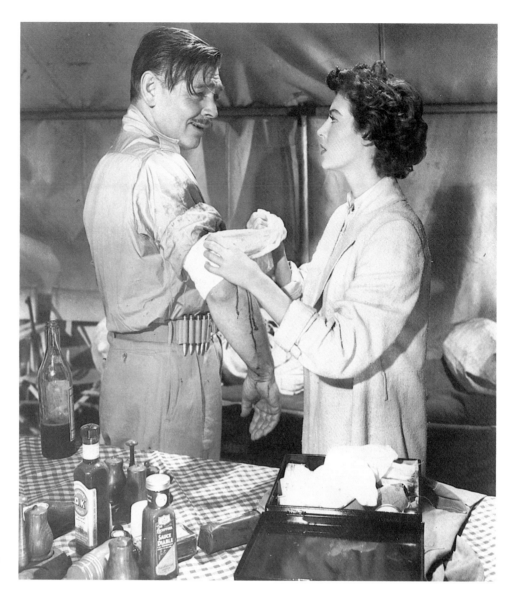

Mogambo. Ava Gardner nurses her white hunter

wife Ava Gardner would be in the bush with the freshly divorced Clark Gable, flew out for Christmas. On Christmas Eve Sinatra serenaded a mildly receptive audience of 175 whites and 350 blacks with 'White Christmas'. Although both were highly professional once the cameras rolled, the only thing that Gable and Ava Gardner shared was alcohol. While Sinatra and Ava Gardner raged at each other in one tent, Gable and Grace Kelly became friends in another. Gable, a fine shot, took eagerly to safari life, once saving a film crew from a crocodile with his Holland & Holland ·375 magnum. Like President Roosevelt forty years before, and like many experienced hunters today, Clark Gable was dressed in the durable, thorn-resistant, pewter-green bush gear made by America's premier safari outfitter, Willis & Gieger.

Mogambo was received as it was made, as a splendid romantic opportunity. The dialogue was crisp and easy to follow, as Ava Gardner purred at Gable, calling him 'My little white hunter', and he snapped at Grace Kelly, 'Out here we have three antidotes for everything: quinine, iodine and castor oil.' One critic referred to Gable as the 'most important gorilla bagged' in the film. Others compared it unfavourably to *King Solomon's Mines* as a safari tale. Film historians noted that the movie was essentially a remake of the 1932 picture *Red Dust*, which was set in the jungles of Indochina, where Jean Harlow bagged the young Clark Gable.

But for the real hunter, who stood in for Gable in some of *Mogambo*'s action scenes, it was all part of the fun of being a white hunter, for Bunny was already tired of shooting. 'As one gets older,' Bunny advised my son in Lamu in 1986, 'one gets more gentle, soft and stupid. Now, anything that God made to wriggle, I want to look after.' Reminiscing with his port, interrupting himself only to chat up the waitress, Bunny continued, 'It's the camp smoke. Watching a fire. Seeing it sparkle. And the stars. The gypsies, too, when I was a boy in England. Their fires caught me. You get the best out of people when they're sitting around a camp fire. The talk is so nice. People forget Belgravia and Fifth Avenue and finally become themselves. And you see the legs of the clients' wives as they pass between you and the fire.'

With *Mogambo*, the African safari was at last reduced to entertainment, without even the sense of mystery, adventure and the magic of wildlife that dignified the 1950 *King Solomon's Mines*. To some old hands, the safari films, and their filming, seem themselves an imposition. Just as many people in different nations feel that they are somehow diminished when their photograph is taken, that something of their private selves is being taken out of them, so perhaps the Hollywood safaris have diminished the reality. As in some churches, where photography is not allowed, the taking of the image can be seen as a selfish, intrinsically disrespectful act. Film-making is a cumbersome enterprise, aggravated by the driven, intense approach of its participants, who often presume that they are involved in a high calling that justifies otherwise intolerable behaviour. In Kenya's small safari world, the making of each film has had an impact.

After dozens of Hollywood films, Africa was less mysterious, distant, unknown. No longer did the word 'Africa' cause the imagination to run quite as before, for much was now commercially displayed, often with a minimum of redeeming, truly educational content. The early books, like radio shows with their listeners, stimulated their readers to fill in the canvas of their imaginations with the extraordinary landscapes, creatures and peoples of the distant continent. But once captured, presented and sold in pictures, to be experienced without risk or effort, Africa seemed somehow the less. As the safari outfitters reduced the effort of going on safari, and as the white hunters reduced the risk, so Hollywood's films reduced the freshness and the sense of personal discovery. To some it seemed that what the film public gained, in entertainment and education, the experience itself lost. A different, and perhaps more democratic view suggests, however, that the film popularization of Africa and safari life, like the almost excessive popularity of the game parks, is not only educational, but has provided the commercial support that makes the preservation of African wildlife possible.

MGM's French film poster of *Mogambo*, 1953, starring Clark Gable, Ava Gardner and Grace Kelly

Thirty years after Bunny Allen's work on *Mogambo*, Universal Studios arrived in Kenya to begin work on a nostalgic movie that concerned many of that old hunter's long-departed friends, the film version of Isak Dinesen's *Out of Africa*. Once again, the first safari problem was logistics, as the top safari firm Ker & Downey struggled to prepare a paramilitary field operation to support a hundred foreign film-makers, a camp to accommodate 340 people under canvas, and even a ten-ton Bedford truck converted into the 'honey wagon', containing four flush toilets. Before the film was finished in 1985, it was to use nearly 10,000 actors and cost about $30m, of which perhaps $8m went into the Kenyan economy.

With the help of K & D's John Sutton, himself a leading professional hunter, director Sydney Pollack strove for authenticity, both for rich period detail and for a moving presentation of the blacks and the land that would convey the Africa that Karen Blixen had found so seducing. It was to be a film that would give something back to Africa. The physical artifacts of the time were assembled with meticulous care. Double rifles, camp furniture, clothing, the Muthaiga Club, the tan cars of the Uganda Railway, and the uniforms of the King's African Rifles as they proudly celebrated the end of the First World War with a torchlight parade through Nairobi, all were true to their day. Many of the African extras were fitted out with traditional drooping open ear lobes, made from latex and costing $15 a pair.

Nature, however, required still more help. When the rains came too late to bring the coffee blossoms to full flower on schedule, puffs of shaving cream were used to supplement the sparkling whiteness that gave the Blixens new hope for their crop each year. With game killing unlawful in Kenya, the animals themselves were brought from California, including six trained lion, three dogs and an eagle. Making discreet gestures to modern conservationist sensibilities, Pollack had his leads, Meryl Streep as Karen Blixen and Robert Redford as Denys Finch Hatton, shoot lion only when the beasts charge. The lion scenes, however, were a subject of fierce dispute off-camera, with lion-trainer Hubert Wells refusing to permit a loaded rifle to be present when his lions were working. Told that Robert Redford's life was more important than any lion's, Wells argued, 'When are you going to use the rifle? When the lion comes towards you? He's trained to come towards you. And, God forbid, if the lion knocks somebody down, are you going to shoot the lion and kill the person beneath it?'

Meryl Streep won the highest marks, both on and off camera. Her highly studied, but hauntingly persuasive Danish accent immediately transports the viewer, as she opens the film with Dinesen's words, 'I had a farm in Ahhfreekaa, at the foot of the Ngong Hills.' Streep was in Africa for 101 days, and was on camera for 99 of them, a gruelling record that would incapacitate many actors. Instead, like Deborah Kerr in 1952, she was an uncomplaining trooper throughout. Redford, too, although straining practicality with his obsession for privacy, travelled light and worked hard, without the usual star's retine of handlers and accountants. Typically, he was more relaxed on film than in person.

Pollack received most criticism for his casting, and Americanization, of the role of Denys Finch Hatton. Redford, in fact, worked hard, and reportedly successfully, to acquire an English accent for the part. But a commercial concern, the notion that audiences wanted the Redford they knew, resulted in a late decision to have him speak as an American. Although one critic found that Redford fulfilled his role with 'nuance and suggestion', some said he appeared like 'a golden yuppie', so American that he lacked only his baseball bat. 'The character of Denys, as written by Kurt Luedtke and played in a laidback, contemporary American manner by Mr Redford, is a total cipher, and a charmless one at that,' Vincent Canby wrote in *The New York Times*, 'It's not Mr Redford's fault. There is no role for him to act.' The complex strength of Finch Hatton's character, and his eccentric English essence, were lost, and with them the magic that drew people to him.

The casting, and the portrayal of Kenya as it was, were enriched, however, with vivid portraits of other strong characters of the day. Klaus Maria Brandauer as Bror Blixen, Michael Gough as old Lord Delamere, Malick Bowens as Karen's loyal servant Farah, Michael Kitchen as Berkeley Cole, all filled their parts with the spirit of their namesakes. Less persuasive was Suzanna Hamilton as Beryl Markham, called Felicity in the film as Beryl Markham was still alive at the time.

Where the film seems to succeed best, and to come together with the work of Isak Dinesen, is in its projection of the romantic ideal of a brief period in the history of east Africa. It was the time of a strangely innocent and benevolent colonial life, lived at its best, when Europeans and Africans seemed cheerfully to exchange paternalism and loyalty, and the beauty of the land and the richness of the game made each safari a voyage into the garden of Eden. Like the book, and like so many Europeans rooted in Africa, the film carries, too, a sense of loss, a sense that we are sharing a special life which cannot last. Virtually every generation of Europeans in Africa has felt that it has seen the last of the old and good days, that, as the great hunter William Cotton Oswell said in 1885, 'Africa is nearly used up; she belongs no more to the Africans and to the beasts.'

As *Out of Africa* closes, we see a shoulder of the Ngong Hills, where Denys Finch Hatton is buried and the lions recline by his grave. Further in the interior of Africa, in Haggard's mythic land of Zu-Vendis, Allan Quatermain and Umslopogaas are also buried, the old Matabele warrior with his knees drawn up under his chin in the manner of his tribe in death, with his face turned towards his own distant land. Both men had died after a great Zu-Vendi battle. Before Quatermain perished, the old hunter calmly observed that 'We had only done our duty, as it is the fashion of both Englishmen and Zulu to do.'

9. THE CHASE GOES ON

As the filtering shadows of the yellow-fever thorn trees lengthen across the ocean-wide bush of southern Kenya's Masai Mara, the last crystals of the afternoon rains still sparkle on the wild olive trees in the elephant hills to the south. At the foot of Cottar's Camp, beyond the stalks of the red-flowered wild aloe and the low whistling thorns, their seed pods singing in the wind as air passes through tiny holes made by termite ants, the duck are calling, flying into the swamp. Then the cicadas begin the evening symphony, beating noisy transparent wings as the huge low sun dazzles briefly under the cloudline and the dusk descends.

At Cottar's Camp, it is the first evening of the Hunters' Reunion, and the tenth anniversary of the hunting ban that stopped all legal hunting in Kenya on 20 May 1977. Soon the lead-wood logs are bright under the shadowy arms of the giant yellow acacia, the encircling stones grow warm, and Kenya's last professional hunters settle down with a drink and a smoke to tell the tales of a thousand African camp fires. A few still hunt, but not in Kenya. For others, it is all yesterday. But the years and the countries do not matter. Respect and a shared ethic bind the hunters, and they speak of a free, wild life that few men know. It is not an evening for outsiders. What other adventurous men would consider the exhilarating moment of a lifetime was to them a daily routine, and they know each other too well for boasting and exaggeration. As they recall stalking sleeping lion in the rocky deserts of Somalia, and long hunts under the high forest canopy of the *galerie forestière* in the Central African Republic, shifting from country to country to keep the profession alive, it is clear that clients served mainly to make the free life possible.

Clients may go unmentioned, but gunbearers and trackers, by far the hunters' best-loved companions, are always in the talk, and none more so than Kenya's skilled Waliangulu. The Waliangulu were a small tribe of perhaps 8,000 hunter-gatherers, who, unlike the agricultural Kikuyu, co-existed easily with nature. One hunter speaks of Barissa, his Waliangulu tracker, who

Okavango swamp, Botswana

291

continued with him after his other trackers were killed by hippo and elephant. One day a startled lion, lashing out viciously as it fled, ripped open Barissa's face, but left him alive to stagger back to his village. The next morning Barissa's twelve-year-old brother took up his bow, followed the lion's trail and killed it with a poisoned arrow. Waliangulus use similar poisoned arrows to hunt elephant, shooting at the belly, because of its relatively thin skin. The hunters pursue the mid-size, young thirty-pounders, less crafty than the old bulls, and their tusks easier to carry. The poison is a black, gluey, tar-like gum made by boiling the bark of the agapanthera or scrub-olive plant, enhanced with puff-adder venom and scorpion's tail. These serve as anticoagulants to stop the blood from scabbing and to keep the poison spreading. The poison is smeared on arrowheads, each one carefully sheathed in leather. Staying fresh for several weeks, the poison will kill a bull elephant in fifteen minutes.

Hovering by the fire, two hunters hang on crutches, like secretary birds in the shadows, reminders of the hazards of the life, laughing with their drinks: Terry Mathews freshly gored by a black rhinoceros, and David Williams enduring still the complications of a 1968 rhino trampling in Uganda, when he declined to shoot, sparing the animal, and rolled sideways as the beast struck him. There is hardly a man who has not taken a serious hammering from several different animals, but the complaints are never about the game. The resentment, instead, is about poaching, corruption and the decline of wildlife since the 1977 Kenya hunting ban, particularly the loss of elephant and rhinoceros. Some are less pessimistic, but others nod as one laments, 'It's getting worse every day. The truth is we need both enlightened African leadership and an active European influence in game policy and management. Otherwise there is no hope.'

Discussing Africa's problems, the conversation inevitably returns to the core issue that aggravates them all. It is one that stalks the game in every country, the demon of population growth. Kenya, once notable for its sparse population, is now the fastest growing country on earth. With medical care outpacing education about birth control, and the average mother bearing eight children, the problem is getting worse. With an annual growth rate of 3.9 per cent, Kenya's population doubles every eighteen years. When I first went on safari thirty years ago, fewer than eight million Kenyans shared their country with the wildlife. Today there are twenty-three million. When Lord Delamere first gazed at the open highlands in 1897, there were something over two million Kenyans. In the year 2000 there will be thirty-eight million, and in 2020 some eighty million. But, as one hunter observes, there will be no more land and no more water than in Delamere's day, and the game will help pay the price.

As the old hunters speak, and the logs are pushed deeper into the fire, after the complaint of changing times is at last exhausted and after absent friends have been remembered, the talk always returns to the wonder of the animals, their peculiar qualities, their distinct magic. One veteran describes how he sought to analyse the charge of a lioness which he survived. Walking back to where she had started, he found there no pad marks on the ground, only deep

Elephant crossing the Ewaso Ngiro river

claw cuts where she rose on her extended talons and whipped herself into a taut fury, until you could see the dust under her like a drag racer as she started, and hear her cut the grass, taking only 'four strides to "full bore", her hind legs in front of her face, rowing at incredible speed, thirty, forty miles an hour.' In rough country, he continues, a charging lion bounds. On flat ground it just flows towards you in a streak. Facing the charge, always holding for a late, close shot, it is best to kneel, improving the odds by firing along the plane of the attack instead of transecting it, thus sighting the animal on its own level, lest the bullet deflect from the flat bone of the face.

Elephant are the missing guests at every camp fire, and so they are this evening. When else can hunters exchange reports of watching in 1964, riveted, while a long grey line of elephant swam across the White Nile to forage in Uganda? Or seeing nine bulls crossing the Kilombero River in Tanzania in 1953, following their ancient underwater trail, only trunk tips showing above the water as they slowly walked the river floor, sometimes too deep even for that, totally submerged for minutes at a time as each one calmly followed the sunken beast in front.

Recalling the days before increased population and cultivation finally stopped the free movement of game in the 1950s, the hunters discuss the old patterns of elephant movement. Very few elephant populations were isolated, although there were small local resident herds. Most moved about, but it was never a migration in the sense of a predictable annual route. The elephants, in their thousands, would be led by weather and food, gathering often in the highlands of southern Ethiopia, then drifting south into Kenya along the eastern side of Lake Turkana, past Marsabit, moving down along the forested Mathews Range. Then they generally proceeded eastwards through the Lorian swamp before dispersing into the south-east and foraging through Tsavo and along the Tana River, where they would concentrate again as the season grew dry. There on the Tana the hunters would find them, in country they loved as well as the elephant, walking for days or weeks to find one perfect old bull, a 100 lb a side.

The hunters after the war were as free as the elephant. Tony Dyer, the final president of the East African Professional Hunters' Association, remembers it well. 'Beginning here in the Mara in 1948, I had thirteen years of the most perfect free hunting. I could wake up in the morning, drink my tea, and just decide then, thinking about the clients, whether I was going to hunt in Kenya, Tanganyika or Uganda. We could even go freely to the Sudan.'

Some think the best large-scale operation after the war, offering both shooting and photographic safaris, was the one launched on 4 May 1945, over a drink or two on the veranda of the Imperial Hotel in Addis Ababa. There two veteran professional hunters, Donald Ker and Syd Downey, celebrated the defeat of Germany and made plans to start their safari partnership, Ker & Downey. Their first client, in 1946, was the film company for *The Macomber Affair*. It was Kenya's first post-war safari.

During the following thirty years, between the Second World War and Kenya's 1977 hunting ban, the safari business enjoyed a second boom. Old and new clients came out, game was still plentiful, and eighty-eight vast shooting blocks covered three quarters of the country and could be rented for moderate fees. In 1967, 1,000 Kenya shillings (then £50) entitled the licensee to shoot sixteen species of non-dangerous game. For dangerous game, in addition to a fee

Safari camp at Namorama, Kenya, 1951

Lake Turkana from the eastern shore

to the local community, the licence charge was one buffalo at 50 s., one lion for 400 s., one leopard for 500 s., one rhinoceros at 2,000 s., and a first elephant at 1,500 s. and a second at 2,500 s. It was unlawful to shoot hippopotamus. About eighteen other species, such as giraffe and kudu, had special fees. A complete bag totalled approximately £750 in licences.

For perhaps £5,000 ($15,000) two shooting clients in the late 1960s could take a three-week Kenya safari. The cost would include all licences, trophy expenses, a Toyota and a Bedford lorry, one professional hunter and a staff of about six, including one or two gunbearers or skinners, a cook, a laundryman and two camp helpers or drivers. Top-grade photographic safaris became increasingly popular and were organized on substantially the same lines in six photographic blocks, at about one third the cost.

Responsible government management and licensed hunting kept the lid on poaching. It was a time of high professional standards and top trophies. The code of the gentleman hunter was law. Shooting was outlawed within 200 yards

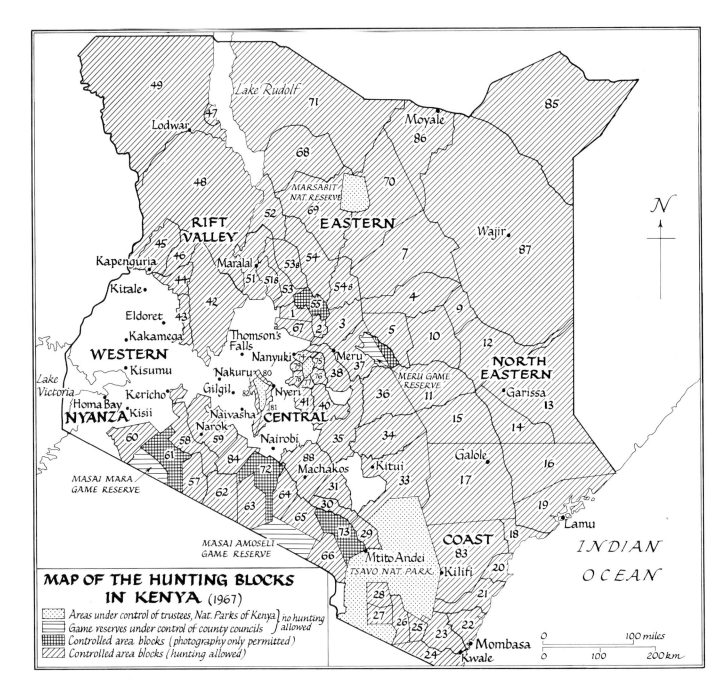

MAP OF THE HUNTING BLOCKS
IN KENYA (1967)

▒ *Areas under control of trustees, Nat. Parks of Kenya* } no hunting
≡ *Game reserves under control of county councils* } allowed
▦ *Controlled area blocks (photography only permitted)*
▨ *Controlled area blocks (hunting allowed)*

of a safari vehicle. The game itself had to be 500 yards from the vehicle. It was unlawful to use aircraft for hunting purposes, despite the early tradition of elephant spotting by Beryl Markham and others in the 1930s. Leaving wounded animals without taking every possible step to kill them was punishable by prison. The Game Department staff, both African and European, was proud and professional, scrupulous in the bush and in Nairobi. By arrangement with the government, all professional hunters were obliged, until 1975, to meet the standards of the East African Professional Hunters' Association, a collection of hardened Africa hands. By no means all colonial English, the Association included such men as the Irish hunter Liam Lynn, the Pakistani Mohammed 'Bali' Iqbal and René Babault from French Equatorial Africa. But there were no blacks. Although they were allegedly welcome, and often highly qualified in the

296

bush, the better-educated Africans seemed not to be drawn to hunting, while others were impeded by their illiteracy and by the language barrier.

After the war everything seemed more intense, less carefree, a little more commercial, a little less romantic. There were fewer European clients, more Americans, all with less time than the old days. Thousands of Africans, after service in the war, took a different view of colonial relationships. Ambition crept into the African attitude. Kenya's whites were less confident of the future. Authority was suspect. One could not so easily take one's staff for granted, although life in camp was less changed than life in town. As the population increased and agriculture spread, wild game and unspoiled bush were always a little harder to find. The good news was the four-wheel-drive vehicle, following the introduction of the military Willys Jeep. The first civilian version was the durable Land Rover, introduced in 1948. Early models provided traction with permanent four-wheel drive. The constant velocity joint permitted the front wheels to be engaged and 'driving' at the same time that they were being turned in different directions. The differential gear allowed the driving wheels to turn at different speeds. On later models, an optional fit raised the air intake pipes so the vehicle would not suck in dust and water. With a relatively light-weight, easy to repair, non-rusting aluminium body, the Land Rover was generally

René Babault

powered by a durable four-cylinder engine sufficient for moderate speeds on hard terrain. The Land Rover made it possible to get deeper into wild country, and to do it faster. As the cars got tougher, the clients got softer, and safari life went on.

Even the Mau Mau guerrilla emergency of the 1950s only slowed down Kenya's safari business. In the tradition of the white hunters who fought in east Africa with the Legion of Frontiersmen in the First World War and in north Africa with the Long Range Desert Group in the Second World War, many professionals turned their bushcraft to pursuing terrorists. With faces blackened, and wearing animal skins and wigs made from the hair of dead Mau Mau, they led hunting teams of pseudo-terrorists. Setting patient ambushes, following bees to their hives to see if men had taken their honey, for months eating like Mau Mau so their bodies would acquire the same smell, they learned to stalk men to the end in the dense wet forests of the Aberdare mountains. As the military campaign against the Mau Mau succeeded in the mid-fifties, the hunters returned to their normal work. It was their country, too, by choice. Most got on well with the men they worked with, for few things are as fraternal as sharing danger and the outdoors.

After Kenya became independent in 1963, poaching and corruption increased steadily, but the old safari traditions continued. Top professional hunters like Harry Selby and Glen Cottar, Reggie Destro and Donald Ker, Eric Rundgren and Syd Downey, led a new generation of hunters and clients. Some new hunters, like Prince Stas Sapieha from Poland, came to Kenya after the war to build a new life. Others, like John Sutton, were colonial products, raised in Africa, still English in many ways, but with the bush in their veins, eager to make an independent, outdoor life their profession.

John Sutton's father arrived in Nairobi while President Roosevelt was on safari in 1909. John was brought up on a farm near Nakuru, chasing eland on horseback before he was twelve, 'with so much wildlife around us that you could not fail but be totally involved with it. As kids we rode and shot everything.' At fourteen, very scared, John shot his first rhino. It was 1941. Opening up new agricultural land was part of the war effort. Hundreds of thousands of acres of wildlife grasslands went under the plough. Then the animals were attracted back by the young green wheat, and keeping down the game became a duty. Although rhino and elephant were beginning to be cut off and squeezed back by farming, they were still all over the country. Calves were taken at night by leopard next to the house. The Suttons' gardener was killed by a rhino. Frequently the hunters coursed, well mounted, following greyhounds in wild chases after reedbuck and Thomson's gazelles, occasionally blundering on lion, or distracted by steenbok, small antelopes too fast and tricky for the dogs.

John Sutton was bored with farm life, drawn by the game, and he started in the great hunting days just after the war, when there were no bookings and no borders. In a single year, shifting camps all over the country, 'we'd do 25,000 miles on really rough roads, before we had Land Rovers, bush bashing in old

Waterbuck by Cornwallis Harris

Chevs and Internationals, with the factory-built bodies cut off, and our own truck bodies, suitable for hunting, fixed on the back'.

The young post-war hunters, often looking for trouble, learned quickly, surviving intense, hazardous experiences. They also learned, as Oswell and Selous did from their mistakes a century earlier, that good hunting habits are essential in the bush, that sloppiness, with weapons or animals, can be fatal. Virtually every incident in which a top hunter is injured contains an element of the unnecessary or the unpredictable. Sometimes it is bad luck or a wild card, an external factor that intervenes in the hunter–quarry contest, like the sudden intrusion of another animal or man. More frequently, trouble or injury in the bush is caused by breaking the rules, even when hunting lesser game. Not reloading promptly, not being familiar with one's weapon, failing to respect the animals, lack of coordination with trackers or other hunters, not enough concentration, too much concentration, all add danger to a dangerous sport.

Like other hunters, John Sutton developed a remarkable affinity with a gunbearer, always the unsung hero. He hunted with Harry Selby, who would generally not let his clients shoot a second lion even when there were four on the licence, learning 'standards, ethics, to work for an animal, not to shoot. The whole thing was in the fair chase. Not in pulling the trigger.' Later, in 1973, John Sutton was among the first Kenya professionals to hunt the Sudan after the brutal Sudanese civil war ended. Today, John Sutton is back in Nairobi, often missing the old days, but busy directing Ker & Downey, now the largest of the firms that operate high-standard photographic safaris.

For at least one young hunter after the war, Glen Cottar, safari life was almost inevitable. His father, his uncle and his grandfather, the redoubtable Charles Cottar, were all professional hunters. Big, rough-looking, harshly independent and full of brass, Charles Cottar was the first American white hunter. Having already moved his family by covered wagon across Texas, Oklahoma and Colorado, he was inspired by President Roosevelt's safari to come to Africa in 1911. Scornful of local colonial authorities, delighted to outrage British social sensibilities, he was a man who did what he wanted, the way he wanted. No one who hunted with Charles Cottar ever forgot it, least of all his own grandson Glen, whom the old man called 'Stewmeat'. Late in life, paralysed on one side, Charles Cottar would order Stewmeat to switch off the Model A and put on the handbrake, while he dragged himself out to shoot once more.

Charles Cottar's son Mike was a mellow, well-loved character, known for his wide Texan hat and quiet humour. He took his own son Glen on safari to Mt Kenya with clients when he was four, and the boy was brought up on Lake Victoria, where his family ran the ferry on Mara Bay. Mike suffered attacks of blackwater fever, passing blood in his urine, a painful result of neglected malaria which had enlarged his spleen. In 1940 a rogue buffalo rushed him. Mike killed it, but it hit him as it fell, damaging his stomach and already weakened spleen. The following year he died of his eighth attack of blackwater fever, when Glen was ten. Growing up, going to school in Nairobi, reading Rider Haggard, Glen

Opposite above: Charles Cottar with his American rifle holster and saddle, 1921

Opposite below: Charles Cottar, Kenya, 1921

Opposite above: Mike Cottar as a young hunter

Opposite below: Mike Cottar

Right: The brothers, Mike and Bud Cottar, in a sand river

Below: Bud Cottar and Masai women

Above left: Glen Cottar, 1938

Above right: Glen Cottar, 1982

Left: Calvin Cottar in the Ruvu river, Tanzania, 1986

continued to spend his holidays in the bush, often out with native hunters. At fifteen he took out his first hunting parties, and at eighteen he joined Eagle Safaris. Due to the Mau Mau emergency, he did not get his professional licence until 1956. He then spent the next seven years hunting with White Hunters Africa, Ltd, in Tanganyika, Kenya and Uganda.

Finally, in 1963, he set up on his own as Glen Cottar Safaris, establishing a permanent camp in Tsavo in 1965, a tough year for him as he suffered severe injuries when trying to kill an immense buffalo which had already been wounded four times by a client. His own heavy ·500 Rigby out of action with a broken lever spring, Glen borrowed his client's ·465 Holland & Holland double rifle and crawled through the thickets, following the blood trail.

After hitting the bull three more times, thinking him almost gone, Glen went in for a final close shot with one barrel empty. As it often happens with even the best hunters, trouble came from breaking one of the old rules: always reload. The buffalo attacked through a heavy bush as Glen fired his only barrel, smashing Glen down and forcing him relentlessly along the ground with the boss of his horns, grinding his legs as the hunter fought to avoid the horn tips. Bleeding heavily from nose and mouth, the buffalo temporarily abandoned the attack. With his skinner's help, Glen lifted himself into a tree by his arms, unable to use his legs, which were slashed open, the torn muscles hanging out like spaghetti. Certainly not the cleanest kill, the buffalo fell after three more shots from the client. Dosed with morphine, penicillin and rum, with the muscles pushed back into his legs by hand, Glen stopped at a nearby camp where Charles Lindbergh was on safari. Lindbergh braced Glen with whisky and he was rushed to Nairobi.

Back in the field the following year, though limping, Glen was sharing a camp with his friend Eric Rundgren, exploring in Bechuanaland. Then in 1968 he secured one of the first hunting concessions in Tanzania, and formed Afriventures with Reggie Destro and the Allen brothers, David and Anton, sons of the professional hunting rascal, Bunny Allen. Soon Glen helped reopen tracks in the wild Moyowosi swamp. But just as things were going well, Tanzania shut down hunting in 1973. As Prime Minister Rashidi Kawawa put it, 'You hunters are the largest single colonial relic left in Tanzania.' So Glen hunted in Uganda for a time, but was finally mistaken for a mercenary and arrested. After attempting the Congo and the Sudan, Glen hunted in Kenya, but by 1975 the country's hunter licensing system was approaching chaos, with unqualified hunters entering the business, and in 1977 it all came to an end with the ban on hunting in Kenya.

What Glen Cottar misses now, as he manages his splendid safari camp in the Masai Mara, hosting the Hunters' Reunion, is 'the exploring, the stalking, not the killing. I always looked for what was over the next hill.' Glen's clients used to complain that they spent all their time cutting tracks. Highly selective in his game shooting, Glen lost clients who were impatient with his anti-killing attitude. But when J. A. Hunter himself went on his last safari, he went with

Glen Cottar. Today Glen misses 'being on the move, with a fly camp at the end of the day. Now it's Botswana-style, base-camp hunting. I miss the evenings by the fire. It makes me homesick to talk about it.'

Stas Sapieha, a friend of Glen Cottar's who began hunting in the same period, came to the profession by a different route. Arriving with his bride at Mombasa by steamer in 1948, buried in a fourth-class cabin under the engines, with $2.20 in his pocket, Stas Sapieha was already a man who had experienced many extremes. Raised in palatial style in Poland, where his father was foreign minister and where a Warsaw avenue is still named after the family, Stas spent the war in German concentration camps. But before the war he had been trained since the age of eight to shoot on family estates in Lithuania, and he was at home with guns and horses.

In 1945, after adventures that would daunt Douglas Fairbanks, Stas liberated from the Germans a farm at Grabau in Schleswig-Holstein that contained 1,200 thoroughbred Polish horses, including Lipizzaners, all stolen by the Nazis and maintained under their control during the war by 300 Polish cavalry NCOs. While the contending armies swarmed about, fighting over more strategic targets, Stas ran the horse farm, earning the title 'the Prince of Grabau', turning captured German officers into meticulous servants and hosting banquets for allied soldiers. There he met Didi Siemienska, married her in Paris the same year, and sailed with her to Mombasa in December 1947.

This spirit of enterprise keeps the Sapiehas young today, as they recall the 1950s, when they walked across Kenya prospecting for rubies, shooting to eat, adding native languages, including English, to the German, French, Polish and Italian they spoke when they arrived. With a struggling ruby mine to maintain,

Left and above: Masai Mara

Stas turned to professional hunting to earn money, often attracting the more eccentric clients whom British hunters found less congenial.

While Glen Cottar thinks back to his fly camps and his favourite hunts in the Mara, in Tanzania on the Ugalla River or in the valleys of the Loliondo deep in the Masai reserve, Stas Sapieha remembers his safari with the finest chefs of France. Two rich clients, one a Hungarian who never shot and waited each morning for his secretary to fly in, the other a French manufacturer of plastic buckets, invited three of France's master chefs to be their guests on a two-week safari at Narosura, in Kenya's hunting block No. 57.

The chefs, of course, were not expected to cook, a duty performed, instead, by the camp baker and Princess Sapieha. Each chef, however, was asked to bring a gastronomic contribution on the safari. One, a seasoned European hunter, brought eight kilos of cheese, kept cool with the large tins of Iranian caviar that accompanied the bucket manufacturer. The second chef, the temperamental Papa Roucou, a Michelin legend and a rigorous gourmand, brought a heavy crate of his own truffled pâté de foie gras. Paul Bocuse himself, rarely seen outside the kitchens of his three-star restaurant near Lyons, brought forty litres of the well-regarded 1976 Beaujolais Nouveau. Challenged at customs in

Nairobi, Bocuse truthfully explained that, for him, it was an essential health drink. Enthusiastic throughout, all three chefs delighted in the camp fire and the lean, fresh meat of different antelopes, particularly relishing broiled eland, fresh camp buns and Didi's bush flambés.

One evening in August of 1986, Ted Roosevelt and I shared a bottle of wine and old tales with the Sapiehas at their house in Kiambu, the garden blazing with the pure colours of Kenya's flowers and the drawing-room rich in geological samples, Turkish rugs, memories of the hunt, and leather-bound crested family histories in Polish. Didi reminded me that in 1959 they took me out on my first safari, and Stas speaks, as old hunters do, of other days and other hunters. He talks about Glen Cottar's former partner Reggie Destro, who died in 1984 after a lifetime of adventurous hunting. With a Scottish mother, an Italian father, but totally English, Destro began at sixteen, when he ran away with a blanket, a teapot and his tracker to spend three years in the bush. By the time he was twenty, Destro did not need a tracker. Like Glen Cottar, Destro was later fortunate to find a wife who became a master of safari management, coordinating logistics, staff and clients. Stas hunted with Destro often, and wishes he could do it once more. Destro was tough, charming, a hard worker, 'the ideal hunter,' recalls Stas, 'a self-made bushwhacker, and a gentleman, not in his manners, in his heart. He was a man.'

While Stas Sapieha was imprisoned by the Nazis in 1941, Tony Archer, at eight, was shooting his first buck, a dik dik, with a ·22 on Impala Farm. Tony's father first came out to Kenya to fight the Germans in 1915, serving with the King's African Rifles. After the first war, he stayed on under the Soldier Settlement Scheme, owning a coffee farm at Thika next door to Elspeth Huxley's. During the Second World War, Tony's father was responsible for

Below left: Stas Sapieha hauling a leopard bait over a tree

Below right: Reggie Destro, 1982

seeing that certain agricultural properties produced food for the war effort. This gave the boy the opportunity, during his school holidays, to enjoy some of the finest shooting in Africa. At sixteen he shot his first buffalo, and by then he had a deep interest in 'the natural-history side'. That year, 1950, Bunny Allen took his son Anton, at fifteen, and Tony Archer and Mike Prettejohn, both sixteen, on their first elephant safari, the boys getting five elephants between them. All three boys went on to become white hunters, with Mike Prettejohn not giving up until he had been mauled by a lion, thrown by a rhinoceros and crushed and shot during a buffalo hunt.

Tony Archer did not become a professional hunter until the Mau Mau emergency began to die down in 1957, when he spent three months on a scientific safari collecting bird specimens in Angola, sponsored by the British Museum and New York's Museum of Natural History. For most of the next twenty years Tony worked with Ker & Downey, hunting across Africa, usually spending 250 days a year in the field, in Kenya, Tanzania, Uganda, Botswana, the Sudan and in Ethiopia, where he opened a K & D branch in 1972.

Although he loved hunting the Loliondo valleys east of the Serengeti, Tony Archer also enjoyed the challenge of hard hunting in the Sudan, even with the curse of swarming stingless bees and the agonizing itching of the tiny penetrating hairs of the buffalo bean plants. He took clients after giant eland, Nile lechwe, white-eared kob, yellow-backed duiker, lowland bongo and other antelope, and sometimes after the great hundred-pound elephant between Kenya's Tiva and Tana rivers. In 1958 and 1959 Tony and his client Raymond Guest sailed the Nile twice between Khartoum and Juba, using the paddle-steam launch *SS Kaibor*, towing a barge with two vehicles, and stopping to hunt on the way. Tony's final shooting safari was a brief one, ten days with Prince Bernhard of the Netherlands in 1977, just two weeks before Kenya's hunting ban. The only animal killed was a kongoni for camp meat.

During all this time, before he finally settled down as an African travel expert in Nairobi, Tony Archer continued as a specialist in scientific safaris, a tradition that began when Selous collected for the British Museum in 1882. Tony worked in the forests of western Uganda with the distinguished Kenyan sculptor Rob Glen, doing ornithological surveys and collecting insects for the Los Angeles County Museum, in Botswana gathering bats for the Royal Ontario Museum and in the Sudan collecting birds and small mammals for Chicago's Field Museum. There he secured fourteen new Sudanese specimen records and introduced the use of mist nets in thick undergrowth to catch skulkers.

Apart from natural history, Tony's favourite delight was hunting with the Africans, studying their bushcraft. For fifteen years his teacher was Abakuna Gumunde, a Waliangulu and former 'prince of poachers', who had killed over 200 elephant with bow and arrow, including three elephant in one day, each with over 100 lb of ivory a side. Abakuna Gumunde hunted with Tony in five African countries, and in Nepal after tiger. Although Tony believes that there is still room for ethical, sporting hunting, he thinks the 'unspeakable, unsporting

Mike Prettejohn being mauled by a lion at night

methods of running down game in cars, using spotlights and the rest, are destroying true hunting'. Bad instincts and inexperience are aggravated by the pressure of time. Most contemporary shooting safaris are limited to two or three weeks, the clients desperate to collect at least one trophy a day, with neither time nor stamina for the long, frustrating stalks that are the heart of hunting. Instead, Tony now sends clients on photographic safaris.

Careers in the bush are often punctuated and remembered by misadventures, and Tony Archer will not forget the day when Terry Mathews, another professional K & D hunter, went after a lion wounded by a Texas client. Hitting his lion in the shoulder at 100 yards with a light ·264, the American's blow was not heavy enough for a bone shot, although it would have sufficed for a heart shot.

Thinking the lion was harder hit than it was, Terry waited, giving it a chance to bleed and weaken. Then he walked alone to the thicket to which the wounded lion and three lionesses had returned. As Terry got to the thicket, he put his 7 mm rifle in his left hand and bent down to pick up a stone with his right, intending to hurl it into the bushes to make the lion stir. As he bent down the lion charged him from four yards. Unable to get his gun up, Terry fired instinctively, using only his left hand, his shooting hand. He killed the lion with a single shot between the eyes. On the way back to camp, where Tony Archer was waiting, the Texan commented, 'Oh, you're sweating. Are you hot?'

'No,' Terry replied, 'I'm scared.'

The incident gives merit to the old Kenya rule that only permitted the hunting of heavy game with a rifle of at least ·400 calibre, the only exception being a ·375. There are many ways, however, to become disabled on safari. In 1968 Terry Mathews was injured in a shooting accident, struck in the face by an American client's shotgun blast while shooting near Selengai, and losing the sight of his left eye, which forced him to give up hunting after thirteen years in the profession. He now wears a black eye patch which makes him still more dashing.

Raised in Uganda, Terry began shooting at the age of ten. After working for the Kenya police in the early 1950s, he started with Safariland and joined K & D in 1956. Terry was fortunate to be Syd Downey's trainee hunter on Downey's last three safaris. He studied the senior hunter's craft in hunting cats, for Downey always seemed to know where they were and how they would react.

Terry also learned from Eric Rundgren, in some ways thought to be the finest hunter of his generation. Rundgren's instinct and knowledge of the country

Right: Lion feeding on zebra

gave him a magical ability to find game. Once after an animal, it was his. The Africans reverently called Rundgren 'Mchangi', after mystical glass beads that scatter in all directions when thrown to the ground. An old hand, a godson of Bror Blixen, Rundgren could be tough on the Africans and impatient with clients, often growling, 'Safari's all right, except for the clients.' A sense of luck and superstition was part of Rundgren's instinct, like the traditional Austrian idea of a hunter's luck, the notion that the animal moves towards you.

Eric Rundgren had no patience with unsporting hunters. He shared the scorn of east African professionals for the techniques used by Portuguese hunters in Mozambique. There clients and white hunters fired from raised seats in the back of safari cars, protected by bars known as 'panic rails', frequently shooting near waterholes at night as the animals froze in powerful spotlights. Himself half Swedish and half Irish, Rundgren once observed that, 'Big-game hunting as we know it was originally a British sport. They created the code. Unless that code is generally followed you can shoot animals, but you can't call it big-game hunting.'

Before his injury made him give up big game, Terry Mathews most enjoyed elephant hunting along the Tana River in August and the excitement of leaving on safari as the tracker ran out with his bedding and tin cup, and Kisiu, Terry's Kamba gunbearer of fifteen years, jumped into the Land Rover with his eyes sparkling. Of all his old hunting companions, Terry enjoyed none more than the tracker Garissa Bhoja, 'a real gentleman of the bush, who wouldn't try to walk you into the ground, as some do, and moved through the bush like a chameleon, never speaking, flicking his hand to point things out, a hornet's nest, a snake. It was an honour to hunt with him.'

As he works at his new profession, sculpting fluid, bronze statues of African game, Terry speaks often of his old clients and hunting friends, like Joe Cullman and Bing Crosby, a particularly fine shotgun shot who shared seven safaris with Terry. Recalling his own schoolboy days in England, Terry looks up from an unfinished elephant carving and remarks, 'I don't read, you know. But I read all of Rider Haggard. As a boy, I was in exile in England. Haggard kept Africa alive for me.'

Early in 1987, a few months after we had talked about the old days over tea at his studio in Karen, Terry suffered one of the maverick accidents that is a product of changing times in the Kenya bush. Assisting Peter Beard, the photographer and the author of the vivid book *The End of the Game*, Terry was on foot with Beard in Nairobi National Park, with a television film crew from the United States. As Terry crouched quietly, unarmed, near a female rhinoceros and her calf, one eager photographer, ignoring Terry's instructions, kept standing up and pressing forward, camera whirring, twice drawing the rhino's anxious attention. Provoked, the rhinoceros finally charged. The photographer ran past behind Terry. Protecting the film crew ten yards behind him by standing his ground, Terry shouted and threw a stone to deflect the charging rhino as the animal lowered its head, coming in fast.

Right: Terry Mathews and Bing Crosby

Below: Terry Mathews

Weighing one ton or more and capable of thirty miles an hour, black rhinos gallop only when charging. They hit with the impact of a small truck. As Terry stood firm, the long front horn entered the pocket of his shorts, punched into his thigh, tore the lining of his colon, and ripped sixteen inches upwards into his pelvic and abdominal cavity. Only Terry's heavy belt saved him from being torn open as the rhino tossed him ten feet into the air.

The long, slender horn missed his spleen, kidneys, major arteries, heart and lungs. Surviving, appreciating his luck, with two ribs and one leg badly broken, Terry complained from his hospital bed that, although he had absorbed sixteen inches of the world's finest aphrodisiac, he had never felt less sexy. Instead of flowers to the hospital, he asked friends to send contributions to the Sheldrick Wildlife Appeal for rhinoceros protection work. A leading conservationist, Terry Mathews had recently completed, as a gift to Kenya, a life-size sculpture of a female black rhino and her calf, destined to stand at the gate of the Nairobi National Park to raise money for rhino rescue operations.

Now that there is no more big-game hunting in Kenya itself, the true safari tradition is kept alive by a few men, largely expatriate Kenyans, who continue the chase wherever the law and the game permit. Scattered across Kenya itself, from Lamu on the Indian Ocean to Marsabit in the north, the network of old hunters stays in loose touch, sharing their own world, with twenty or thirty gathering together each May at the Hunters' Reunion to raise the odd drink and retell a few tales. The rest of the year they pass around the news of the hunters who are still in the field, some faithfully tuning in their shortwave radios at home each evening to listen in, eager for details, as the safari camps call in to their bases.

When the hunting ban hit Kenya in 1977, most professional hunters based in Nairobi took it as the end of the traditional African safari. For several years standards had already been declining, with government officials sometimes being suspected of involvement in organized poaching. Of 150 hunters active in 1977, over a hundred were not members of the association. Many of these were not fully qualified, and the government took to licensing hunters directly and tried to assign them to clients, disregarding the intensely personal nature of the business. The Professional Hunters' Association made it a clean kill, disbanding that August after a final banquet. Many veteran professional hunters went into photographic safaris, some with large-scale mini-van tourism, others trying to keep some of the old style, with small parties and first-class camps in more remote locations, but it was not the same. Not for the hunters, not for the clients and not for the game.

As in many other countries, the end of licensed hunting was the beginning of the end for the big game. The professional hunters had every reason to protect both game and habitat. They trained generations of game wardens to their own high standards, and actively held government officials to their duty. Where hunting is allowed on private land, as in Zimbabwe, the owners have reason to protect the game for paid cropping by hunters, but where there is no legal hunting they have no economic reason not to kill the game that threatens their crops and livestock. Under Kenya's 'concession system' that prevailed just prior

Herd of buffalo, Zimbabwe

to 1977, local tribes had received money from the hunting licensed on their land. So they too benefited from the game. But in 1977, as one veteran game warden put it, 'The hunting ban made wildlife the enemy of the people.'

When the hunters moved out, the poachers moved in, not just local tribesmen hunting for meat, but large-scale commercial poachers. The rhinos and large bull elephants were largely destroyed. Elephant have the power to influence the environment they inhabit. As the elephant populations changed, either declining if poached or multiplying if concentrated in parks, the ecology changed for other wildlife, whether birds, carnivores or antelopes. If the elephant overgraze, vegetation perishes and small dustbowls are created. If there are too few elephants to hold down the acacia trees, then the lower vegetation is smothered, the open plains shrink and antelopes like reedbuck lose their food supply.

As in Tanzania, the hunting ban meant death for any elephant with heavy ivory. As the available tusks became smaller and smaller, young cows were also killed. Iain Douglas-Hamilton, the leading expert on elephant populations, estimates that the elephant population of east Africa is declining by 7.5 per cent annually. When Tanzania's Selous Game Reserve permitted controlled hunting, such animals as lion and elephant multiplied. Dominant old male lions were shot on licence and breeding increased. In 1969 there were about 30,000 elephant left in the Selous, Africa's largest wildlife sanctuary. Under the effective wildlife management system set up by the celebrated game warden Brian Nicholson, that population recovered to 120,000 elephant, largely due to strict enforcement of regulations that permitted licensed shooting, but only of elephant carrying tusks of less than 60 lb or more than 80 lb. The typical eighty-pounder is a forty-year-old male that is no longer breeding. With licensed shooting no longer allowed in the Selous, poaching has now taken over. By 1988 the population was down to perhaps 50,000, with virtually no large bulls, and the total numbers were still dropping.

Despite the hunting bans in Tanzania and Kenya, and the difficulties of finding good game country elsewhere, a few determined hunters refused to give up. They started over again, sometimes more than once. Continuing the tradition of a century and a half, confronting problems every bit as severe as those that faced the old hands, they broke camp and adapted like the hunters before them, seeking out whatever countries had decent game and tolerable regulations. Thinly scattered across about ten countries, perhaps fifteen top professionals today maintain the safari ethic of the early hunters. They have different advantages and face different sets of problems from those of the white hunters who came before them, but they share the spirit and pursue the same adventure.

Most of today's professional hunters were brought up in the bush, an advantage that even Oswell and Selous, J. A. Hunter and Denys Finch Hatton did not possess. Like Cotton Oswell, these modern hunters require the wild life, and they respect most those Africans who remain closest to nature, for they understand how truly sophisticated and demanding that is. Most of their clients are serious hunters. In 1988 a typical first-class hunting safari for two shooting clients costs approximately £4,500 ($8,000) per week for each hunter, in addition to perhaps Tanzania government royalty fees of $8,000 and game licences and trophy costs of approximately $4,000. A comparable photographic safari in traditional tented camps, organized by Robin Hurt Safaris or another top outfitter like Ker & Downey, for a party of four led by a knowledgeable professional guide, often a retired hunter, would cost from $2,000–3,500 for each client per week.

The surviving, active professional hunters are not, however, the bush chauffeurs who take tourists 'on safari', pausing at predictable game spots and escorting photographers as they peep through the roof decks of recreational vehicles and upholstered zebra-painted mini-vans, although some have done that work.

They are eccentric characters like Tom Mattanovich and Nassos Roussos, who lead safaris into the Ethiopian hunting grounds, walking fifteen hard miles a day after elephant with one or two clients, in the high country near where Cornwallis Harris first hunted with the King of Shoa 150 years ago. Operating in a land elsewhere ravaged by civil war, forced resettlement and famine, these hunters know the mountainous rain forests and meadows of eight-foot grass of the Mizan Taferi as few other men do. When it seemed impossible to continue, these individuals hung on, confident that their reputation among the best clients and professionals would see them through. When nobody came, they looked after their gear, held their men together and tirelessly searched out the best game habitat. Now they are back on safari.

In Botswana, Harry Selby and Tony Henley are two Kenya hands still taking out tented shooting safaris and doing it the old way. Like two other top Botswana hunters, Fred Bartlett and Lionel Palmer, they operate out of Maun near the Okavango swamp, and their clients know what a full day means. As two of the very few professionals who have never stopped hunting in over thirty years, Selby and Henley know the game. As a competitor puts it, 'They still produce such successful safaris that they keep us younger hunters on our toes.'

In Zambia, where the job is getting harder as the poaching gets worse, a few men, like John Knowles, still lead real safaris. As a boy of twelve, out with an Afrikaaner friend on the Erasmus family farm outside Lusaka, John Knowles learned his lessons. Normally the boys hunted rabbit and duikker with slingshots, spears and bows, usually failing, but 'learning the wind, stalking, anticipation, keeping down'. When the farm was short of meat, old Erasmus, the Boer farmer, would wake the boys before daybreak, handing them his ·300 Savage and one cartridge, looking carefully into their eyes, slowly saying, 'Go out and bring back the meat.' If they came back without an antelope, whether a reedbuck or an oribi, a duikker or a bushbuck, it meant 'the old rhino jambok, and a proper hiding. Erasmus would just say, "I didn't send you out there to play the fool." '

Later, at school in Devon, lying in his dormitory at night, John Knowles recalls, 'I would hear the wind of Africa, and I'd miss the sun on the long grass. I could smell it. I could smell the first rain after the dry season. God, I missed Africa.' Back in Africa in the late 1950s, still young, John finally learned the rest from an old African village hunter called Jacobi. 'He taught me tracking. The habits of the animals. How to look at an elephant. Never straight on. Never directly, until you shoot. They feel you looking at them, just like people.' When Jacobi himself was young, hunting elephant with a bow and arrow, having to get in close, he would first strip and smear his body with fresh, moist elephant dung, masking his own smell, and then creep into the middle of the herd.

But today, John says, there are no more village hunters growing up like Jacobi in Zambia. Today they just poach, using guns and cable snares. Clearly, too, there are no more hunters growing up like John Knowles. Wire-lean, sun-wrinkled, John still makes the best of Zambia's game and landscape.

Like Erasmus, but in his different way, John teaches his clients to respect each shot, never to shoot unless confident of bringing an animal down, and never to lose it once hit. A stickler for fair chase, working hard on foot in Zambia's lovely Luangwa Valley, John and his clients still find lion and leopard, buffalo, kudu and sable. But each year the poaching and population mean less habitat and less game. John Knowles has not seen a decent elephant in eight years. In 1986 an African villager in Chifunda told him, 'Bwana, the only elephant my boys will see will be in a photo.'

The pining for Africa that afflicted John Knowles at his Devon boarding-school is a common complaint of young white Africans sent 'home' for school. One of the painful lessons of colonialism, it is a sense of loss shared by many colonials for whom a life in Europe can never be complete. It strikes most of all at school, or when old in retirement, as they miss the end of the day on the veranda in Malaya, or the scents and sounds surrounding a tent in the Congo. When J. A. Hunter returned to Scotland in 1950, after forty-five years in Africa, he found the fields and the trout smaller than he remembered. On the farms the smell of petrol had replaced the scent of clover of his youth. Fences, gates and vermin possessed the countryside. The old hunter sailed home to Africa.

Sometimes, in schoolboys, the shock of adjusting to Europe has come early enough to change their lives, as it did for Wilfred Thesiger, perhaps the greatest explorer of the post-war period. Thesiger, who once shot seventy lion in five years, is celebrated for hunting bareback on a difficult Arab mare, with the reins in one hand, his Rigby ·275 held in the other like a pistol as he shoots a wild boar dead with each shot. Born in Addis Ababa in 1910, and sent home to boarding-school at eight, Thesiger had already witnessed more fantastic things than he could hear in any bedtime adventure tale read in England. He once told me that when he spoke of Africa, his schoolmates told him he lied, that it could not be. So he turned for nourishment to the books of Gordon Cumming, Baldwin and Selous. As a boy at Eton, which he loved, 'dreaming of big-game shooting and exploration', he thought of his early days in Ethiopia, when he saw, in 1916 at the age of six,

> . . . the priests dancing at Timkat before the Ark of the Covenant to the muffled throbbing of their silver drums . . . the triumphant return after the battle of Sagale . . . the chiefs in their panoply of war, lion's mane headdresses, brilliant velvet cloaks stiff with silver and golden ornaments, and great curved swords . . . a frenzied tide of men surging past to the thunder of the wardrums . . . like the Zulu impis parading before Shaka . . .

In 1930, Wilfred Thesiger attended the coronation of Haile Selassie as Ras Taffari, or Emperor of Ethiopia. Haile Selassie was himself the great-grandson of King Sahala Selassie, with whom Cornwallis Harris hunted in the Abyssinian highlands in 1842. Reflecting later, considering how missing Africa affected his life, as a boy deeply influenced by the tales of the early white hunters, Thesiger identified the sensibility that still draws the hunters to Africa. He wrote in *Arabian Sands* that,

> I have looked back into my childhood for a clue to this perverse necessity which drives me from my own land. Perhaps it lies in the background of my memory: in journeys through the deserts of Abyssinia; in the thrill of seeing my father shoot an oryx when I was only three; in the smell of dust and acacias under a hot sun; in the chorus of hyenas and jackals in the darkness round the camp fire . . . I tasted freedom and a way of life from which there could be no recall.

One decision that every safari client and professional hunter must make today is how truly close to Africa they want their safari to get. Will they camp in luxury, sit in a Toyota and step out to shoot or photograph? Or will they welcome a leaner camp in a more inaccessible place, see fewer, but wilder animals, earn their game with hard stalks on foot, and try to understand the lives of the Africans around them? Ideally, one would walk across Africa, like a Selous or a Thesiger. Believing that language, colour and culture are barriers enough, Thesiger sought to get as close as possible to the lands he travelled, rejecting mosquito netting, boiled water and tinned foods as further insulation from experience, as distinctions that would distance him from his native companions.

Today's safaris cannot meet Thesiger's standards, but an understanding of his ethic is a useful influence. Every professional hunter must assess what his client truly wants, not necessarily what he says or thinks he wants. For many clients, the idea and the impression of testing themselves on safari are more welcome than the reality. For most, the modern safari is a holiday in which stress and hardship may not be desirable. Often it is easier for a professional hunter to set standards of moderately luxurious camping and undemanding hunting, which can then be adjusted either for the really spoiled or for the serious hunter.

Across the Zambesi River from Zambia, in Zimbabwe, a country long neglected by foreign hunters despite its magnificent game and healthy climate,

An elephant in Matabeleland, 1985

two young hunters, Barry Duckworth and John Stevens, maintain the highest standards of bushcraft and sporting ethics, although Zimbabwe safaris are not traditionally as comfortable as those of east Africa. Like the best of the Kenya hunters, Duckworth and Stevens began early. When they applied to be cadet game rangers at seventeen, they were two of the top twenty applicants, all of whom Bruce Austen, the celebrated game warden who developed Hwange National Park, sent to the Rhodesian training camp of the Special Air Service for evaluation. The SAS picked Duckworth and Stevens as the best, and wished to keep them both.

Today, there are few better adventures in Africa than to take a small, mixed safari with John Stevens, whether shooting or photographic. First a few days learning the land, canoeing the mile-wide Zambesi, watching for crocodiles as you drag the canoe across sand bars, silently drifting up to drinking elephant, alert for hippos lest they surface and capsize your craft, pausing to drink from the river with your hand, pulling into the bank for a long stalk after buffalo, finally camping out by a fire on the river bank. Then a couple of weeks on foot, hunting or stalking with John, travelling light, John with his old ·375, impossibly fit, always enthusiastic, loving Zimbabwe, sharing the intricate detail of his bushcraft. For those who like to stalk without shooting, as I do, or to photograph on foot, Zimbabwe today has an advantage over Kenya, in that about a dozen professional guides, like John Stevens, are authorized to carry a gun in the parks and to walk with non-shooting clients. In Kenya, guides today may not carry guns, and so it is generally forbidden to leave the vehicle.

On the Zambesi in 1984, with my fourteen-year-old son and me in one canoe, and John alone in the other, I was considering his difficult instruction that if a hippo capsized the canoe we should not surface, but must swim quietly downstream underwater, lest thrashing on the surface draw the crocodiles.

Aware that each year hippos kill more people than do any other African animal, recalling Selous's description of hippos 'crushing canoes in their huge jaws like nutshells', I was discussing the alternatives with my son. Just then an immense dome of water rose a foot or two from where I sat paddling. A hippo exploded to the surface like a submarine or breaching whale, hitting the back of John's canoe, sending it planing forward as John grabbed his gun to save it and the hippopotamus crashed on into the shallows with the force and noise of a locomotive. With a dozen hippos now visible in the narrowing channel ahead, my son and I paddled frantically for the bank, forgetting all instructions.

A week later, after days of teaching my son the mysteries of tracking, a skill John had also taught to his troopers in the army, John tapped the boy's shoulder as he bent low over an elephant print, trying to estimate the animal's height, age, sex and weight of ivory. 'No, Bartle,' said John, 'get your nose off the ground. When your father drives, does he stare at the front edge of the car, or does he look down the road? You're on a road, too. An elephant road. Look ahead. What would your path be if you were an elephant? If his trail leads straight up the hill, he was scared and running. If he picks the easy path, he was going slowly, eating as he went. Check the broken acacia branches.'

As a cadet game ranger himself in the early 1960s, John Stevens was lucky to be trained by Bruce Austen, a classic of the African hunting scene. Bruce's grandfather, a Finn who ran away as a cabin boy in 1876 and then jumped ship in East London, South Africa, came to Rhodesia in a pioneer wagon train in 1894. Known as a pioneer of pioneers and the 'uncrowned king of Que Que', he relished hunting on his horse Rifleman. When a lion once jumped on Rifleman's hindquarters, he leaned forward, turned in the saddle and beat the

Opposite above and below: Bruce Austen on his first safari in Rhodesia, 1920s

Boat attacked by hippopotamus

320

clinging lion across the face with his riding crop until the cat sprang down. It was a rare experience, for Selous reported that lion generally prefer to attack horses by pulling them down at the shoulder or haunches, rather than by leaping on to them. Bruce himself cannot remember when he did not hunt, going after steenbok and other small antelope with his single shot ·22 when he was eleven. Intensely loyal to England, like his grandfather who personally financed a small Royal Navy vessel in the First World War, Bruce, under age, joined the RAF at the outbreak of the Second World War.

Later, when he was not running Hwange Park, Bruce would lead shooting safaris, never more than two clients, with a professional hunter for each, because 'you can't mass produce good hunting'. Before the shooting started, Bruce warned that if any blood was found after a shot, the client would have to pay the trophy fee, so they should shoot carefully and get what they hit. Bruce himself only shot either in an emergency or if the client asked for help, usually when they got buck fever and their hands began to shake. Only one client, a distinguished Frenchman, asked Bruce to shoot all the trophies while he himself went after *le gros gibier* under canvas, revelling in his tent with his girlfriend.

Today Bruce, chairman of Zimbabwe's Professional Hunters and Guides Association, reminiscing at his farm in Ruwa, his grandfather's old Finnish sea chest near his chair, is proud to say that Zimbabwe now has the highest standards of professional hunting left in Africa. To be a licensed professional, a Zimbabwe hunter must study first aid, law, firearms, vehicle maintenance, Rowland Ward animal records, and wildlife habits and habitat. Then he undergoes two sets of written examinations, two years of apprenticeship in the field, a practical proficiency test in the bush and an interview by an examining

panel. Bruce is convinced that, 'proper, licensed shooting is the only hope for wildlife in modern Africa. It's the hunting that controls the poaching.'

In Kenya, where game laws and dwindling habitat make big-game shooting impossible, a half dozen serious professional hunters still make Nairobi their base. One of the best is Tony Seth-Smith, the son of Donald Seth-Smith. Today's Seth-Smith is little different. But Donald Seth-Smith could just ride up into the Ithanga hills on a Sunday to chase roan antelope, while Tony now leads his clients on expensive safaris into Tanzania. Like his father, Tony is known for his uncompromising hunting ethics. God help the Seth-Smith client who wounds a young animal or wants the trophy without the chase. Very much an Englishman, with generations of Coldstream Guards stiffening his spine, famous as a lightning wing shot, Tony tries not to favour his right foot, injured by a charging buffalo in 1985.

Perhaps most of all, Tony relishes still a long safari into the southern Sudan in 1974, hunting bongo in the thick finger-forest jungle of the Yambio region, part of the great central African forest that once reached into western Kenya. In the Yambio, near Zaïre, long sections of heavy forest are split by tongues of open savannah and dotted with glades of ten-foot grass. After seventeen years of warfare, the population had fled, the land had reverted to forest, trees grew through abandoned mission buildings and the game had taken over once again.

Mangoes grew everywhere, spread by the elephant that ate the fruit and left the seed in their dung to germinate. Occasionally, among the isabellina trees in the savannah's orchard country, Tony found large elephant herds containing both savannah and forest elephant. Bongo were plentiful, for the local Zandi never hunted them, believing that they carried leprosy, and Tony tracked one bull bongo right through a destroyed building. A Christian tribe who worshipped in open churches formed by rows of logs under a canopy of mango trees, the Zandi were reduced to selling scorched fruit bats, flying foxes with the hair singed off, to passing travellers.

Discussing the old days in Kenya, Tony laments 'I wish I'd been here thirty years earlier. Those were romantic days. It was unbelievable. Now everything we loved is being destroyed. The game, the romance, even the African, from a wild, proud, free man to a homogenized man like us. Coca Cola, platform shoes, sun glasses.'

When he wants to remember what it was like, Tony Seth-Smith goes up to the remains of the Mau forest that once stretched for three hundred miles. There he visits an old Dorobo, Tony's Baba Kidogo, or 'Little Father'. As a lad, Tony spent every possible moment in the forest with the Dorobo, out overnight with his ·22 at the age of eight, learning to live with fear. He shot his first leopard at eleven as it came at him on a forest trail. Stalking, collecting roots and honey, calling birds, he learned which plants are good for glue, for poison, for malaria and for poultices. Now the animals and the old man's forest are gone. The honey trees are cut down. The Kikuyu have moved in, planting maize.

Tony Seth-Smith, December 1987

Robin Hurt is another top Kenya professional who believes in fair chase and still does things the right way. Many hunters believe he has done the best job, after punishing tries in different countries, of adapting to the hunting conditions of today's Africa. A number of today's hunters share some of the qualities that distinguished Cotton Oswell and Frederick Selous, and some of those described here deserve a more complete introduction. Few, however, have the hunting background of Robin Hurt, or have led the hunter's life with Hurt's consistency.

A six-month apprenticeship in the Selous Game Reserve earned Robin Hurt his full professional hunting licence in 1963, when he went to work with what became the Tanzania Wildlife Corporation. At eighteen he became one of the youngest professionals ever licensed to take out hunting clients in east Africa. After several years hunting professionally in Kenya, Tanzania and Uganda, Robin joined Ker & Downey in 1967, staying with them until he had so many clients that he set up on his own in 1975, two years before the hunting ban shut down the traditional Kenya safari.

During all these years, Robin's favourite client was Stas Radziwill, 'the best sport I've ever seen'. Joining Robin on eight safaris, shooting rarely, generally hunting on each safari only for the best specimen of one specific species, Radziwill became the closest friend in a diverse list of clients. When Robin first started on his own, being scrupulous with K & D, he asked Radziwill with whom he would like to hunt. Upset even at the question, Radziwill replied, 'How can you ask me? Of course I'm hunting with you.'

A camel safari in northern Kenya, 1960s. Robin Hurt as a young man in the dark jacket

Robin Hurt's clients follow him not because he is the most fun to share a drink with by a fire at the end of the day, although he is not bad at that, but because of his persistent ability to find unspoiled country and get the best trophies under the most difficult conditions. On safari in 1973, Robin and his client came back with an immense, fifty-four-inch set of buffalo horns, which won the Shaw and Hunter Trophy, perhaps the high point of Robin's hunting career. Then given annually in Kenya by the Professional Hunters' Association to the hunter who secured the single finest trophy for a client, the trophy was considered 'the hunter's Oscar', the highest recognition of hunting ability. The standard for this prize was so demanding that, despite all the game killed annually in Kenya, it was not awarded in a year when no trophy was sufficiently distinguished.

In the years preceding the 1977 hunting ban, the Ian MacDonald Trophy was awarded to the professional hunter who obtained for his client the best buffalo of the year. During the six years of the award, Tony Seth-Smith won it twice, and Robin Hurt three times. In order to encourage the shooting of only the better trophies, for three years the Professional Hunters' Association, under its 'Measurement Scheme', gave an award for the best combined standard of trophies taken by a hunter during the year. Robin Hurt won this award two years out of three, and was runner-up in the third year.

When Kenya's hunting ban hit, Robin moved his operation to the Sudan and Zambia. He had already been hunting in the Sudan for two years, and now he led safaris there from January to May, and took clients to Zambia from July to October. All the traditional logistical problems became vastly more difficult, and there were new ones, like different languages and habitats, but at least the game could go on. Nairobi was still home base, and Janet Hurt, Robin's wife, organized an intricate support operation that spanned much of Africa. Working outside his own environment, Robin hunted in the Sudan more than any other east African hunter.

Sudan in the hunting season is hot, thick country. Very large tuskers were still plentiful, over 100 lb a side, and Robin and his clients followed the game favoured by hunters who relish long stalks: Lord Derby's eland, Mrs Gray's lechwe and the elusive bongo, the rarest of all antelope. In the more temperate climate of Zambia, a thousand miles to the south, hunting in the hill country of the Kafue was less strenuous, but invariably exciting, going after big lion, sitatunga, kudu and large sable, the striking black and white antelope once called the 'Harris buck'.

Each year, making the life more difficult, politics was becoming an increasingly important factor in the survival of wildlife and the African safari. In some countries the post-colonial pattern of independence, political strife, tribalism, the collapse of game management, military conflict, population explosion, economic decline and official corruption conspired to encourage poaching and make the safari business more difficult. At the same time, however, African game rangers and government administrators have become more experienced,

A Robin Hurt safari with clients
and staff

and each new generation of African politicians has acquired a better understanding of the complex interrelationships of wildlife management, land use and tourism.

By 1983 the Sudan, Africa's largest country, was in chaos. Civil war flared again between north and south as Muslim fought black and the government sought to impose Muslim law on the Christian and animist tribes of the southern Sudan. Undisciplined troops and armed gangs roamed the country, ravaging villages and slaughtering the game with automatic weapons. Gone were the old days of artful hunting, when the Dinkas in the Sudan used bow traps, digging holes containing hidden triggers that released snares of twisted buffalo hide up the legs of passing elephant that stumbled into them. For a time some safari operators tried to carry on despite the violence, avoiding troublespots and hunting in remote areas. Finally there was skirmishing between safaris and poaching gangs, and some hunters were kidnapped. In

1983, shortly after taking a new record bongo, Robin decided it was time to move on.

Starting once again, Robin began hunting in Zaïre, taking clients after the big rain-forest tuskers. It was a risky enterprise, for Zaïre had already imposed one hunting ban. Shortly after Robin got started, with his equipment and logistics in place, Zaïre re-imposed its hunting ban and the work was lost.

Conveniently, Tanzania had recently ended its six-year ban on hunting. The game had declined drastically during the ban, and the government now sought to rebuild the positive links between conservation and proper hunting. Recognizing that licensed hunting was the best way to earn revenues while preserving the game from poaching and habitat destruction, in 1984 the government authorized ten hunting concessions through the Tanzania Wildlife Corporation, Tawico. One-year concessions, renewable for three years, were awarded on the basis of experience, projected hunting revenues to the government, and other factors. Government revenues were to be derived from specific fees, payable only in US dollars, for each licensed animal taken, such as $110 for hyena and $1,165 for leopard or lion, plus a royalty fee of $376 per day for each hunter and $53 for each observer. In this way the game were made to earn their own preservation. Robin Hurt's company, Tanzania Game Tracker Safaris, secured the tenth concession, and Janet Hurt had a new campaign.

The concept that licensed, properly conducted hunting is consistent with wildlife preservation, and sometimes even essential to it, is now recognized by CITES, the United Nations' Convention on International Trade in Endangered Species, which, with ninety-five member nations, determines world policy on endangered animals. As Eugene Lapointe, the Secretary-General of CITES, remarked to me in 1987, 'hunting can be an important conservation tool for even endangered species. Properly, a hunter's role is as a predator, as a part of nature. Economics, including hunting, must support conservation. We are trying to make wildlife conservation realistic and practical.'

As part of this programme, CITES, at its headquarters in Geneva, now assigns a computerized number to each elephant tusk legally exported anywhere in the world. With the total African elephant population estimated at roughly one million in 1987, the CITES concept is to treat that population as 'capital', and to accept the shooting of 50,000 African elephant annually, as the natural increase or 'interest' on the capital. Each country is then assigned a quota of elephants, and tusks for export, depending on its elephant population. Each tusk has its number placed on it. Tusks may not be dispatched in commercial shipments, but only as the property of individuals. This system is thought to encourage the taking of only the larger, male tusks, as they will yield the largest amount of ivory under the quotas.

Some experts estimate that there are now only 730,000 African elephants. They contend that most elephant populations are already at an unacceptably low level, and should be allowed to recover. Others argue that government elephant control, or 'culling' campaigns, which are not part of the CITES quota

Above: Assembling Robin Hurt safari vehicles

Left: Camp supplies

Opposite above: Camp beds and first-aid supplies

Opposite below: Tent-makers and lamp-fitters

system are frequently based on inflated estimates of elephant populations, partly motivated by the value of elephant meat and hide, as well as ivory. Without active control in the field, most bush poachers just continue with their work, indifferent to CITES, simply selling ivory for whatever it brings.

In 1984 Robin Hurt's Game Tracker Safaris started operations in Tanzania with four professional hunters. Headquarters was an office and radio base in Nairobi. A forward headquarters was set up in Tanzania at an old coffee plantation outside Arusha. There clients and supplies are gathered and boarded into light planes for flights to ten tented bush camps scattered among Tanzania's game reserves. Other hunters face the hassles and crises that go with running a safari in the bush, but Robin and Janet Hurt also have to master the complex day-to-day organizational and logistical problems that keep many safaris in the field simultaneously.

Every evening, after long days telexing clients around the world and organizing permits, transportation, staff and supplies, Janet Hurt at home in Nairobi turns on her shortwave radio, organizes logistics through the Arusha base and calls in the senior hunter at each Tanzania safari camp. Crouching forward to hear the radio, with a hand-mike in one hand and a list of supplies and a drink in the other, the hunters report in. In 1987 Game Trackers earned $900,000 for the government in hunting fees, approximately 10 per cent of the total foreign exchange earned by tourism in Tanzania.

Today about a dozen hunters take clients out from Robin Hurt's camps, hunting the plentiful game in the Maswa reserve on the edge of the Serengeti plain, or going after the large black-maned lion and heavy-horned buffalo in the

Janet Hurt calls in a safari camp on the radio telephone

Owen McCallum and client, Kenya,
1950s

miombo forests and swamplands of the Moyowosi reserve. They include top
professionals like Tony Seth-Smith, Danny McCallum and Nick Swan.

Like his father Owen McCallum, Danny is a leading hunter of his day, bone-
hard, ethical, savvy in the bush. Poachers never linger long near a Danny
McCallum camp, and clients learn, at once, to be restrained in their shooting. As
the Moyowosi camp manager puts it, 'Danny's a diamond. And can he drink!'
Danny McCallum's grandfather came north from the Transvaal in 1906, and at
fourteen Danny's father Owen roamed the bush hunting on the family farm in
Tanganyika, practising the tricks of the local Dorobo, often forgetting time and
sleeping out on his own. A romantic figure, Owen was known for his gentle
side, and as a boy cried when he shot a lion. Even in the days when every farmer
hunted big game, he was considered a 'natural', becoming a successful professional without the formal apprenticeship that launches most hunters.

Owen McCallum was slight but tough, once surviving a rough hammering
by an old buffalo bull that caught him between its horns and pressed him into a
thorn bush without being able to gore him with either tip. Trying to avoid
hitting Owen, his companions took twenty-one shots to kill the buffalo.
Claiming not to be an ace shot himself, Owen specialized in getting in close, to
make certain kills at twenty yards. His favourite double rifle, his 'drainpipe',

Above left: Danny McCallum, Nairobi, 1986

Above right: Iris McCallum

was an 1898 Watson .450 No. 2, which sometimes fired both barrels when only one trigger was pulled, an explosive quirk in the weapon which he never set right. On at least one occasion, thanks to the immediate double impact, it was an idiosyncrasy that saved his life.

But Owen McCallum died at forty-one in 1964, denying Danny the boy's dream of hunting with his father. So Owen's friend Glen Cottar took on the job, teaching Danny to hunt elephant at Lake Rukwa and training him as a professional hunter in the late 1960s. Glen Cottar always looked for what was over the next hill, and the two men hunted in Uganda and the Sudan and cut many trails in the Moyowosi. Twenty years later, Danny is repaying his debt to Glen Cottar, helping to train Glen's son Calvin, perhaps the only fourth-generation European now hunting professionally in Africa.

Today Danny McCallum himself is sought after by respected hunters who come to Tanzania to hunt the heavy black-maned lion that feed on the Cape buffalo that still roam Moyowosi in thousands. Whenever it might be needed, Danny carries his insurance policy, his father's old drainpipe, now reblued and in proper firing trim. Danny McCallum knows why he does the work. 'What I really love about it are the early mornings and the late evenings. The bloody sounds. The smells. The cloud formations. There's something different every day. I love the trees. I love the birds. The calmness. Being away from homo sapiens himself. The hunting and shooting is just a sideline. It's being out there.'

Danny's sister Iris understands. She herself continues the Beryl Markham tradition of crack lady bush pilots, ferrying hunters into narrow dusty strips cut into the bush near the safari camps, first buzzing in low to clear warthogs and zebra from the runway. Like her brother, Iris is admired for her cool skill in emergencies, having once walked away from a crashed twin-engine plane, with all her passengers alive and unhurt, after both engines caught fire in the air. This incident won for Iris the Guinness Stout Effort Award, and is still discussed around the camp fires when talk turns to the hazards of modern safari life.

In the nineteenth century, Cornwallis Harris and Frederick Selous ventured through the bush among regiments of Zulu and Matabele. Today's professional hunters have survived hunting bans and civil wars. They have learned to run a business among roving guerrillas, poachers and undisciplined government troops. As in the days of Mzilikazi and Lobengula, tribute and tribalism are still part of the game. Harris used Cape wagons and oxen. Today's hunters move in by Land Cruiser and light plane. Replacing the ironwood axle under the old wagons was a cruel job, and so it is today to lift the front of a Toyota by its own winch over a tree branch to replace the mainspring, pounding it out with stones used as improvised mallets. Radios, medical kits and high-powered rifles all help, but in the end an honest safari is still tough sport, and is finished on foot.

In the old days there was competition from native hunters, who starved hippos to death in pen traps in rivers, caught buffalo in deep pits, poisoned elephants and hunted lion with circles of spearmen. Today the competition is gangs of paramilitary poachers armed with AK-47s, and licensed hunting safaris are sometimes their only restraint. Faced with these obstacles, why do today's hunters struggle on, living a life so long past its time?

Russ Broom, at twenty-nine probably the youngest of today's top professional hunters, exemplifies the reason why. Now leading shooting safaris in Tanzania with Robin Hurt's operation, Russ formerly operated out of Lusaka, Zambia, with his father Geoff Broom, a veteran of the old school. Originally a Rhodesian, Geoff Broom is proud of his great-grandfather, who rode into the country with Selous in the original pioneer column in 1890. Today the only elephant herds left in Cape Province roam Addo National Park, which his great-grandfather gave to South Africa. Always gathering information from the network of hunters still scattered across Africa, young Russ Broom speaks the dialects, knows the game and makes his life in the bush. One day he may be the last. Like all the hunters still working, he understands the words J. A. Hunter wrote in 1952:

> I am one of the last of the old-time hunters. The events I saw can never be relived. Both the game and the native tribes, as I knew them, are gone. No one will ever see again the great elephant herds led by old bulls carrying 150 lb of ivory in each tusk. No one will ever again hear the yodelling war cries of the Masai as their spearmen swept the bush after cattle-killing lions. Few indeed will be able to say they have broken into country never before seen by a white man. No, the old Africa has passed, and I saw it go.

10. BREAKING CAMP

Tanzania, 1987

If the true safari still exists, it lives in the tent of Robin Hurt on the edge of the Moyowosi swamp. The only human living place in 38,000 square miles of Tanzania wilderness, Hurt's camp is a base for one third of the top professional hunters still operating in Africa.

Whenever he can, Robin Hurt himself leads hunting clients into the Moyowosi, setting off briskly across the burned grass that covers the hard black cotton soil around the swamp, carrying only fieldglasses and his buffalo sticks, three five-foot, worn bamboo poles, which make his favourite gun rest. In August 1986 Ted Roosevelt and I hunted with Robin for three weeks, with Ted shooting and me stalking, and we started in the Moyowosi. When the first rains flood the plain in November, the rich soil turns to black glue, making the swamp deep and unapproachable until May, when the ground dries iron-hard and is split by fissures. By August it is just right, soft at the swamp's periphery, preserving buffalo prints for tracking, crusty at the edges if the track is old, wet at the bottoms when fresh.

Before first light every morning, from July to November, hunters and clients are woken at five or six o'clock by the sound of the tent zipper rising, and a murmured, 'Morning, Bwana, *chai*,' as strong morning tea is set down between the camp beds. Resisting getting up, one is drawn into the day by the hissing of the lanterns freshly lit outside the tent. Finally, the splash of steaming water into the shaving basin leaves no choice. At the edge of camp another early riser, a tropical boubou, is calling through the branches.

Soon a sturdy English breakfast, porridge, sausages, eggs and grilled tomatoes, is eaten by lamplight. Green wooden lunchboxes are heaved into Land Cruisers. Rifles are strapped to gun racks. Eager with expectation, hunters, trackers and gunbearers scramble in as the vehicles head into the dark bush. These are not the conventional, closed Toyotas and Land Rovers that carry photographers through the game parks of east Africa. No production-line

Mt Kilimanjaro at night

335

machine can endure a Hurt safari. Robin himself designs and builds heavy steel underplates, a rig of roll bars behind the cab and a shell of two-inch pipe and steel screening that surrounds bumpers and fenders.

Gripping the roll bar, bracing for violent bounces, hunched against the cold wind, clients and trackers squint into the dark, trying to duck heavy branches and escape the lashing thorns. With the early grey light, old Makanyanga, once a leading Wakamba ivory poacher who hunted with a seven-foot elephant bow with a 140 lb pull, starts looking out for game. At first a tight red circle on the horizon, the sun finally bursts up with a rush. The truck is left under an acacia tree, guns are loaded and the long stalk for buffalo begins.

Versatile grazers, the buffalo drift in and out of the swamp in vast black herds, moving into the deep water when threatened, often in groups of one or two thousand, the largest buffalo herds left in Africa. Today their enemies are poaching and agriculture. Their best protection is neither the swamp itself nor the severe government hunting restrictions. Their guardians are the hunting revenues they earn, the professional hunters who fight off the poachers, and the innumerable tsetse flies that infest the swamp and discourage both sport and settlement. Robin calls the tsetse eradication programme in Botswana and Zimbabwe 'a catastrophe for wildlife. I reckon the tsetse is the best game warden in Africa.' For each buffalo shot on a hunting licence, Tanzania collects $525, plus thousands in safari costs, and the good professionals allow clients to shoot only the old, wide-horned bulls whose breeding days are generally over.

Robin Hurt checks the wind and steps eagerly into the swamp as if he is coming home, with Ted Roosevelt and myself tight in line behind him, followed

Ted Roosevelt and the author scan the Ruvu escarpment for kudu

Right: Laboso, gunbearer and tracker, with professional hunter Ray Stanley, stalking buffalo in the Moyowosi swamp, Tanzania, 1986

Below: Saddle-billed stork

by Makanyanga carrying Robin's ·375 Ruger, and the head tracker Laboso with the heavy 1915 William Evans ·500 double rifle. Ted is armed with a new, left-handed, bolt-action ·375 H & H made by David Miller, the master gunsmith of Tucson, Arizona. Last comes Ray Stanley, a top shot who was once welterweight champion of Tanzania and now is assigned to the safari as the required government hunter. Also known as 'TR-4', Ted has been an active outdoorsman and conservationist ever since he set his first trapline for muskrat as a boy of twelve, selling the pelts for 75 cents each after his mother taught him how to skin. Although he is not quite as fit as when he led his SEAL frogmen ashore in Vietnam, observing him and the rest of our hunting party reminds me that I, the oldest, am in pretty fast company. All six of us carry fieldglasses and wear green and khaki: Ted in a heavy, worn cotton shirt with the faded letters 'USN' barely showing where the insignia has been removed, myself in a twenty-year-old shirt from Ahmed's in Nairobi, and Makanyanga and Laboso in long, one-piece green coveralls.

Soon we are up to our knees. A saddle-billed stork retreats among the yellow waterlilies. The only sound is the sucking of mud and buffalo dung as our feet plunge in and out. Robin has the nasty job of moving first through the tall, sharp swamp grass that cuts our knees until they bleed and makes the muddy water feel fresh and cool. Finally Makanyanga, his legs covered, steps out in front.

It is heavy work, there is no falling out, and it is none too soon when the file climbs on to an island of hard ground, crowned by a six-foot ant-hill, actually a rock-hard termite mound, cooled by a palm thicket and littered with small brown snail shells abandoned by swamp otters under the mauve claw orchids. We are reassured that although bilharzia flourishes in the swamp water, the snails that play host to bilharzia are a smaller variety. Most African orchids are parasites, growing on trees, but claw orchids grow independently on the ground. Laboso and Makanyanga climb the ant-hill to look for buffalo, giving us time to pick off leeches, slap at tsetses and enjoy tales about the green mambas, spitting cobras and pythons that enrich the swamp life.

Robin recalls coming on the choking, foul smell of decomposition while elephant hunting in Uganda. A python had swallowed a bushbuck up to the antelope's head, with the head and horns sticking out of the python's mouth, the snake's flexible, hinge-less jaws strained wide like a rubber collar. Unable to swallow the head, as the horns would pierce the walls of its stomach, the python

Buffalo in the long grass

The author and his son Bartle in the Okavango Swamp, Botswana, 1986

Bartle Bull on Amber in Matabeleland, Zimbabwe, 1986

was waiting for maggots to sever the head by eating away the antelope's neck. Hard at it, eating only the dead flesh, the maggots completely covered the python's mouth and the head of the bushbuck.

Lowering his fieldglasses, Laboso points with his hand, Robin checks the wind, and we slip back into the swamp, with the herd feeding a mile away. Every hundred yards we crouch low, stuck in place, as Robin scans the herd with his glasses, trying to spot a good bull with a heavy boss. Bent low over the water, trying to make no sound, I become absorbed in the rich detail of the swamp, forgetting the anticipated drama with the buffalo. The swamp seems still, but close to my eyes everything is moving. Insects search across the water, long green grasshoppers with shimmering blue wings cling to the reeds, unseen creatures move along my legs, purple, orange and red flowers, pungent pink and white thistles are hidden in the grass, spiders are at work.

Suddenly there is a massive splashing thirty yards to the right and a large bull stares directly at us, his wide head now raised above the swamp grass, the heavy shoulders just visible, his body buried in deep water and thick grass. We stare back. Where could he have been? He is seconds away, and I wish I carried a rifle. Nobody moves, each of us knowing that single old bulls are the most dangerous. Slowly Ted takes his ·375 from his shoulder, but Robin gestures to us not to shoot. Alarmed, the big bull plunges off with astonishing speed. Robin explains he had a damaged horn and we should do better: 'There's no way we're going to shoot that.'

Thinking back, remembering old buffalo stories, I recall an evening fishing in Botswana's Okavango swamp with my son Bartle and our friend Richard Randall, a Zimbabwean. As we took our boat back to camp through the reeds under a lush orange moon, our faces sticky with swarming gnats, Richard taught us old Rhodie hunting slang, 'flat dogs' for crocodiles, and 'dagga boys' for the ageing buffs that hang about in ones or twos or threes, named for the Shona word for the mud they enjoy so much. He warned us that the old bulls are less alert than the cows and that they are dangerous if you startle them as they doze in the bush. This time, with Robin, we were lucky.

A week after Richard Randall had warned me about the lone buffalos, he and I were rafting near Victoria Falls with Paul Connelly, the 'double-rugged' pioneer of white-water safaris on the Zambesi. Charged by a bull hippo, forced into shore with one of our two oars snapped off, losing control, we jumped out, dragging the raft through the shallows on foot, wary of the flat dogs we could not see, but even more scared of the angry hippo we could see waiting in the deep-water passage. I recalled J. A. Hunter's account of hippos biting canoes in two, and his finding a dead rhinoceros with its back torn open by the jaws of the gored hippopotamus lying dead near by. The next day Richard and I shared the fraternity of flipping in the rapids and hurtling a mile down the Zambesi as we hung on to our overturned kayak, not even thinking of the flat dogs and hippos as we desperately struggled to save Paul's kayak and make land, mindful only of the world's largest waterfall, twice the height of Niagara Falls, waiting six miles downstream.

Baldwin's horse trampled by a buffalo, 1856, by Whymper

I put the Zambesi from my mind, and bring myself back to the swamp. We labour on for four hours, but now the herd is spooked, and we never get close enough to single out a good bull for a confident shot. Whenever we sneak within a hundred and fifty yards and Ted starts isolating a target, they stop grazing and a few scouts raise their heads and begin to shuffle. Soon the entire herd is splashing off, with a roar that sounds like crashing surf as a thousand hooves beat the water. We try again. Our approach sets them off again, and I remember Isak Dinesen observing that civilized people have lost 'the aptitude for stillness' and should take lessons in silence.

As we push along, never speaking, my mind drifts again. Contemplating as if in church or at the ballet, I recall old buffalo tales, Cotton Oswell out with Dr Livingstone, hunting in the tall reeds near the Limpopo, or Baldwin in Zululand chasing buffalo on horseback with his dog Smoke, his mare rearing and crashing with the hunter tangled between her legs as a buffalo thundered over them both, injuring only the horse's eye with a glancing hoof. Or Selous himself near the Nata river, 'pitched into the air like a dog', dying horse and all.

It was these tales of hunting on horseback that had finally led me to try it myself only three weeks before our Moyowosi safari, although I never achieved my ambition of following Cornwallis Harris's 1836 experience of galloping after giraffe, said by that old hunter to be 'the most thrilling passage of all my adventures'. Staying in the camp of Alan Elliott, an enterprising old Rhodesia hand and encyclopaedic naturalist, just outside Zimbabwe's vast Hwange game reserve, I went riding with a local English horsewoman. Carrying no gun, we rode on old Rhodesian cavalry saddles once used by the Selous Scouts. Riding Amber, a tall chestnut, I was far better mounted than I deserved. Soon I was led

galloping through the acacia forest until both my legs bled from saddle sores, and we ended up, in my case scared and exhilarated, chasing forty buffalo along the edge of the forest. Back in the saddle on Amber at six the following morning, riding to a waterhole before daybreak, I turned a corner in the trail to find a baby eland thrashing on its back, all four legs kicking in the air, its neck broken but its throat and fat stomach uncut. Amber jumped violently sideways, panicked, smelling cat, and crashed into the trees, ripping my jacket. Looking down, we see lion prints all about and realize the lion must have broken the eland's neck a second before we startled it from its kill. Frightened, lucky, we head back to get Alan and a gun for safety, so that we can track the lion on foot. Thinking of lions and horses, I remember Baldwin, writing in his diary of 1857, years before a lion chased him and leapt on his horse, that lions are 'proverbially fond of horseflesh'.

Back in the Moyowosi swamp, concentration gone, I commit the stalker's sin of not following precisely the man ahead. Disappointed, knowing I know better, Robin impatiently gestures at me to crouch down. We go on. But the buffalo retreat into deep swamp, the afternoon begins to shade, and we give it up, concerned that a late shot could mean an uncertain sunset chase after a wounded bull, unfair to the animal and dangerous to the hunters.

Robin recalls a nasty incident in 1984, demonstrating again that a wounded buffalo is hard to put down, particularly once it starts running and adrenalin pumps through its system. Charged from a few yards by a wounded bull, Robin shot the animal an instant before it tossed him in the air. Holding on to his rifle as he crashed down, Robin struggled to reload from a sitting position while the bull attacked his gunbearer, Joseph Sitiena. Before Robin could shoot again the buffalo collapsed, leaving Sitiena with internal injuries and Robin brutally bruised. They were lucky, for buffalo, unlike rhinoceros, have a cruel instinct for pursuing their adversaries. Even J. A. Hunter once had both his gunbearer and his tracker killed in a single buffalo incident.

Slogging back to the truck, Robin and the trackers are relieved that we did not press for a late shot. Fed up with clients who demand a trophy every day, they are pleased that Ted did not try for a bad bull. Most of all they dread the clients who hunt and even shoot from a vehicle, sometimes stepping down to fire as the animals bolt away, occasionally bringing one down up the rump with a 'Texas heart shot'. For Ted and me, the Moyowosi swamp was enough, good training, exhilarating, the stalk a feast in itself. For the professional hunter, the first days define the client, as he learns how much rigour and risk the safari can bear.

Above: Cornwallis Harris hunting giraffe

Right: Baldwin on horseback attacked by a lion, 1857, by James Wolf

Back at the Toyota, we enjoy cool Tusker beers and biscuits from the lunchbox, and then a cold, swinging ride back to camp. Stripping off the mud-cemented boots, we take a brief hot shower from a canvas bag hanging from a tree and, finally, experience for ourselves the camper's great truth, that drink and food taste best in the field. A second Toyota has not yet returned, presumably kept out by late sport, but by 9.30 our gas lamp is out.

Two hours later a voice calls sharply at the tent flap, 'Get up. Something terrible has happened.' We pull on shorts, rush to the camp fire and get the news. Bilu Deen, a professional hunter driving the other Toyota, out hunting with two clients, a gunbearer and two trackers, was killed, burned alive in a grass fire. The survivors have just made it back to camp, picked up on the trail by a search party sent by Robin. An Indian from Kenya and a third-generation professional hunter, Bilu Deen was an experienced hand. Driving along, he had directed the trackers to set grass fires as they moved. Each dry season the government encourages hunters to burn the dead grass, a customary technique of Masai herders, so that fresh grass grows in to feed the game. Cooperating, the hunters routinely throw out matches as the vehicles cross the dry bush. For nearly two centuries, European cattle farmers have burned off the dry grass in South Africa, and Bushmen hunters did it long before. Cornwallis Harris reported in 1836 that Matabele cattle drovers did the same.

Early in the afternoon, passing through dense, eight-foot grass, Bilu Deen's Toyota ran up on an ant-hill, grinding stuck with all four wheels off the ground. The truck had been moving slowly, with the fires dancing in the distance behind it, occasionally stopping when grass jammed the fan and made the engine overheat. Then the wind began to shift. As the wheels turned without catching, the hunting party heard fires crackling and chasing behind them. The trackers jacked up the front end, but it was too late. The clients ran from the truck, grabbing a shovel and abandoning three valuable antique rifles. Cutting a fire break with the shovel, they escaped through the fire into the burned-out grass, followed by a tracker.

The other tracker and gunbearer escaped in a different direction, but Bilu Deen stayed with the truck, trying to rock it off the ant-hill and save the equipment. At the last moment he bolted, but instead of running through the fire into the burned-out bush, he fled before the flames until they caught him 300 yards later.

Hearing the story, Robin and Makanyanga climbed into a Toyota and were out until 3 a.m. searching for the body by moonlight, hoping to save it from lion and hyena. Unable to find it at night, they were out again at dawn, returning, horrified, with the body. After a long, silent day in camp, we held a service by the camp fire. We each read a prayer, and Robin spoke quietly of Bilu Deen, a hunter now 'home from the hill'.

Heading back to the swamp after two days in camp, we see thick new grass rising green among the blackened stalks of the old bush fires, and we set new fires when we come to the dead grass. As we pause to admire a lilac-breasted

Above left: A Robin Hurt camp

Above right: Vultures

roller, proudly displaying the pure intense colour of his brilliant chest to the early morning, three vultures spiral down near by. Pulling off the track we find a male buffalo down in the flattened grass, a fresh kill, his throat torn, his white stomach open on the ground. An old bull, but not large at 1,500 lb, he is the sort of lonely straggler lions favour.

It is usually the old and the young who play a close game with survival. Many baby antelope, especially topi, a favourite dish of leopard, have a 70 per cent mortality rate. For ostrich it is worse. With their eggs hatching on the ground, and with many enemies, perhaps 90 per cent die early. Even vultures, who normally wait for the end of life and are highly interactive with the frailties of other species, go after the huge shining eggs. They wait to descend until the parents are scrabbling for food, and then, clutching sharp rocks in their beaks, smash the shells to get to the gangly chicks.

Examining the old bull, we find clean open bone on the left hind leg where the lion, always too lazy for a long chase, ripped at the hamstring and brought it down. The hard black face is lacerated where the lion grabbed the muzzle and suffocated the animal before eating its tongue, a favourite delicacy for many lions and hunters. It looks like an easy kill. Noticing the flattened grass where the lion lay to eat, I remember the great debate among the early hunters. Which is the better fighter of these old adversaries? Lions hunt buffalo, but a buffalo can kill a lion. Unlike many animals, lion, particularly males, rarely have to test their full power and speed to survive. When lions are challenged, however, the enemy is usually a male Cape buffalo.

A student of this issue, William Cotton Oswell, contributed to the debate in 1846 by first-hand observation. Hunting along the banks of the Limpopo, he was pursuing a large buffalo, already hard hit with a two-ounce ball in the shoulder. Suddenly three lion attacked the wounded bull. Even then it was a fierce match, as the lion on their hind legs 'tore away with teeth and claw in

345

most ferocious style', the bull lifting one lion off the ground as his tormentors attacked from the flanks to avoid his horns.

Finally the buffalo died of his bullet wound, and Oswell and his companion shot all three lion. Examining the bodies, Oswell found the lion had taken a beating, but had barely torn the buffalo's shoulder, never weakening the mighty hump of muscle at the base of its neck. The centre of a buffalo's strength, this is the same muscle, the *morillo*, that Spain's mounted picadors gore with their lances to lower the head of a fighting bull before the matador starts his work on foot. Like Oswell, Selous himself, while conceding that an adult male lion may have more strength relative to its weight than any other large African animal, was sceptical that one lion could kill a big male buffalo in its prime. 'Not so,' argues Robin Hurt, 'a big male lion can kill any buffalo, albeit not without some danger to himself.'

Looking back as we leave the buffalo, we see the patient vultures descending. A scaly francolin darts off to the side as we pass by, and Laboso's panga flashes down from the back of the truck, just missing the francolin, although the machete's sharp blade stabs quivering into the bird's footprints. We laugh and shout as Laboso jumps down to recover the panga, for Laboso rarely misses, and his name means 'darling' in Nandi. Respected both in the bush and in camp, Laboso is widely acclaimed for having the best game-spotting eyes of all the trackers in the business. As he climbs back into the truck, Ted notices that Laboso's hands are mangled by old wounds, and we learn that a year before he was badly chewed by a female leopard, which had been wounded by a client who had been told not to shoot.

After a long morning buffalo stalking in the swamp, working close to three herds, spotting some reasonable heads, but still searching for the right one, Robin stops at the edge of the swamp, 'Let's tank up with a drink.' We rinse our hands and collapse under a tree, wolfing our fresh camp bread, sardines, cold

Above: Hippos in the Mara River, Kenya

Left: Three lions attempting to drag down a buffalo

eggs and oranges, lounging back with our hats over our faces, napping. After a time I ask Robin how he became a professional hunter at sixteen. Interrupted by the harsh bird cry of a fiscal shrike, he explains how these aptly named bankers build larders by impaling grasshoppers on long acacia thorns and hoarding them there for later.

Robin's father, Lt Colonel Roger Hurt, DSO, after Sandhurst and wartime service with the King's African Rifles in north Africa, became a game warden in the elephant country near the Kenya coast. At eight, when his English cousins were bowling cricket balls and snaring rabbits, Robin was out with his father, tracking the great hundred-pounders along the Tana River. Even back at home, he thought only of the game, studying the globe as a vast collection of habitats, at school excelling in geography because that connected with his animal world.

At ten Robin began to shoot on the family's farm at Lake Naivasha in the Rift Valley, going out with his ·22 and his father's buffalo pack, mixed hounds led by a combination of airedales and bull terriers, even finer big-game dogs than the lion-hunting Rhodesian ridgebacks. Airedales run better than ridgebacks, and bull terriers are more aggressive. At first he hunted all the light antelope, dik-dik, steinbuck, reedbuck and bushbuck, letting the dogs finish what the ·22 could not.

Often he would not shoot at all, but spend the days crawling and watching and running, learning why the dik dik is grey and the reedbuck tan, why shorter antelopes need different camouflage from those that move against the higher branches. Inevitably, this early field training included ornithology, for Lake Naivasha's lavish birdlife includes 450 species. Even the United States, for example, a country that is sixteen times the size of Kenya and has extremely diverse habitats, has 700 species of birds, whereas Kenya has 1,054.

There were many leopard and a few lion on the Hurt farm. Robin always carried a gun, but 'The shooting side was always secondary. I was far more interested in where the animals were, what they were like, where the biggest ones went.' Lying in bed at night, or by a fire with his father in a fly camp, Robin read Cornwallis Harris, Selous and Rider Haggard. For Robin, and English boys like him all over the world, Haggard's Allan Quatermain was as much a part of the bush as the next giraffe.

When his son was thirteen, Roger Hurt gave him a ·303, and Robin went after his first buffalo, hunting with his friend Tinia, a Masai of the same age. The boys worked together, making mistakes, competing to follow the track over hard ground, staying out overnight in the bush, teaching each other the hunting lore learned from their families. Superstition was part of the lessons, a sense that animals and man share certain mysteries, that there are rules, that it is bad luck to kill a hyena: 'Maybe we subconsciously know the hyena has his essential function. Even today, my skinners would never touch a hyena.'

Sometimes Tinia and Robin would go off with the buffalo pack, hunting warthog with long-bladed Masai spears. Occasionally they speared buffalo that were bayed up by the dogs. Stamina, reflexes and mutual confidence were the heart of this game, and Robin remembers it as, 'The greatest sport I ever had.'

At fifteen and sixteen Robin hunted more with his father, and spent weeks patrolling the reserve with the Wakamba game scouts, learning the special tricks of each, particularly Ndaga, a hunter with an uncanny ability to anticipate what each animal would do. From Ndaga Robin learned that, beyond all the skills and experience that are essential to hunting, the key, irreplaceable element is the ability to release one's instinct: 'At the critical moments, it's all instinct.'

Hunting buffalo one day with a borrowed ·404, Robin hit a good bull. Following as it took the shot and plunged off, they soon found the bull dead and began to cut it up. Ndaga, with his extraordinary instinct, sensed that something was unusual. Troubled, he rose from the work, searched in an arc, spotted another blood trail, followed it and found a dead buffalo cow, killed, incredibly, by the same hard-nosed bullet that had passed through the bull.

Robin's intimacy with wildlife made it difficult for him to understand formal religion, 'because I found it hard to see how we are different from the animals. They are as much a part of the world as we are. Everything's got a story. God is nature. We must live by our conscience about how we behave with nature. The skeletons in the bush made me recognize the total finality of shooting an animal. And us, do we not totally die too?'

Ray Mayers, a farmer near Thika, hired Robin at sixteen to hunt the buffalo that were damaging his coffee plantation and spreading disease among his cattle. It was tough hunting in thick country, particularly difficult on the forested slopes, but at £10 a head it was a schoolboy's bonanza, filling his pockets with money for school, although his housemaster at the Duke of York School outside Nairobi was appalled when Robin brought smelly buffalo heads back to school.

By seventeen Robin had shot all the big five, and he secured his second professional hunting job, culling hippopotamus by moonlight on Kongoni Farm, where the hippos were emerging from Lake Naivasha at night, trampling on the irrigation pipes and eating the lucerne grass that fed the cattle. Hippos are surprisingly dangerous, and it was exciting work. He was so careful to kill only the offending animals that Major Lyn Temple-Boreham, the redoubtable warden of Masailand, made Robin an honorary game ranger at seventeen, and assigned him to buffalo and hippo control.

Before he was eighteen, Robin had done more big-game hunting than most hunters would do in a lifetime, but Sandhurst was calling. He was due at the Royal Military College, where his father, grandfather, and great-grandfather shared a long Hurt tradition. For two hundred years the oldest Hurt son had always started life as a professional British soldier. The Royal Welch Fusiliers, the Distinguished Service Order and the Crimean War were part of the family drill. The military tradition is traceable to 1377, to Roger Hurte of Kniveton, Derbyshire, a stalwart champion of Edward III. Family legend has it that the king rewarded Hurte by taking him to a hilltop in Derbyshire, directing him to draw his longbow, and granting him all the land within the circumference from the spot where his arrow fell, some two thousand acres.

But Robin wanted to be a game warden or professional hunter, and he consulted his employer at Kongoni Farm, Mrs Miller, one of the gritty frontier-school English ladies who made east Africa work. With 50,000 acres to manage, Mrs Miller got straight to the point, 'Do what you want to do. Be a hunter.' By then Robin was already working as a trainee hunter for John Cook, an old professional who 'always did everything properly'. When safaris were scarce, Cookie and Robin did zebra control for farmers who were too busy, shooting several hundred a month under Game Department authorization, and splitting the skins with the farmers and the government. Sandhurst fell by the way.

Learning the trade, Robin did some early safaris with the veteran hunter Andrew Holmberg, a crack shot and a master at judging game trophies precisely before shooting. Holmberg, a godson of Isak Dinesen, was the hunter who pioneered horse and camel safaris in northern Kenya. Holmberg was a natural teacher, as he once showed me when he used a wooden matchbox to illustrate where to aim for a mortal hit from every angle. After working with Holmberg, Robin then did rhino and elephant control work for the Game Department, specializing in hunting the 'shamba raiders' that were damaging the native crops.

Finally, Jack Block, chairman of the firm then called Ker, Downey & Selby Safaris, hired Robin as a trainee hunter. Pending a vacancy in the field, he put Robin to work at K & D's warehouse and store in Nairobi, fixing vehicles, outfitting, repairing equipment, struggling with supplies, and 'generally being a stooge'. The boy hated it, but he learnt the critical lessons of safari logistics and organization.

The following year, 1963, Robin began work as a young hunter in Tanzania. In the twenty-five years of professional hunting that followed, always sticking with it, repeatedly opening up inaccessible, untouched country when politics and poaching, land development and government regulation made the old hunting grounds impossible, Robin struggled to maintain the tradition of the great safaris. Having adapted in five countries and moved camp through three hunting bans and a civil war, today Robin is once again on safari in Tanzania and the Central African Republic.

Understanding, after hearing his story, why Tony Dyer, the last President of the Professional Hunters' Association, calls Robin 'the hunter's hunter', we tighten our boots and walk back to the swamp. Slogging along in the water we spot three pale grey humps rising on the grass horizon as we advance. Elephant. Working quietly closer, we find not three, but six, three cows and three calves just visible. We stay back, not wanting to be forced to shoot if an anxious female charges. Ivory poachers have done such damage in Moyowosi that now even young bulls are hard to find. Despite their small tusks, these females are in danger, and Robin laments, 'The sad thing is I may never see these three again.' Across Africa, a reverse of natural selection seems to be taking place, for the bulls never live long enough to grow big ivory. Every bull elephant is potentially a hundred-pounder, as his ivory keeps growing until the day he dies.

Right up until the 1977 Kenya hunting ban, top hunters like Reggie Destro and Glen Cottar used to get hundred-pounders on almost every safari to the Tana River. There was always some poaching, but as Robin says, 'it never got out of hand until the end of hunting. Now they're finished. There wouldn't be any elephant or heavy game here either if there weren't professional hunters and clients and trackers and rangers in here reporting back and keeping the pressure on the poachers.'

Moving back through the swamp, we again fail to find the right buffalo. We head back to camp in the truck, Robin reminiscing with us about Bilu Deen. Then we discuss the ivory trade, the engine that drives the poaching. Like many hunters, and like the writer and pre-eminent elephant scholar Iain Douglas-Hamilton, Robin considers the key is to create an enforced international system

Robin Hurt and Makanyanga

that only permits ivory to cross borders when it is whole tusks and is accompanied by a licence of origin. Otherwise there is a market for small tusks from females and young males, which are then carved up in the Far East for export.

Burundi, which has no elephants, is the world's largest illegal exporter of ivory, most of it poached and smuggled in from Zaïre and Tanzania. Zaïre is now closed to all hunting, although elephant poaching is said to flourish there under government protection. Tanzania, Botswana, Zimbabwe and Ethiopia still permit licensed hunting of elephant. Today Robin Hurt strongly discourages his clients from shooting elephant, because of the lack of old trophy bulls carrying ivory of 70 lb or more a side. In recent years only one elephant has been shot in Tanzania on a Game Tracker safari. In Botswana the elephant are getting hammered by both poaching and by authorized, but badly managed, native hunting. The best elephant hunting is now in Ethiopia, where since 1986 several hundred-pound tuskers have been found following the reopening of hunting. Oppressed by the poaching, sometimes the work of soldiers with vehicles and automatic weapons, some of the Sudan's savannah elephant may have left their natural habitat to retreat to the forests of Ethiopia. Where Robin hunted ten years ago in the Sudan, not far from where Wilfred Thesiger once saw 1,000 elephant in a single day on the banks of the White Nile, there is not one elephant left. Native forest elephant tend to have a superior quality ivory, with longer, thinner tusks, and the best of them are now thought to be in the Central African Republic and Zaïre, where the alternating habitat of rain forest and savannah is ideal for elephant.

Where we are, in the Moyowosi swamp, poachers are generally not as well armed and mechanized as in some parts of Africa. Skilled bush gunsmiths, the poachers often make their own muzzle-loaders, powder and percussion caps, using pipes, matches and occasionally actions from old guns. Sometimes they use nails as bullets; Robin has found them in wounded hippos. Often poison is placed inside the round, yellow fruit of the barasus palm tree, an elephant favourite, and the fruit are then left near a waterhole. Each morning the poachers check to see if any fruit are missing. Then they follow the track from the missing fruit to the dead animal. Occasionally the poachers poison entire waterholes.

Buffalo are also poaching targets, as the meat of one animal will bring 6,000 shillings (£23, $40), in the villages. Near the Serengeti plain, in the Maswa Reserve, poachers dig traditional pit traps 15 feet deep, 10 feet long and 5 feet wide, with no stakes, but with the sides tapering down to wedge the animal in. Their most effective technique is to spread steel-cable snare lines, sometimes in groups of traps over a mile long. A cruel combination of old and new techniques, these traps indiscriminately kill hundreds of animals in a single day.

Still discussing poaching techniques, we suddenly see a long line of buffalo galloping across the trail ahead of us. Pulling up, we jump out, grabbing the bamboo buffalo sticks, reloading and running after the buffalo deep into the bush. At first we find no old males with exceptional heads, and as we stalk they keep moving off. Each time the pattern of the herd changes, and as we check with our glasses we spot different animals. After five approaches Laboso and Robin find a good head. Ted and I zero in with our fieldglasses, finding him. We advance in a tight line to 120 yards. Robin opens the gun rest. The three bamboo poles, tied together near the top, open into a natural tripod, easily adjusting to the uneven ground. Ted rests his gun, sights carefully, squeezes, and the buffalo stumbles after the retreating herd. We run after it through the bush, Ted fires again, and the buffalo falls dead. Checking, we find that the first shot took him in the heart. A buffalo's spine hangs relatively low, and a good vital shot must hit only one third up the shoulder, whereas for most animals it is half-way up.

In moments Laboso and Makanyanga have sharpened their skinning knives and are into the animal. Opening the stomach, they spill out the damp green grass that fills it like a lawnmower bag. As they peel the skin back over the ribs, the flesh of the chest is still twitching, a sign of good luck, Robin tells us. By now Makanyanga is at his favourite delicacy, fresh liver, which he cuts into slices, dips in the buffalo's stomach grass for seasoning and gulps down. He reminds me of his namesake, another Makanyanga and expert tracker, who accompanied the elephant hunter James Sutherland in Nyasaland in 1903, and once condemned unwitting Muslim villagers to their hell by bartering 'unclean' elephant meat with them, deceiving them that it was buffalo whose throats had been cut in the prescribed Muslim manner. Noticing us watching him, Makanyanga dips two sleek moist slices into the spicy half-digested grass and presents them to Ted and me on the point of his skinning knife. Finding them warm, fibrous, surprisingly good, and rather like *sushi*, we bolt them down and quickly take a beer. Laboso, seeing no charm in this dish and eager to return to camp for a proper buffalo feast, cuts off the head and finishes cleaning out the eight or nine stomachs and dozen kidneys, remarking that the layers of lower intestine resemble the pages of a book.

Eight hundred pounds of buffalo meat work like champagne for camp morale, but it is never enough. The next morning we are back in the swamp. We stalk without shooting, relaxed, stopping to sit by an ant-hill. We talk about the tropical bees of the Moyowosi, called *Apis mellifer*. These small, energetic bees make a thick, smooth honey that I stir into my tea at breakfast. In the afternoon we drive on to the hard plain next to the swamp. We stop, dazzled, to admire two beautiful male lions, father and son, that dominate the view. As Beryl Markham once wrote, they are 'huge, black-maned, and gleaming with life'.

Wild and alert, unlike the jaded lions of the game parks, but with the confidence of lions that have not known shooting, they rise to watch us and then settle down thirty yards away. Whenever we move even slightly, the father grows protective, going into first alarm, his tail not yet rigid, but twitching on the ground from side to side, his ears up, and then flattened back. The son is five or six years old. The father, lordlike, is the finest lion I have ever seen, perhaps fourteen or fifteen, at least nine feet nose to tip, 450 lb, with a thick black mane, some grey under the muzzle, his coat golden-grey, his body heavy, sleek and fit. Not wanting to shoot, doing our best not to disturb them, we back quietly away. 'This is their land,' Robin whispers, 'we are the intruders.'

As the afternoon ends, knowing it is feeding time for the buffalo, we walk in and out of the edge of the swamp, finally spotting one splendid buffalo with a heavy boss and a wide spread. He is packed thick in the edge of a huge herd that keeps drifting about him. We stalk forward, crouching low. Stopping to spot him with our fieldglasses, he now is hard to find, but a grey patch on his shoulder helps. As we approach closer, a few heads rise and the herd goes off. On the third try Ted studies him with his glasses at 120 yards as other buffalo drift across. Settling with his gun on the rest, Ted sights patiently through the scope, waiting for a clear shot. The old bull is never fully exposed, but he is tempting. It is getting dark, and Ted decides to go only for a sure shot, so we try moving up, but again they run before us, and we leave the Moyowosi for the last time.

Early the next morning Iris McCallum flies us 430 miles east across Tanzania to the Ruvu Game Reserve on the Ruvu River. Close to Mt Kilimanjaro, near the Kenya border, it is Masai country, a broad dusty plain with the river on one side and the Ruvu escarpment rising on the other. The camp is set on the lush jungled bank of the Ruvu, under heavy acacia and fig trees, with vines dropping to the water. There are catfish and crocodile, but no hippos. The Juluwa, a tribe of skilful fishermen, have stretched elaborate wattle traps across the river. The nights are warmer, the days hotter and, with the camp cook Gideon at the fires, the food is even better. It is a rare pleasure on safari to have a glass of wine by a fire as a river, eighty yards wide, slips black and smooth through the shadows just behind you.

Excited to be hunting in new country, we are up early, but as we load up we miss Makanyanga, who stayed at Moyowosi to hunt with Danny McCallum. Laboso is still with us, already bundled in his dark grey, strangely formal overcoat, and we meet Diwani, famous even among the trackers for the gift of his eyesight, for in the bush Diwani literally sees what other men do not. He is handsomely wrinkled, lean and quietly merry, delighted to be going out with Robin, keen to get started. Conferring, we agree to spend several days walking and learning the country, perhaps shooting francolin or guinea-fowl for lunch, and going after gerenuk or oryx for meat if we find good ones.

Diwani, the finest eyes in Tanzania

Heading out, we stop to measure large lion tracks that cross the dusty trail just outside camp, and already we are caught up in the detail of the bush. It is baobab country. With fat, warty trunks and spindly witch-like arms, these mysterious trees are the source of cream of tartar, and of much tribal mythology. Ted points out a yellow wagtail, questioning whether it is also called the 'Sudan wagtail'. Before Robin resolves this, they spot another bird, debating whether it is a pengoni pipit or a yellow-throated longclaw. Soon we stop to study an orange-bellied parrot resting brightly in one baobab. Then we notice short wooden climbing pegs driven into the side of the tree by honey hunters and we see a lesser honeyguide swooping about, perhaps ready to lead us to the bees, trusting us to perform the traditional courtesy of leaving the last bit of honey for him, lest bad luck follow. A member of the family aptly named Indicatoridae, honeyguides do in fact lead their followers to honey.

The honeyguide recalls me to a hot afternoon in Matabeleland five years before, stalking in Zimbabwe with Alan Elliott. He punished my scepticism about honeyguides by leading me on a running chase over burned-out bush, as we dashed after the twittering bird from one blackened, bare tree to another. Finally the honeyguide swooped in circles around one tree, drawing us with shrill, chattering calls. Alan pressed his ear to the trunk. I joined him, exhausted and annoyed, but astonished by the din of humming bees in the hollowed tree.

The traditional technique is to run after the honeyguide, whistling back to it in encouraging conversation as the chase proceeds, and then gathering dry grass to burn next to the hive to suffocate the bees. In 1850 the pioneer hunter Gordon Cumming observed that one must be wary of the honeyguide's signals, for they are also known to lead one into danger, running up to a sleeping lion, or, in Cumming's case, to an immense crocodile hidden in the banks of the Limpopo. Eight years later, Baldwin reported that a honeyguide led his Bushman companion to within five feet of a crouching lion.

Moving on, we see dik dik scamper off to our left, dainty grey antelope fifteen inches tall, with longer hind legs, fleeing like jack rabbits in a jagged, leaping flight that makes them hard to chase. Ted and I take a walk with the shotguns.

Baobab tree, Tanzania

Vulterine guinea-fowl

He gets a yellow-necked francolin, while I shoot a vulterine guinea-fowl, my only bag of the safari, and admire its iridescent blue feathers, monk's fringe and red eyes encircling tight black pupils. Then we join Robin and the trackers, climbing through rocky hills, looking for vantage points for spotting. We soon learn that the Ruvu, instead of swamp to impede movement, has thorns. These include straightforward acacia thorns of all sizes, clever wait-a-bit thorns that will not let you ignore them, hooking and clinging deep under the skin with the branch bent like a fishing rod until you stop to release them, and merciless iron thorns that will pierce a shoe or a tyre, artfully designed so that one point is always up, like medieval cavalry snares.

Finally we reach a jagged clifftop with a wide, curving horizon over the plain. We each sit down with our fieldglasses to scan different sectors of rock and valley, searching for greater kudu, a magnificent tall antelope with spiralling horns four feet long. Because of their beauty and illusiveness, and the hard chase they give, the greater kudu is a favoured quarry of serious hunters. It ranges from South Africa up to Ethiopia. The southern greater kudu of South Africa, Zambia and Zimbabwe is larger and darker, with nine or ten light vertical stripes. The east African greater kudu, with six to eight stripes, is more like the mountain nyala of Ethiopia, favouring high ground and steep rocky landscapes.

The wind is sweeping up from the plain in gusts, like a balmier Scotland, with a clean strong smell of thornbush, grass and dust. It reminds me again of Alan Elliott explaining what he misses when he leaves Zimbabwe: 'Most of all, it's that strange smell of the African dust.' We see giraffe in the distance, then nimble klipsringers leaping among the rocks, and a Wahlberg's eagle, with its yellow eyes, furry brown feathers and white underwings, but not even Diwani spots a kudu. Instead we find a lion fly, gold in front, with a strong pincered grip, a flying tick that feeds on leopard and lion. Climbing down, Robin stops us with his hand, showing us many tracks of a lioness and her cubs, a dangerous combination. Then we see the flattened grass still rising where they were lying near a rock, 'Don't go back there. We don't want to have to shoot her.'

At the base of the hill, Laboso cleans the birds, and we make a fire and share lunch. After long mornings on foot, it is easy to get lazy in the afternoon. We talk about Robin's father, and how he kept Robin in touch with England, and with the family history since Norman days. Robin recalls the time when he was a boy of twelve, and his father took him to Derbyshire, to visit Alderwasley, their old family house with its two-hundred-year-old deer park. Always there was a link with nature. As they walked about, Robin's father told him that at Robin's age he used to lie by the stream under the oaks, with his hand in the water under a rock ledge, tickling trout, touching a fish lightly so that it would not get alarmed, and then quietly moving all his fingers until it lay in his palm. Lying down, his father reached gently under the ledge. He could not see the fish, but after twenty years away, he still knew where they were. Closing his

Author and son stalking rhinoceros, Zimbabwe, 1985

hand, he threw a small trout up on the bank and then brushed it back into the river. Today, Robin still loves England, visiting it every year to see his children in school and shooting pheasant each November in the Cotswolds.

Like Cornwallis Harris, Selous and J. A. Hunter, who transported the country gentleman's hunting ethics and enthusiasm to the Eden they discovered in Africa, Robin seems to find in the bush a wild extension of the English countryside. As Ted puts it one evening in our tent, Robin has an English affinity with the land. He is tirelessly fascinated by the interrelationships of nature, and cares for each plant and animal in the game reserves as if they were on his land in Gloucestershire. But he is not all English. Part of his instinct is African. After thirty-five years of hunting and tracking with Tinia, Ndaga and Laboso, Robin, like a very few of the best professionals, brings together the key qualities of both African and European hunters. Due to his background, he combines the bushcraft, instinct and superstitions of the local African hunter with the sporting attitude, discipline and broad hunting horizons of a British sportsman and officer.

Returning to the escarpment the next day, we pass two secretary birds. Tall, elegant creatures that eat lizards and trample snakes to death, these 'pedestrian eagles' remind Ted of the ornithologist David Bannerman describing a secretary bird 'striding majestically through the savannah'. On a tree we find the claw marks of a large male leopard, with porcupine quills on the ground near by. Not knowing I am offending a Robin Hurt superstition, I pick up a quill, admiring the strength and lightness of its cylindrical architecture. Ted observes a pile of white shell fragments from the exoskeletons of centipedes, several inches long, the chalky excrement of the civet cat that ate them. Civets like to pass

Above: Secretary bird

Left: Leopard carrying a dik dik

Kudu, by Cornwallis Harris

excrement in the same spot, a habit fatally shared by the endangered white rhinoceros, which helps make them easy to poach. Then we see a colony of basket-like weavers' nests dangling from an acacia tree like Christmas tree ornaments, a sign that there is water near by. Continuing on foot, we find eland, a female kudu and kongoni, a gregarious, small-horned antelope much favoured by lion. The kongoni are 250 yards off across mostly open country. We try stalking by tacking at angles towards them, walking erect without concealment, as Diwani suggests, as if we were Masai just walking by. It does not work; the kongoni run off.

On the way back Diwani spots a fine male gerenuk, perhaps thirteen years old, nearing the end of his time, browsing in wait-a-bit thornbush, a favourite food, although it is hard to imagine this slender, long-necked gazelle relishing such a hostile plant. Named after the Somali word for 'giraffe-necked', generally three feet at the shoulder with a neck eighteen inches long, these large-eyed antelope require no water at all, except the moisture they find in small leaves and shoots. Frequently they stand on their hind legs to eat. Ted makes a clean kill with his ·375 and we look forward to our dinner. We notice the small, open pocket between the nose and the eye, where male gerenuks secrete drops of musk, which they leave on branches to mark their territory. Then Robin flicks off his arm an unwelcome 'Nairobi eye', a small crawling insect resembling a thin beetle which, if crushed on the skin, yields an acid secretion that causes the skin to blister, scab and peel.

As we walk back to get the truck, I deplore the absence of elephant in country so suited to their tastes, dotted with the sansevieria plants that only elephant love to eat. Last year Robin saw fifty elephant in the area, this year none. Ten years ago there were black rhino and thousands of elephant all through Masailand, including hundred-pounders. Instead we spot female kudu, but no males. With the shy antelopes, like bongo, eland and kudu, it often appears that there are more females. This is not so, but the bulls are instinctively even more shy than the females. Kudu generally drink only at midday, avoiding predators and other animals that come to the water early and late.

Climbing the Ruvu escarpment again the next day, searching for kudu, we open up a new trail with the pangas, proud as Boy Scouts when Robin says he knows of no Europeans being there before us. It is thick, dry, rocky country. I learn again why early hunters elsewhere in Africa complained that the thorns literally cut the clothes from their backs during hard chases, and it is difficult to imagine Gordon Cumming surviving in his kilt. I know of one professional hunter who has had an eye torn from its socket by a thorn branch that lashed his passing Land Cruiser.

After six hours Laboso spots a male kudu among the trees on a rocky hillside a mile off. We go into our centipede mode, nearly touching each other as we advance crouching in single file, footstep for footstep, passing back hand-to-hand the bending thorn branches, then crawling on our stomachs, bare legs scraping along, imprinted with burrs and thorns. As Ted finally rises to shoot, three impala appear on the hillside, spooking the kudu and destroying our stalk. We plan to return for another chance. On the way home we are lucky, Ted spotting a handsome oryx in more open country. Seen from the side, with only one straight, ridged horn visible in profile, one understands why the oryx may be the source of the unicorn legend, particularly when one horn is lost and the other naturally edges towards the centre. While we stalk I recall the remarkable durability of an oryx twenty years before in Kenya when a hunting friend, Dominic Cadbury, had to hit it five times before it died, each time the animal struggling to rise once more before we finally held it down and cut its throat. Ted shoots. The oryx runs off, hit, and we pursue it hard, Ted finally killing it with three more shots.

Early the next morning we head back to the escarpment, Laboso amazing us all by spotting a male kudu among the trees a mile and a half from the moving vehicle. Stepping down quietly, Ted loading his ·270 for a longer, flatter shot with a lighter bullet than the ·375, we start another circuitous stalk from one sheltering tree or rock to another, crawling again on our stomachs, finally clambering up steep rocks as Ted moves into position for a long shot from 400 yards. Pointing the ·270 out between some rocks, brushing the side of a cactus,

Ted aims through his scope and squeezes off three shots. All miss. Incredibly, the kudu does not move, not knowing whence the shots are coming. Laboso explains that a branch of the cactus, not visible in the scope, blocked the barrel, deflecting the light bullets. Ted switches to the ·375 and fires one shot as the kudu moves off, and we start climbing after him. On the summit, Diwani finds his trail among the rocks, but no blood, and then spots him breaking cover. Ted fires twice more, missing, and we tear down the hill after him, slipping and panting, forgetting the thorns. But he has gone, running off across a distant slope, unharmed, his splendid spiralled horns bobbing as he canters.

On the way back, I try to recall Cornwallis Harris writing about his first 'princely kudu', reminding myself that while all else has changed on safari in a century and a half, the central qualities of the animals endure, and the closer one is to the game, the more it is like the old days. As Harris wrote about the kudu on the first safari in 1836,

> . . . his great sagacity, wildness and self-possession demanding the most skilful generalship to outmanoeuvre him, the pursuit differs altogether from the usual stamp of African hunting, and involves no inconsiderable acquaintance with the subtleties of woodcraft. We have here no dashing among countless herds, no helter-skelter riding by the side of a closely packed phalanx; yet have we a quarry well worth the hardest day's fag on foot.

Back at camp, we are exhilarated by the chase, revelling in the details, repeating ourselves, proud of the hard stalk and our small wounds, exclaiming at the beauty and luck of the kudu. I remind Ted of Joseph Stalin's characteristic adage, 'Patience is the hunter's greatest weapon.' We doubt that Stalin was referring to either a kudu or romance. Soon my own satisfaction is interrupted by a scorpion, hidden in a damp towel, that lashes his raised tail and stings me in the thigh after my shower. Fortunately, most east African scorpions are less poisonous than the occasionally fatal scorpions found to the north. Then we feast on Gideon's oryx shepherd's pie, guava jelly and carrots flown in from Arusha. Robin lifts a glass of our familiar camp claret, predicting that tomorrow we will get our kudu.

By the fire after dinner, our conversation returns to animals, this time to the dreaded ratel, the most fierce of all African animals. A type of honey badger, the ratel frequently follow honeyguides to bees' nests, ignoring the stings and sharing the spoils with the bird. Known to go berserk in combat, the most dangerous animal for its weight and size, the ratel is the hero of numberless camp fire jokes across Africa, due to its propensity to swarm up the legs of its adversary and ravage his genitals. Robin confirms that he has seen even a leopard driven from its kill by a ratel, at 24 lb a creature one sixth of a leopard's weight. In Zimbabwe it is said that buffalo, after nosing in a ratel's burrow, are known to have bled to death after the badger has torn off their nose or genitals.

The renowned wildlife photographer Hugo van Lawick, who has lived twenty-five years under canvas studying animals in east Africa, once photographed a male ratel as it attacked his Land Rover. In Zambia, a friend of mine in a safari camp one evening saw three fearless professional hunters leap up on to the bar when a ratel entered the tent. I was told in Zimbabwe of a ratel found caught in a poaching snare, its hind legs pinned in the pointed teeth of the trap. Released, the snarling ratel attacked the metal trap, savaging it hysterically, and then turned on its saviour, who crushed its skull with the shovel he had used to release it and flung the body into his Land Rover. Later, in camp, the man reached into the vehicle and the ratel struggled up to attack him again.

On our way back to the escarpment in the morning, the fifth day of our kudu hunt, Robin spots a hoopoe, prominent on an acacia branch with its orange body and black and orange crest. By now the trackers and I just roll our eyes when Robin stops the car while he and Ted dispute whether indeed it is an African hoopoe, or the more rare European hoopoe that migrates to east Africa. Bird books are consulted, the discussion lingers on. Finally we drive on to the escarpment and begin our march. Diwani spots three kudu bulls at a great distance, we start our stalk and Robin gets a good view with the glasses: 'Two definitely aren't shootable. Only one turn to the horns. I'm not sure about the other one.' We keep after them, but the third is also too young for a fair shot. I remember J. A. Hunter's account of two older bulls, with two full turns to their horns, locked dead together, their horns fatally tangled in combat.

For several hours we move across the red clay-based soil and short dry grass, trying to avoid the wait-a-bit thickets and other thorns, slowly moving up the escarpment, now punctuated by abrupt, rocky hills and dry *luggas*, or sand rivers. The country becomes thick with *Acacia albida*, and we move more discreetly, for it is the season when kudu concentrate under the albida to eat the seeds, burrs and thistles that gather there.

Then Diwani spots him. At first we see nothing, even with our glasses, as the off-white vertical stripes of the kudu break up the shape of his body and echo the vertical lines of the grey trees, his curling horns lost in the twisted branches. Robin picks him out for us at 200 yards. We study him through the branches, trying not to move. Painfully we stalk up to 100 yards, but there is no way to get closer. Only his head is partly visible through the branches, facing us straight on. We wait ten minutes. Longer. The kudu does not move. Ted sights his ·375, trying to estimate the rest of the figure from the fragment he can see. We wait again. Carefully calculating where it must be, Ted shoots for the neck, which he cannot see. The kudu breaks away, running with two other bulls, confusing us. We rush down to where he stood, finding blood, and start a long jogging run through the thorns.

Determined not to lose the wounded animal, Robin pushes hard, for the first time brusque with his client, 'Don't shoot. It's the wrong one. Careful, you could blow someone's head off.' Once or twice, as he pauses between sprints, hoping to get the kudu before it moves on again, Robin begins to raise his own rifle. The blood trail grows heavier. Diwani reckons he was hit in the jaw, damaging his sense of smell. The other bulls, frightened and stronger, abandon

The hunting party on the Ruvu
Escarpment, 1986
Left to right: Robin Hunt, Ted
Roosevelt, Bartle Bull, Diwani and
Laboso

The kudu

him, a sign that we should get him. After four miles, we come on him, hiding in
a thicket in a lugga. Ted shoots perfectly and the kudu is dead.

He is beautiful. Five years old, five feet tall at the shoulder, perhaps 650 lb,
two and a half open spiral turns to his heavy twisted horns, a smooth grey coat
with a white tufted spine and eight vertical stripes starting behind the shoulder,
with a small grey-white beard and the tiny bump of a third horn growing below
his eyes. Cut and exhausted, we cheer and clap shoulders with excitement,
proud of the animal and loving the chase. It is that ageless, fraternal moment of
the hunt that is happy and sad and thrilling.

Robin is proud of his trackers and his clients, pleased with our teamwork, grinning like a boy, 'Instinct is everything in hunting. I told you last night, this was our day.' I remember him telling us earlier that, for him, the challenge still left in hunting is 'getting the client in the position where he can hunt an animal, and do it cleanly, the right way. You lose some control. That's the hard part. You know what you can do, not what your client can do.'

Another day we decide to sleep out in a fly camp, a light camp with no tents. First we climb a tall, bare rounded rock, sloping smoothly down from one end like a sperm whale, perhaps a hundred feet high, a remarkable twin to Ayer's Rock in the Northern Territory of Australia. The coincidence startles me, because for days I have thought that the Northern Territory is the only place outside Africa where I have seen *kopjes*, groups and mounds of large stones set together in open, flat country, as if by the hand of a giant at play. After the climb we go hunting for our dinner. Ted drops a fine impala and we build fires and lay our blankets at the base of the hill, naming it 'Bilu's Rock' after Robin's friend Bilu Deen. We drink red wine, smelling the smoky impala steaks grilling on acacia sticks between slices of onions, tomatoes and peppers. We talk about the future of hunting in Africa. Is the true safari nearly over?

Without enlightened government action, and the paradoxical support of professional hunting, it cannot last long, but there will always be somewhere to go on safari, Robin says. It just gets harder. 'I can see a new generation of hunters coming along. After skipping a generation, it's all now starting again. Calvin Cottar's hooked. But the new hunters have to learn that the shooting side is secondary. Most important is finding the game, which is pretty well an instinct. Most lads brought up in east Africa have it. Next, it's logistics.'

Fly camp near Bilu's Rock, Tanzania, 1986

Today's young trainee hunters have a problem new to Africa, virtually no opportunity to shoot dangerous game. Some learn by going from country to country, to Zimbabwe to help cull elephant, to Zambia on lion hunts, to Tanzania for buffalo. Many try to work for Robin Hurt or other top hunters. But no new hunter can ever again have the background, the boyhood experience with African game of the old hands. 'The biggest difficulty for the new chaps,' Robin explains, 'is getting the experience of handling dangerous game and difficult situations. Will their instincts and reflexes be OK? We were brought up with it.'

What is it that still draws these young men to give their lives to a profession that could be dead in five years? For the clients, Ted speaks of 'the distance, the stalking, the solitude, not seeing another human being. No matter where you go at home, there are always airplanes, power lines, roads, lights. We come to Africa to let our senses roam free.' For the young hunters, it is much the same, a sense of freedom, and nature. Robin says the key is still 'the animals, being out in the land, peaceful, hearing the lion roaring at night. It takes you back in history so you can relax and be yourself.'

By now we are ready to tear the impala steak from the roasting sticks like angry ratels. We eat everything we can, and stretch out by the camp fire. We talk about the changes on safari since the early hunters came to Africa, how it is impossible not to love what they loved best, a drink and a smoke with a friend by the fire as the stars brighten, the bush comes alive around you and the African night settles in. I take out my scruffy copy of Selous's *A Hunter's Wanderings in Africa*, and we read aloud in turn from the great elephant chase in Mashonaland in 1878, knowing that tonight we will look up at the stars as he did, and hear the lion roar.

Two evenings before, back at camp on the Ruvu River, I had asked young Calvin Cottar, aged twenty-two, on the day he took out his first client, why he wanted to be a professional hunter. Brought up in Glen Cottar's tented safari camp, studying correspondence courses, shooting meat at thirteen for his father's safari camps, Calvin is determined to be 'one of the few fourth-generation professional hunters in Africa'. Calvin told me his great-grand-father explained it all as he lay dying in the bush in 1940. Charles Cottar, the first American white hunter, began hunting as a boy of eight in Cedar County, Iowa, paying for his bullets by selling mink pelts for 15 cents apiece. Never able to give up the outdoor life, he was killed hunting rhinoceros twenty-nine years after he came to Africa. Already gored by a buffalo, knocked down by an elephant, three times mauled by leopard, partially paralysed by a stroke, at sixty-seven Charles Cottar was unable to get his lever-action ·405 Winchester up in time to stop the charging rhino, although he hit it twice. Crushed as the rhino fell on him, bleeding to death from a severed femoral artery, with his last words he stopped his son from raising a canvas to protect him from the hot sun, 'No. I want to see the sky.'

GLOSSARY

Aardwolf – A small member of the hyena family, with long, pointed ears, weighing up to thirty pounds.

Acacia – A large genus of African trees and shrubs, bearing many varieties of thorn. Some forty species of acacia occur in Zimbabwe alone.

Afrikaans – A modified form of the Dutch language that is spoken in South Africa.

Afrikaaners – The Afrikaans-speaking white people of South Africa, of predominantly Dutch descent.

Assegai – An iron-tipped African spear with a hardwood shaft.

Askari – An east African native soldier or policeman.

Bantu – Generally defined as the five major ethno-linguistic peoples of southern Africa: the Nguni (including Zulu, Swazi, Xhosa, and Ndebele or Matabele), Sotho (including Tswana and others), Venda, Tsonga and Lamba.

Bilharzia (or schistosomiasis) – A chronic tropical disease associated with the tiny flatworm of the same name that becomes a parasite in the pelvic region.

Biltong – strips of sun- and wind-dried meat.

Black cotton soil – Dark terrain, common in certain regions of east Africa, that is rock-hard when dry and becomes swampy and glue-like if wet.

Blackwater fever – A tropical disease caused by malarial infection, characterized by the passing of blood in the urine.

Blesbok – A mid-size antelope, three feet at the shoulder, with the face and legs partly white.

Boers – South Africans of Dutch descent.

Boma – An enclosure or stockade.

Bongo – The largest forest antelope, up to 500 lb and four feet at the shoulder. Chestnut red, with white stripes on the sides and massive spiralling horns.

Boss – The protuberant, massive base of horn that bridges across the forehead of Cape buffalo.

Buffalo sticks – A gun rest made of three bamboo poles lashed together near one end.

Bushbuck – A small chestnut-coloured antelope, up to three feet at the shoulder, with a high rump and long bushy tail.

Bushmen – Tribes of San in southern Africa, generally diminutive hunter-gatherers.

Chigger (or chigoe) – A burrowing flea that can penetrate and grow its eggs under human skin, generally afflicting the feet.

CITES – The United Nations' Convention on International Trade in Endangered Species, which establishes the listing of 'endangered' species and has its headquarters in Geneva.

Cordite – An efficient, smokeless explosive made from gun-cotton, nitroglycerine and Vaseline.

Dik-dik – Tiny, shy, largely nocturnal antelopes, averaging about fifteen inches at the shoulder, dik-dik are browsers generally found in dry bush country. Their flight is characterized by zigzag leaps.

Donga – A gully or dry stream bed, often thick with bush.

Duiker – A family of small, ungregarious antelopes, subdivided into two groups, bush and forest duiker. The largest of all duiker, the yellow-backed duiker, is about two and a half feet at the shoulder and prefers high forest country.

Eland – The largest antelope, up to 2,000 lb and nearly six feet at the shoulder. Fawn-coloured and bovine, with a prominent dewlap.

Elephant shrew – The size of a rat, this shrew is distinguished by a long, trunk-like snout and by hind legs that are far longer than its front legs.

Flat dog – Old Rhodesian slang for a crocodile.

Fly camp – A light camp without tents. Camping 'on the fly'.

Francolin – An African partridge, of which there are many species. Rotund, gregarious and terrestrial, this gamebird can fly fast over short distances.

Gerenuk – A slender, brown gazelle with an exceptionally long neck, given to browsing while standing erect on its hind legs.

Gnu – See wildebeest.

Guinea-fowl – A large gamebird, related to the pheasant.

Hartebeest (or kongoni) – A large reddish-tan antelope,

over four feet at the shoulder, with a sloping back and narrow head.

Honey badger – See ratel.

Honeyguide – A family of small birds of the genus *Indicator*, named for their propensity to lead honey hunters, including humans and ratels, to bees' nests, chattering and dipping in flight as they do so.

Hottentots – Tribes of Khoi in southern Africa, generally diminutive nomadic herdsmen.

Impi – A Zulu or Matabele regiment.

Induna – A Zulu or Matabele officer or councillor.

Jambok – A short, heavy whip, once usually made of rhinoceros or hippopotamus hide.

Kaffir – A generally pejorative term for Africans, derived from the Arabic word *kafir*, or non-believer.

Kaross – Cloak made of animal skins, usually with the hair left on.

Karroo – Barren tracts of land that are desert-like in the dry season.

Klipspringer – A small antelope, twenty-two inches at the shoulder, with a thick, olive-yellow coat and unusual, blunt hoof tips. Remarkably nimble on rocks, extraordinary jumpers, frequently standing silhouetted on boulders, klipspringers are confined to rocky, hilly habitat.

Kob – A mid-sized antelope, three and a half feet at the shoulder, varying in colour, with a whitish area around the eyes and thick horns with a double curvature, from the side seeming to rise in the shape of the letter S.

Kongoni – See hartebeest.

Kopje – A group or hill of large stones, often balanced on each other as if assembled by a giant at play.

Kraal – An African enclosure, whether for a household, a village or cattle. Generally made of thorn bushes.

Kudu – A large, greyish antelope with vertical white stripes. Up to 700 lb and over five feet at the shoulder. Horns up to four feet long, spreading into open spirals.

Laager – Afrikaans term for an encampment or defensive circle of wagons.

Lechwe – A medium-sized antelope, three feet at the shoulder, with elevated hindquarters and lyre-shaped horns.

Lugga – A dry ravine or stream bed.

Maggot – A soft-bodied legless grub or larva that consumes dead flesh.

Mamba – A family of extremely venomous snakes of the genus *Dendroaspis*, including green and black varieties.

Related to the cobra, but with no hood, mambas grow up to twelve feet and can be remarkably swift in moving through the grass.

Mimosa – A genus of pod-bearing shrubs common in Africa.

Mopane – A deciduous tree growing to a height of almost forty feet, common in Botswana, Zambia and Zimbabwe.

Moran – A Masai warrior, or mature male member of the tribe.

Mountain nyala – A large antelope, over four feet at the shoulder and up to 500 lb, with a shaggy, greyish-chestnut coat and heavy horns in two open spirals.

Ngoma – A tribal feast and dance.

Oribi – A small antelope, two feet at the shoulder, with large, pointed ears and a short bushy tail. A grazer, when alarmed it springs into the air with all four legs stiff.

Oryx (or gemsbok) – A tall antelope, four feet at the shoulder, 450 lb, with a grey body and black and white face. Horns nearly straight and up to four feet long.

Panga – An African machete.

Quagga – An extinct member of the zebra family.

Ratel (or honey badger) – A fierce, stout, greyish badger, the upper body lighter in colour. Ten inches at the shoulder and up to twenty-five pounds, with a massive head, short legs and powerful claws, the ratel is said to attack the genitals of larger animals.

Reedbuck – A small antelope, under three feet at the shoulder, with a longish, heavy, fawn-coloured coat and thick horns (except for the Sudanese variety, which has long, thin horns). Grazers, they run with a rocking-horse motion and during the day lie down in reed beds or tall grass.

Roan antelope – The third largest African antelope (after the eland and the kudu), five feet at the shoulder and up to 600 lb. Fawn-coloured, with black and white face markings, a dark mane and ridged horns with a sharp backward curve.

Roer – A heavy, Boer muzzle-loader.

Sable antelope (or Harris buck) – A large, dark antelope with a generally glossy-black body and white belly. Long, ridged horns sweeping back in a sharp curve.

Sais (or syce) – The Arabic and Swahili term for a groom.

Sassaby – A generally chestnut-coloured antelope with a black face and curved horns, nearly four feet at the shoulder.

Schutztruppe – The German forces that fought in east Africa in the First World War.

Secretary bird – Four and a half feet tall, with a dignified, haughty appearance, this bird has pink and black legs, a white body, black and white tail feathers, and a tiara of projecting black head feathers. Utters a deep croak when mating, and enjoys a diet of snakes, lizards, rodents and domestic fowl.

Shamba – A cultivated plot of ground or native farm.

Shoa – A Coptic, Christian kingdom that was once part of Abyssinia.

Sisal – A tough fibre made from the large, spiky leaves of certain agave plants, used for ropes and cordage. Once the basis of a major plantation industry in east Africa.

Sitatunga (or nakong) – A grey-brown, swamp-dwelling antelope, three and a half feet at the shoulder, with distinctive elongated hoofs and spiral horns.

Springbok – A seventy-five pound gazelle, reddish and with small horns, given to leaping in the air. Highly gregarious, they used to gather in vast herds.

Swahili – The common language of much of Kenya and Tanzania, derived from a mixture of coastal African dialects influenced by Arabic, Portuguese and English. The term itself is derived from the Arabic word *sawahil*, or coasts.

Topi – A large, highly gregarious antelope, up to four feet at the shoulder and 300 lb. Reddish-brown in colour, with lyre-shaped horns and high shoulders sloping down to its rump.

Tsetse – An African fly, with about twenty species, that carries disease to people and animals. A brown blood-sucker with a grey mid-section, the tsetse is slightly larger than a housefly and gives a sharp sting as its jaws bite.

Waterbuck – A large antelope, four feet at the shoulder, 450 lb. Grey-brown, with rounded ears and a white ring across the rump.

Wildebeest (or gnu) – A large, ox-like antelope, four and a half feet at the shoulder. Dark grey, with massive shoulders and head, and a black mane on the neck and shoulders. Rather prehistoric in appearance.

Zareba – A thorn-branch enclosure.

Zimbabwe – Shona word meaning buildings of stone or temples.

BIBLIOGRAPHY

Chapter 1

Becker, Peter, *Path of Blood*, Harmondsworth, Penguin Books, 1979.

Becker, Peter, *The Pathfinders*, London, Viking, 1985.

Burchell, William J., *Selections from Travels in the Interior of Southern Africa*, London, Oxford University Press, 1937 (first published 1822).

Cambridge History of Southern Africa, Vol. 5 (of 8), Cambridge, Cambridge University Press, 1976.

Cattrick, Alan, *Spoor of Blood*, Cape Town, Howard Timmins, 1959.

Child, G., and Le Riche, J.D., *Recent Springbok Treks*, Paris, Centre National de la Recherche Scientifique.

Cronwright-Schreiner, S.C., *The Migratory Springboks of South Africa*, London, Unwin, 1925.

Harris, Sir William Cornwallis, *Portraits of the Game and Wild Animals of Southern Africa*, Alberton (RSA), Galago, 1986.

Harris, Sir William Cornwallis, *The Wild Sports of Southern Africa*, 5th ed., London, Henry G. Bohn, 1852.

Hibbert, Christopher, *Africa Explored*, London, Allen Lane, 1982.

Ingham, Kenneth, *A History of East Africa*, London, Longmans, Green, 1965.

Leakey, Louis S.B., *Animals of East Africa*, ed. National Geographic Society, Washington, NGS, 1973.

Longford, Elizabeth, *Wellington – The Years of the Sword*, New York, Harper & Row, 1969.

Malecot, Georges, *Les Voyageurs Français . . . 1835 à 1870*, Paris, Société Française d'Histoire d'Outre-Mer, 1972.

Morris, James, *Heaven's Command*, Harmondsworth, Penguin Books, 1982.

Ritter, E.A., *Shaka Zulu*, Harmondsworth, Penguin Books, 1978.

Chapter 2

Adams, H.G., *Dr Livingstone*, London, Houlston & Wright.

Baldwin, William Charles, *African Hunting and Adventure*, London, Richard Bentley, 1894.

Becker, Peter, *Path of Blood*, Harmondsworth, Penguin Books, 1979.

Birkinshaw, Philip, *The Livingstone Touch*, London, Macdonald, 1973.

Brodie, Fawn M., *The Devil Drives*, New York, Norton, 1984.

Butcher, T.K., *The Great Explorations: Africa*, London, Dennis Dobson, 1959.

Cattrick, Alan, *Spoor of Blood*, Cape Town, Howard Timmins, 1959.

Coupland, Reginald, *Livingstone's Last Journey*, London, Readers Union/Collins, 1947.

Cumming, Roualeyn Gordon, *The Lion Hunter of South Africa*, London, John Murray, 1904.

Fehr, William, *Caldwell's Animals*, Cape Town, Art Reproductions, [undated].

Greenwood, James, *Wild Sports of the World*, London, Ward Lock, [1884].

Hall, Richard, *Lovers on the Nile*, New York, Collins and Random House, 1980.

Haresnape, Geoffrey, ed., *The Great Hunters*, Cape Town, Purnell, 1974.

Hibbert, Christopher, *Africa Explored*, London, Allen Lane, 1982.

Hobusch, Erich, *Fair Game*, New York, Arco, 1980.

Jeal, Tim, *Livingstone*, London, Heinemann, 1973.

Kemp, Kenneth, *Tales of the Big Game Hunters*, London, The Sportsman's Press, 1986.

Livingstone, David, *Missionary Travels and Researches in South Africa*, London, John Murray, 1857; Philadelphia, Bradley, 1858.

Morris, James, *Heaven's Command*, Harmondsworth, Penguin Books, 1982.

Phillipps-Wolley, Clive, *Big Game Shooting*, London, Longmans, Green, 1894.

Schillings, C.G., *In Wildest Africa*, New York, Harper, 1907.

van der Post, Laurens, *Lost World of the Kalahari*, Harmondsworth, Penguin Books, 1962.

van der Post, Laurens, *A Story Like the Wind*, Harmondsworth, Penguin Books, 1978.

Chapter 3

Bryden, H.A., 'Captain F.C. Selous', *Cornhill Magazine*, London, 1917, vol. 43, pp. 470–83.

Clements, Frank, *Kariba*, London, Methuen, 1959.

Cranworth, Lord, *Kenya Chronicles*, London, Macmillan, 1939.

Farwell, Byron, *The Great War in Africa*, New York, Norton, 1986.

Fehr, William, ed., *Caldwell's Animals*, Cape Town, Art Reproductions, [undated].

Finaughty, William, *The Recollections of an Elephant Hunter*, Bulawayo, Books of Zimbabwe, 1980.

Greenwood, James, *Wild Sports of the World*, London, Ward, Lock, [1884].

Hubusch, Erich, *Fair Game*, New York, Arco, 1980.

Kerr, Walter Montagu, *The Far Interior*, London, Sampson, Low, Marston, Searle & Rivington, 1886.

Meinertzhagen, Richard, *Kenya Diary*, London, Eland Books, 1983.

Millais, J.G., *Life of Frederick Courtenay Selous D.S.O.*, London, Longmans, Green, 1918.

Miller, Charles, *Battle for the Bundu*, London, Macmillan, 1974.

Morris, James, *Heaven's Command*, Harmondsworth, Penguin Books, 1982.

Neumann, Arthur H., *Elephant Hunting in East Equatorial Africa*, London, Rowland Ward, 1898.

Outlook Magazine, New York, 1917, vol. 115, pp. 410–11.

Pease, Sir Alfred E., *The Book of the Lion*, New York, Scribner's, 1914.

Selous, Frederick C., *African Nature Notes and Reminiscences*, Alberton (RSA), Galago, 1986.

Selous, Frederick C., *A Hunter's Wanderings in Africa*, London, Macmillan, 1920.

Selous, Frederick C., Phillipps-Wolley, Clive, and others, *Big Game Shooting*, vol. 1, London, Longmans, Green, 1894.

Selous, Frederick C., *Travel and Adventure in South-East Africa*, London, Rowland Ward, 1893.

von Lettow-Vorbeck, General Paul E., *My Reminiscences of East Africa*, London, Hurst & Blackett.

Chapter 4

Bell, W.D.M., *Bell of Africa*, Saffron Walden, Neville Spearman, 1985.

Bell, W.D.M., *Karamojo Safari*, Saffron Walden, Neville Spearman, 1984.

Bell, W.D.M., *The Wanderings of an Elephant Hunter*, Saffron Walden, Neville Spearman, 1976.

Blunt, David Enderby, *Elephant*, Ottley, Holland Press, 1985.

Buxton, Edward North, *Short Stalks* (Second Series), London, Edward Stanford, 1898.

Churchill, Randolph, *Men, Mines and Animals in Africa*, Bulawayo, Books of Rhodesia, 1969 (first published 1892).

Herbert, Agnes, *Two Dianas in Somaliland*, London, Thomas Nelson, 1908.

Johnston, Sir Harry H., *British Central Africa*, London, Methuen, 1897.

Kingsley, Mary, *Travels in West Africa*, London, Virago, 1983 (first published 1897).

Manchester, William, *The Last Lion*, Boston, Little, Brown, 1983.

Neumann, Arthur H., *Elephant Hunting in East Equatorial Africa*, London, Rowland Ward, 1982 (first published 1898).

Pringle, John, *The Conservationists and the Killers*, Cape Town, Bulpin, 1982.

Roberts, Brian, *Churchills in Africa*, New York, Taplinger, 1971.

Schillings, C.G., *Flashlights in the Jungle*, New York, Doubleday, Page & Company [c. 1905].

Schillings, C.G., *In Wildest Africa*, New York, Harper & Brothers, 1907.

Sutherland, James, *The Adventures of an Elephant Hunter*, London, Macmillan, 1912.

Chapter 5

Ardrey, Robert, *African Genesis*, London, Collins, 1961; New York, Dell Publishing, 1972.

Cranworth, Lord, *A Colony in the Making*, London, 1912.

Cranworth, Lord, *Kenya Chronicles*, London, Macmillan, 1939.

Cutright, Paul Russell, *Theodore Roosevelt – The Making of a Conservationist*, Urbana, University of Illinois, 1985.

Grogan, Quentin O., 'Safari Through the Soudan and Upper Egypt', *Reveille* magazine, 1910.

Grogan, Quentin O., Unpublished memoirs, property of his daughter, Diana G. Wasbrough.

Huxley, Elspeth, *White Man's Country*, London, Chatto & Windus, 1956.

Jackson, Sir Frederick, *Early Days in East Africa*, London, E. Arnold, 1930.

Leakey, Louis S.B., *Animals of East Africa*, ed. National Geographic Society, Washington, NGS, 1973.

Life Magazine, vol. 51, no. 19. 10 Nov. 1961.

Lundeberg, Axel and Seymour, Frederick, *The Great Roosevelt African Hunt*, McCurdy, 1910.

Millais, J.G., *Life of Frederick Courtenay Selous, D.S.O.*, London, Longmans, Green, 1918.

Morris, Charles, *The Marvelous Career of Theodore Roosevelt*, Scull, 1910.

Morris, Desmond, *The Naked Ape*, London, Cape, 1967; New York, McGraw-Hill, 1967.

Morris, Edmund, *The Rise of Theodore Roosevelt*, New York, Coward, McCann & Geoghegan, 1987, vol. I.

Pakenham, Valerie, *The Noonday Sun*, New York, Random House, 1985.

Pease, Sir Alfred, *The Book of the Lion*, New York, Scribner's, 1915.

Roosevelt, Kermit, *A Sentimental Safari*, New York, Knopf, 1963.

Roosevelt, Theodore, *African Game Trails*, New York, Scribner's, 1910.

Roosevelt, Theodore, Letter to Henry Rider Haggard, 22 August 1911, in *The Letters of Theodore Roosevelt*, Cambridge, Mass., Harvard University Press, 1954.

Schillings, C.G., *In Wildest Africa*, New York, Harpers, 1907.

Schullery, Paul, Introduction to *American Bears*, Selections from the Writings of Theodore Roosevelt. (In Theodore Roosevelt Collection, Harvard College Library.)

Stewart, Kate M., 'Theodore Roosevelt, Hunter–Naturalist on Safari', *Quarterly Journal*, Library of Congress, vol. 27, no. 3, July 1970.

Trzebinski, Errol, *The Kenya Pioneers*, London, Heinemann, 1985.

Wilson, R.L. *Theodore Roosevelt – Outdoorsman*, New York, Winchester Press, 1971.

Chapter 6

Aschan, Ulf, *The Man Whom Women Loved*, New York, St Martin's Press, 1987.

Cambridge History of Modern Africa, vol. 6, Cambridge, Cambridge University Press, 1985.

Churchill, Winston S., *My African Journey*, London, Holland Press/Neville Spearman, 1962.

Cranworth, Lord, *A Colony in the Making*, London, 1912.

Cranworth, Lord, *Kenya Chronicles*, London, Macmillan, 1939.

Dinesen, Isak, *Out of Africa*, Harmondsworth, Penguin Books, 1954; Vintage, 1972 (first published 1937).

East African Standard, Nairobi, 1909–14.

Farwell, Byron, *The Great War in Africa*, New York, Norton, 1986.

Hill, Clifford, 'Ostriches', unpublished manuscript, 1948.

Hunter, J.A., *Hunter*, New York, Harper Brothers, 1952.

Hunter, J.A., and Mannix, Dan, *African Bush Adventures*, London, Hamish Hamilton, 1954.

Huxley, Elspeth, *White Man's Country*, London, Chatto & Windus, 1980.

Ingham, Kenneth, *A History of East Africa*, London, Longmans, Green, 1965.

Lovell, Mary S., *Straight on Till Morning*, New York, St Martin's Press, 1987.

Markham, Beryl, *West With the Night*, San Francisco, North Point Press, 1983.

Memories of Kenya, ed. Arnold Curtis, Introduction by Elspeth Huxley, London, Evans, 1986.

Miller, Charles, *Battle for the Bundu*, New York, Macmillan, 1974.

Pakenham, Valerie, *Out in the Noonday Sun*, New York, Random House, 1985.

Pretorius, P.J., *Jungle Man*, Sydney, Australasian Publishing Co., 1948.

Roosevelt, Theodore, *African Game Trails*, New York, Scribner's, 1910.

Thurman, Judith, *Isak Dinesen*, Harmondsworth, Penguin Books, 1986.

Trzebinski, Errol, *The Kenya Pioneers*, London, Heinemann, 1985.

Trzebinski, Errol, *Silence Will Speak*, Chicago, University of Chicago, 1985.

von Blixen-Finecke, Bror, *African Hunter*, New York, St Martin's Press, 1986.

von Lettow-Vorbeck, General Paul E., *My Reminiscences of East Africa*, London, Hurst & Blackett.

Chapter 7

de Watteville, Vivienne, *Out in the Blue*, London, Methuen, 1927.

East African Standard, Nairobi.

Eastman, George, *Chronicles of an African Trip*, privately printed, New York, Rochester, 1927.

Fox, James, *White Mischief*, London, Jonathan Cape, 1982.

Gide, André, *Travels in the Congo*, Harmondsworth, Penguin Books, 1986.

Johnson, Martin, *Safari*, New York, Putnam, 1928.

Johnson, Osa, *Four Years in Paradise*, Philadelphia, Lippincott, 1941.

Johnson, Osa, *I Married Adventure*, Philadelphia, Lippincott, 1940.

Percival, A. Blayney, *A Game Ranger's Notebook*, London, Nisbet, 1925.

Percival, Philip, 'Notes', unpublished manuscript, Nairobi, 1948.

Wales, Prince of, *Sport and Travel in East Africa*, compiled from his diaries by Patrick R. Chalmers, London, Philip Allan, 1934.

Chapter 8

Baker, Carlos, *Hemingway – A Life Story*, London, Collins, 1969.

Curtis, Charles P., jr., and Curtis, Richard C., *Hunting in Africa – East and West*, Boston, Houghton Mifflin, 1925.

East African Standard, Nairobi.

Haggard, H. Rider, *Allan Quatermain*, London, Longman's, Green, 1887.

Haggard, H. Rider, *King Solomon's Mines*, Harmondsworth, Penguin Books, 1958 (first published 1885).

Hemingway, Ernest, *Green Hills of Africa*, New York, Scribners, 1963 (first published 1935).

Hemingway, Ernest, 'The Short Happy Life of Francis Macomber', first published in *Cosmopolitan*, September 1936.

Hemingway, Ernest, *The Snows of Kilimanjaro*, London, Panther, 1977 (first published in *Esquire*, August 1936).

Look Magazine, New York, vol. 18, no. 2, 26 January 1954.

Lynn, Kenneth S., *Hemingway*, New York, Simon & Schuster, 1987.

ILLUSTRATION ACKNOWLEDGEMENTS

The author and publishers are grateful to the following for permission to reproduce photographs:

Brenthurst Library (Oppenheimer Collection), Johannesburg, 14, 15, 16, 28, 50, 53, 57 (top and bottom), 63, 81, 82, 96, 97; African Museum, Johannesburg, 19, 22, 52; State Library, Pretoria, 124, 125; Victoria & Albert Museum, 18; Holland & Holland Ltd, London, 51 (middle and bottom), 146 (all pictures); Miss K. M. Gordon Cumming, 54; Royal Geographical Society, 66 (top and bottom), 79 (top and bottom); Rugby School, 67, 116; Hulton Picture Library, 72, 124, 227; National Archives, Harare, Zimbabwe, 85, 104, 105, 201; Robin Hurt, 120, 206 (top and bottom), 323, 325, 336, 345 (both), 351; Royal Commonwealth Society, 131 (right), 198 (bottom), 251 (top and middle); Earl of Scarbrough, 128, 129 (top and bottom); Army & Navy Stores, London, 135; T. Roosevelt Collection, Harvard College Library, 156, 164, 167, 170 (top and bottom), 177, 180 (top and bottom); Mike Prettejohn, 171, 187 (top and bottom), 209, 294, 310; Mrs Dorothy Percival (The Percival Collection), 173, 175, 185, 230, 242, 252, 253, 256, 259, 261, 275; Tony Seth-Smith, 174, 196, 218, 219 (bottom), 223, 229, 232–3 (all pictures), 237; Q. O. Grogan Collection, Nairobi Archives (Mrs Diana G. Wasbrough), 178; Lord Cranworth, 165 (top and bottom), 189, 190, 194–5 (all pictures), 196 (both), 199, 200, 202, 211, 219 (middle); J. Allan Cash, 184, 205, 314, 347; Bryan Hook Collection, Nairobi Archives, 198; Martin and Osa Johnson Safari Museum, Inc., 244 (both pictures), 245 (both pictures, 247, 254–5 (all pictures); The Kobal Collection, 263, 272, 273, 278, 285, 287; Frank Lane Picture Agency, 307, 327, 337, 345, 358 (top); Royal Archives, Windsor, 209 (middle and bottom); Topham, 228; Ullstein Bilderdienst, 215 (top), 221; Bundesarchiv, Koblenz, 215 (bottom), 216; Imperial War Museum, 219 (top); Bruce Coleman Ltd, 222, 235, 290, 295, and 334; G. Fleming, 224; Berne Museum, Switzerland, 241; Miguu Anderson's Albums, 251 (bottom); Popperfoto Ltd, 265 (left); Jerry Ohlinger's Material Store, New York, 280; still from the film King Solomon's Mines (1938) by courtesy of the Rank Organisation Plc, 271; Cinema Bookshop, London, 262, 270, 279; Mouse McConnell, 284 (top), 356; Charles McConnell, 293; Mrs Réné Babault, 297; Sonia Ryrie, 284; Glen Cottar, 301–3 (all pictures), 304 (top left and right); Survival Anglia, 306, 311, 358 (bottom); Cecilia Destro, 308 (left and right); Terry Mathews, 313 (top); Bruce Austen, 321 (top and bottom); Sarah Seth-Smith, 322; Richard Randall, 339 (top); Richard Hall 51 (top), 131 (left); Alan Elliott, 339 (bottom), 357; Bartle Bull, 6, 203, 304 (bottom), 313 (bottom), 319, 328 (all pictures), 330, 332 (left and right), 337, 338, 354, 355, 363 (both), 364.

Illustrations have been taken from the following books: W. Cornwallis Harris, Portraits of the Game and Wild Animals of South Africa, 33, 35, 45, 92, 204, 299, 359, and Wild Sports of Southern Africa, 3, 12, 30, 36, 39 (left), 39 (right), 42, 48, 73, 113, 342; William Finaughty, The Recollections of William Finaughty, Elephant Hunter, 183; Sir Samuel Baker, Ismalia, Macmillan, 1874, 70; David Livingstone, Missionary Travels and Researches in South Africa, 13, 49, 68, 74, 78, 93, 123, 157, 346; James Greenwood, Wild Sports of the World, 80; F. C. Selous, African Nature Notes and Reminiscences, 117; C. G. Schillings, Flashlights in the Jungle, 134, 138, 142; C. G. Schillings, In Wildest Africa, 141, 143; Arthur Newmann, Elephant Hunting in East Equatorial Africa, 1898, 147; Rider Haggard, Days of My Life, Volume 2, 1926, 265 (right); W. D. M. Bell, Bell of Africa, 150 (all pictures), 152, and The Wanderings of an Elephant Hunter, 153; J. G. Millais, The Life of Frederick Courtenay Selous, D.S.O., 101 (left), 121; Frans Lassan, ed., The Life and Destiny of Karen Blixen, Michael Joseph, 1970, 225; Peter Beard, The End of the Game, Collins, 1979, 25, 186; Look Magazine, 26 January 1954, 282 (top and bottom); Agnes Herbert, Two Dianas in Somaliland, 137 (both pictures); William Burchell, Selections from Travels in the Interior of Southern Africa, 20, 21, 26; Gordon Cumming, A Hunter's Life in Southern Africa, 58, 60; H. Faulkner, Elephant Haunts, 1868, 108; William Charles Baldwin, African Hunting from Natal to the Zambesi, 64, 77, 83, 86, 88, 89, 320, 341, 343; Valerie Packenham, The Noonday Sun, 158, 189, 210; F. C. Selous, A Hunter's Wanderings in Africa, 101 (right); K. Roosevelt, A Sentimental Safari, 168, 180 (both pictures).

INDEX

Page numbers of illustrations are in *italic* type

Index